MW00803847

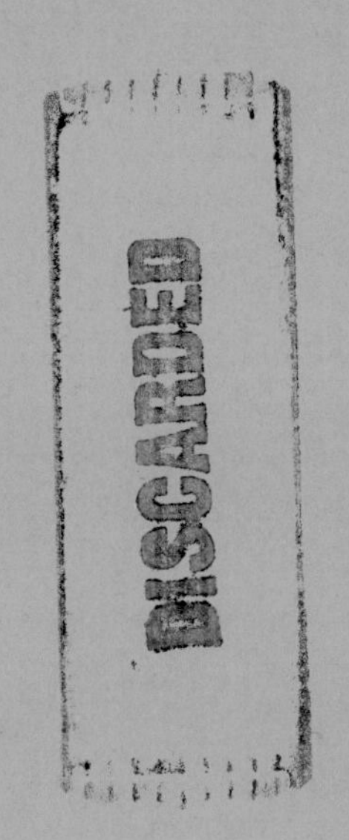
DISCARDED

Senator Richard B. Russell and My Career as a Trial Lawyer

Charles Campbell's amazing life story gives us a rare and valuable insight into Georgia's political history and a sharper understanding of why Richard B. Russell was the most respected and powerful United States Senator of his era. Moving from the inner circle of Washington influence to his own experiences at the pinnacle of Georgia's legal arena, Campbell reveals the good, the bad, and the ugly of today's legal profession. Charles' own prescriptions of what must be done about the bad and ugly will be of interest to all who are a part of the legal profession, as well as to those who want to improve it.

Charles also most importantly reminds us that Senator Russell believed that effective governance requires "the ability to consider, at least on a theoretical basis, that the other side may be correct." This book is a must-read for all who believe that today's leaders and citizens have much to learn from yesterday's giants.

—Sam Nunn

Very few people know Georgia politics of the last half century like Charles Campbell does. He has participated in it and observed it up close and with an unerring eye and shrewd analysis. He lays it out as no one else could. He also describes the legal profession of Georgia. The great lawyers and judges and important trials he was part of and saw first hand. This is a well done work and a significant contribution to the history of Georgia.

—Zell Miller

Charles Campbell's career spans an era of profound changes in the practice of law from a profession to a business, and those changes are recounted for us by someone in a unique position to shed light on their meaning. He has for four decades been in the trenches experiencing the pain in defeat and the exhilaration in victory while representing clients of all varieties in a very general law practice in small local and large multinational firms. If you think you want to be a lawyer, read this book.

—Robert E. Hicks

This is a very good and important book, direct and revealing. Mr. Campbell displays an innate skill in observation, a mature sense of meaning, and a fresh, powerful, writing ability. This book presents significant ideas and previously unknown facts with clarity. Vibrant with life, abundant with real people, full of memorable scenes and revelations, this is a "must-read."

—Ted Maloof

Senator Richard B. Russell

and

My Career as a Trial Lawyer

An Autobiography

Charles E. Campbell

MERCER UNIVERSITY PRESS

MACON, GEORGIA

MUP/ H867

1400 Coleman Avenue
Macon, Georgia 31207

First Edition

Books published by Mercer University Press are printed on acid-free paper that meets the requirements of the American National Standard for Information Sciences—Permanence of Paper for Printed Library Materials.

Mercer University Press is a member of Green Press Initiative (greenpressinitiative.org), a nonprofit organization working to help publishers and printers increase their use of recycled paper and decrease their use of fiber derived from endangered forests.
This book is printed on recycled paper.

ISBN 978-0-88146-432-0

Cataloging-in-Publication Data is available from the Library of Congress

Contents

Endowed by
Tom Watson Brown
and
The Watson-Brown Foundation, Inc.

Prologue

It was spring 1960. Juniors and seniors—like myself—were looking forward to career day at Jackson High School in Jackson, a small middle Georgia town. On that day, we were permitted to take a day off from school to visit the office of a doctor, pharmacist, lawyer, businessperson, or government official to explore a possible career interest. By career day, I had pretty much decided to become a lawyer. Several things moved me in that direction. First, I had watched the *Perry Mason* television program and dreamed of starring in an important courtroom drama. Second, I had participated in high school debate, which was supposedly a good training ground for a future trial lawyer. Finally, and perhaps most important, I observed that attorneys were among the most respected, influential, and affluent citizens in my hometown. They seemed to occupy most of the significant political offices or positions of civic responsibility. Few lawyer jokes were heard in Jackson in those days.

On career day, I did not have to visit the office of a lawyer because the school gave me permission to attend a spectacular trial taking place at the Butts County Courthouse. In fact, I was allowed to miss school for up to one week since the trial was expected to last that long. The case involved a horrific traffic accident outside Jackson that resulted in serious injuries to a number of local people. Well-known local lawyer Benjamin B. Garland, a former district attorney, represented the plantiffs. Mr. Garland's son, Ben, Jr., was my debate partner at Jackson High School. He went on to enjoy an outstanding career as a lawyer in Macon, Georgia. Mr. Garland brought in his more famous brother, Rueben Garland from Atlanta, to help him try the case. Rueben Garland was a highly successful trial lawyer who was known for taking on unpopular clients and for his courtroom antics that often got him in trouble with the trial judge. For example, he had represented the accused bomber of the Jewish Temple in Atlanta and ~~he~~ had been held in contempt of court by a number of trial judges.

If I needed any encouragement to finalize my decision to become a trial lawyer, attending the trial did the trick. I arrived early each morning to claim a seat in the packed courtroom. I found the trial very exciting, particularly Rueben Garland's cross-examination of hostile witnesses.

The result of the trial was that the plaintiffs received the largest jury verdict in the history of Butts County to that point in time.

After graduating from high school and college, I enrolled in law school in Washington, DC. Quite by accident, I was given the opportunity to join the staff of Senator Richard B. Russell and ~~was~~ allowed to go to law school at night. Working for Richard Russell was a life-transforming experience that greatly helped ~~in~~ my later career as a trial lawyer. After graduating from law school and following Senator Russell's death in 1971, I returned to Atlanta, where I practiced law for almost forty years before retiring at the beginning of 2009.

I decided to write this book for two principal reasons. First, Richard Russell had such a profound impact on my life that I want to pay respect to his outstanding career of fifty consecutive years in public office. Second, I owe a tremendous debt to the practice of law. It afforded me an exciting career and allowed me to practice with outstanding lawyers, represent interesting clients, and retire to a comfortable standard of living. However, I also practiced law during a period in which it deteriorated from a respected profession to essentially just another business. There are various reasons for that, some of which are not the fault of lawyers. I will discuss some of them in this book with the hope that I can make a small contribution to returning the practice of law to the status of a respected profession.

As will be apparent to any reader of this book, this is not a scholarly biography. It is based largely on my recollection. As everyone knows, relying on one's memories is a tricky business. That is particularly true when the memories are fueled by a mind that is now past its seventieth year. I have tried to verify facts stated in this book where possible, but much of it is simply what I remember. As my great friend, Jasper Dorsey, told me, "My problem is not what I cannot recall but is what I recall that did not happen." Any factual errors contained in this book are entirely my own.

I dedicate this book to my dear wife of more than thirty-five years, Ann, and to our wonderful son of thirty years, Garrett.

The Butts County Courthouse in Jackson, Georgia.

1

The Early Years

I was born Charles Edward Campbell on January 12, 1942, at the St. Joseph Hospital in downtown Atlanta, Georgia. At the time, my family lived in the far northwest corner of Georgia in Dalton. I was born in Atlanta because my mother's sister, Edna Barton, or "Aunt Nig" as we call her, was a registered nurse at St. Joseph. For that reason, my family elected to have me and my two brothers delivered at the hospital. (St. Joseph Hospital has subsequently relocated to the North Atlanta suburbs. The site of the old hospital is now the downtown Atlanta Hilton Hotel.)

After I was born, we lived in Dalton for only one year. My father, Borden Burr Campbell who was born in Heflin, Alabama, was the assistant county agent in Whitfield County, employed by the Cooperative Extension Service of the United States Department of Agriculture to advise local farmers on the latest and best agricultural practices, administer the various USDA farm assistance programs in the county, and supervise the 4H Club rural youth program. When I was about a year old, my father received a promotion when he was named as the county agent in Pike County, Georgia. At that time, our family moved to Zebulon, Georgia. While I remember nothing about my time in Dalton, I recall that my best friend in Zebulon was Dan Baker, whose father was the local pharmacist. At the time we moved to Zebulon, my older brother, Borden, was about four years old. Our younger brother, Kenneth, was born while we lived in Zebulon.

When we had lived in Zebulon for several years, my father received another promotion and was named the county agent in Butts County, Georgia. At that time, we moved to a place we called "the Kelly Place" because my parents rented the property from a man named Mr. Kelly. I remember that the Towaliga River flowed near the Kelly Place, and we maintained fish baskets in the river and caught a lot of catfish, which we ate at least once each week. I have a vivid recollection of getting a fish bone caught in my throat during a meal and being extremely frightened by the pain and difficulty in extracting it. To this day, I try to avoid eating meat with bones. I also remember my father assembling a tractor for use in cultivating the family garden at the Kelly Place. He got aggravated with me for distracting him while he tried to follow the assembly instructions.

I started school while we lived at the Kelly Place. For one year, I attended class in a three-room community schoolhouse that served eight grades in the Towaliga community of Butts County. Also, my parents joined the Towaliga Baptist Church. The church was important in our lives. My father was the superintendent of the Sunday school, and my mother taught the intermediate class. We went to church every Sunday morning and Sunday night, and we attended a one-week revival and Vacation Bible School each summer.

When I was about six years old, I joined the church and was baptized in O. L. Weaver, Jr.'s fish pond. While my parents thought I was imagining it, I am confident that a fish bit my foot when the preacher immersed me in the water. As I grew in the faith, I remember participating in a "Bible Sword Drill" program and becoming somewhat of an expert at finding a particular verse or part of the Bible during Bible drill competitions. I also remember attending camp meetings at the Holiness Campground of the Southeast, located between Jackson and Indian Springs. The meeting, with hundreds of people attending, lasted for about four weeks each summer. Guest preachers spoke about "fire and brimstone," and music groups performed each evening. I liked the music—not so much the preaching.

We lived at the Kelly Place for several years, and then my parents bought a large white frame house with four bedrooms that stood on approximately one hundred acres of adjacent land on the Barnesville highway about six miles from Jackson. This is where we lived until I left for college. We had a large barn, and my father usually had anywhere from twenty-five to one hundred head of beef cattle. We also had an extensive garden that provided fresh vegetables during the summer. My father would prepare the garden and my mother would gather the vegetables. My brothers and I provided little assistance, and I recall having a strong dislike of working in the garden.

I can remember my brothers and I walking two miles to a country store and buying a Royal Crown Cola and a Moon Pie. The three of us spent time playing, fighting, and eventually being a part of the city baseball league. We also discovered the advantages of living on a farm. For example, we had shotguns and hunted rabbits and other game. We also maintained rabbit boxes that we used to catch rabbits. We would put food in these wooden boxes, each of which had a door at one end, and place them in the woods on trails we had observed, When a rabbit entered to eat the food, the little door shut and trapped the rabbit in the box. Occasionally, our mother would even agree to skin the rabbits and serve them at the evening meal. It was a matter of pride for my brothers and me to know we had put food on the family table.

We attended school in Jackson and participated in the usual school activities. The public schools in Butts County were strictly segregated even after the Supreme Court's 1954 landmark decision declaring segregation unconstitutional (*Brown v. Board of Education*, 347 US 483 [1954]). Shortly thereafter, large billboards began to appear on Butts County roads bearing the message "Impeach Earl Warren," calling for the removal of the Chief Justice who had written the desegregation decision. We also took part in the 4-H Club program administered by my father. I became particularly interested in cattle judging and grew proficient in this activity. One year, I made it all the way to the southeastern finals of the cattle-judging contest.

When we moved to the big house, we did not have a television, but a neighbor had one and invited us to visit and watch it one evening. I recall falling asleep in my mother's lap and our neighbor dangling a rubber spider before me when I awakened. I have never been so frightened in my life.

Summer was my favorite time of year. I enjoyed being off from school and participating in a variety of activities, a few of which earned me some money. For a while, I mowed grass for customers in Jackson. One day a friend told me that I could make more money picking cotton. There was a large cotton field across the Barnesville Highway in front of our house. I investigated and discovered that my friend was right.

I remember a large black man named Gus who was the champion cotton picker in the field. Most of us picked one row of cotton at a time, but Gus picked two rows simultaneously. While we strapped one cotton sack to a shoulder and picked one row with both hands, Gus slung a sack over each shoulder and picked one row with his right hand and the other with his left. At the end of the day, he had picked more than twice as much as anyone else in the field. We placed the picked cotton on large blankets, and it was weighed. Each picker received a certain amount of money for each pound picked that day. I remember being so impressed with the amount of cotton Gus picked that I went home and tried to calculate how much he had earned. While I made more money picking cotton than mowing grass, I soon quit because the work was hard, hot, and long.

I also started going to visit my grandparents in northwest Georgia during the summer. They were my mother's parents and were farmers who lived on a 100-acre farm outside Bremen, Georgia. I never considered my father to be a real farmer because he did not grow crops. My grandparents, though, were real farmers who grew corn and other crops. My grandfather, Hoke McPherson, was a small man, probably weighing less than 130 pounds. He was serious minded and worked from sunup to sundown. My grandmother, Nellie McPherson, whom we called "MoMo," was a huge woman who often weighed almost 300 pounds. She was lighthearted and believed in having fun. She taught me to smoke rabbit tobacco, a wild weed, rolling cigarettes from used newspapers and putting the rabbit tobacco in the paper to make a cigarette.

My grandfather arose before the sun came up so that he could finish breakfast and be on his way to the fields. My grandmother got up even earlier to prepare a huge country breakfast for my grandfather. She cooked it on a large, wood-burning stove in the kitchen. I will never forget those breakfasts of eggs, grits, and ham, sausage, or bacon all served with country biscuits and sorghum syrup. When my grandfather worked in the fields close enough to the house, he came home for lunch. If not, he took his lunch with him. I accompanied him to the fields almost every day and brought him water as he plowed a field with a mule or did his other farming chores.

Both of my grandparents were among the most hard-working people I have ever known. They relaxed for about one hour after dinner in the evenings and after the day's work was done. We would all adjourn to the front porch, where we sat in chairs or in a swing and talked. In 1952, I remember my grandfather saying that he was going to vote for a Republican for president for the first time in his life. Dwight Eisenhower was running that year, and my grandfather reasoned that if General Eisenhower could successfully see us through World War II, he could surely do a good job in the less-demanding position of president of the United States.

My grandparents had few modern conveniences. For example, the only heating in the house was the large stove in the kitchen that burned wood and the smaller, coal-burning stoves in two of the bedrooms. There was no air-conditioning. When I first started visiting them, they did not have a telephone. One year when I arrived in the summer, I found that they had gotten a telephone, but it was on a party line shared with four other customers. My grandparents counted the number of rings to determine if the call was meant for them. They could also tell which of their neighbors was the intended recipient of a call. It was a good way to keep up with the neighbors' business. Many of our front-porch conversations in the evening focused on the gossip my grandmother reported after listening in on her neighbors' phone calls.

My grandparents did not have a television during any of the summers that I visited them, though my grandfather told me of a neighbor who had one. My grandfather said he bought the television because he enjoyed watching professional wrestling matches that invariably involved a good guy and a bad guy. The bad guy would engage in such impermissible activities as pulling his opponent's hair. My grandfather said that his neighbor would become incensed at the bad guy. On one occasion, according to my grandfather, his neighbor shouted at the bad guy in a wrestling match that if he pulled his opponent's hair again, he would shoot him. When he did, the neighbor retrieved his shotgun and shot the television set. I do not know if this story is true, but my grandfather told it as if he believed it.

Their house had no indoor plumbing, and we had to go outside the house to a two-seater located near the garden. Also, while my grandmother had a car, she seldom drove it because my grandfather thought gas was too expensive. They used the car on Sundays when we went to church about ten miles from their house or when we went into Bremen, about six miles away, on the weekend. My grandfather normally traveled by mule or mule and wagon. I remember going with him to the mill to have corn ground for bread. He hitched up the two mules and we climbed into the wagon for about an hour to ride to the gristmill. I enjoyed those trips. The only indulgence during the week was on Tuesday, when the "peddler" came by the house. This small, bus-like vehicle offered candies, drinks, and other treats that my grandmother bought for me. Tuesdays were the only days that I did not accompany my grandfather to the fields.

My summers in Bremen ended when I started working at the New York Store in Jackson at about fourteen years of age. It was an old, large retail department store that sold everything from men and women's clothing to furniture. Each year, the store's owner traveled to New York to view the latest fashions—thus the name. My mother kept the books for the owner and, when the owner grew infirm, she ran it herself. I started working in the men's clothing department. At first, I simply assisted Joe Moore, who ran the department. I worked there for a number of years and eventually became familiar with the clothing lines, including suits, shirts, shoes, and hats among other offerings. I sometimes worked after school and all day on Saturdays. One of the things I noticed was that the attorneys purchased the most expensive items. They did not seem concerned about the cost of the items they bought. That was when I first thought it might be good for me to become a lawyer.

My mother worked five and a half days each week at the store; like most stores in small southern towns at the time, the New York Store was closed on Wednesday afternoons. On those free afternoons, Mother kept the books for a cattle auction barn located outside Jackson. It was her longest working day of the week, and she did not often get home until ten o'clock at night. Sometimes I went with her to the auction and enjoyed observing the interaction between the auctioneer and the purchasers. He would speak so rapidly I could barely understand, and the experienced cattle purchasers, who represented large meatpacking producers, would signal their intent by either a wink of the eye or a nod of the head. I tried to use my 4-H cattle-judging knowledge to predict the amount the purchasers would pay per pound for the livestock.

I did not have an opportunity to travel widely during those years. When my parents took a vacation, we either went to the Great Smoky Mountains in North Carolina or to the beach at Daytona, Florida. Another trip was to a national county agent convention meeting at Michigan State University in East Lansing, Michigan. We drove for long hours in my father's automobile. I remember that my mother was driving and had left the interstate to get gas outside Cincinnati, Ohio. We thought my father was asleep in the back seat, but when Mother exclaimed that she didn't know what to do, Father woke right up and said, "If I was driving and you were back here, you would." My mother's usually good sense of humor apparently escaped her that time. When we finally got to Michigan State, we stayed in one of the college dormitories. It was an exciting experience that made me eager to go to college.

We made several memorable trips to Atlanta. My brothers and I wore braces on our teeth, and we saw an orthodontist in Atlanta. The worst part of those trips came in the morning, when the orthodontist modified our braces. I dreaded that experience. Afterward, though, we got to eat lunch at the Varsity—reputedly the world's largest drive-in restaurant, offering chili dogs, orange drinks, and other delicacies. As soon as our vehicle entered the property, an employee would jump on either the running board of the car or the back of the car until we pulled into a parking spot. He then took our orders and soon delivered the food to our car. We could finish our meal without ever entering the restaurant!

After lunch, we traveled to the Fox Theatre where we sat under a ceiling of sparkling stars and listened to organ music by Bob Van Camp before watching the latest movie. Our trips to Atlanta usually concluded with a stop by the Sears Roebuck and Company store, where Mother shopped and my brothers and I selected items to buy as well. I remember these trips fondly—except the parts at the orthodontist's office—and would be happy to relive them.

My final memory about growing up before my high school years is not pleasant. My brothers and I were playing in a wooded area near our house and decided to cut some vines so we could swing on them. Unknown to us, the vines contained thunderwood, a particularly strong cousin of poison oak. By the next day, we had all developed an itchy rash, so our mother took us to the pharmacy. The pharmacist was sort of a surrogate doctor. While I don't remember his exact diagnosis, I recall that he told us to eat ice cream. I particularly liked that recommendation. The rash and itching intensified, however, and we finally went to see a doctor, who prescribed a lotion to apply several times each day. By the time we started taking the medicine, the poison had spread so far that it basically affected our entire bodies. My older brother, Borden, was the most severely affected as it had spread to his eyes, face, and genital area. We eventually overcame it, but we all missed at least one week of school, and Borden stayed out even longer. To this day, I am cautious around poison oak or poison ivy.

Charles at about 5 months.

Daddy with my older brother, Borden, and me when I was about 13 months.

My maternal grandparents, Nellie and Hoke McPherson.

Towaliga Baptist Church in rural Butts County, Georgia.

2

High School

The class of 1960 at Jackson High School consisted of forty-nine students. When we had our fiftieth reunion in 2010, thirty-one of my classmates attended. Eight had passed away. At this small rural school not known for academic achievement, I found the courses to be quite easy and was able to make almost straight A's without much study.

I do remember several outstanding teachers. Mrs. Edwards, who taught science, chemistry, and physics, was one of the most demanding teachers I had in high school but also the one from whom I learned the most. Mr. Comer taught agriculture and was the advisor for the Future Farmers of America program, in which students learned agricultural skills, including carpentry. I remember making a bookcase in FFA class that has traveled with me through the various stages of my life—college, law school, and law practice. Now, in my retirement, it still holds books in our Atlanta home.

While in high school, I continued participating in 4-H Club. In addition to judging cattle, I became involved in public speaking. I attended a 4-H Club camp for several years that was located at Rock Eagle, Georgia. This camp, as well as my church, offered me numerous opportunities for public speaking that eventually led to my decision to join the high school debate team. Perhaps more than anything else, debate piqued my interest in becoming a lawyer.

Though I still worked at the New York Store, I was able to make time for baseball. Each year at Jackson High School, I played on the school team, and I was one of the star pitchers during my junior and senior years. We won a number of tournaments, and I particularly enjoyed the travel involved in competing against teams within a fifty-mile radius of Jackson. During the summer, after I grew too old to participate in the Babe Ruth League, I played in the Connie Mack League for boys between 16 and 19 years of age. Jackson had an active team and won a number of tournaments. We played most of our games at night or on the weekend, which permitted me to work during the daytime in the summer. When I outgrew Connie Mack baseball, I continued as the team's manager for several years. One year, we had an excellent team that reached the finals of the southeastern tournament. Several players in the Connie Mack League went on to play professional baseball.

I did not have a serious girlfriend in high school, and there was little for young people to do in Jackson aside from attending various ball games. We frequented the Tasty Freeze and occasionally spent time at Indian Springs State Park about ten miles from Jackson, where businesses offered a bowling alley and a roller-skating rink. Whenever we went out of town, we traveled to Macon, about fifty miles away, and visited several clubs and music establishments.

Because of the conduct of the senior class the year before I graduated, the school would not permit us to take a senior trip. One of my best friends, Douglas Bryant, and I decided to take our own senior trip to New York City to watch New York Yankee baseball games. It is a wonder our parents allowed us to go alone to New York, and it is also a wonder that we got back in one piece. We checked into a substandard hotel in New York and traveled by subway to Yankee Stadium in the Bronx each day. At that time, the Bronx was not a safe area. But Doug and I thoroughly enjoyed our trip, and I especially remember New York Yankee reliever, Ryan Duren, who threw a fastball up to 100 miles per hour. He wore thick glasses and often pitched nowhere near home plate. My good friend Doug later became a minister and served for many years as a missionary abroad.

My goal was to graduate number one academically in my class at Jackson High School, but I ended up finishing second. I did receive three senior superlatives: Most Intellectual (which I did not deserve), Most Likely to Succeed, and Most Dependable. I was proudest of the last superlative because my parents had always taught me to be dependable and to do what I said I was going to do.

In the summer after graduation, I took a job at the Georgia Experiment Station in Griffin, Georgia, where I worked for the Entomology Department that tested insecticides for various agriculture crops. At the time I began my employment and throughout the next several summers when I worked there during college, we applied a different insecticide to several plots of cotton and then monitored each poison's ability to kill the boll weevil. I helped monitor plots near

Clayton in North Georgia and near Plains (the home of Georgia governor and president Jimmy Carter) and Blakely in southwest Georgia.

After several summers of employment at the Experiment Station, I was entrusted to travel on my own at least once a month to Clayton, Plains, and Blakely to record the results of the tests. When I was in Blakely once, battling the intense South Georgia heat and doing my work, I met an attractive waitress at the local café. A junior in high school, she lived on a farm outside Blakely with her poor, uneducated parents. I could tell they were somewhat dubious about me as they probably thought I was from Atlanta. This smart young lady had a wonderful personality. On one of our dates, she showed me her straight-A report card. I hoped she would have a chance to go to college. Once I quit work at the Experiment Station, I lost touch with her. I wondered if she would have an opportunity to go to college and what a shame it would be if she did not. She certainly would have had an opportunity if the Hope Scholarship Program that Governor Zell Miller established twenty years later had been in existence.

As I graduated from high school and prepared to go to college, I looked forward to a new stage of life. While my brothers and I enjoyed a satisfying environment growing up in Jackson, I was ready to move on to a fresh challenge.

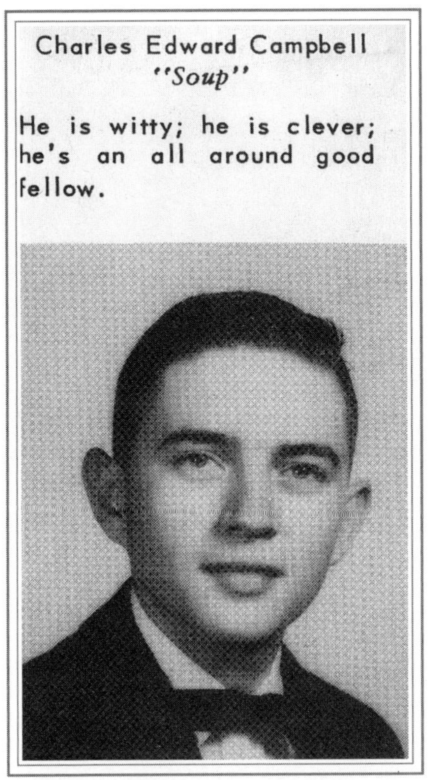

My senior photograph in the Jackson High School Yearbook in 1960.

As recipient of senior superlative for "Most Dependable" with Margaret Fletcher.

As President of the Jackson High School Beta Club along with the other officers.

The 1960 Jackson High School baseball team. I am on the front row, far left, and my younger brother, Kenneth, is the second from the left on the back row.

3

College

Emory University

It was a tradition in Jackson for the best students to attend Emory University in Atlanta, which is still one of the most expensive private schools in the Southeast, if their parents could afford the tuition. My parents could not afford it, but they made me a proposal I could not refuse. They would pay my expenses to attend Emory if I made straight A's. Largely ignorant of the quality of education I had received in Butts County public schools and naïve about the level of competition I would face at Emory, I readily accepted their offer.

I did not have an automobile at the time. Atlanta is about fifty miles north of Jackson, so I traveled to the city by Greyhound bus and then took a street-car trolley, which ran on tracks with an overhead wire connector from the Atlanta bus station to the Emory campus in Northeast Atlanta. My trip from the downtown bus station to the Emory campus took about thirty minutes. The entire trip was about three hours.

When I arrived at Emory in fall 1960, I was assigned to the Longstreet Dormitory since all freshmen were required to live on campus. I was immediately surprised that the roommate assigned to me was from New York State—along with about 20 percent of the freshman class. At the time, Emory was known as "the Harvard of the South." Many talented students from the northeast attended Emory when they were unable to gain admittance to an Ivy League school.

The center of social life at Emory was the fraternities and sororities. About ten fraternity houses stood on a street on campus known as "Fraternity Row." Each fall, the fraternities staged a "rush" so that the new students could become acquainted with each one and decide which fraternity to pledge. I went through this process and decided that Sigma Nu was the best fit for me, but I decided not to pledge my first year for several reasons. First, it would be an unexpected expense for my parents. Second, I knew I would spend much of my time on debate. Finally, based on the students I had met and the classes I had attended, I realized that the competition was steep at Emory, and I was suddenly unsure whether I would be able to meet my parents' conditions.

The latter concern turned out to be justified. As I began taking classes, I learned that most courses were graded on the "curve system." That is, each class would produce a certain number of A's, B's, C's, and D's. A student's grade in those classes was determined not by the absolute quality of his or her work but on how it measured against the work of other students in the class. Since most students had attended more demanding high schools and were more prepared for college, I felt that this system put me at a significant disadvantage. But I was determined to try.

Surprisingly, my favorite course at Emory was geology—the study of rock formations, minerals, and other solid substances of the earth. I had no prior knowledge of or interest in geology before I took the course, but Professor Lester made the subject fascinating. Our class frequently took field trips ten miles from campus to Stone Mountain, reputedly the largest outcropping of granite in the world. Though many ride a cable-car system up the mountain, our class climbed it by foot to its peak, noting the unusual rock formations along the way. On one occasion, I remember being at the top of the mountain near the steep side when Dr. Lester asked me to retrieve a rock near the edge. I almost slipped over the edge of the mountain. Dr. Lester never asked me to retrieve a rock after that.

In addition to classes like geology, I enjoyed college debate. Emory had an excellent debate program known as the "Barkley Forum." Dr. Glenn Pelham, a man weighing almost three hundred pounds, was the director of debate. I was one of about twenty students in the program. The freshmen participated in the "novice" program. While a number of my team members had received debate scholarships to Emory and were far more experienced and accomplished at it than I was, I won as many debates as I lost in our tournaments, and I thoroughly enjoyed myself.

By the spring of my freshman year, however it was clear I would not be able to make the straight A's I had promised to my parents. Thus far, I had made almost equally A's and B's with an occasional C. I started considering which school to attend as a transfer student after my freshman year. We had debated the University of Georgia team, which was not nearly as talented as the Emory team but was still respectable. While UGA was the state's flagship university and the oldest land-grant college in the United States, it was not the academic powerhouse that it is today. (In the last ten years, it has consistently been ranked as one of the top twenty-five public universities in America.)

As we approached my sophomore year in fall 1961, my parents were not disappointed with my choice to transfer to UGA, which cost about one-tenth of the tuition for Emory. In fact, they were so elated that they bought me an automobile, which I would need at Georgia.

The University of Georgia

When I arrived at the University of Georgia in fall 1961, the first decision I had to make was where to live. As a sophomore, I was not required to live on campus When my older brother, Borden, was at UGA, he had rented a room in the home of chemistry professor Cecil N. Wilder, who lived on University Avenue approximately two miles from campus. Fortunately for me, the professor favorably recalled my brother and agreed to rent the room to me. I lived there at the front of the house through my senior year, using the Wilders' front or back door and occasionally joining them for meals. Professor Wilder, whose sole interest was teaching, never earned a PhD or conducted research. He would not survive today in the major college environment but he taught chemistry at the University of Georgia for fifty years before retiring.

Another early decision was whether to participate in the honors program UGA had started the previous year. It was reserved for the top students who were generally given the best professors. Today, the UGA honors program is one of the best in the nation. I decided not to participate primarily because I did not want academic demands to interfere with the amount of time I intended to devote to debate. After all, debate was the primary reason I had come to the University of Georgia.

Since I planned to go to law school, I decided to major in political science, which was a popular major for pre-law students. The university had an excellent political science department. One of my principal professors, Dr. Robert Clute, was an outstanding teacher of international and comparative politics. He had been a soldier in World War II and told many interesting stories. He became one of my advisors and a close friend.

Aside from the honors students, who were probably competitive with the general student body at Emory, the students at the University of

Georgia were much less academically inclined. In fact, some of them did not belong in college at all. Georgia was known at the time as one of the top party schools in the country. Although UGA had an active Greek organization, being in a fraternity or sorority was not as socially important at Georgia as it had been at Emory. I decided not to pledge a fraternity due to my time commitment to debate.

I was, however, active in several other campus organizations. In my senior year I served as vice president of the Blue Key National Honor Society chapter at Georgia and as vice president of Omicron Delta Kappa, a national leadership organization. I was also a member of Phi Kappa Phi, one of the two main literary societies on campus. In my last year, I was selected for Who's Who in American Colleges and Universities. I was also elected to the Gridiron Secret Society. Based on my academic record at UGA, I was elected to Phi Beta Kappa.

I continued to work at the Experiment Station in Griffin and to manage the Connie Mack baseball team in Jackson during the summers until my senior year at UGA, when I accepted a summer job with a local fruitcake company, Benson's Bakery. The bakery employed UGA students in the summers to sell contracts to civic clubs throughout America as fundraising projects for the holiday season. A friend had recommended the job. I was assigned the eastern half of the lower peninsula of Michigan, a station wagon filled with fruitcake samples and promotional materials, and given a weekly allowance.

During my month in the Detroit area, I spent most of my allowance attending Detroit Tiger baseball games. I often ran out of money about midweek and had to start eating the fruitcake samples. I came to detest fruitcake, but I sold a lot of it that summer. In fact, I was the top-selling student in the nation for Benson's. The primary reason for my success was that the Rotary Club in Warren, Michigan, had as its president the regional vice president of a paint company. He put the fruitcake in his company's locations throughout the upper Midwest. The fruitcake job was one of the most interesting I have ever had, but I do not desire to repeat it.

As I had planned when I transferred to the University of Georgia, my central focus was college debate. I debated for three years at Georgia and served as the captain of the debate team my senior year. The director of debate when I arrived at UGA was Dr. Merwyn Hayes, an excellent coach who greatly improved the Georgia program during my time there.

While our team never made it to the national tournament, we steadily improved each year.

Debate taught me many skills that were essential for my later career as a trial lawyer. The popular myth is that the main advantage of debate for future lawyers is the honing of speaking skills. That is not the case; speaking in college debate is nothing like trying lawsuits in a courtroom. In debate, the challenge is to cover as much information as possible in the allotted time, so we spoke rapidly. A trial lawyer, on the other hand, has to concentrate on speaking slowly and effectively communicating with lay jurors. The most helpful skills I learned in debate were the ability to analyze issues, to research the facts, to organize an argument, and to think quickly under pressure.

Each year, the National Debate Association established a debate topic. Two that I debated were (1) whether the federal government should substantially increase federal aid to education and (2) whether there should be a compulsory national health insurance program in the United States. Each debate team of two people had to prepare to defend both the affirmative and the negative response with respect to the debate question. The preliminary rounds of the debate tournament generally consisted of six debates—three on the affirmative and three on the negative. We did not know when we would be placed on the affirmative or the negative side or who our opponents would be until a random assignment took place prior to the tournament. Some of the tournaments also involved a cross-examination format in which the students cross-examined each other as a part of the debate. Debate coaches from the participating schools served as judges. At the end of the preliminary rounds, the top sixteen teams proceeded to the elimination rounds. The process continued until the final debate, at which point the winner was declared. Awards were also given for the top speakers in the tournament, whether or not their teams reached the elimination rounds

While I was a debater at Georgia, we traveled from Athens to attend tournaments as far away as Texas, Washington, DC, Illinois, and Miami, as well as a host of tournaments in the Southeast. The two principal competing debate schools in Georgia were Emory and Mercer University in Macon, Georgia. There were also less well-known debate programs at various other colleges in Georgia. Two of the most skilled debaters from Georgia that I recall were Nathan Deal of Mercer and Ben F. Johnson III of Emory. Both went on to become lawyers. Nathan became the eighty-second governor of Georgia in January 2011, and Ben is the former chairman of the Alston and Bird law firm in Atlanta.

During my time at UGA, there were no debate scholarships and we had limited financial support from the university. In contrast, today the UGA debate program offers a number of scholarships and receives significant financial support from the administration. It is consistently ranked among the top ten debate programs in the country. In my days as a debater in Athens, we traveled to tournaments not by airplane but by piling into the coach's Volkswagen bus. We journeyed as far as Texas Christian University, Northwestern University, Georgetown University, and the United States Naval Academy. On these trips, we generally left on Thursday morning and drove until late in the evening. Most tournaments started on Friday morning and lasted through noon Sunday.

Of all my debates, I recall two experiences in particular. When I was a junior, we attended a debate tournament at Northwestern University in Evanston, Indiana, near Chicago. It was the middle of the winter, and I had neither an overcoat nor a wool suit. The weather was the coldest I had ever endured, and the biting wind made it worse. I thought I would freeze to death. In spite of this, though, we did quite well at the tournament and I received one of the top speaker awards.

Probably the most interesting debate tournament I ever attended was held at the United States Penitentiary in Atlanta. The topic that year was whether or not there should be substantial prison reform in the United States. We debated teams of prisoners who were incarcerated at the federal prison in Atlanta. I noticed that the prison debaters were much more enthusiastic about affirming prison reform than arguing against it. Some of them were quite good. I remember a lawyer from Boston who was in jail for income tax evasion. A graduate of Harvard Law School, he was a talented debater. Interestingly, I also remember the prison debates from the food served at the prison. We went through the food line just as the prisoners did. I finally selected a bowl of split pea soup and a brownie. The split pea soup was so bad that I have never had it again, and the brownie was not much better. If I needed any incentive to stay out of the federal prison system, the food alone was sufficient. I still have my trophy from that memorable trip: it is cast in the form of a jail door.

As my undergraduate and debate careers drew to an end, I began planning to enroll in law school at the University of Georgia. Then something happened to redirect me. The debate coach, Dr. Hayes, decided to leave Athens to coach at Wake Forest University in Winston-Salem, North Carolina. Dr. Richard Huseman, who previously coached at the University of Illinois, succeeded Dr. Hayes as the Georgia debate coach. I was asked to stay on after my senior year to be an assistant debate coach during the transition from Dr. Hayes to Dr. Huseman. I also received an offer from the political science department for a teaching assistant position while I did course work for a Master's degree in political science. I decided to take these offers, primarily because of my loyalty to the debate program.

As a graduate student and assistant debate coach, I received an offer from Congressman John J. Flynt, Jr., for a position on his staff in Washington, DC. Thinking of my original plans to attend UGA law school, I hesitated to accept Congressman Flynt's offer. I told him that I was inclined to stay in Georgia for law school but would inform them if I changed my mind. That settled the matter, as I did not hear from Congressman Flynt's office again for many months.

In October 1965, Georgia's senior United States senator, Richard B. Russell, received a homecoming award and made a speech before the annual Blue Key National Honor Society Chapter banquet at the University of Georgia. Franklin Freeman, my roommate at the time and a fellow debater, was president of the Georgia Chapter of Blue Key. He asked if I would be willing to introduce Senator Russell at the banquet, and I said I would. Though I knew who he was, I went to the library and researched Senator Russell's career. I learned that he had been in the United States Senate since 1933, was one of the nation's most respected and powerful senators, and had brought many important federal projects to Georgia, including the Lockheed C-5A contract. I decided to make my introduction a tribute to what the senator meant to Georgia. At the time, I was unaware that Russell and his supporters were concerned about rumors that Georgia's young and progressive governor, Carl Sanders, was considering a race against Senator Russell when he was next up for reelection in 1966.

The senator apparently liked my introduction. The following week, his office called and invited me to join his staff in Washington, DC. Unlike the offer from Congressman Flynt, I felt that I could not turn this one down. Once Russell and his staff agreed to the condition that I could attend law school at night, I decided to accept. I did not negotiate a salary and was not even told what my position would be. All I knew was that it was a great opportunity for me. It was even worth giving up law school at UGA. As I made plans to leave Athens at the end of fall quarter 1965, I looked back on my decision to transfer from Emory as one of the best choices I had ever made. I felt ready to go until a tragic automobile accident took the life of one of my friends a few days before my departure. Tucker Dorsey, who was traveling from Athens to Washington, DC, to be with his parents for Christmas, was killed in a car crash on his journey. I had known Tucker's father, Jasper Dorsey, as a supporter of the debate program at Georgia. He was also head of lobbying for AT&T in Washington. Tucker was his only son, and the loss devastated him. After I arrived in Washington, Jasper and I became close, and he grew to be like a second father to me. We played golf almost every week at his private club, which was one of the most exclusive golf clubs in the Washington area. It was not unusual to see members of the United States Senate or cabinet officials on the course or in the locker room. After several years, he returned to Georgia as head of Southern Bell Telephone Company's operations in the state. When I moved back to Georgia a few years later upon Richard Russell's death, Jasper and I renewed our friendship, and I attribute part of my success to him. We remained good friends until he died in 1990.

Leaving Texas in November of 1963 after a debate tournament at Texas Christian University. Atop the sign is the trophy we won at the tournament. Pictured from left to right is UGA Debate Coach, Dr. Merwyn Hayes, me, Ron Shelp and Franklin Freeman.

One of the "jailhouse door" trophies from the debates at the United States Federal Prison in Atlanta.

4

Richard Brevard Russell, Jr.

Richard Brevard Russell, Jr., served in elective office in Georgia for fifty consecutive years. He was elected to the Georgia Legislature in 1921 and became Speaker of the Georgia House of Representatives before he was thirty years of age. He was the youngest governor in Georgia history in 1931 and the youngest United States senator in 1933. He served in the United States Senate for thirty-eight years, becoming the first person to serve more than half a lifetime as part of that body. He died on January 21, 1971, at Walter Reed Army Medical Center outside Washington, DC. At the time, he was serving as president pro tempore of the United States Senate and was third in line of succession to the presidency.

Working for and getting to know Richard Russell as a senator and as a man was a once-in-a-lifetime opportunity for me. He was, quite simply, the finest public servant and one of the best people I have ever known. I learned so much from him that beneficially affected my life that I owe a debt of gratitude to him. Because of my great respect for him as a person and for his remarkable career of public service, I provide a summary of his life in this chapter.

One of the Russells of Georgia

In early summer 1864, Union general William T. Sherman was on the march from Chattanooga to Atlanta. His mission was to disrupt the Confederate supply lines and destroy manufacturing facilities, thereby diminishing the ability of the Confederate States of America to wage war. Directly in the path of General Sherman and his army was the town of Marietta, some fifteen miles north of Atlanta. Marietta was the home of an enterprising young couple, William John Russell and his wife, Harriette Brumby Russell. Their oldest son, Richard Brumby Russell, Senator Russell's father, was barely two years old at the time. A successful young businessman not yet forty years old, William John Russell, owned and operated various properties, including manufacturing facilities that supplied shoes and cloth to the Confederate Army. The destruction of such properties was a principal mission of General Sherman.

By the time General Sherman arrived in Marietta, William John Russell had joined the Confederate Militia and was stationed at the Confederate Arsenal in Augusta, Georgia. He left his properties and son in the care of his wife. As the sounds of General Sherman's artillery grew louder in Marietta, Harriette Russell decided to flee. Her husband had urged her to go to South Carolina or North Carolina where she had kin but she did not want to be so far away from him and chose to flee south and wait out the war in rural Georgia, approximately fifty miles from Augusta. The mill workers and their families employed at the properties of William John Russell who did not flee were boarded on trains and shipped north. Most of them wound up in Indiana and never returned to Georgia. The Union Army destroyed all of the Russell properties.

At the end of the war, William John Russell returned to Marietta, but he had nothing on which to rebuild his prior lifestyle. He would be a hired hand for the rest of his life. He shortly accepted a job in a small community near Athens, Georgia, some seventy-five miles northeast of Atlanta, where he became the superintendent of a textile mill owned by an absentee landlord He raised his family there, including Senator Russell's father. The young Richard Russell was a precocious child, known for reading and intellectual pursuits. As he grew into manhood, he graduated from the University of Georgia School of Law and became a lawyer in Athens. In addition, like his father before him, he became an enterprising young businessman, starting a bank, newspaper, and railroad.

Senator Russell's father had previously been married, but his wife died during childbirth. They had lost two previous children. He remained a widower for some five years after the death of his first wife before he married Ina Dillard, a beautiful young schoolteacher in Athens. The couple eventually had thirteen surviving children. (They were a remarkable group. In addition to Richard Russell, his brothers included a federal court of appeals judge, a doctor, a university professor, a minister, a career military officer, and a farmer. His sisters included a lawyer at a time when there were few women lawyers, several school-teachers, and the wife of a United States congressman and member of the Georgia Board of Regents.)

Richard Russell, Sr., did well in Athens in business and law, but his major goal was to hold high political office. He succeeded in being elected to the local school board and to the state legislature, where he was a progressive legislator who championed increased educational opportunities for women. Notwithstanding this success, Senator Russell's father felt that he was not fully accepted in the university-dominated social structure of Athens. He announced to his wife that they would be moving to Winder, Georgia, some thirty miles west of Athens. Ina was not pleased about her husband's decision to leave Athens because she loved the intellectual stimulation of the university environment, but of course she acceded to his wishes. At about this same time, the elder Richard Russell decided to change his middle name from "Brumby" to "Brevard" because two members of the Brumby family were known to have alcohol problems and he was afraid that would damage his planned political career.

Richard Russell, Sr., did achieve a certain measure of success in politics. In addition to being elected to the state legislature, he was elected district attorney and eventually became a member of the first Georgia Court of Appeals and then Chief Justice of the Georgia Supreme Court. He was not able to achieve his highest ambition to be elected governor of Georgia or United States senator. When his first son was born on November 2, 1897, he named him Richard B. Russell, Jr. From the beginning, he intended that his oldest son and namesake would achieve the political offices that he had failed to achieve. Letters written to Senator Russell when he was a young man make it clear that both his father and mother expected him to achieve in politics what had been denied to his father. The father's lack of success was not for lack of trying. He ran for public office seventeen times, including for Congress, governor, and United States senator. He failed in each of the latter instances. A particularly futile race occurred in 1928 when he opposed the legendary United States senator Walter F. George. He had no chance of winning, and the race was an embarrassment to the Russell family.

The precocious young Dick Russell liked to read and to pretend that he was a general commanding Southern forces in the Civil War. When he was growing up, he heard conversations among neighbors who had actually fought in the Civil War, and the subject became his lifelong interest. He read so many books about it that he eventually became as much of an expert on the subject as the most accomplished university professor. Senator Russell's early education consisted of home schooling and then attending a small school near his home. When he was about thirteen or fourteen years old, his father decided to enroll him in the Gordon Military Institute (now Gordon College) in Barnesville, Georgia, which was considered one of the best prep schools in Georgia. His father believed that he would make contacts invaluable to his political career. The young Russell, however, disappointed his parents at Gordon. His grades were mediocre at best, and he appeared to be more interested in social activities than in his studies. Numerous letters from his parents emphasized that he would be a great disappointment if he did not adequately prepare for a life of significant achievement. The admonitions apparently did little good. After several years at Gordon, Senator Russell's father decided that he should transfer to the Powder Springs A&M School in Powder Springs, Georgia. He hoped this would instill greater discipline in his son, but within a year, the younger Russell was back at Gordon. He did eventually graduate from Gordon, although he admitted later in his life that it was due more to the mercy of his teachers than the state of his learning.

A Rising Political Star

Upon graduating from Gordon, Dick Russell immediately enrolled in the University of Georgia Law School, his father's alma mater. While his grades were never outstanding, they were somewhat better, and he graduated on schedule. He also joined the Navy during this time, though his brief stint at the Navy Supply School in Athens was the extent of his military career—a bit ironic since he later served for more than fifteen years as chairman of the Senate Armed Services Committee. Immediately upon graduating from law school, Senator Russell returned to Winder and began practicing law with his father. Within a year, he entered a race for the Georgia House of Representatives. He later said that he did not enter the race expecting to win but to become better known to prospective jurors who would decide his cases. Regardless of his intent, he won against a much more experienced opponent. It was a habit-forming result. The young Richard Russell was a member of the Georgia Legislature before he was twenty-five years of age. He went on to serve in the State House of Representatives for ten years, the last four as Speaker. In the legislature, he aligned himself with a group of young representatives who intended to change state government. He generally worked behind the scenes and often gave others credit for work he had done. Russell also became known as one who was completely dependable, and his word was his bond. These traits, in addition to his familiarity with the procedural rules, benefited him greatly when he later arrived in Washington.

In 1930, Richard Russell shocked the political establishment by announcing that he was a candidate for governor. Several seasoned candidates were contending for the position, and he was given virtually no chance of winning. In fact, many thought it evidenced the same lack of judgment his father had demonstrated in undertaking unrealistic political campaigns. The younger Russell, however, mounted an energetic statewide campaign and simply outworked the other candidates. His most formidable opponent was Georgia Secretary of State George Carswell. In the campaign, Carswell made the unusual charge that Georgia would have no first lady if the unmarried Richard Russell were elected. Responding to this issue, Russell assured the people of Georgia that if they elected him governor, there would be a Mrs. Russell in the governor's mansion. Everyone assumed he meant that he would marry one of the several young ladies he was dating at the time. But he meant that he would install his mother as Georgia's First Lady, which is exactly what he did. Later in his life, he said that he could never decide whether the young ladies he dated were in love with him or with the governor. Utilizing his contacts at Gordon and in the state legislature, he won the governorship by a substantial margin. In 1931, when he took the oath of office from his father, who was chief justice of the Georgia Supreme Court, Richard B. Russell, Jr., became the youngest governor in Georgia history.

Governor Russell served for two years during the depths of the Great Depression. When he took office, teachers in public schools were paid with script, and the state was practically bankrupt. He engineered a massive reorganization of state government in which the number of state agencies and bureaus were reduced from more than one hundred to less than twenty. The state budget was slashed, including his own salary as governor. He reorganized the way in which Georgia purchased schoolbooks and used some of the scarce state funds to jumpstart Georgia's turpentine industry. Soon, teachers were paid with real money, and the state budget was balanced. Probably the most significant accomplishment of his term as governor was a complete reorganization of Georgia's higher education system. Prior to the Russell Administration, each of Georgia's numerous colleges and universities were considered completely separate and managed their own affairs. Political considerations had priority over educational ones. The Russell Reorganization Plan created a unified Board of Regents that oversaw all public colleges and universities in the state. That system still exists in Georgia today. Many other states, including New York, adopted similar systems patterned after the Georgia plan.

It was widely assumed that Richard Russell would run for a second two-year term as governor in 1932, but then Georgia's senior United States senator, William J. Harris, died in office. Governor Russell appointed the editor of the *Atlanta Journal* newspaper as an interim senator and announced that he would run as a candidate for the office. Again, many in the state thought this was audacious and presumptuous, since a highly respected longtime congressman from Georgia, Charles Crisp, had already announced his plans to run. Just as when he ran for governor, the young Richard Russell had little chance of defeating Congressman Crisp. Almost all the major newspapers in Georgia, except the *Atlanta Journal*, endorsed Crisp. Crisp accused Governor Russell of buying the endorsement of the *Atlanta Journal* by appointing its editor as an interim senator. Of the out-of-state papers, all supported Congressman Crisp, including the *Washington Post* and the *New York Times*. Undaunted, Richard Russell ran the same kind of intensive statewide campaign he had run for the governor's race. He accused Congressman Crisp of being a tool of the special interests, including the power company lobby, and referred to him as "Kilowatt Charlie." When the votes were counted, Richard B. Russell, Jr. was installed as the United States' youngest senator.

A Senator's Senator

Richard B. Russell, Jr., arrived in Washington in early 1933 as the newest and youngest member of the United States Senate. He was welcomed by Georgia's senior senator, Walter F. George, against whom Senator Russell's father had made the ill-advised campaign in 1928. Senator George greeted Russell warmly and helped him in every way he could. As he built a powerful career in the Senate—due both to luck and to his unique abilities, Russell never forgot this courtesy.

In early 1933, Huey Long, the populist United States senator from Louisiana, was making life miserable for the Senate leadership. He had resigned all of his committee assignments and devoted himself full-time to harassing Senate Majority Leader Joe Robinson of Arkansas. Without the burden of attending committee meetings, he stayed on the Senate floor and offered procedural delaying motions to block the processing of legislation. Majority Leader Robinson approached the new senator from Georgia about his committee assignments. Senator Russell told him that his predecessor, Senator Harris, had been on the Appropriations Committee, and he wanted to follow in Harris's footsteps. Senator Robinson tried to explain to the young upstart from Georgia that such an appointment was out of the question because a number of long-time senators were waiting to be appointed to that committee. He asked Senator Russell for his second and third choices. Russell replied that he did not desire to be appointed to any committees if he could not be on the Appropriations Committee. After all, his people expected him to be on that committee. Senator Russell later said that he did not insist on the appointment because of the activities of Senator Long; at the time, he was not fully aware of them. Regardless of his reason, Senator Robinson decided to buy his peace with Senator Russell by giving him his appointment as a freshman senator to the Appropriations Committee. That was almost unprecedented in the Senate. It assured that Richard Russell would be a senator of influence from the beginning of his career. He served on the Appropriations Committee for his entire thirty-eight years as a member of the Senate and was its chairman at the time of his death in 1971.

Even more remarkable was his next stroke of luck. The Appropriations Committee operates primarily through subcommittees, and the subcommittee chairmen have immense power. One of the most important subcommittees at the time was the Agriculture Appropriations Subcommittee. It was particularly important to Georgia, whose economy was primarily agricultural. The Agriculture Appropriations Subcommittee provided the funds to finance the various Department of Agriculture programs that assisted farmers. The senator who should have been appointed chairman of this subcommittee , Senator Cotton Ed Smith of South Carolina, was an archenemy of the chairman of the Appropriations Committee, Senator Carter Glass of Virginia. Despite the seniority rules, Senator Glass had no intentions of appointing Senator

Smith as subcommittee chairman. Instead, Chairman Glass decided to appoint the newest member of the committee, Richard B. Russell, as Agriculture Appropriations Subcommittee chairman. Therefore, Russell immediately secured not only an almost unprecedented appointment to the Appropriations Committee as a freshman senator but also won the even more improbable position of chairman of one of the most important subcommittees.

Richard Russell's unique abilities also helped propel him into a position of influence in the Senate early in his career. He studied and mastered the far more complex and arcane procedural rules of the United States Senate, and he also asked the Senate parliamentarian to provide him with a copy of the extensive precedents interpreting those rules through the years. Soon, he was known in the Senate as the person most knowledgeable about Senate rules. Other senators who had been there for years came to him for advice as to how they could utilize the rules in supporting or opposing legislation. As he had done in Georgia, he also developed a reputation for working behind the scenes in the legislative process and not being concerned about who received credit for the legislation that passed. Senators felt comfortable confiding in him because they knew he would honor those confidences. In its Marble Room, the Senate maintains at least one newspaper from each state. Richard Russell read newspapers from across the country, and it soon became apparent to other senators that he understood the important political issues in their states as well as they did. Richard Russell was becoming a "senator's senator."

Another main reason for Russell's immediate influence and prestige was his relationship with President Franklin Roosevelt. Good friends since they had served as governors of their respective states[,] with Russell having given a nominating speech for Roosevelt at the 1932 Democratic National Convention when Roosevelt secured the first of his four nominations for president, they both arrived in Washington in early 1933. Richard Russell became one of the most consistent and enthusiastic supporters of the New Deal in the Senate. He supported almost all of Roosevelt's early legislative proposals, and his support was decisive in passing a number of the agriculture bills. He was known as someone who had the ear of the president.

Senator Richard Russell's committee assignments, work ethic, knowledge of the rules, and relationship with the president were important, but most significant to his standing with the other senators were his relationships with those senators. Whether they were Democrats or Republicans, he was a friend of them all. The committees he chaired were models of bipartisanship. His best friends in the Senate included the ranking Republicans on the committees he chaired, such as Senator Leverett Saltonstall on the Armed Services Committee and Senator Milton Young on the Appropriations Committee. In 1952, when Richard Russell was seeking the Democratic presidential nomination and Senator Young was up for reelection in his home state of North Dakota, Young announced that he would vote for Richard Russell if he received the Democratic nomination. This created a firestorm of criticism in North Dakota and threatened Senator Young's own reelection. Senator Russell wrote him a handwritten letter in which he said, "If I had to choose between being President or having the confidence of Milt Young, I would choose the latter."

Senator Russell also particularly cultivated newly elected senators. While he went to few social events, he regularly attended the opening receptions of new senators, going out of his way to try to help them early in their careers. They came to him not only for his advice but also for his help in obtaining their desired committee appointments. In 1962, when Senator Edward Kennedy was elected to the Senate, he asked his brother, President Kennedy, who had served in the Senate with Senator Russell, what he could do to get off to a good start. President Kennedy told him to go see Richard Russell. Senator Robert C. Byrd of West Virginia, who came to the Senate in 1959, wrote Senator Russell a letter at the end of his first two years in the Senate, thanking him for making such a difference in his Senate career and for helping him learn the ropes in the Senate.

In addition to Senator Russell's appointment as a freshman to the Appropriations Committee, he was also appointed to the Immigration Committee and to the Naval Affairs Committee, which was later reconstituted into the Armed Services Committee. In fact, the first committee chaired by Richard Russell was the Immigration Committee. His power on that committee is exemplified by an experience that Alan Cranston had with him. At the time, Cranston was a lobbyist in Washington, and his clients included various Jewish organizations. When World War II broke out, certain Jewish citizens who were abroad could not return to the United States due to a quirk in the immigration laws. Cranston was told that the only person who could solve this problem quickly was Richard Russell. He discovered that Russell was in an Atlanta hospital but was able to get through to him on the telephone and bring the problem to his attention. Within a few days, Chairman Russell got legislation through both houses of Congress from his hospital bed. Senator Alan Cranston related this story in his eulogy [for] Senator Russell after Russell died in 1971. Alan Cranston later became the majority leader of the United States Senate.

Senator Russell also used his famous sense of humor in dealing with his fellow senators. I saw this on display in regard to Senator Thomas McIntyre of New Hampshire, one of the few Democrats New Hampshire had sent to the Senate in a long time. Senator Russell welcomed him and assisted him in being assigned to the Armed Services Committee. When Senator McIntyre was up for reelection a few years later, he wanted to have his picture made with Chairman Russell for use in his campaign literature. As the photographer was about to take the picture, McIntyre asked Russell if they could switch places so that his better side could face the camera. Senator Russell, who was almost completely bald, quipped, "You are lucky to have a good side." Russell was also famous for needling Lyndon Johnson when he served in the Senate. Even after Johnson became president, the needling continued. One night Russell and President Johnson were having dinner together at the White House when Johnson complained about a certain senator and observed that he had no place in the Senate. Senator Russell responded, "Mr. President, is that not the same man you were praising a week or so ago as one of the finest members of the Senate?"

By the time of World War II, Richard Russell's attention was increasingly focused on national security. He had already earned a reputation in the Senate as being one of the most knowledgeable members in regard to military matters. When the Senate decided to have a group of senators visit each theater of the war to observe how well American soldiers were supplied and equipped, they selected Richard Russell as the head of the delegation. The group traveled around the world for some eight weeks and visited each theater, meeting with such leaders as Winston Churchill and Dwight Eisenhower. When the senators returned to Washington, Senator Russell made a speech to the Senate that had a major influence on America's post-World War II policy. He became a vigorous supporter of the Marshall Plan to rebuild Europe after the war and to establish NATO.

The Senate created the Senate Space Committee in 1958 and the Joint Committee on Atomic Energy in 1946. Richard Russell was appointed as one of the first members of both committees. He became an avid supporter of the space program and civilian control over it. He also warned of future energy shortages in America and of the necessary role atomic energy would have to play in meeting those shortages. History has judged him to be correct. These additional committee assignments by no means lessened his interest in agriculture. His proudest legislative accomplishment was the National School Lunch Act, which he started as a pilot program as chairman of the Senate Agriculture Appropriations Subcommittee. He saw that an excellent use of surplus agricultural products would be to provide free lunches to America's schoolchildren. At a time when the administration did not support this program, each year he would insert in the agriculture appropriations bill monies (what would today be considered an " earmark") to continue the program for another year. Finally, in 1947, he was able to get the Senate to authorize the program permanently. In the late 1990s, primarily because of the efforts of Georgia senator Max Cleland, the legislation was renamed "The Richard B. Russell National School Lunch Act." Millions of American children have received free school lunches under this program.

Richard Russell and Civil Rights

No discussion of Richard Russell's Senate career would be complete without considering his steadfast opposition to civil rights legislation. It is not my purpose here to offer excuses or apologies. Richard Russell's record on civil rights is what it is. I do believe, however, that it is important to consider his position in the context of the times in which he lived and that the positives not be ignored or the negatives exaggerated. In 1896, the year before Richard Russell was born, the United States Supreme Court declared segregation to be legal and constitutional as long as it was separate but equal. That did not materially change until the Supreme Court's landmark *Brown v. Board of Education* decision in 1954. In that decision, the court declared segregation to be inherently unequal and therefore unconstitutional. By that time, Richard Russell was almost sixty years of age. He had lived all of his formative years under a system of strict segregation that was seemingly sanctioned by the highest court in the land.

It is difficult for us today to accept some of America's practices in past times. For example, it is difficult to understand how the most respected founding fathers of this country—including George Washington and Thomas Jefferson—could have owned slaves. Or how the family of one of the most popular presidents in the next century—Andrew Jackson—could have bought and sold slaves while he was in the White House. The answer, of course, is that we are all products of our generation. Just as the segregation policies of fifty and sixty years ago are difficult to understand now, undoubtedly many policies now in effect will be difficult to understand in the coming years.

One thing that set Richard Russell apart on civil rights was that he was not a demagogue or a racist, as were many Southern politicians of his era. He did not raise the race question in his political campaigns. When his opponents did so, such as Eugene Talmadge in 1936, Russell would simply accuse them of trying to divert voters' attention from the real issues. To be sure, Richard Russell was a segregationist. He opposed all civil rights bills that were brought before the Senate during his tenure. In fact, if it had not been for his influence and standing in the Senate, meaningful civil rights legislation would probably have passed twenty years earlier. Richard Russell's opposition to civil rights legislation was based principally on his constitutional arguments that policies related to operation of the schools, public accommodations, and similar matters were reserved for the states and not within the province of the federal government. When he officially became chairman of the Southern Caucus in 1948, a number of powerful southern senators were outright racists. In prior civil rights debates, they had regularly used the word "nigger" on the Senate floor and had engaged in such irrelevancies as reading southern recipes during the debates. Richard Russell put a stop to this. He insisted that unless senators had something relevant to say[,] they should let other senators do the talking.

Aside from the fact that the Supreme Court had declared segregation unconstitutional, a principal fallacy of the position of southern senators on civil rights was, of course, that the South made no real effort to make segregation separate but equal. All emphasis was on separate and none of it was on equal. I know this from personal knowledge. When I was growing up in Butts County, the black schools had inferior facilities, teachers, and textbooks. After my five years of working for Senator Russell, I was asked on occasion what I thought might have changed his position on civil rights other than being born in a different era. I replied that I thought if he had had some of the experiences I had in my early years, he might have been able to overcome the prejudices that were so prevalent when he grew up. For example, while debating at the University of Georgia, I was defeated fair and square by black debaters from schools outside the South. When I enrolled in law school at Georgetown, I had black law professors. When I started practicing law, I was defeated in the courtroom fair and square by black lawyers. Richard Russell had none of those experiences. The only blacks he knew when he was growing up were field hands and house servants. I believe he would have benefited by knowing and working closely with African Americans such as Barack Obama, Colin Powell, Condoleezza Rice, or Andrew Young.

Richard Russell's correspondence with constituents in the 1950s and early 1960s make clear that he knew segregation was coming to an end. He apparently believed that it would be easier to gain acceptance of this new day in the South if southern senators put up the strongest possible fight in the Senate. He led the longest filibuster in Senate history before cloture was invoked and the 1964 Civil Rights Bill became law. When President Johnson signed it into law, widespread tension, unrest, and violence swept the South. In Georgia, a black military reserve officer was brutally murdered on a Georgia public highway. At a time when many southern politicians were condoning if not encouraging unrest and violence, Richard Russell addressed the issue in his first public speech in Georgia after President Johnson signed the legislation into law. The speech, given at Berry College in Rome, was about economic development in northwest Georgia and not civil rights. However, in departing from his prepared remarks at the end of the speech, Richard Russell said,

> The signature of President Johnson has placed it on the statute books of our country.... It is the understatement of the year to say that I do not like these statutes.... However, they are now on the books and it becomes our duty as good citizens to learn to live with them for as long as they are there.... It is therefore our duty as good and patriotic citizens, in a period that will undoubtedly be marked by tension and unrest as this statute is

implemented, to avoid all violence. Violence and law violation will only compound our difficulties and increase our troubles.

From the White House, President Johnson said that this statement by Senator Russell was the most important one made by any public official in the period after the Civil Rights Act became law. Editorials in newspapers across Georgia praised the Russell speech and called on other southern politicians to cease their efforts to stir up unrest and violence.

During the five years I worked for Richard Russell, I never heard him use the word "nigger" in public or private. I saw him almost every day, traveled with him extensively, attended meetings with county school superintendents from Georgia as they tried to desegregate the schools, and attended his family reunions in Winder. I never saw the slightest evidence of animosity from him toward African Americans. I observed him dealing with African Americans in three different settings—his maid in Winder, the dining room staff in the Senators' Private Dining Room, and Senator Edward Brooke of Massachusetts.

Modine Thomas, a longtime maid for the Russell family, was Senator Russell's maid in Winder. She must have started when she was a young girl because she was in her fifties when I knew her. After Senator Russell's parents died, he continued to employ Modine as his maid. From the numerous times I traveled with the senator to Winder, there is no doubt in my mind who [controlled] the Russell household. Richard Russell and Modine had a wonderful relationship based on mutual respect and even affection. She came the closest of anyone I have ever observed in being able to tell Richard Russell what to do. I remember one day at lunch when Modine had prepared her usual noonday meal. It included an assortment of vegetables as well as a tasty sweet potato dish that was almost like a dessert. Senator Russell, as usual, was pigging out on the dessert at the expense of the vegetables. Modine suddenly came into the room and said to Senator Russell, "Mr. R. B., you are eating too much of them sweet potatoes and none of your vegetables." Senator Russell responded, "Well, Modine, you are, of course, correct, but it is all your fault because if you did not make it so damn good, I would not eat so much of it." Their appreciation for each other was evident in the easy banter that went on between them. In Russell's final illness, he was disappointed that he would not be able to go to Georgia for Christmas. I remember him saying, "Modine will be expecting me." After reaching seventy years of age, I think I know a little about judging the relationships of people. There is no doubt in my mind that Richard Russell and Modine Thomas enjoyed a relationship of mutual respect, concern for each other, and affection.

Senator Russell's relationship with the staff in the Senators' Private Dining Room in the Capitol is also instructive. From my time spent in the dining room when Senator Russell was eating, it was clear to me that he was the staff's favorite senator. Most, though not all, were African American. He would ask them about their family members and other personal matters. They would occasionally seek his advice on family matters. They sent him flowers on a number of occasions when he was in the hospital. One of the staff members did an oral history interview for the Russell Library in Athens and talked about how kind he was to her. She specifically said that he frequently asked about her son who was in college.

The final interaction Senator Russell had with African Americans that I observed was with Senator Edward W. Brooke of Massachusetts. Brooke was a former attorney general of Massachusetts who was elected to the Senate in 1967. I can remember going to the Senate floor one day to get Senator Russell for a constituent meeting. He was sitting next to Senator Brooke, and the two were engaged in a private conversation. It was clear to me that it was not the first talk that had occurred between them. I interrupted and told Senator Russell that his constituents had arrived. He indicated that I would have to wait because he was talking to Senator Brooke. When Senator Russell died, one of the finest eulogies given on the Senate floor was by Senator Brooke. He did not mention civil rights but talked about the wonderful things Richard Russell helped bring to pass, including electricity for rural people; support for education, science, and technology; and the school lunch program. One would have thought that Richard Russell would have little in common with Senator Brooke because he was an African American Republican senator from the Northeast. However, from my observations and from Senator Brooke's eulogy, one can only conclude that they had a relationship based on mutual respect. In his recent autobiography, *Bridging the Divide* (New Brunswick, N.J. Rutgers University Press, 2007), Senator Brooke says this about the southern senators he met after he was elected to the United States Senate: "I felt that if a senator truly believed in racial separatism I could live with that, but it was increasingly evident that some members of the Senate played on bigotry purely for political gain" (p. 149). Richard Russell believed that segregation was the best policy, particularly for states like Georgia that had large numbers of whites and blacks, and he also believed that the Constitution of the United States left these decisions to the individual states and not to the federal government. History has adjudged him to be wrong on both counts, but no one has suggested that he was not sincere in his beliefs.

The senator who fought Richard Russell the hardest on civil rights was probably Hubert H. Humphrey of Minnesota. As the mayor of Minneapolis, he had electrified the 1948 Democratic National Convention with his civil rights oratory. In fact, in response to Humphrey's speech and the Democratic Party platform, Southern delegates persuaded Richard Russell, who was far away in Winder, Georgia, to permit his name to be placed in nomination for president so that southern delegates would have someone for whom they could vote and would not have to walk out of the convention. Shortly thereafter, Humphrey was elected to the United States Senate. He was brash and not at all deferential to the Senate elders. The southern senators, including Senator Russell, isolated him and ostracized him. Humphrey later said that it was the most difficult and depressing period of his life. During that time, he heard Richard Russell ask several of the southern senators, "Why do you suppose the people of Minnesota would send a damn fool like that down here to represent them?" Soon, however, because of Humphrey's outgoing personality and with the aid of Lyndon Johnson, who helped build a bridge to the southern senators, the animosity and isolation decreased. And Richard Russell found that he had things in common with Hubert Humphrey. One day Russell walked through the Senate chamber as Humphrey made a speech on agriculture to an almost empty Senate. Minnesota's economy was as heavily agricultural as Georgia's. As Senator Russell heard some of the points Humphrey made, he sat in a nearby chair and listened to the speech. Soon, Russell was saying "Amen" almost as if he were at a southern revival.

Russell and Humphrey became friends and worked together on a number of legislative matters. Russell once said of Humphrey, "I like Hubert a lot. He can charm the birds right out of the trees. The only problem I have with Hubert is that he has more solutions than the country has problems." Their political philosophies were different, but their respect for each other was great. When Russell died in 1971, Senator Humphrey gave one of the most effusive eulogies on the Senate floor. He said in part, "He displayed an acute understanding of the issues and problems facing our government. And whether you agreed with him or not, you could not fault Richard Russell's sincerity, dedication, honesty, and integrity." Senator Humphrey concluded his eulogy by quoting an editorial from the *New York Times* that appeared on the day after Russell's death: "Public men, whether they are right or wrong, are measured by their character and by the size of the issues which concern them. By these standards, Richard Russell was a big man."

A President's Senator

Richard Russell was a serious candidate for the Democratic presidential nomination in 1952. He won the Florida primary and campaigned across the country. At the convention, he received delegate votes from twenty-seven states and finished second to Governor Adlai Stevenson of Illinois. He was offered the vice presidential nomination but declined, indicating that he preferred to stay in the Senate. He was asked to recommend someone for the vice presidential nomination , and he named Senator John Sparkman of Alabama, one of the more moderate of the southern senators. The Stevenson/Sparkman ticket was decisively defeated in the general election by the Republican ticket of Dwight Eisenhower and Richard Nixon.

While Russell was never elected president, he was a confidential adviser to six American presidents. Every president from Franklin Roosevelt to Richard Nixon knew Richard Russell well before they entered the White House[,] and he became one of their most important advisers. Several of them thought he should have been president. Harry S. Truman said that Russell probably would have been president if he had been from Indiana, Missouri, or Kentucky. At a public dinner in Washington honoring Senator Russell, Lyndon B. Johnson, while serving as vice president to John F. Kennedy, said that if he could personally select the president of the United States, he would select Richard Russell. At the time of Senator Russell's death, Richard M. Nixon said if Russell had been born ten years later and served in the Senate ten years later, he would have been president of the United States. Nixon aptly described Russell as a "president's senator." A brief review of Senator Russell's relationship with the six presidents with whom he served will reveal why President Nixon was correct.

Franklin D. Roosevelt

As discussed earlier in this chapter, Franklin Roosevelt and Richard Russell were close friends before they arrived in Washington in early 1933. Russell became one of the most consistent and reliable supporters of Roosevelt's New Deal program in the early years of his first presidential term. However, one characteristic of Richard Russell would result in problems in his relationship with Roosevelt as well as with a number of other presidents—Russell's independence. No matter how close his friendship was with a president, Russell insisted on voting in a manner that he considered to be in the country's best interest.

The first source of friction in the Roosevelt–Russell relationship was over Roosevelt's "Court Packing Plan." The Supreme Court of the United States had declared several of Roosevelt's legislative proposals, which Richard Russell had uniformly supported, unconstitutional. Roosevelt proposed to deal with the Supreme Court problem by purging certain justices and creating additional vacancies that he would fill by appointing justices who agreed with him. Specifically, Roosevelt proposed to impose strict age limits on members of the Court and to increase the size of the Court from nine members to fifteen members. This proposal caused Russell great concern because, under the Constitution, there were supposed to be three co-equal branches of the government: the executive, the legislative, and the judicial. If a president could arbitrarily enlarge the size of the Supreme Court and impose age limits on its members because he disagreed with court decisions, Russell was concerned this would undermine the constitutional principle of separation of powers. The senator from Georgia was in a tight spot. He was one of Roosevelt's strongest supporters and did not want to have to oppose, for the first time, an important legislative proposal of the president. Russell decided to seek a compromise. He and a handful of other senators who had generally been supportive of Roosevelt proposed that the Court be increased by two members but that there be no age limits. They took their proposal to the White House and presented it to Roosevelt. President Roosevelt would have none of it. Senator Russell and the other senators returned to Capitol Hill and opposed the proposal, which basically doomed the Court Packing Plan[,] although there were a few more unsuccessful efforts at compromise. It was Roosevelt's first major legislative defeat.

Not long after the disagreement over the Court Packing Plan, Roosevelt and Russell had another disagreement that involved Georgia politics. Just as Roosevelt wanted to purge the Supreme Court of justices who did not agree with him, he also wanted to purge the Senate of senators who did not agree with him. One of those senators was Russell's colleague from Georgia, Walter F. George. Russell was summoned to the White House to meet with one of Roosevelt's key aides. The Roosevelt staffer outlined the plan to defeat Senator George. Roosevelt would select an opponent in Georgia to run against George and give him strong support. He also expected Richard Russell's support. Russell explained to the Roosevelt aide that his policy was not to become involved in the politics of other people in Georgia. He said he would not be in a position to oppose Senator George. Roosevelt was not happy. To put maximum pressure on Senator Russell, Roosevelt decided to select Lawrence Camp of Atlanta, a former United States attorney, as the candidate to oppose Senator George. Camp happened to be one of Richard Russell's closest friends and strongest supporters. If Roosevelt thought this would force Russell off the sidelines, he was badly mistaken. Senator Russell maintained strict neutrality in the race, and Camp was decisively defeated. It not only further weakened Richard Russell's relationship with President Roosevelt but also destroyed his friendship with Lawrence Camp. Senator Russell was undoubtedly affected in his decision in this matter by the kind treatment he received from Senator George when he arrived in Washington (notwithstanding Senator Russell's father having opposed George in 1928) as well as Senator George's strong support of Russell in 1936 when Eugene Talmadge had challenged him.

In a series of interviews with WSB Television toward the end of his career, which resulted in the film *Georgia Giant*, Russell was asked about his assessment of President Roosevelt. He said he thought that Roosevelt was a great man and a great president. When asked what he considered Roosevelt's greatest weakness to be, he said "ego." Russell went on to say that every person should be able to consider whether at least on a theoretical basis the other side might be correct. The implication clearly was that Roosevelt was unable to do that. While Russell continued to be generally supportive of Roosevelt's policies, particularly in foreign affairs, they no longer had the close personal relationship that had existed before the Court Packing Plan and the campaign against Senator George.

Harry S. Truman

In 1945, when Franklin Roosevelt died in Warm Springs, Georgia, Vice President Harry S. Truman became president. No one has ever entered the office of president at such a critical time but with such little preparation. Truman was Roosevelt's afterthought choice for vice president in his fourth term. Roosevelt was not in good health at the time. Nonetheless, he did not include Truman on any consultations with respect to American policy, even in regard to World War II. He did not brief Truman on his negotiations with Joseph Stalin, and Truman was not even told that the United States was working on an atomic bomb.

Harry S. Truman and Richard B. Russell knew each other well before Truman became president. They occupied adjoining seats in the Senate for several years. Russell liked the senator from Missouri because of his down-home and frank personality. He did not consider him a particularly outstanding senator, but he recognized Truman for his hard work and integrity. Russell would later say that Truman grew tremendously in the presidency and was faced with some of the most difficult decisions of any president. Russell was generally supportive of the Truman policies, including the decision to drop the atomic bomb on Japan to bring World War II to a conclusion, the Marshall Plan to rebuild Europe after the war, the establishment of the North Atlantic Treaty Organization (NATO), and the creation of the Jewish State of Israel. He was frequently at the White House in the Truman years and was recognized by the president as one of the most important members of the Senate, particularly in regard to military policy.

The only major disagreement Russell had with Truman was over civil rights. In an address to a joint session of Congress, President Truman proposed sweeping civil rights legislation. Truman likely knew from his years in the Senate that he would not be able to pass major civil rights legislation over the objection of Senator Russell and the other southern senators. He decided to do the next best thing. He desegregated the armed forces by executive order and also created a Civil Rights Commission to study and report on the nation's failings in the area of civil rights. While Russell and the other southern senators could and did bottle up the proposed civil rights legislation, there was little they could do about the executive orders. Truman probably did more to advance civil rights than any modern president prior to Lyndon Johnson.

In 1951, President Truman fired Army General Douglas McArthur from his command in Korea. This was at the height of the Korean War and created a tremendous controversy in the United States. McArthur favored a much more aggressive policy in Korea than Truman was pursuing, even at the risk of a war with China. He made statements to the press inconsistent with Truman's policy and generally acted as if he were the commander in chief instead of Harry Truman. Harry Truman was not someone to trifle with either as president or as a senator. He dismissed General McArthur for insubordination. When the general returned to the United States, he was given a hero's welcome. It was reported that nearly one hundred thousand people greeted him when he landed in San Francisco. At each stop he made across the country en route to the nation's Capitol, large crowds cheered him. When he arrived in Washington, McArthur was invited to address a joint session of Congress. The capitol was in a frenzy. There were calls for Truman's impeachment and talk about McArthur challenging Truman for the presidency in 1952.

The Senate decided that there was no choice but to investigate Truman's firing of General McArthur. They decided to appoint a special investigative subcommittee consisting of key members of the Armed Services and Foreign Relations Committees. Richard Russell was chosen to chair the subcommittee. Russell was a great admirer of General McArthur and considered him one of America's greatest military leaders. However, he also believed strongly in the constitutional principle of civilian control over the military and that the president was the commander in chief of the armed forces. He did not disagree with President Truman's dismissal of General McArthur, but he did disagree with the way in which it was done. He thought it could have been done with more respect and that Truman could have told McArthur directly as opposed to having McArthur learn about it indirectly.

The first explosive issue the investigative subcommittee had to tackle was whether the hearings would be open or closed. The Republicans pushed strongly for open hearings because they thought it was a great opportunity to embarrass Truman. The Democrats generally wanted closed hearings because of a concern about the amount of classified information that would be disclosed in the testimony of numerous witnesses. Russell came up with an ingenious compromise. The hearings would be closed, but at the end of each day a verbatim transcript of the hearing would be released to the press and the public after classified information had been redacted. While most Republicans opposed Chairman Russell's proposal, a few of Russell's key supporters on the Armed Services Committee, including the ranking Republican, Senator Leverett Saltonstall of Massachusetts, voted for the compromise, and it carried the day.

General McArthur was the lead witness on the first day of the hearings. Russell treated him with the utmost deference and respect, allowing him to complete his statement without interruption. However, he also asked the general some tough questions. One of them was what the general thought the actions of China would have been if his recommendations had been followed in Korea. General McArthur responded that he did not know and that the answer to that question was beyond his pay grade. The general's answer made the point—it was not beyond the president's pay grade. Other witnesses from the Pentagon, including several members of the Joint Chiefs of Staff, openly disagreed with General McArthur's position when they testified. The hearings continued for approximately six weeks, during which the subcommittee heard from numerous witnesses with a hearing record of more than three thousand pages. Gradually, McArthur's position was weakened and the furor died down. By the time the hearings concluded, there were no longer calls for Truman's impeachment and no further discussion of McArthur being a candidate for president in 1952. Russell had skillfully defused the crisis.

There was one remaining contentious issue. The Republicans were sure to use the opportunity afforded by a final report of the subcommittee to launch new attacks on Truman. Russell again came up with an ingenious solution. The subcommittee would issue no final report. Instead, it would rest on the record of the hearings that had been released to the public. In a close vote, the Russell proposal was adopted.

Many felt that the McArthur hearings were Russell's finest hour. His picture was on the cover of *Time Magazine*, and he immediately became a national figure. His name was prominently mentioned as a presidential candidate in 1952 when Truman announced that he would not seek reelection. In a private meeting at the White House, Truman told Russell that he wished he could be elected president but that the liberals in the Democratic Party would never accept him. Truman was correct.

Richard Russell's adroit handling of the McArthur investigation was still being praised some sixty years after the event. On April 10, 2011, two historians, Steven Casey of the London School of Economics and William Stueck, a history professor at the University of Georgia, published an article in the *Atlanta Journal Constitution* that they titled "MacArthur Hearing Revealed a Statesman." In it, they wrote, "...Russell performed an enormously valuable service to the nation. He exercised enormous tact and patience in reducing the temperature on Capitol Hill. He helped to build bridges between the two parties.... Russell's willingness to put aside differences with the president, and to manage a congressional hearing in a calm, nonpartisan manner, ought to be remembered today, when vicious partisanship all too often trumps unruffled statesmanship."

Dwight D. Eisenhower

To the best of my knowledge, Richard Russell first met Dwight Eisenhower when Eisenhower was stationed at the Pentagon before World War II. He also met with Eisenhower on Russell's around-the-world trip during World War II. He talked to him occasionally thereafter and became a great admirer of General Eisenhower. Russell was willing to run against him, however, if Russell had secured the 1952 Democratic presidential nomination. That not being the case, Russell was probably not disappointed when Eisenhower won the election.

By the time of Eisenhower's election as president, Lyndon B. Johnson had already become the Democratic leader in the Senate with critical assistance from Richard Russell. Since Eisenhower had won such an overwhelming election victory and was so popular in the country, Russell told Johnson that the best strategy for the Senate Democrats would be to work with the Eisenhower Administration where possible, modify its proposals where necessary, and vote against them only as a last resort. Johnson generally followed Russell's advice. This ushered in a degree of bipartisanship that has not been seen again in this country. It also tremendously helped Lyndon Johnson because he was given most of the credit for the effectiveness of the Senate Democratic effort. Russell supported almost all of Eisenhower's foreign policy and much of his domestic policy.

That is not to say there were no disagreements. One was over agriculture policy. Eisenhower's secretary of agriculture, Ezra Taft Benson, significantly changed agriculture policy by substantially reducing price support payments to America's farmers. This hit southern farmers particularly hard. Russell organized a coalition of southern Democrats and midwestern Republicans to oppose the new policy. They were successful in defeating some, but not all, of the Eisenhower farm program.

Another area of disagreement was civil rights. Eisenhower did not push civil rights nearly as hard as his predecessor, but he did send federal troops to Little Rock to put down a disturbance over the desegregation of schools there. Russell opposed that move because he believed it should have been left to local law enforcement agencies. Primarily at the urging of his attorney general, Herbert Brownwell, Eisenhower sent a Civil Rights Bill to the Senate in 1957. It was advertised as a modest proposal that should not be controversial. It would allegedly have made it easier for blacks to vote and would have also provided a statutory basis for the Fair Employment Commission. The southern senators, of course, were opposed to the bill and started a filibuster.

During a congressional recess while other senators were out partying, campaigning, or raising money for their campaigns, Richard Russell was in his office studying the civil rights bill and the record made before the Senate Judiciary Committee in regard thereto. He saw several references to an 1800s law that mystified him. Upon further research, he found that the enforcement mechanism for the 1957 Civil Rights Act was the same law used in the period after the Civil War to send federal troops to the South during Reconstruction. Russell immediately knew that this discovery would be dynamite. He kept his discovery to himself, however, because he wanted to use it at a time when it would be most effective. The debate continued. Finally, Russell asked for floor time.

At the beginning of his speech, Russell indicated that for the first time during his twenty-five years in the Senate, he would not entertain questions during the course of his remarks but would answer questions at the conclusion. A senator was overheard saying to one of his colleagues, "This is going to be good." As Russell spoke, the Senate floor filled up with senators. He started in a low-key manner by noting that the proponents of the bill both from the Eisenhower Administration and from within the Senate had advertised it as a modest and non-controversial measure. He said it was a "wolf in sheep's clothing." He then traced the history of the enforcement provision. Silence fell across the Senate, and one could tell from the expressions on the faces of both proponents and opponents that there was a feeling of shock. Russell said he doubted that the president knew about this provision because he did not believe Dwight Eisenhower would ever support such a proposal.

The Washington newspapers the next day carried headlines such as "Senator Russell drops bombshell on Eisenhower Civil Rights Bill." At a press conference on the day after the Russell speech, President Eisenhower was asked about it. He said he was not familiar with the charges Senator Russell had made and that he would have to talk to the attorney general about them. A reporter asked the President if he planned to meet with Senator Russell to discuss the matter. He replied that he was always available to meet with Richard Russell at any time and on any subject. A meeting at the White House was hastily arranged. More than ten years later, Russell referred to it as "the most unusual meeting I have ever had with a president." He said Eisenhower "poured out his heart" not only about the Civil Rights Bill but also about his other many frustrations in serving as president. Russell said that he was at first taken aback by the directness and frankness of Eisenhower's comments, but then, on reflection, he realized Eisenhower knew he was talking to a close friend who would keep the conversation confidential. Russell never revealed what Eisenhower said at that meeting.

The administration immediately modified the Civil Rights Bill by deleting the most objectionable features. Lyndon Johnson, the Democratic leader in the Senate, further watered down the bill in an effort to cut off the southern filibuster. Richard Russell believed that he and his colleagues should discontinue the filibuster, reserving the right to vote against the measure on final passage. After all the concessions that had been made by the proponents, he was afraid that if they did not discontinue, there was a chance cloture would be invoked for the first time on a civil rights legislative measure. He did not want to take a chance on that precedent in future fights. Not all the southern senators agreed with Russell. Strom Thurmond of South Carolina, for example, conducted his own one-man filibuster, which resulted in the longest continuous talking by one senator in Senate history. Most of the southern senators accepted Russell's advice, and the measure passed. The liberals in the Senate were so disappointed in the outcome that they accused Lyndon Johnson of being "Richard Russell's lapdog."

Then there was the question of Vietnam. The French had been defeated and were withdrawing from Vietnam. Some in the Eisenhower Administration, particularly his secretary of state, John Foster Dulles, were afraid the vacuum in Vietnam would be filled by Communists from the North. They proposed, and Eisenhower agreed, that the United States send military advisers to Vietnam to help train the South Vietnamese Army. Russell was adamantly opposed. In the first place, he did not believe that America had any vital strategic interest in Vietnam. He did not subscribe to the "domino theory" that held that the fall of Vietnam would result in numerous other countries in that region also becoming communists. He also feared that sending American military personnel to Vietnam would be a forerunner to the introduction of American ground troops. He asked what would happen if one of the American military advisers were killed or captured.

Senator Russell and Lyndon Johnson went to the White House to meet with Eisenhower. They presented their case against any military personnel from the United States being sent to Vietnam. The strength of the opposition was so great that the Eisenhower Administration put the proposal on the back burner. They would later resurrect it and send, over Russell's opposition, a limited number of military advisers to Vietnam. It would be the first step down a dangerous road that would result in numerous American casualties, untold amounts of American tax money being spent, and ultimate defeat and embarrassment. Ironically, it would also be the issue that would destroy the presidency of Lyndon Johnson.

John F. Kennedy

Richard Russell did not consider John F. Kennedy to be a particularly effective senator, but he liked his charisma and outgoing personality. The two also had in common an intense interest in the Civil War, often discussing Civil War battles when they served in the Senate together. This continued after Kennedy became president. In the book *True Compass* (New York, Twelve Hachette Book Group, 2009), published shortly before his death, Senator Edward Kennedy tells the story about a phone call President Kennedy made to Russell during Christmas holidays one year. The Kennedys were at their home in West Palm Beach, Florida, for the holidays, and Senator Kennedy and the president were discussing the Civil War. Neither of them could recall the name of a key battle that took place near the Georgia–Tennessee line. President Kennedy said that Richard Russell would know the answer. He asked the operator to get Senator Russell on the phone. The operator said she would try the senator's home in Winder, Georgia, as he would probably be there for the holidays. According to Edward Kennedy, President Kennedy told the operator that he was probably in his office at the Capitol and to try him there. Russell answered the phone. He was quickly able to tell President Kennedy that [it] was the Battle of Chickamauga, one of the bloodiest battles in the Civil War. He proceeded to describe the details of the battle and the commanding generals on both sides. The president and the senator from Georgia then got into a spirited discussion about which side had won the battle.

When Kennedy became president, he needed Russell's muscle and know-how to implement a campaign promise to build up the American military, as he had charged the Eisenhower Administration with allowing it to deteriorate. Russell was a key supporter in shepherding the Kennedy program through Congress. Kennedy also consulted Russell on his cabinet. He was considering Russell's fellow Georgian, Dean Rusk, as his secretary of state. Russell told the president that he liked Rusk. He said his only question was whether Rusk was strong enough to deal with the entrenched bureaucracy at the State Department, which Russell viewed as a weak link in times of crisis. Rusk was eventually appointed secretary of state and served with distinction in both the Kennedy and Johnson administrations. Russell had heard rumors that Kennedy was considering his brother, Robert F. Kennedy, for the position of attorney ceneral. Russell told the President that would be a bad mistake because his brother did not have the necessary experience and because it was not a good idea to have the brother of the president of the United States as the nation's top law enforcement officer. He pointed out that the president's lawyer was the White House counsel, and the attorney general was supposed to be independent and above politics. Kennedy, nonetheless, appointed his brother, allegedly under pressure from their father. Russell was disappointed.

Kennedy asked Russell if there was a particular person he would like to have appointed to the cabinet. Russell recommended his close friend and agriculture advisor, Dr. D. W. Brooks, who was president of the forerunner of the Gold Kist agriculture cooperative in Georgia. Kennedy responded that he had already promised the secretary of agriculture position to Minnesota governor Orval Freeman. He said that he would be glad to appoint Dr. Brooks to the number two position in the department and commit to name him secretary should Governor Freeman leave the position. Dr. Brooks declined the offer.

The Cuban missile crisis occasioned intense discussions between the president and Senator Russell. Senator Russell had sponsored a resolution the prior year that passed the Senate and warned the Russians that the introduction of offensive military weapons in Cuba would be considered by the United States as an act of war. Russell likely knew from Vice President Lyndon Johnson and/or CIA briefings of the weapons in Cuba before Kennedy consulted the congressional leaders. Russell was head of the Senate subcommittee with oversight over the Central Intelligence Agency, and he regularly received one-on-one briefings from the director of the CIA in his office at least once a month with respect to the latest intelligence. It is likely that he learned of the missiles in Cuba in those briefings. What is certain is that he requested a briefing on Cuba from the White House before he left Washington for a congressional recess. This caused an intense discussion at the White House over how much Richard Russell should be told. On the one hand, the missile information was closely guarded and known by few people. On the other hand, the administration could not refuse to give Russell a briefing, and there would be hell to pay later if it was not a full and truthful briefing. A memorandum written by a key White House aide, Ted Sorensen, suggested to the president that Russell should be given a full briefing. It is possible Russell asked for the briefing to see if he would be told the whole story.

After Russell left Washington and was in Winder for the congressional recess, Kennedy called the congressional leaders back to the White House for a briefing on the Cuban situation. He outlined the certainty that Russia had introduced offensive military weapons in Cuba. He said that after intensive consultations, he had decided on a quarantine as the safest and most effective way to deal with the problem. Russell spoke up immediately and advised a much more aggressive policy. He told the president that he did not doubt a quarantine might work and get the missiles out of Cuba, but it would leave Castro in power and a thorn in the side of the United States for years to come. He recommended military action to remove the missiles and Castro while the United States had a credible excuse. To his surprise, Senator J. William Fulbright, chairman of the Senate Foreign Relations Committee, spoke up in support of Russell's position. So did several other congressional leaders. However, the president indicated that he had already decided on the quarantine and was going to announce it on television within the hour.

The quarantine did eventually result in the removal of the missiles from Cuba, but the United States also agreed to remove missiles from Turkey and made certain other concessions. Russell continued to believe that the United States had missed the best opportunity it would ever have to rid the hemisphere of Fidel Castro. He thought Castro would cause numerous problems for the United States in South America and elsewhere. He turned out to be correct.

Richard Russell was not an emotional person. He was known as one who could control his emotions at all times. That quality failed him at the time of the assassination of John F. Kennedy. CBS newsman Roger Mudd reported Russell hunched over a teletype machine off the Senate floor reading the latest dispatches to a group of senators who were following Kennedy's condition after his shooting in Dallas. Tears were flowing down Russell's cheeks. Later that afternoon, after it was announced that Kennedy had died, Senate Majority Leader Mike Mansfield asked Russell to accompany him to the Senate TV Gallery for a series of interviews to pay tribute to the fallen president. Russell was barely able to get through the interviews without breaking down. A few days after Kennedy's funeral, he wrote Jackie Kennedy a letter in which he commended her for the way she conducted herself and represented the country in the days after the president's assassination. A copy of this letter can be found at the end of this chapter. It reflects not only Russell's great admiration for Mrs. Kennedy but also his considerable skill as a writer.

Lyndon B. Johnson

When Air Force One landed at Andrews Air Force Base outside Washington with the slain president's body, his widow, and the newly sworn-in President Lyndon B. Johnson on board, almost all of official Washington met the plane. Lyndon Johnson searched the faces in the crowd for that of his mentor, Richard B. Russell. He was not there. Russell had gone to his apartment to mourn alone. His participation in the television interviews earlier that afternoon had convinced him that he was not in an emotional state for further public appearances. When Johnson reached the White House, he immediately called Russell. They talked for about ten minutes, and the new president asked Russell to be at the White House early the next morning. It would be the first of many private meetings Richard Russell would have with Lyndon Johnson in the early days of the Johnson Administration.

The friendship between Lyndon Johnson and Richard Russell was a strange one. They seemed to have little in common, and they had completely different personalities. Russell, the quintessential southern gentleman—humble, reserved, urbane, and patrician—was one of the most widely read members of the United States Senate. Johnson, the brash Texan—profane, backslapping, and boorish—hardly ever read any book. Once, when President Johnson was unable to get in touch with Russell at a time of crisis, he exploded to an aide, "Hell, he is probably off somewhere reading Plato."

The reason a friendship developed was because Lyndon Johnson made it happen. He came to the Senate in 1948 under less-than-auspicious circumstances. His Senate victory in Texas was so narrow and the allegations of voter fraud so widespread that he was referred to as "Landslide Lyndon." When he arrived at the Senate, one of the first things he did was sit down and talk with the powerful Democratic aide, Bobby Baker. Baker knew the Senate as well as anyone. Johnson asked him what he could do to get off to a good start in the Senate. Baker told him the best way was to try to become close with Richard Russell. Johnson set out to do exactly that.

Years later, Johnson admitted that he knew the only way he could become friends with Richard Russell was to secure a seat on Russell's Armed Services Committee. Otherwise, Johnson said that he knew he and Russell would be nothing more than passing acquaintances. Securing a seat on the Armed Services Committee as a freshman senator was not easy. It was one of the most-desired committee positions in the Senate. Senators often waited years for a seat to open on the committee. For example, Senator Strom Thurmond of South Carolina, a general in the Army Reserve, waited a number of years for his seat on the committee. Johnson, however, had several advantages. First, he had met Russell while Johnson was serving in the House of Representatives and both men were working on making electricity available to rural areas of the country. Russell wanted it for Georgia and Johnson wanted it for the Hill Country of Texas. Second, Johnson had served on the House Armed Services Committee, which was chaired by the legendary Georgian, Carl Vinson. It is likely that Vinson put in a good word with Russell on Johnson's behalf. Finally, Johnson was good friends with his fellow Texan, Sam Rayburn, who was Speaker of the House of Representatives and also a good friend of Russell.

Regardless of how he did it, Johnson succeeded in being appointed to the Armed Services Committee as a freshman senator. He made the most of it. Richard Russell worked longer hours than any other senator, in part because he was not married and had no family to go home to at night. Johnson was determined that he would be the one senator who was still there when Russell left each night. He started inviting Russell to go home with him and eat with his family. Russell was reluctant at first, but Johnson insisted, saying he had to eat somewhere and Lady Bird Johnson liked to cook good southern food. Russell immediately took a liking to Lady Bird. Johnson encouraged his daughters, Lynda Bird and Luci, to call Russell "Uncle Dick." Soon, Russell was being invited to have Sunday brunch with the Johnsons, at which time they would read newspapers and talk politics.

Johnson also learned that Russell was an avid baseball fan. He started going with Russell to Washington Senators games. John Connolly, a young Johnson aide at the time who would later become governor of Texas and be shot when President Kennedy was assassinated, ridiculed Johnson for going to the baseball games. "Lyndon," he said, "you do not give a damn about baseball. The only reason you are going to those games is to butter up Richard Russell." Russell was invited to deer hunts at the LBJ Ranch in Texas. By then, Russell was not much of a hunter, but he accepted the invitations nonetheless. He particularly disliked the way Johnson staged the deer hunts with a bunch of old men shooting wildly at a herd of deer as they were stampeded past the senators. While Russell continued to accept the invitations, he stopped going on the deer hunts and started staying back at the house to talk to Lady Bird.

Johnson's strategy paid off. When the Armed Services Committee established a Preparedness Investigating Subcommittee, Russell appointed Johnson as chairman. This resulted in Johnson receiving substantial publicity and earning credibility in the Senate. When the assistant Democratic leader was defeated, Johnson expressed an interest in the position. Russell saw to it that Johnson received the post. A few years later, the majority leader of the Senate was defeated in his reelection bid. Russell's Democratic colleagues urged him to accept the position of majority leader, but Russell declined. Instead, he supported Lyndon Johnson. With Russell making the nominating speech for Johnson, Johnson was elected and quickly on his way to becoming the most powerful majority leader in Senate history. One of his first actions was to insist that Richard Russell relocate his Senate seat from the third row from the back of the chamber to the second row immediately behind the seat of the majority leader. Johnson wanted him there for help on procedural and parliamentary questions. Russell would, on more than one occasion, rescue Johnson by various procedural maneuvers.

In 1956, capitalizing on his influence and national media attention as a result of being Senate Democratic leader, Lyndon Johnson made a tepid effort to run for president. Richard Russell strongly supported him. When John F. Kennedy secured the Democratic presidential nomination in 1960, Lyndon Johnson was offered the vice presidential nomination. Russell advised him against taking it because he told him that someone as active and accustomed to the spotlight as Johnson would not do well as vice president. He was also concerned that Johnson would not be accepted by Kennedy's inner circle. Nonetheless, Johnson accepted the vice presidential nomination and was responsible for carrying Texas, which made it possible for the Democratic ticket to win. He soon discovered, however, that Russell was right. He was miserable as vice president. He was given little of importance to do and was ostracized by Robert F. Kennedy and others in the Kennedy Administration. This was not true of President Kennedy, but it was true of almost everyone else in the Kennedy inner circle at the White House. They did not even meaningfully utilize him in his area of greatest expertise—his great knowledge of Capitol Hill and the levers of power in Congress. His position did result, however, in Johnson becoming president when Kennedy was assassinated.

One of the first things Johnson had to address as president was whether to order a federal investigation into the assassination of John F. Kennedy. He initially resisted calls for a blue-ribbon commission, preferring to leave the matter in the hands of the Texas authorities. He eventually relented, however, and agreed to name an investigative body. He discussed the matter with Senator Russell on a number of occasions. In the first conversation, Johnson briefly alluded to the possibility of appointing Russell to the commission, which Russell flatly rejected. Since President Johnson did not mention it again, Russell assumed that the matter had been put to rest. Russell urged him to appoint as chairman of the commission a highly respected judge on the United States Court of Appeals in New York. Johnson wanted to appoint the chief justice of the United States Supreme Court, Earl Warren. Russell told him that would be a bad idea because matters relating to the Kennedy assassination could come before the Supreme Court. During these conversations, Johnson did not give any hint that he also still had Richard Russell in mind for the commission. Finally, at about nine o'clock one evening, President Johnson phoned and told Senator Russell that Warren had agreed to serve as chairman of the commission and that he, Russell, had been appointed as a member of the commission as well. Russell protested greatly but was told by Johnson that the membership of the commission had already been announced to the press. Russell said that he could not remember ever having been so disappointed at anything in his life. He did not like Earl Warren and did not have time to serve on the commission in view of the demands on him as a result of being chairman of the Armed Services Committee, chairman of the Defense Appropriations Subcommittee, and a member of the Senate Space Committee, the Joint Committee on Atomic Energy, and the Senate Democratic Steering and Policy Committees. Russell also suspected it would not be long before Johnson would start pushing civil rights legislation that Kennedy had introduced but had been unable to move forward, and Russell knew it would fall to him as leader of the southern senators to direct the inevitable filibuster. He protested so much that Johnson put on the phone an old deer-hunting friend of Senator Russell from Texas who happened to be with Johnson. Russell eventually agreed to serve on the Warren Commission because he had no choice.

He clashed with Warren from the beginning. He thought Warren had already prejudged the evidence and was stacking the staff of the commission with ultraliberal members. To calm Russell down, Warren offered to appoint Morris Abrams of Georgia as a member of the staff, but that did not placate Russell because he considered Abrams to be an extreme liberal as well. Russell did not have much time to devote to the work of the commission because, as he feared, shortly after it was organized, Johnson started to push a sweeping civil rights bill that Kennedy had introduced but had been unable to move forward. In one of their private meetings at the White House, Johnson told Russell, "Dick, I am going to push the civil rights bill and I will not compromise. If you get in my way, I will run you over." Russell replied, "You may very well do that, Mr. President, but, if you do, you will destroy the Democratic Party in the South." The president indicated that he would pay that price if it were necessary to get the civil rights legislation passed. Russell led the longest filibuster in Senate history against the legislation.

Since Senator Russell did not have the time to attend all the hearings of the Warren Commission, he recruited a young law clerk who worked at the Georgia Court of Appeals in Atlanta, Alfreda Scobey. She would be his eyes and ears and would attend the commission hearings. Russell read all the transcripts of the hearings and kept abreast of the proceedings. He was dissatisfied with what he considered to be kid glove treatment Lee Harvey Oswald's widow received when she was questioned by the commission. He persuaded Earl Warren to appoint him and two other members of the commission as a special subcommittee to go back to Dallas and question Marina Oswald again. No significant new information developed. Russell would later say that this was the most stressful period of his life with his responsibilities as chairman of both the Senate Armed Services Committee and the Senate Appropriations Subcommittee on Defense as well as leading the southern senators and the extra work required by his service on the Warren Commission. At one point, he prepared a letter of resignation from the Warren Commission, but President Johnson persuaded him not to submit it. Many evenings during this period, Russell did not leave his office at all, opting to sleep on a sofa there so he could work through the night. He believed until the day he died that all this work and stress compromised his health and led to an illness in early 1965 that almost took his life.

Earl Warren was determined that the report of the Warren Commission would be unanimous. There was conflicting testimony on whether the same bullet that hit Governor Connally of Texas also struck President Kennedy. That was important because, if it was a different bullet, that raised the possibility if not the likelihood that there was another gunman in addition to Oswald. Governor Connally had testified strongly that the bullet that hit him did not also hit the president. That was also Russell's view. In the draft report of the commission, it was stated that Oswald acted alone to kill the president, and the evidence established that conclusion "beyond a reasonable doubt." Russell was not willing to go that far since Oswald had made a trip to Russia and a secret trip to Mexico City during which he visited the Soviet and Cuban Embassies just weeks before that fateful day in Dallas, and the details of what he did on those trips were beyond the reach of the commission. Russell prepared a dissent to the Warren Commission Report in which he stated that from the evidence available to the commission, Oswald killed Kennedy. It also stated, however, that Oswald had been to Russia and Mexico and that information on those trips was not available to the commission. Earl Warren was so insistent on a unanimous report that he agreed to change the language in the final report to a version closer to that of the views of Richard Russell. Although Russell was not fully satisfied with the revised language and the time pressure to get out a final report, he reluctantly signed the report. Richard Russell's draft dissent and resignation letter are included in his papers at the Richard B. Russell Library for Political Research and Studies at the University of Georgia.

The other matter that occupied a good deal of the time of Richard Russell and Lyndon Johnson in their private meetings related to the Vietnam War. By the time Johnson took office, the United States had a contingent of less than 30,000 military personnel in Vietnam as advisors but no fighting ground troops. Kennedy had been weighing options on how to proceed. Russell had urged him to withdraw from Vietnam, and he believed Kennedy would have done so if he had lived. In his conversations with President Johnson early in the Johnson Administration, Russell urged Johnson to figure out a way to withdraw gracefully. He warned him that ground troops would simply bog the United States down in a land war in Asia that it likely could not win. Primarily at the urging of Secretary of Defense Robert McNamara,

Johnson escalated the war by sending in ground troops and by commencing the bombing of North Vietnam. After his reelection in 1964, again principally on McNamara's advice, with Russell unavailable and seriously ill in the hospital, President Johnson continually escalated the level of ground forces and the bombing. He also stated repeatedly at press conferences and in speeches that the United States had a vital security interest in Vietnam and that all of Southeast Asia would likely fall to the communists if the United States were defeated or withdrew. Of course, Richard Russell agreed with none of this. At an appearance on the *Meet the Press* Sunday talk show, Russell said that if they held a completely free election throughout Vietnam, it was his opinion that the North Vietnamese leader Ho Chi Minh would win. Russell viewed the Vietnam War as essentially a civil war. Johnson, at a press conference the next day, asked when Richard Russell had become an expert on Vietnamese elections. Russell knew more about the history and culture of Vietnam than Johnson, McNamara, or Johnson's other advisers because he had read so widely on the subject. Books on Southeast Asia littered the huge table in his office.

Richard Russell was in a difficult position in regard to the Vietnam War. He had consistently opposed it and did not believe it to be in America's best interest. But he was chairman of the Senate Armed Services Committee, which was charged with the responsibility of providing the funds to equip and supply American soldiers. He stated that it was the most agonizing issue he confronted in his entire Senate career. When he was unsuccessful in convincing Johnson to withdraw and after Johnson repeatedly stated publicly that the United States had a vital security interest in Vietnam, Russell started urging him to pursue a more aggressive bombing strategy, including the closing of the main port of North Vietnam at Haiphong. His position was that if Johnson insisted on fighting the War, it should be fought in a way to bring it to a conclusion at the earliest possible time. He recognized that this more aggressive strategy might bring China or even Russia into the war, but he was adamant that it was not acceptable to send American servicemen to their deaths or crippling injuries and to spend billions of dollars in taxpayer money if the country was not willing to do everything possible to end the war at the earliest opportunity.

The Vietnam War and President Johnson's deceit relating to it eventually destroyed the Johnson presidency. The war protests grew, and the Senate Foreign Relations Committee started hearings on the conduct of the war. Hundreds of protesters were heard around the clock across from the White House. It was reported that Johnson and his family had difficulty sleeping at the White House because of the noise of the protests. In early 1968, Johnson announced that he would not run for reelection. Richard Russell was given a little advance notice of the announcement. He was disappointed that his old friend's presidency had come to such a conclusion, but he faulted Johnson to a considerable extent for failing to do what was necessary to end the Vietnam War and for blindly following Robert McNamara's advice as opposed to the contrary advice of Russell himself, Senate Majority Leader Mike Mansfield, an acknowledged expert on Asia, and George Ball.

There was also friction between Russell and Johnson over Johnson's Great Society programs and the War on Poverty. Russell had no disagreement with the goal of eliminating poverty, and he initially supported a number of the Johnson proposals such as the expansion of the Appalachian Regional Commission. He soon became discontented, however, because he felt that every time Johnson identified a problem, he created a new government program. Russell viewed this maze of overlapping government programs as wasteful and poorly run. He started voting against almost all of it. He also questioned Johnson's fiscal policies of trying to pursue his domestic agenda and the War in Vietnam at the same time. He warned of looming budget deficits. One year during the Johnson presidency, the budget deficit exceeded $25 billion, a considerable sum at the time.

The Russell–Johnson friendship could perhaps have survived all these difficulties if it had not been for a bitter dispute over a judicial appointment in Georgia. It was customary in the Senate that when the president and the senators from a state were of the same political party, the senators had the right to choose federal district court judges who sat in their state. In Georgia, there are three judicial districts—the southern, middle, and northern districts. Russell and his Senate colleague, Herman Talmadge, agreed that Russell would make the appointments in the southern district, Talmadge in the middle district, and they would agree on appointments in the northern district. A vacancy occurred in the southern district in late 1967 when the longtime United States District Court Judge Frank Scarlett died. Russell initially proposed Mack Barnes, a lawyer from Waycross, Georgia, to fill the vacancy. Barnes died of cancer before he could be confirmed.

Russell then proposed his longtime friend Alexander Lawrence of Savannah. Lawrence was a distinguished lawyer and a former president of the Georgia Historical Society. After the Supreme Court of the United States issued its desegregation decision in 1954, Lawrence was highly critical of the Court in a speech to a civic club in Savannah. Russell thought so much of the address that he put it in the Congressional Record. When Russell announced his selection of Lawrence, it was immediately opposed by the NAACP and other civil rights groups. It was also opposed by Johnson's attorney general, Ramsey Clark. Russell had several meetings with the president about the Lawrence nomination and understood that Johnson would direct Ramsey Clark to send the nomination to the Senate. He also had at least one meeting with Clark. But time dragged on with no action. Russell had several additional meetings with Johnson on the subject at the White House, but there was still no action. During this time, a vacancy occurred on the United States Supreme Court. Its chief justice, Earl Warren, announced his retirement. Johnson nominated Justice Abe Fortas to become chief justice and Judge Homer Thornberry from Texas as a new member of the Court. Apparently, during some of the meetings and discussions about the Lawrence nomination, Russell agreed that the southern senators would not filibuster the nomination of Fortas to become chief justice, although they reserved the right to vote against it.

Cartha (Deke) Deloach was one of the principal assistants at the FBI under J. Edgar Hoover. DeLoach, originally from Claxton, Georgia, was a confidant of Richard Russell. He was the person Russell went to when he wanted sensitive information from the FBI. He was also the point man on the Alex Lawrence judgeship nomination investigation into Lawrence's background. Russell had discussed the matter with him on several occasions as the FBI's background investigation of Lawrence proceeded. According to Russell's notes of a conversation with DeLoach on June 11, 1968, DeLoach told him that Attorney General Ramsey Clark was not cooperating with the investigation. In another conversation on July 2, 1968, DeLoach told Russell that the Department of Justice was trying to figure out a way to trade its support for the Lawrence nomination for Russell's support for the Fortas nomination. It is not clear whether Russell's concerns about how the Lawrence nomination was being handled by the attorney general and the president were prompted by the information he received from DeLoach or whether that information simply confirmed the suspicions that Russell already had based on his own conversations with the attorney general and the president. What is clear is that Russell's patience was being exhausted and his temper was reaching a boiling point.

In late June 1968, Senator Russell went home to Winder during a congressional recess. I did not accompany him because, as I recall, I was in the midst of exams at law school. When Russell returned to Washington, he had the draft of a letter to President Johnson concerning the Lawrence matter and the Supreme Court vacancy. He called me into his office and asked me what I thought about the letter. I was taken aback by the harshness of the language since I knew of Richard Russell's great respect for the office of president, to say nothing of his relationship with President Johnson. He basically accused Johnson of trying to bribe him and stated that he could do what he wished with the Lawrence nomination and that Russell considered himself released from any commitments he may have made to Johnson concerning the Supreme Court nominations. In his letter, Senator Russell stated,

> To be perfectly frank, even after so many years in the Senate, I was so naïve I had not even suspected that this man's nomination was being withheld from the Senate due to the changes expected on the Supreme Court of the United States until after you sent in the nominations of Fortas and Thornberry while still holding the recommendations for the nomination of Mr. Lawrence either in your office or in the Department of Justice.... I...dislike being treated as a child or a patronage seeking ward heeler.

I asked Senator Russell if he really wanted to use this kind of language in his letter to Johnson. He was in no mood for such advice. He immediately took the letter back and finalized it. He did call his Senate colleague, Herman Talmadge, down to his office to review the letter. Talmadge thought it was an excellent letter and offered to cosign it. Russell declined, saying this was a matter between him and the president.

The letter got the attention of the White House. Johnson telephoned Russell and told him how disappointed he was in the letter and that he had not intended to tie the Lawrence matter to the Supreme Court vacancy. He said he would be responding in writing but that he thought the correspondence so misrepresented the nature of the relationship between the two of them that both letters should be destroyed because he would not want his grandchildren to see them. Within a few days, the president dispatched Tom Johnson (no relation to the president) with his written response. Tom Johnson was from Macon, Georgia, and had gone to the White House as a White House Fellow in the press office. After his internship was over, he had stayed on as a member of the press secretary's staff. He was one of Johnson's favorites and was known by Johnson to be one of Russell's favorites. After the Johnson presidency ended, Tom Johnson would go with him back to Texas where he would be his chief of staff in retirement. He later became editor of the Dallas newspaper, editor and publisher of the *Los Angeles Times*, and eventually the president of CNN. Today, he is chairman emeritus of the Board of Trustees of the Lyndon Johnson Foundation and a trustee of the Richard B. Russell Foundation. After Tom Johnson left the office, Russell called me in and showed me Johnson's letter. The letter concluded with this paragraph: "I am sure that you will vote for or against the nominations of Justice Fortas and Judge Thornberry as your conscience dictates. I am frankly surprised and deeply disappointed that a contrary inference would be suggested. Both my standards of public administration, and my knowledge of your character, would deny such an inference." Senator Russell told me to be sure that copies of both letters were preserved in his files because he knew they would be in the White House files notwithstanding Johnson's statement that he was going to destroy his copies. He was correct in that copies of both letters can be found at the Richard B. Russell Library for Political Research and Studies in Athens, Georgia, and at the Johnson Presidential Library in Austin, Texas.

Johnson immediately called Ramsey Clark and told him that he had destroyed one of the great friendships he had ever enjoyed. He directed Clark to send the Lawrence nomination to the Senate. Lawrence received a "well-qualified" recommendation from the American Bar Association and was overwhelmingly confirmed by the Senate. He served with distinction as a District Court judge for many years and received great praise for his handling of a number of difficult civil rights cases.

Shortly after this dispute over the Lawrence nomination, I started seeing Senator Robert Griffin of Michigan going into and coming out of Senator Russell's hideaway office in the Capitol. The most senior and influential members of the Senate have these private offices near the Senate floor so they do not have to return to their Senate office building offices between votes. As Senator Russell's health deteriorated, he used his office at the Capitol more frequently. Senator Griffin was the Republican point man in the opposition to the Supreme Court nominations. I immediately surmised that his meetings with Senator Russell resulted from the fact that Senator Russell was consulting with the Republicans about the Supreme Court nominations. During this process, it was revealed that Justice Abe Fortas, while a member of the Supreme Court, had written speeches for Johnson and had continued to accept speaking fees and payments from his former law firm, which had numerous cases before the Supreme Court. These revelations torpedoed the Fortas nomination. It was soon withdrawn.

The dispute over the Lawrence nomination pretty much ended the friendship between Richard Russell and Lyndon Johnson. There were no more private dinners at the White House and no more expansive phone calls. Johnson did try to patch matters up, but Russell was largely unresponsive. In his final address to a Joint Session of Congress before his presidency ended, Lyndon Johnson paid tribute to Russell as a friend and one who had made a real difference in his career. In Johnson's retirement, there was little contact between Russell and Johnson, although Russell did receive Christmas cards at the end of each year that were usually signed by Lady Bird. On one occasion, Russell endorsed an invitation to Johnson to speak at commencement at the University of Georgia School of Law. Johnson acknowledged the letter, but, to my knowledge, the two never talked.

One other matter illustrates how complete the breach was between Johnson and Russell from Russell's viewpoint. After Johnson left Washington, a professor at the University of Texas headed up a program of oral history interviews with various people in Washington who had been close to Johnson. He, of course, requested an interview with Senator Russell. Russell did not make any response. As time passed, almost everyone in Washington who had anything to do with Lyndon Johnson's career had recorded an interview except Richard Russell. The requests continued to come. Senator Russell continued to fail to respond. I received a call from former Secretary of State Dean Rusk as to why Senator Russell had not granted an interview. I finally decided to discuss the matter with Senator Russell. I told him that the failure to respond was becoming embarrassing, and I felt that we had to say something. He responded, "If I did the interview, I would have to tell the truth. That would not help anyone. Just tell them that I am planning to write a book and I am not available." Russell never granted the interview. After similar requests continued to come in from other groups, he eventually authorized his press secretary, Powell Moore, to prepare a written submission to one such request. Richard Russell, who was known to extensively rewrite speeches or other written materials presented to him by his staff, accepted the paper from Powell Moore with only one change. He added a few sentences about him and Johnson attending professional baseball games.

I have been asked many times about my assessment of the Russell–Johnson relationship. Admittedly, I saw it in a narrow window of time when it was winding down. I may be mistaken in my assessment because I was not there in the forties, fifties, and early sixties when the friendship was at its peak. It is my assessment, however, that it was essentially a friendship of convenience. In the early years, the convenience flowed to Lyndon Johnson as Russell helped him get off to a good start in the Senate, become part of the Senate leadership, and eventually become president. In the later years, the convenience flowed principally to Richard Russell. He could get administration support for almost any project he wanted in Georgia, and his position in the Senate was strengthened by the knowledge that he was one of the people closest to the president. Georgia benefited greatly during those years from the Russell–Johnson friendship. For example, it is given credit for Lockheed's Marietta, Georgia, plant receiving the huge government contract for the C-5A Air Force Transport Plane. The news was conveyed to Senator Russell by President Johnson personally. A handwritten note by Russell at the time reads, "brought home the bacon." To my way of thinking, one essential element of a true friendship is mutual trust. By the time I arrived in Washington, I do not believe Richard Russell trusted Lyndon Johnson. This is evident by his letter about the Lawrence matter as well as his belief that Johnson lied to him or at least misled him by not being forthcoming concerning his appointment to the Warren Commission. There is no question that Richard Russell had genuine affection for Lady Bird Johnson and the Johnson girls. However, Richard Russell was the most astute judge of people I have ever known, and I do not believe it is possible that he did not recognize the qualities in Lyndon

Johnson that were so unlike himself and so criticized by others. Johnson's press secretary, George Reedy, wrote a perceptive, readable, and entertaining book about his boss's personality and character traits titled *Lyndon B. Johnson, A Memoir* (Andrews and Mc Meel, Inc., 1982).

Richard M. Nixon

Richard Russell only lived for the first two years of Richard Nixon's presidency. He did not live to witness the Watergate Scandal. He would surely have been highly critical of Nixon and certain members of his administration, because one thing Richard Russell would not tolerate was improper, unethical, or illegal conduct on the part of public officials. He also did not live to witness Richard Nixon's overtures to China that eventually led to full diplomatic recognition. Russell would surely have been in the front row of supporters for that policy; he had told Lyndon Johnson when he was in the White House that it would not be long before the United States would be required to extend full diplomatic recognition to Red China. This is particularly surprising since Richard Russell was one of the most committed warriors of the Cold War, but early on he recognized China's growing importance in the world. He also believed that better relations with China might help the United States in the Cold War with the Soviet Union.

Russell did live long enough to advise Nixon on his Cabinet, particularly in regard to his selection of a secretary of defense. While Nixon and Russell were not particularly close during the years in which they served in the Senate together or during Nixon's eight years as vice president, Nixon made it a point to court the Georgian when he became president. He immediately requested that Russell, as president pro tempore of the Senate, be included in the weekly meetings between him and the congressional leaders. The office of president pro tempore was largely a ceremonial position reserved for the senator with the longest period of service. The position had not previously been included in the Senate leadership or participated in leadership meetings with the president. Russell attended a number of the meetings before his health took a serious downturn. Russell and Nixon also discussed the Vietnam War, and Russell encouraged President Nixon to do whatever was necessary to bring it to the earliest possible conclusion. Nixon did that, although probably not as swiftly as Richard Russell would have liked.

In 1970, in one of his meetings with Nixon at the White House, Russell was asked by the president if he had seen *Patton*, the recently released movie on the career of army general George Patton_(dir. Franklin J. Schaffner, Twentieth Century Fox, 1970). Russell had known Patton in World War II. He told Nixon that he had not seen the film but hoped to do so. Nixon was about to leave the country on one of his foreign trips, and he asked Russell to view the film in the White House Theater following a dinner and reception. He said Russell could invite anyone of his choosing, and Nixon arranged for Mamie Eisenhower and also his daughter, Julie Nixon Eisenhower, to host the event. Senator Russell invited several other senators and a number of staff, myself included.

It was a wonderful occasion with a nice reception and a good dinner. I had an excellent time except for an incident that occurred as we viewed the film. Sitting on the front row next to Mrs. Eisenhower, Senator Russell carried on a constant conversation about the historical inaccuracies in the film. His conversation was audible to others in the theater who were trying to watch the movie. Senator Sam Ervin of North Carolina, one of Senator Russell's best friends and the future folksy chairman of the Senate Watergate Committee, called me over during the film and asked me to tell Senator Russell to tone down the conversation because he could not hear the film. This put me in a tough spot. I did not want to ignore the request of Senator Ervin, but I was certainly not going to tell Senator Russell to tone down his conversation. I went up to the front row, kneeled down, and asked Senator Russell if he needed anything. He said he did not. I then went back to my seat, hoping Senator Ervin would believe that Senator Russell's chatter continued notwithstanding my best efforts.

Also in 1970, the film on Senator Russell's career, *Georgia Giant*, was commissioned and financed by Cox Broadcasting Corporation through its WSB television station in Atlanta and premiered in Washington at the Washington Hilton Hotel, the same hotel where President Reagan was later shot during his first term as president. President Nixon attended the premiere. Senator Russell and I met President Nixon in a room reserved for the president, and he and Senator Russell had a cordial conversation. When we walked into the ballroom of the hotel, there was a large carving of Senator Russell in the middle of the room. It appeared, at first glance, to be carved of ice. Senator Russell, who was not in good health at the time, told me as we entered , "I hope that thing doesn't melt while we are in here." It turned out that it was carved from lard.

During Senator Russell's final illness, President Nixon visited him several times at the hospital. On one visit shortly before the Christmas holidays in 1970, Senator Russell told Nixon that he most regretted not being able to go home to Winder for Christmas. The president told him that there was no reason why he should not be able to go home and offered to make Air Force One available to fly him and his doctors to Winder. At first, Senator Russell seriously considered this offer, but as his condition deteriorated, it become out of the question. President Nixon called the hospital at least once after his offer to see whether Senator Russell would be able to go.

When Russell died on the afternoon of January 21, 1971, the president immediately ordered all flags lowered to half staff. In his State of the Union Address several nights later, he praised Richard Russell as one of the greatest senators of all time and asked for a moment of silence. He also provided Air Force One to fly Senator Russell's body and any members of his family or staff who were in Washington, DC, to Georgia. It was the first time I had ever been on the president's jet. I confess that I do not remember much about it because it was such a sad occasion. While Senator Russell's body lay in state in the Rotunda of the State Capitol in Atlanta, President and Mrs. Nixon flew to Georgia to pay their final respects. The president met privately with the Russell family and then addressed the news media. In these remarks, he referred to Richard Russell as "a president's senator."

Georgia's Senator

Many times when a member of Congress achieves the fame and prestige on the national stage that Richard Russell achieved, he or she often forgets home-state constituents. Such was not the case with Richard Russell. He never forgot who had sent him to Washington, DC. He was fond of saying, "I have been elected to represent Georgia's interest in Washington and not Washington's interest in Georgia." He worked tirelessly to bring federal money to Georgia, and he was uniquely successful. He not only obtained the money to maintain and expand the numerous military installations in Georgia but was also active in bringing federal research facilities to the state. For example, he played a major role in the location of the Communicable Disease Center (now known as the Centers for Disease Control and Prevention) in Atlanta. He also brought to Georgia federal research laboratories for water conservation, poultry, and peanuts. He obtained funds for the widening or deepening of the ports at Savannah and Brunswick and for numerous Corps of Engineers dam projects, as well as for the Federal Court Building in Atlanta. Many of these facilities bear his name. Once when the Appropriations Committee was considering a new federal research laboratory, one of Russell's good friends on the committee said, tongue-in-cheek, that he was going to oppose the project because he knew from past experience that if it was appropriated, Richard Russell would locate it in Georgia, and he was worried about Georgia falling into the Atlantic Ocean because of all the federal money that Senator Russell had put there. While Russell generally had a good sense of humor, it escaped him on this occasion when he replied, "If the project is authorized, you are damn right I am going to try to get it for Georgia."

There was no quicker way to get on the bad side of Richard Russell than to interfere with one of his Georgia projects. I remember one in particular. He started putting money into the Interior Appropriations bills for a visitor center at the Okefenokee Swamp near Folkston, Georgia. Even though the Johnson Administration supported almost any project in Georgia desired by Richard Russell, they did not support this project because there was already a visitor center entrance to the swamp at Waycross, Georgia, some seventy-five miles away. Senator Russell still put funds into the appropriations bills for the project, which came to be known as Camp Cornelia, and he stoutly defended the money in the Appropriations Committee and in conference with the House of Representatives. One year a new senator from California appeared on the scene who was determined to eliminate what he considered to be pork-barrel spending. When the Interior Appropriations Bill was considered by the subcommittee, he offered an amendment to delete all projects that had not been recommended by the administration. Senator Russell was in the hospital at the time, and Camp Cornelia was eliminated. Senator Russell was furious. He sent word to the California senator, I believe through Senator John Stennis of Mississippi who was a key member of the Armed Services Committee, that Chairman Russell was having second thoughts about a large buildup at a military base in California—a matter that was then pending before the Armed Services Committee. The senator from California got the message. When the

Interior Appropriations Bill was considered by the full Appropriations Committee, with Senator Russell present, the California senator stated that he had gotten carried away in his earlier amendment, and there were several projects he wished to have restored. Camp Cornelia was one of them.

There is much discussion these days about earmarks. If Senator Russell were still around, he would be a strong supporter of earmarks. The difference between Russell earmarks and the current ones is that Senator Russell did his openly. He would strongly oppose the idea now in vogue that members of Congress should not put funds for special projects in their states in appropriation bills. He thought the executive branch of the government had already become too powerful, and this would simply be another way of increasing its power at the expense of Congress. If Congress is going to be called upon to appropriate funds, what sense does it make to say that Congress should not have a say in how those funds are spent? I am confident that Russell would rather have members of Congress determining these matters than some unelected bureaucrat in a department of the executive branch.

Richard Russell was a fiscal conservative. He consistently voted for a balanced budget and opposed many expenditures. He routinely returned unused office funds to the treasury. If Congress voted to authorize the money, however, he was determined that Georgia would get more than her fair share. He viewed that as one of the reasons the people of Georgia had sent him to Washington. While he took his national responsibilities seriously, he also took seriously his obligation to work tirelessly in the best interest of Georgia.

Richard Russell became the most popular officeholder in the history of the state of Georgia. He ran for public office thirteen times and never came close to being defeated. His only serious campaign for reelection to the United States Senate came in 1936, when he was opposed by Georgia governor Eugene Talmadge, a populist on the order of Huey Long and an arch segregationist. His core support in Georgia came from the rural areas of the state, as did Richard Russell's. Known as the "Wild Man from Sugar Creek," Talmadge wore bright red suspenders at his campaign rallies and was one of Georgia's most colorful politicians. Talmadge said once, "I am not seeking any votes in any county that has a streetcar." That meant Atlanta. He was also fond of saying, "The people of Georgia have only three friends—God Almighty, Sears Roebuck, and

Gene Talmadge." Talmadge could not stand Franklin Roosevelt, and the central thrust of his 1936 campaign against Richard Russell was that Russell was a stooge for Roosevelt. He accused Senator Russell of supporting Roosevelt's plan to replace white postmasters and other federal officeholders with blacks. Russell defended his support of Roosevelt by saying that Roosevelt was successfully lifting Georgia and the nation out of the Great Depression. He accused Talmadge of trying to divert the attention of the voters of Georgia from the real issues and of being a Republican in disguise and a tool of the Northeast Republican Establishment.

Russell also ridiculed Talmadge for the large security detail of state troopers that accompanied him everywhere he went. Russell would ask at campaign rallies what Gene Talmadge was afraid of that would necessitate such a security detail at taxpayer expense. To further ridicule the governor, Russell had the Girls Bugle Corps from Winder attend several of his rallies. He would tell the crowds that he was better protected than the governor, and it was not at taxpayer expense. Talmadge's strategy in attacking Roosevelt was a bad mistake because President Roosevelt was popular in Georgia. Talmadge's son, Senator Herman Talmadge, maintained until he died that his father would have defeated Russell if he had not made Roosevelt such an important issue in the race. When the results were counted at the end of the race, Talmadge had suffered a humiliating defeat. The race was not even close either in the popular vote or in the county unit vote. The race did not destroy the public career of Gene Talmadge because he was elected to public office on a number of occasions thereafter, including governor. It did assure, however, that Richard Russell would never have serious opposition again to his reelection to the Senate. He was reelected either with no opposition or with token opposition in 1942, 1948, 1954, 1960, and 1966.

When Senator Russell's official biographer, Dr. Gilbert Fite, wrote his award-winning biography of Richard Russell, he titled it, *Richard B. Russell, Jr., Senator from Georgia* (Chapel Hill: University of North Carolina, 1991). While Richard Russell was very much a senator's senator and a president's senator, he was also Georgia's senator, and working with him changed my life.

Senator Russell's paternal grandparents, William John Russell and Harriette Brumby Russell.*

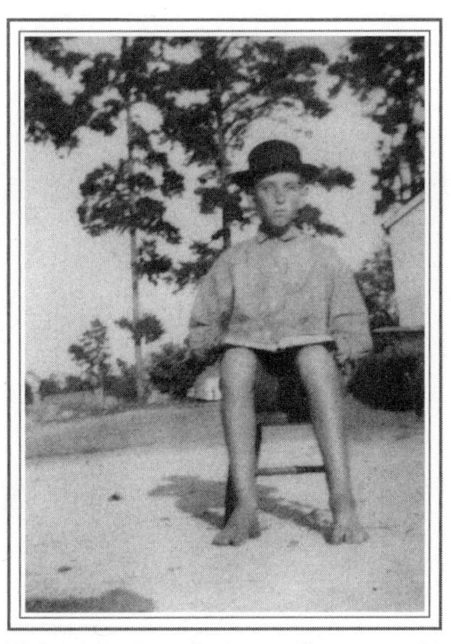

Richard B. Russell, Jr. at about age 10 engaged in one of his favorite pastimes—reading a book.*

Senator Russell with his mother, Ina Dillard Russell, when she was named "Mother of the Year" in Georgia.*

Senator Russell, the youngest member of the United States Senate in 1933, meets the Senate's previous youngest member, Senator Robert M. La Follette, Jr. of Wisconsin.*

Richard B. Russell, Jr. being sworn in as the youngest Governor in Georgia history in 1931 by his father, Richard B. Russell, Sr., who was at the time the Chief Justice of the Supreme Court of Georgia.* *(Courtesy of Corbis)*

Senator Russell, far left, meets with General Douglas MacArthur second from the left, and other leaders in New Guinea in 1943 as a part of a Senate mission in World War II led by Russell during which he visited all the theaters of the War and met with other Allied leaders such as Winston Churchill and General Dwight Eisenhower. Following the trip, Russell made a speech to the Senate that had a significant effect on America's post-war policies.*

Senator Russell presides over a meeting of the Southern Senate Caucus of which he became the leader in 1948.*

Senator Russell with Senate Republican Leader Everett Dirksen of Illinois and Senate Democratic Leader Mike Mansfield of Montana.*

Governor Richard B. Russell, Jr. meets with Governor Franklin D. Roosevelt in 1932 at Warm Springs, Georgia when Roosevelt was running for President and Russell was running for the Senate. Russell made a nominating speech for Roosevelt at the 1932 Democratic National Convention.*

Senator Russell shakes hands with General Douglas MacArthur immediately before his testimony before the investigating subcommittee chaired by Russell inquiring into President Truman's dismissal of the General from his command in Korea. Russell's deft handling of the hearings over six weeks helped to diffuse a national crisis. Many felt it was Russell's finest hour.*

President Truman signs the Legislative Reorganization Act of 1946 in regard to which Russell played a pivotable role. Senator Russell is the second to President Truman's left.*
(AP Photo/Henry Griffin)

The White House
Washington

AUG 7 9 05 PM 1945

WU80 LG GOVT

WINDER GA AUG 7 427P

THE PRESIDENT

(PERSONAL DELIVERY) THE WHITE HOUSE

PERMIT ME TO RESPECTFULLY SUGGEST THAT WE CEASE OUR EFFORTS TO CAJOLE JAPAN INTO SURRENDERING IN ACCORDANCE WITH THE POTSDAM DECLARATION. LET US CARRY THE WAR TO THEM UNTIL THEY BEG US TO ACCEPT THE UNCONDITIONAL SURRENDER. THE FOUL ATTACK ON PEARL HARBOR BROUGHT US INTO WAR AND I AM UNABLE TO SEE ANY VALID REASON WHY WE SHOULD BE SO MUCH MORE CONSIDERATE AND LENIENT IN DEALING WITH JAPAN THAN WITH GERMANY. I EARNESTLY INSIST JAPAN SHOULD BE DEALT WITH AS HARSHLY AS GERMANY AND THAT SHE

SHOULD NOT BE THE BENEFICIARY OF A SOFT PEACE. THE VAST MAJORITY OF THE AMERICAN PEOPLE, INCLUDING MANY SOUND THINKERS WHO HAVE INTIMATE KNOWLEDGE OF THE ORIENT, DO NOT AGREE WITH MR. GREW IN HIS ATTITUDE THAT THERE IS ANY THING SACROSANCT ABOUT HIROHITO. HE SHOULD GO. WE HAVE NO OBLIGATION TO SHINTOLISM. THE COMPTEMTUOUS ANSWER OF THE JAPS TO THE POTSDAM ULTIMATUM JUSTIFIES A REVISION OF THAT DOCUMENT AND STERNER PEACE TERMS.

IF WE DO NOT HAVE AVAILABLE A SUFFICIENT NUMBER OF ATOMIC BOMBS WITH WHICH TO FINISH THE JOB IMMEDIATELY, LET US CARRY ON WITH TNT AND FIRE BOMBS UNTIL WE CAN PRODUCE THEM.

I ALSO HOPE THAT YOU WILL ISSUE ORDERS FORBIDDING THE OFFICERS IN COMMAND OF OUR AIR FORCES FROM WARNING JAP CITIES

x692-A

Senator Russell's telegram to President Truman immediately following the Potsdam Conference in which he urges Truman to use the atomic bomb against Japan to force its unconditional surrender and the end of World War II.*

THAT THEY WILL BE ATTACKED. THESE GENERALS DO NOT FLY OVER JAPAN AND THIS SHOWMANSHIP CAN ONLY RESULT IN THE UNNECESSARY LOSS OF MANY FINE BOYS IN OUR AIR FORCE AS WELL AS OUR HELPLESS PRISONERS IN THE HANDS OF THE JAPANESE, INCLUDING THE SURVIVORS OF THE MARCH OF DEATH ON BATAAN WHO ARE CERTAIN TO BE BROUGHT INTO THE CITIES THAT HAVE BEEN WARNED.

THIS WAS A TOTAL WAR AS LONG AS OUR ENEMIES HELD ALL OF THE CARDS. WHY SHOULD WE CHANGE THE RULES NOW, AFTER THE BLOOD, TREASURE AND ENTERPRISE OF THE AMERICAN PEOPLE HAVE GIVEN US THE UPPER HAND. OUR PEOPLE HAVE NOT FORGOTTEN THAT THE JAPANESE STRUCK US THE FIRST BLOW IN THIS WAR WITHOUT THE SLIGHTEST WARNING. THEY BELIEVE THAT WE SHOULD CONTINUE TO STRIKE THE JAPANESE UNTIL THEY

ARE BROUGHT GROVELING TO THEIR KNEES. WE SHOULD CEASE OUR APPEALS TO JAPAN TO SUE FOR PEACE. THE NEXT PLEA FOR PEACE SHOULD COME FROM AN UTTERLY DESTROYED TOKYO. WELCOME BACK HOME. WITH ASSURANCES OF ESTEEM

RICHARD B RUSSELL US SENATOR.

Russell and other Congressional leaders meet with President Eisenhower following a luncheon at the White House. Senator Russell is on the front row, far left. His Senate colleague from Georgia, Walter F. George, is just to the right of President Eisenhower.*

(Courtesy WSB-TV)

Senator Russell and a small group of Senators are photographed after a meeting with President Kennedy. Russell is second from the right of Kennedy. Other Senators, from left to right, are Senator Allen Ellender of Lousiana, Senator Leverett Saltonstall of Massachusetts, Senator George Aiken of Vermont and Senator Carl Hayden of Arizona.*

November 26, 1963

Dear Mrs. Kennedy:

At the danger of being thought presumptuous, I am writing to express my unbounded admiration of your demeanor and every act and deed during the past four tragic days.

No queen, born to the purple, could have acquitted herself more admirably. Your calm dignity banished the hysteria which threatened millions of your fellow Americans who followed your every movement on the television screen.

I am so old-fashioned as to believe that those who have departed this earth still know what transpires here, and I therefore believe that President Kennedy was prouder of you then than he had ever been in this life. Only a great lady in the finest traditions of the old school could have displayed such magnificent courage.

Thanking you for what you did to steady our national morale and to improve our nation's image, I am, with assurances of deep respect and esteem,

Sincerely,

Mrs. John F. Kennedy
The White House
Washington, D. C.

Senator Russell's letter to Jackie Kennedy three days after the President's assassination.*

Richard Russell and Lyndon Johnson confer at the White House during the Johnson presidency.*

United States Senate
COMMITTEE ON ARMED SERVICES
WASHINGTON, D.C. 20510

July 1, 1968

The President
The White House
Washington, D. C.

Dear Mr. President:

Without adding to the voluminous file or the record of the many conversations we have had on the subject, I remind you that on February 13th of this year -- over four and a half months ago -- my colleague, Senator Talmadge, and I forwarded to you an urgent request based on public need for you to appoint Mr. Alexander A. Lawrence as United States District Judge for the Southern District of Georgia.

I desire to avoid as much as possible repetition of the innumerable conversations and communications that I have had with you on this subject. I, therefore, content myself with saying that I explained my position as the primary mover of this recommendation and on a number of occasions assured you of the unquestioned capacity of Mr. Lawrence to serve as Judge.

Over three months having elapsed, on May 20th, at your suggestion, I wrote you again with respect to this appointment and concluded by making a personal appeal (the fi that I have made to any President of the United States) for you to forward the nomination of Mr. Lawrence to the Senate. I stated in that letter that I had not requested any executive or administrative appointment at your hands during the six years you have served as President and I was only insisting on that which every Democratic Senator has had a right to expect since the formation of our Party.

Also, I did this out of my knowledge that no name ha been submitted during my time in the Senate to any President for nomination as a District Judge of a lawyer who was better qualified than Mr. Lawrence and with the further knowledge

Senator Russell's letter to President Johnson concerning the Alexander Lawrence judgeship nomination.*

that no lawyer had been more universally endorsed for appointment by the bench, bar, and those who are likely to be litigants in the courts of this District.

For some reason, a minister or former minister of Savannah, Georgia, decided to demonstrate the power which he later claimed to have over you or your Attorney General and set out, with surprising success, to block the naming of Mr. Lawrence as Judge. It is only incidental that he displayed poor taste to boast of the successful use of this power in a address he made recently to a civic club in Savannah.

An overwhelming majority of the leading citizens of all races, creeds and colors in the Southern District have, however, expressed their complete confidence in Mr. Lawrence and his fairness as Judge.

From our conversations, I had about become convince that, despite the protests of the person who serves as your Attorney General, you would name Mr. Lawrence, and in additi you stated to me on my visit with you on the evening of the 26th instant that you would appoint him as United States Circuit Court Judge if he, Senator Talmadge, and I desired that this be done.

To be perfectly frank, even after so many years in the Senate, I was so naive I had not even suspected that th: man's nomination was being withheld from the Senate due to changes expected on the Supreme Court of the United States until after you sent in the nominations of Fortas and Thornl while still holding the recommendations for the nomination Mr. Lawrence either in your office or in the Department of Justice.

Whether it is intended or not, this places me in t position where, if I support your nominees for the Supreme Court, it will appear that I have done so out of my fears t you would not nominate Mr. Lawrence.

Mr. Lawrence and I enjoy a close friendship that is the heritage of three generations, but for your information, when placed in a similar position by former President Truman when he nominated my own beloved brother to be a Judge of the United States Circuit Court, I told Mr. Truman that he had bes withdraw that nomination as I did not intend to be blackmailed into voting for a District Judge in my own Federal Judicial District even to secure a Circuit Judgeship for a brother who was as close to me as two men could be. I still dislike being treated as a child or a patronage-seeking ward heeler.

When I came to the United States Senate some thirty-odd years ago, I did not possess much except my self-respect. When I leave -- either voluntarily, carried in a box, or at the request of a majority of the peopleof Georgia -- I still intend to carry my self-respect back to Georgia.

This is, therefore, to advise you that, in view of the long delay in handling and the juggling of this nomination I consider myself released from any statements that I may have made to you with respect to your nominations, and you are at liberty to deal with the recommendations as to Mr. Lawrence in any way you see fit. I shall undertake to deal objectively with the nominations you have made to the Supreme Court, but however, I may vote, I want you to understand that it is not done with any expectation that I am buying or insuring the nomination of Mr. Lawrence to either the District or the Circuit Court and that I do not propose to make any future endorsements to you for judicial appointments even in my own state.

I would have made this statement to you on Thursday when we were talking over the phone, but I desired to have an opportunity to see Mr. Lawrence and apprise him of what I proposed to do. He and his family have already been humiliate beyond what decent and honorable people should be required to bear at the hands of a motley collection of fanatics, mystics and publicity seekers.

With respect, I am

Yours very truly,

THE WHITE HOUSE

WASHINGTON

July 3, 1968

My dear Senator:

I have received your letter of July 1 relating to the nomination of Mr. Alexander Lawrence as United States District Judge for the Southern District of Georgia.

As your letter recognizes, I indicated to you several times in past weeks that I intended to send Mr. Lawrence's nomination to the Senate.

I did so because I was convinced that he was qualified for the post. I was pleased to act upon your recommendation, and that of Senator Talmadge. All of this transpired weeks before I was notified by the Chief Justice of his intention to retire.

In early May, you first informed me in my office of the opposition which had been expressed to Mr. Lawrence's appointment. I concluded that it was advisable to go ahead and complete the investigations then underway.

Pursuant to this, we agreed that other prominent citizens would be contacted to get their views on Mr. Lawrence and his qualifications. You will remember that over a hundred additional names were supplied to Tom Johnson by your office on May 24. The FBI was immediately asked to interview and write a report on each name submitted. The American Bar Association was asked to complete their investigation promptly.

On Wednesday, June 19, the last and final FBI report was completed. I reviewed with you in my office at the White House Tuesday evening, June 25, the Lawrence file, including reports received ~~just~~ that day. The Department of Justice informed me today that they have not yet received the final American Bar Association report. We hope to obtain a formal report this week.

I consider these steps, which require time, to be prudent in the interest of Mr. Lawrence, the sponsoring Senators, this Administration and the Judiciary.

President Johnson's reply to Senator Russell concerning the Alexander Lawrence judgeship nomination.*

My decision to nominate Mr. Lawrence was based entirely upon his qualifications and upon the recommendations of yourself and Senator Talmadge.

It had and has no relationship to anything else.

Certainly it had and has no relationship, direct or indirect, to the nominations of Mr. Justice Fortas as Chief Justice and of Judge Thornberry as Associate Justice of the Supreme Court.

It is my intention to send Mr. Lawrence's name to the Senate. We will communicate with you when the final ABA clearance is received.

I am sure that you will vote for or against the nominations of Justice Fortas and Judge Thornberry as your conscience dictates. I am frankly surprised and deeply disappointed that a contrary inference would be suggested. Both my own standards of public administration, and my knowledge of your character, would deny such an inference.

With respect,

Lyndon B. Johnson

Honorable Richard B. Russell
United States Senate
Washington, D. C.

6

Russell, as President Pro Tempore of the Senate, with President Nixon on inauguration day in 1969 along with Senate Democratic Leader Mike Mansfield and Senate Republican Leader Everett Dirksen.*

Senator Russell acknowledges applause, after being introduced by President Nixon, in 1970 at the Washington Hilton Hotel at the premier of the WSB-TV film on Russell's career, "Georgia Giant."* *(Courtesy WSB-TV)*

5

Law School

When I arrived in Washington, DC, to work with Richard Russell, I did not immediately enroll in law school. I had not yet finished the research for my Master's thesis at the University of Georgia, and I had not even started writing it. Thus I decided to devote the first nine months of my spare time in Washington to completing this requirement for my Master's degree. I had already selected a topic, "Basic and Fundamental Freedoms in the Old Commonwealth," in conjunction with my advisor at the University of Georgia. This topic was basically a study of individual freedoms in Canada, Australia, and New Zealand, which comprised the Old Commonwealth in the British Empire. I had already done about half the research at the University of Georgia Library and in one trip to the Duke University Library in Durham, North Carolina. Fortunately, the Library of Congress was located only about two blocks from the Old Senate Office Building, and I was able to use the research facilities there on nights and weekends. It took me about two months to complete the research and about six more months to finish the thesis. I then submitted it to the university and waited for them to schedule a conference with the graduate faculty at which I would defend my work. That did not happen until 1967, when I received my Master's degree from the University of Georgia.

In the meantime, I had to decide which law school to attend. I had applied to what were generally regarded as Washington's two best law schools: George Washington University School of Law and the Georgetown University Law Center. I was accepted at both schools. The specialties at George Washington—commercial law, taxation, securities and creditor rights—probably fit better with my future plans to become a commercial trial lawyer. Georgetown, on the other hand, had as its main specialties constitutional law, criminal law, and international law, subjects that would not be terribly relevant to a commercial litigator. Nonetheless, I selected Georgetown for a practical reason. At that time, the school was located at Fifth and E Streets Northeast in Washington between Capitol Hill and downtown Washington. I could get from my office in the Old Senate Office Building to law school classes at Georgetown in about fifteen minutes, whereas it would take me at least twice as long to get to George Washington. Since I already had to leave Senator Russell's office before the day was over, I decided to enroll at the Georgetown Law Center.

I attended law school classes either five nights a week or four nights a week and on Saturday morning[s]. The classes lasted two hours. Almost all the students in the night law school program at Georgetown had full-time government jobs. A number of them worked on Capitol Hill. They were generally diligent and committed to their studies. Many were married and had families. I knew the competition would be stiff and that it would be difficult to attend law school and hold down a full-time job in Senator Russell's office at the same time. Fortunately, I am a person of habit. I got into a constant routine each day of attending class, returning to my apartment to study for about two hours with the assistance of a couple of drinks, eating dinner either in the apartment or in a nearby restaurant, and going to bed by 11:00 PM. Then I would be back at the office the next morning at about 7:30 AM. I also studied on the weekends. By committing to this routine, I was able to make decent grades in law school and graduate in five years. It is probably not the best way to get a legal education, but it allowed me the unique experience of working for Richard Russell while going to law school.

The professors at the Georgetown Law Center were excellent. I intentionally took courses that I thought would be the easiest and for which I felt most prepared due to my undergraduate and graduate studies at UGA. For example, I took constitutional law and international law, which had been major parts of my education in Athens. I also took courses in professionalism and trial practice. I particularly remember one trial practice course that was taught by a well-known trial lawyer in private practice in Washington. I remember a student asking him one day what he thought was the most important attribute of a successful trial lawyer based on his thirty years of trying lawsuits. He answered, "a reputation for integrity." That made quite an impression on me because I was having difficulty understanding the secret of Richard Russell's power and influence in the Senate. A light went off in my head at the professor's words. Richard Russell's integrity was one of the principal reasons other senators had such confidence in him. In essence, this professor/lawyer said that a reputation for integrity with judges before whom you try cases would be a tremendous asset. I never forgot that after I became a lawyer.

Since I took a lower course load and took off two semesters for extensive travel with Senator Russell's office, it took me a little longer to graduate from law school. The timing of my graduation in June 1971 worked out well for me. Senator Russell had died that January, and I had my law degree a few months later.

One of the victims of my going to law school and having a full-time job was my social life. In the first nine months I was in Washington, before I started law school, I enjoyed the social circuit. Senator Russell was invited to all kinds of receptions and other events and hardly ever went to any of them. Before I started law school, I went to several receptions at different embassies in Washington that I enjoyed very much. I also dated from time to time. After law school started, this social life largely came to an end.

6

Working for Senator Russell

While I was a student at the University of Georgia, I met George Watts of Brinson, Georgia, who was a journalism student at UGA. Before I went to Washington, George had accepted a job as press secretary to Congressman Maston O' Neal from Georgia. He and I decided to room together and rented a two-bedroom apartment on Ridge Road in Arlington, Virginia, near the Pentagon. We lived together for about a year and a half before George got married. We have remained friends through the years and served as best man at each other's weddings. George went on to become president of the National Broiler Council, now known as the National Chicken Council, the principal poultry trade group in Washington, DC. We used to refer to George as "President of NBC" or "Chicken Watts." George retired on March 31, 2011, after almost forty years in that position.

After George married, I moved to a basement apartment in Southeast Washington, where I lived for the next two years. In 1968, when Dr. Martin Luther King, Jr., was assassinated, that area of Washington suffered considerable damage in the riots. I decided to move back to Arlington to the River House Apartments near where George Watts and I had lived. This time I rented a two-bedroom apartment with Proctor Jones, a fellow staffer in Senator Russell's office, as my roommate until I graduated from law school and returned to Georgia.

Legislative Assistant in Name Only

I got off to a rocky start in Richard Russell's office at the beginning of 1966. On the first day I was to report for work, a snowstorm hit Washington, DC. No more qualified to drive in it than many of the other drivers, I had an automobile accident on the way to work and did not arrive until almost noon. When I did arrive, more bad news awaited me. Congressman John Flynt's office had called and accused Senator Russell's office of pirating his employees. This apparently resulted from my earlier conversations with Congressman Flynt's office when I was still at the University of Georgia. I had told them that I wished to stay in Athens for law school but would let them know if I changed my mind. I certainly never committed to work for Congressman Flynt, but, in hindsight, I should have been more explicit in declining his offer of employment. William H. Jordan, Jr., Senator Russell's executive secretary and the person who ran his office, devised an ingenious strategy to deal with the problem: Senator Russell would offer me to Congressman Flynt if Flynt still wanted me. I must admit that I was not too enthusiastic about this strategy. What if Flynt accepted? Bill Jordan did not seem worried. His strategy worked, as Congressman Flynt's office made it clear that they would not accept me as a staff member under any circumstances in view of what had happened.

A further bump in the road occurred shortly thereafter when Senator Russell requested that someone buy him a new white shirt for an event he was attending at the White House. Since I was the low man on the totem pole and the newest member of the staff, I was given the responsibility. I, of course, knew nothing about shopping in Washington, DC. One of the ladies in the office suggested that I go to the Woodward and Lothrop Department Store downtown. Utilizing my vast experience in men's clothing from having worked at the New York Store in Jackson and the limited shopping I did as a student in Athens, I purchased what appeared to me to be an acceptable shirt at a reasonable price. When I gave Senator Russell the shirt and a receipt for the purchase, he did not appear to be overjoyed. Several days later, a member of his staff told me that he had remarked about questions he had concerning the judgment of the boy from Jackson based on the amount he paid for a shirt. I had learned firsthand that Richard Russell was as frugal with his own money as he was with taxpayer money.

Shortly after I arrived in Washington, I received good advice from William H. Darden, the chief of staff for the Armed Services Committee. Bill Darden is from Union Point, Georgia, and had come to Washington in the 1950s to work on Senator Russell's staff. When Russell became chairman of the Armed Services Committee, he moved Bill Darden, whom he trusted with matters of national security and intelligence, to the committee staff. Bill was privy to the highly secret information available to Senator Russell from the Pentagon and the CIA. Bill and I became great friends and often played golf on the weekends. He is now retired and living in Florida. The advice he gave me at the beginning of my employment in Washington was not to stay more than five years if I wanted to return to Georgia. He explained that after five years[,] it became difficult to leave because of one's entrenched interest in the Washington retirement system. Though it was not because of any great design on my part, I did end up following Bill's advice, returning to Georgia about five and a half years after my employment began.

When I accepted a job in Senator Russell's office, I did not try to negotiate a salary or a title. Upon my arrival, I was told that I would be Russell's first legislative assistant, and my starting salary was approximately $15,000. The position of legislative assistant, in those days, was important in most Senate offices. The legislative assistant worked with the senator on all legislative matters, including the drafting of bills, committee work, and floor consideration of legislation. That was not the case in Senator Russell's office. He did his own legislative work and did not need anybody to advise him, particularly not a young non-lawyer with no Washington experience. He also had access to the large staffs of the Armed Services and Appropriations committees. My principal responsibility insofar as it related to legislation was answering mail.

The answering of the mail was given much more importance in Russell's office than in most Senate offices. On an average day, Russell received approximately one hundred letters from Georgians. When controversial questions were in the news, the total letters each day might reach one thousand. Every letter from Georgia had to be answered within no more than three days after its receipt. Most of the staff was involved in answering mail, but we were not free to make up our own answers to mail from Georgia constituents. A dictation file was maintained of Senator Russell's language in answering letters on virtually every subject, and staff members were expected to use that language in answering inquiries. If a staffer tried to branch out and use his or her own language, the letter was frequently returned with a note from Senator Russell: "I like my language better." Senator Russell saw between twenty and thirty letters a day. Sometimes, he redraft[ed] the letter prepared by the staff member, and his language would then be placed in the dictation file for future reference. The letters he saw included letters from fellow senators, cabinet officials, and friends from Georgia. If a constituent Senator Russell did not know wrote a particularly good letter, Bill Jordan or whoever screened the mail also selected it for personal review by Russell. A particularly hostile or derogatory letter was placed in the "nut" file without response. If Russell received out-of-state mail on matters relating to the work of his committees, that mail was sent to the committee staffs for response.

The office also maintained an elaborate set of name cards filed by county. If the person was a good friend of Senator Russell, the name card indicated how to address him or her. If the person was not known to Senator Russell but was from Georgia, the manner of address was "Dear Friend." For the letters that were not personally reviewed by Senator Russell, automatic signing machines affixed his signature to the response letters. Young interns working in his office operated these machines, which contained three different signatures. "Richard B. Russell" was the most formal and was used for people he did not know or for government officials. "Dick Russell" was used on letters from personal friends or people he knew. "Dick R" was used for very close friends or family members. A staff person reviewed every letter and every response. In the first couple of years I was on the staff, I would say that fully fifty percent of my time was devoted to mail. It did teach me one quality that would benefit me in my later law career—the ability to quickly proofread a letter or document for typographical errors.

In the five-plus years I worked for Richard Russell, I can only recall being involved in two substantive legislative assignments. The first came not long after I started working there. Senator Thomas Dodd of Connecticut was accused of violating the Senate rules with respect to the use of his office and campaign funds. Senator Russell asked me to look at the record before the Senate Ethics Committee and prepare him a memorandum on what I thought he should do when the matter came before the Senate for action. In hindsight, I think he probably asked me to do this because he wanted to see if his new aide had the ability to analyze an issue and write a coherent memorandum. I reviewed the record and concluded that Senator Dodd had undoubtedly acted in a manner inconsistent with the normal behavior expected of members of the Senate but that his actions were not greatly different from those of a number of other senators at the time. I concluded that it was a case of selective prosecution. Senator Dodd was eventually censured by the Senate. Censure is the strongest sanction that can be taken against a senator short of expulsion. Senator Dodd's son, Christopher Dodd, wrote a book, *Letters from Nuremberg: My Father's Narrative of a Quest for Justice* (New York: Crown Publishing Group, 2007), about numerous letters his father wrote the family while he served as one of the principal prosecutors in the Nuremberg War Trials after World War II. The younger Dodd also said in his book that his father lost his Senate seat after the Senate censure and that he and his wife died shortly thereafter. Chris Dodd blamed his father's death at age sixty-four partly on the action taken by the Senate, which he says the Dodd family viewed as unjustified. Christopher Dodd later became a powerful senator himself and retired at the end of 2010.

The Dodd matter presented Senator Russell with a difficult question. He was friends with Senator Dodd, as he was with almost all senators. He and Thomas Dodd were among the fiercest cold warriors and saw eye to eye on how to deal with the Soviet Union from a position of strength. As a delegate from Connecticut at the 1952 Democratic National Convention, Dodd had cast his vote for Richard Russell for president. On the other hand, Russell did not condone improper, unethical, or illegal behavior by public officials. In addition, the chairman of the Senate Ethics Committee bringing the charges against Senator Dodd was Russell's close friend, Senator John Stennis of Mississippi. Senator Dodd's chief defender was Senator Russell's friend, Senator Russell Long of Louisiana. Even Dodd questioned whether some of Senator Long's arguments defending him were effective. Dodd was not particularly well liked by a number of his Senate colleagues because of the stridency of some of his positions and because, on more than one occasion, he had violated the Senate's unwritten rule never to speak ill of a fellow senator. A series of amendments to the Censure Resolution was offered by Senator Long and Senator John Tower of Texas to reduce the punishment or temper the language used in the Censure Resolution. All of these amendments failed. Richard Russell did not vote on any of them. He also did not vote on final passage of the Censure Resolution. Russell had a good excuse. He was in Winder attending the annual Russell family reunion, which he hosted each summer. While he did not vote, he had it announced at the time that if he had been present, he would have voted for the Censure Resolution.

The other substantive legislative matter in which I became involved related to the Education Bill in 1967. This came at a time when I had been attending Senator Russell's meetings with various county school superintendents from Georgia who were struggling with the desegregation of their schools. Some were trying to desegregate in good faith and some were not. Some were making progress and some were not. All of them complained about what they viewed as the arbitrary decisions of the Department of Health, Education, and Welfare (HEW) concerning the cutoff of funds to southern school systems that were not making sufficient progress toward desegregation. They complained that they did not get sufficient warning, which created havoc during the school year. After attending a number of those meetings, I asked Senator Russell if he thought it would be a good idea to offer an amendment to the Education Bill that required HEW to give more advance notice. He said he thought it would be an excellent idea and asked me to draft a bill. In consultation with the Senate Legislative Office, which assisted senators in drafting legislation, I came up with an amendment that Senator Russell filed for floor consideration.

By the time the Education Bill became the pending business before the Senate, Senator Russell and I were in New York where he was undergoing a week of medical consultations at Doctors Hospital in connection with his growing emphysema problem. Senator John Stennis was left in charge of southern senators' amendments to the Education Bill. He announced that he would not allow a final vote on the bill until Senator Russell returned and was able to present his amendment. This had the effect of holding up important legislation over one amendment. After talking with Senator Stennis on the telephone, Senator Russell asked me to return to Washington and work with Stennis in regard to his amendment. When I arrived back in Washington, Senator Stennis told me that HEW had indicated a willingness to negotiate a compromise with respect to the amendment. He asked me to take charge of the negotiations with HEW. For a number of days, I negotiated principally with Peter Libassi, who was the head of HEW compliance. HEW made several compromise offers that I thought were not adequate, and, after consulting with Senator Stennis, I declined them. We eventually agreed that before funds could be cut off to any school system, an advance written notice had to be given no later than March 1 of the prior school year. This compromise resolved the Russell amendment.

By the time the Education Bill was ready for final vote, Senator Russell had returned. In thanking various people for their efforts in his absence, he said this about me on the Senate floor: "I also wish to thank...Charles Campbell of my staff who showed a profound understanding of this question which I really did not know he possessed." Senator Russell rarely praised a member of his staff in public or private. He may have done so because of the profuse praise heaped on me by Senator Stennis and Senate Majority Leader Mike Mansfield. Peter Libassi of HEW offered me a job on his staff. It was an easy offer to decline, as I already thought I had one of the best jobs in Washington. Notwithstanding the successful outcome of this legislative matter, Senator Russell did not ask me for substantive work on future legislative questions. He continued to do his own work.

In addition to answering mail, I also occasionally represented Senator Russell in meetings with executive agencies on matters of concern to Georgians. One occasion I particularly recall involved a meeting with the Federal Highway Department concerning an interstate highway question in Georgia. Senator Talmadge's office was to take the lead in the meeting, with Senator Talmadge personally presenting the state's position. I planned to be there to represent Russell's office. When we arrived at the meeting, I was surprised that Senator Talmadge was not there. His administrative assistant, Ronald B. (Bo) Ginn, handled the meeting well. When I returned to the office, I told Senator Russell of my surprise that Talmadge was not present at the meeting. "Don't worry," he said, "Herman is probably off on a drunk. He will be back." It apparently was not unusual for Senator Talmadge to go on a drunk and be gone for a week or so.

When I arrived in Washington, DC, Senator Russell's staff was run by Bill Jordan. He did not have the title of administrative assistant (AA) because Leeman Anderson, who had been Russell's AA almost since he was first elected to the Senate, held that position. By early 1966, Leeman was aging and also battling a serious drinking problem. Because of his long service and loyalty, however, Senator Russell would not replace him as AA Leeman died several years after I joined the staff. Also on staff when I arrived was Proctor Jones. Proctor had come to Washington as a 4-H Club intern and stayed on as a member of the staff after the internship ended. He became Senator Russell's personal aide and was probably closer to him than anyone else in the office. Shortly after I arrived, Proctor was drafted into the Marine Corps, where he served for about two years. This resulted in my assuming most of Proctor's duties and having the opportunity for a much closer relationship with Senator

Russell. For example, I traveled with him extensively in Georgia in the first half of 1966 when there was still some possibility that Governor Sanders would run against him. I remember going with Russell to the Georgia Press Association Meeting, the County Commissioners Meeting, the State Bar Association Meeting, and the Hibernian Society Meeting in Savannah on St. Patrick's Day. I also made a number of trips with Russell to his home in Winder.

The other principal members of the staff when I started included Bill Bates, who was Russell's press secretary. Bill had several tenures as press secretary and had come back in 1964 to help with Russell's speeches and relations with the press. When Governor Sanders announced that he was not going to run in mid-1966, Bill left and Powell Moore replaced him as press secretary. Powell served in that position until Russell died in 1971. When I became executive secretary, the office hired Joel Williams, a young attorney from Dacula, Georgia, to replace me as legal counsel. Additional principal members of the staff included Babs Raesley and Jane McMullan of Athens, personal secretaries who took dictation from Senator Russell and handled his appointments. Finally, a woman named Marge Warren had been there for many years as an assistant office manager. Other women worked in the office, but these were the people who dealt with Richard Russell on a regular basis.

Traveling with Richard Russell

Shortly after I joined Richard Russell's staff in January 1966, Proctor Jones, his personal aide, was drafted into the military. He would be away from the office for approximately two years. During this time, I assumed many of his duties, including traveling with Senator Russell. This was a wonderful opportunity to get to know the senator better, since he was more uptight and much busier in Washington. In addition, after September 1966, I left to go to law school at 5:30 in the afternoon four or five nights a week. Often, Richard Russell had not even returned to the office by that time from his activities on the Senate floor or in committee meetings.

Most of our travel in the first nine months of 1966 related to the possible campaign by Governor Sanders against Russell. Fortunately, this was a window of time in which Russell enjoyed relatively good health. I traveled with him for a number of campaign speeches throughout Georgia. Before September 1996 when I entered law school,

Governor Sanders had announced that he would not run against Senator Russell but would support his reelection. Some of the people in Russell's office thought this was because he ran some polls that indicated he could not defeat Russell. In any event, this took the pressure off Russell to do extensive travel in Georgia.

Both before and after September 1966, I traveled with Russell on a number of occasions to his home in Winder. With the exception of one car trip that I will discuss later, we always flew on an Air Force jet from Andrews Air Force Base outside Washington to the airport in Winder approximately two miles from his home. The airstrip there had been lengthened to accommodate the Air Force jets. Within about two hours after we walked out of the Old Senate Office Building in Washington, we would be walking into Senator Russell's home in Winder. On the flights, Russell would typically lie on a couch and sleep for almost the entire trip. Once I started law school, I usually spent the time studying my law books.

The routine in Winder was almost the same on every trip. Russell's longtime maid, Modine Thomas, fixed three meals a day of country foods. Richard Russell typically got up at about 8:30 and ate breakfast. He read the Atlanta newspaper and returned any telephone calls he had from the office or from other senators, cabinet officials, or constituents. About midmorning, we often walked to the Russell family cemetery located about half a mile from the house. We usually spent about an hour there among the graves of his parents and other members of his family. Sometime after I started working for him, the Georgia Forestry Commission converted about twenty acres of land he owned adjacent to the cemetery into a park. In the park, they planted one of each species of tree that was indigenous to Georgia. Russell spent a lot of time reviewing the growth of the trees on our trips to Winder.

At about noon on these trips, he usually ate lunch and then took a one-hour nap. Afterward, we drove around Barrow County or one of the adjoining counties. During our trips, he reminisced about his time growing up. I particularly recall him telling about conversations he had with people who fought during the Civil War. That is one of the reasons he developed such a great interest in that topic. After our car trips, we returned to the Russell house to watch the evening news and have dinner. Then we watched Atlanta Braves baseball games if the team was playing. Senator Russell usually went to bed by ten o'clock in the evening.

I remember being in Winder with Senator Russell one election night. He followed the election returns closely. He also received telephone calls from a number of newly elected senators seeking his assistance in being assigned to committees of their choice. I also remember one night in early 1969 when he received calls from a number of senators wanting to know if he planned to oppose Senator Edward Kennedy's effort to defeat Senator Russell Long for the position of Democratic Whip. Russell told the senators that he was going to vote for Senator Long, but he was not going to "throw any stones in Senator Kennedy's path." I was somewhat surprised at that, since Russell Long was a good friend of Richard Russell and was the incumbent Senate Democratic Whip. However, Long was developing a reputation with a serious drinking problem. I assumed that was the reason Richard Russell refused to go all out to support Long. I had a personal introduction one time to Senator Long's drinking habits. When I arrived at the office one Saturday morning , Senator Long and his administrative assistant, Bob Hunter, were walking down the hall singing with their arms around each other. It was clear to me that neither of them had been home during the night. Senator Long's office was adjacent to our office for the entire five years I worked for Richard Russell.

On another trip I made to Winder with Russell, we drove by car to Ailey, Georgia, for a party related to the wedding of Senator Russell's nephew, Hugh Peterson. This was an interesting trip because Senator Russell told stories about his early campaigns for governor and the Senate. We stopped often in small towns so he could talk to people at a filling station or restaurant he had visited during his earlier campaigns. Hugh Peterson, one of Russell's favorite nephews, became the co-executor of Russell's estate following his death in 1971. Also a good friend of mine, Hugh has been a trustee of the Richard B. Russell Foundation for many years.

One memorable trip we made to Winder was during the race for governor of Georgia in 1970. Jimmy Carter was running against Carl Sanders. Most of Russell['s] people supported Carter because of lingering resentment of what they viewed as the thwarted plans of Sanders to run against Russell in 1966. The Carter campaign actively encouraged the perception that Russell was supporting Carter. Russell, however, had a long-standing policy of not becoming involved in the Democratic primary of any race in Georgia other than his own. He had religiously followed this practice since his initial election to the Senate in 1932. During a visit to Winder in early 1970, Jimmy Carter and Ford Spinks, a state senator from Tifton, Georgia, and later a member of the Georgia Public Service Commission, came to visit Senator Russell at his home. I remember the four of us sitting on the front porch in rocking chairs along with Senator Russell's sister, Ina Stacy. Ford Spinks was a friend of Senator Russell, and the meeting was clearly for the purpose of trying to get Russell to endorse Carter. The conversation was pleasant, but Russell gave no indication of any endorsement. Finally, Mrs. Stacy, who supported Carter, became exasperated and left the porch with the statement, "Well, I am supporting Jimmy Carter." Russell steadfastly maintained his policy of not becoming involved in the race.

The most interesting trip I took with Richard Russell to Winder was by car. He called me into his office one day and said that he had been thinking about the fact that he never drove to Georgia anymore because of the availability of the Air Force jets. He asserted that a senator who could not drive to his home state should not be in the Senate. He announced that he and I would leave Washington by car shortly after noon on Thursday with me driving. I had an important date with a young lady that weekend, and I immediately formulated a strategy to block this ill-advised car trip to Winder. I first observed that many senators could not drive to their home states. I cited as an example his good friend, Senator Daniel Inouye of Hawaii (Inouye, the last serving senator with Russell, died 17 December 1012). Russell brushed this off by observing that he was unaware of any ocean between Washington, DC, and Georgia. I then tried the weather routine. I told him that I had heard on the news that snow was expected in the Carolinas. He dismissed that concern by saying that we could handle the weather. I reluctantly canceled my date and packed my bags.

The first noteworthy happening on the trip occurred shortly after we left the Washington area. Senator Russell turned on the radio, selected a music station, and reclined as if he were going to sleep. Within about ten minutes, the radio changed stations. He sat up and asked if I disapproved of his music selection. I told him not at all. He then asked me why I had changed stations. I told him I had not touched the radio. He looked at me skeptically and turned the radio back to the station for more music. Before long, the radio changed stations again. He sat up again, looked at me, and turned off the radio. I learned later that his Chrysler New Yorker automobile had a button in the floorboard that activated a scanning device that would change stations. Looking back on the incident now, I am confident that Richard Russell was toying with me.

When we reached the area around the Virginia/North Carolina border, it started snowing. The snow grew heavier, with a number of cars slipping off the highway or stopping. My only experience driving in snow was from my first day driving to work in Washington when I had an accident. As the traction became more difficult, Senator Russell told me to let some air out of the tires. I had never heard of such a thing, but I did as I was told. Amazingly, the traction greatly improved. We arrived on the outskirts of Durham, North Carolina, around dark. Senator Russell announced that we should try to get a hotel in Durham, but he had not been there in many years and did not know of any hotels. He asked me if I knew of any. I told him that on a debate trip to Duke University while I was at the University of Georgia, we had stayed at the Jack Tar Hotel in downtown Durham. He said that was fine with him if I recommended it. We stopped at a gas station to get directions to the hotel.

When we arrived at the hotel, there was a considerable line of people waiting to get rooms. Registration took place by remote television across from the main lobby of the hotel. As I was in the process of registering, the clerk asked me whether we needed one or two rooms. Senator Russell immediately broke in and took over the registration process. He told the clerk that he had emphysema and he proceeded to explain, in considerably more detail than the clerk or the people standing in line behind us were interested in hearing, his emphysema affliction. We did finally get two rooms, and on the elevator Senator Russell observed that we had had a hard day and he thought we needed a drink. He complimented me on doing a good job with the driving. He suggested that I take my bags to my room and then come back to his room. By the time I did so, he had turned on the television and the movie, *Pork Chop Hill*, about the Korean War was just beginning. Russell told me that he had attended the premiere of the movie in Washington and met the actor Gregory Peck there. Russell's nephew, Walter Russell, Jr., had fought in the battle. Senator Russell mixed a strong drink of Wild

Turkey Bourbon and water. I was somewhat surprised that he included me in the cocktail hour because he had never done that for me or any other member of his staff when he had cocktails in Washington. I preferred scotch, but I was certainly not going to decline Richard Russell's offer of a drink. The strong drinks continued throughout the movie. By the end of the movie, I was drunk. I had not had anything to eat since before noon that day, and it was now almost nine o'clock in the evening.

When the movie ended, Russell said he thought we should go eat before the dining room closed. The restaurant was located in the basement of the hotel, which was accessed by crossing the lobby and descending a flight of stairs. I stumbled along behind Richard Russell and somehow made it down the stairs. I was relieved when the waitress showed us to a table and I could sit down. Almost immediately, Senator Russell said he had not read a paper that day and asked me to go back to the lobby and get him one. That was quite a challenge in my drunken state. Somehow, I was able to get the paper and get back to the table in one piece. Finally, much to my joy, food arrived. I slept well that night but woke up with a terrible hangover the next day. Fortunately, the snow had largely melted and the rest of the trip to Winder was uneventful.

I learned three important lessons from this car trip. First, be careful where you put your foot when you are driving Senator Russell's car and he is listening to the radio. Second, letting air out of the tires when driving in snow actually improves traction. Third, never feel badly when Richard Russell does not invite you to join in cocktails with him.

Another interesting trip I made with Senator Russell occurred in March 1967. We flew from Washington to McDill Air Force Base near Tampa, Florida. The trip was ostensibly for the purpose of Richard Russell being briefed by military officials. An equally important purpose, I learned, was for him to attend several Atlanta Braves exhibition baseball games in nearby Bradenton, Florida. At one of the games, Richard Russell noticed that one of the principal sports writers for the Atlanta newspapers was in the press box. He asked me to go tell this writer that Russell would be glad to give him a prognosis for the upcoming season. I did so, and Russell and the writer had a long conversation. Russell was an avid baseball fan and kept up with the Atlanta Braves throughout the season.

A highlight of this trip to Florida was a dinner at the famous Columbia Restaurant in Ibor City. A grand affair, it was hosted by the commanding general at the Air Force Base. Richard Russell gave an after-dinner speech to the group, and a photograph was made of him speaking, with the commanding general sitting next to Russell and me sitting next to the commanding general. The military provided me with a copy of the photograph, and I asked Senator Russell if he would autograph it. He signed it as follows: "To my friend and comrade, Charles Campbell, with appreciation and affection." That picture appears on the jacket to this book. I kept it as one of my most treasured possessions throughout my law practice career and gave it to the Russell Library upon my retirement in 2009.

The Perks of Working for Richard Russell

It is a wonderful opportunity to work for any United States senator. Richard Russell, however, was not just any United States senator. He was *the* senator. His prestige and respect in the Senate were so great that in the periodic polls taken of Senate staffers as to the most effective senator, Richard Russell's name was often at the top of the list. This was even true when I joined the staff in 1966, at a time when Richard Russell was not in the best of health and was on the downside of his career. His voting pattern was clearly outside the mainstream of the Senate. In addition to opposing the civil rights legislation in 1964 and 1965 and voting against almost all of Lyndon Johnson's Great Society Programs, he also voted against almost all foreign aid. Yet the Senate staffers who voted in these polls were generally young and liberal. The huge respect their bosses had for Richard Russell apparently filtered down to them.

Senator Robert C. Byrd of West Virginia, who would go on to become the longest-serving United States senator in the history of the country before dying in 2010, was notorious for hounding Senate aides and interns if he thought they were not behaving properly. I remember one instance when King Askew, a Russell intern who is now a successful lawyer in Rome, Georgia, encountered the Byrd treatment. King's job was to operate one of the elevators in the Senate Office Building. The operators were taught to drop everything else when a senator rang for the elevator and to immediately pick up the senator, as he or she might be rushing to a vote on the Senate floor. As King related it to me later, one day he did not immediately recognize Senator Byrd when he rang the elevator. Senator Byrd criticized him in public and told him it would cost him his job. King was terrified. He apologized profusely, but Senator Byrd continued to berate him. Finally, Byrd asked him the name of his sponsoring senator. King said it was Senator Russell of Georgia. According to King, Byrd's demeanor changed completely. He smiled and said to be more careful in the future. King was so concerned about the encounter with Senator Byrd that he went back to the office and told Bill Jordan about it. Bill talked to Senator Russell, who said King should not worry, as his position was not in danger.

I observed Senator Byrd's strict code of conduct for Senate staffers whenever I went onto the Senate floor. Top aides, such as legislative assistants, were given floor privileges to the extent necessary to assist their senators with legislation. Some of us abused the privilege by going onto the Senate floor when we should have been in the Senate gallery. When Senator Byrd observed that, he would go up to the aide and ask him what business he had on the Senate floor. If the aide did not have a good answer, Byrd would ask him to leave. I occasionally went onto the Senate floor and sat on a couch at the rear of the chamber to listen to floor debate. That, of course, was completely improper and would have resulted in Senator Byrd's wrath if it had been someone other than Senator Russell's staffer. When Byrd walked by and observed me sitting on the couch, however, he would simply smile and pass by.

The perks of working for Richard Russell were not limited to the Senate itself. I enjoyed a number of nice trips because of my position on his staff. Some of these were government-sponsored trips, and some were sponsored by companies from Georgia or elsewhere. Of the government trips, I particularly recall being flown from Washington to an aircraft carrier that was conducting sea trials off the coast of Florida. We spent one night on the carrier and were able to observe the impressive sight of the airplanes taking off and landing from the deck. I was even given an opportunity to fly in one of the aircraft. While it was exciting, it was also a scary experience. When a plane landed on the deck of the aircraft carrier, it was stopped when a hook on the bottom of the plane caught one of three cables on the deck of the carrier. The pilot got the highest score for catching the middle cable and the lowest score for catching the first cable. The reason is that the worst kind of accident is for the airplane to land short and crash into the aircraft carrier. When the plane lands on the deck, its engines are accelerated until the pilot can feel the effect of the cable stopping the aircraft. If the pilot misses all three cables, the acceleration of the engines results in the aircraft touching down but then taking off again for another attempt at landing. I had assumed that landing would be far more harrowing than taking off, but I found the opposite to be the case. When an aircraft took off, it would dip as if it were going to drop into the ocean when it reached the end of the aircraft carrier deck. After that experience, landing was a breeze.

Another interesting government-sponsored trip was to Cape Kennedy in Florida to observe a space launch. We were taken on a tour of Cape Kennedy prior to the launch. The amount of training that the astronauts undergo is amazing, and I came away impressed with the space program. As chairman of the Armed Services Committee and the ranking member of the Space Committee, Senator Russell received invitations to go on all of these trips, but he almost never went. The Pentagon or the Space Agency was glad to have a staff member from Russell's office there to represent him.

In addition to government-sponsored trips, I went on a number of trips paid for by corporations. In those days, there were fewer restrictions on the entertainment of Senate staffers and almost no disclosure requirements. One trip I remember particularly, paid for by the Southern Railway Company, was to Super Bowl IV in New Orleans, which the Kansas City Chiefs won. We went by train from Atlanta to New Orleans. On the way, we stopped to review the damage from Hurricane Camille that had struck the Gulf Coast a few months earlier in 1969. The devastation was unbelievable. I remember a large boat that had washed inland in a small Mississippi town. Some four or five months after the hurricane, it still had not been removed. Also, large trees were leveled miles inland from the coast.

I also went several times on trips sponsored by the Union Camp Corporation to its retreat on the South Carolina coast. The lodge, known as Palmetto Bluff, housed about forty people at a time. We were given the option of engaging in a number of activities such as hunting, fishing, or golf. I generally chose golf. Union Camp had a large manufacturing plant outside Savannah, Georgia. We usually stayed at the retreat for three or four days and were flown from Washington to Savannah and back.

It was while I was working for Richard Russell that I also had my first opportunity to attend the famous Masters Golf Tournament at

Augusta National Golf Club in Augusta, Georgia. I have forgotten now who provided the tickets, but I am sure it was some company in Georgia. Those tickets were hard to come by. In fact, after I returned to Georgia, I found that they were exceedingly difficult to obtain, as there was a long waiting list for the tickets.

In 1968, Earl Leonard of the Coca-Cola Company invited me to the Republican National Convention in Miami Beach. I had never been to a national political convention and accepted his invitation. Earl was a former press secretary to Senator Russell and was in the Government Affairs Department at Coca-Cola. The 1968 convention nominated Richard Nixon for president and Spiro Agnew for vice president. I stayed in Miami Beach for three or four days at Coca-Cola's expense and attended all of the Coca-Cola parties and other convention activities. Earl also invited me to join him at the 1968 Democratic National Convention in Chicago. However, I decided not to go because I thought one national political convention in a year was enough. That Democratic Convention suffered from widespread protests and altercations between the Chicago police and the protesters, so I did not regret my choice. Earl's boss at Coca-Cola was Senior Vice President Ovid Davis. Ovid was quite a character with a good sense of humor and was interesting to be around in a social setting. He was also a favorite of Richard Russell. One time, after a meeting with Ovid and other senior officials of the Coca-Cola Company, Russell said to me, "I like that Davis fellow. He could be a druggist in Douglasville." That was Russell's way of paying Ovid the ultimate compliment, meaning that he was not all consumed with his lofty position at Coca-Cola but was a down-to-earth, regular guy.

The Assassination of Dr. Martin Luther King, Jr.

When word reached the nation's Capitol of the assassination of Dr. Martin Luther King, Jr., in Memphis, Tennessee, on April 4, 1968, I was attending a Democratic Senate Campaign Committee dinner at the Shoreham Hotel in Northwest Washington. Senator Hubert Humphrey of Minnesota was giving the keynote address. In the middle of his speech, he was handed a note. After a brief pause, he read it, announcing the murder of Dr. King. Following a brief prayer, the dinner was summarily adjourned.

I returned to Capitol Hill and went to a bar behind the Senate Office Building. There, I watched television for a time, as the riots that would sweep Washington and other major American cities were just starting. I was living in a basement apartment in Southeast Washington, which was not the safest area in the best of times. I seriously considered checking into a hotel for the night instead of returning to my apartment, but I finally decided to take my chances. During the night, I heard a lot of shouting and gunfire on at least one occasion. Thankfully, my apartment was not disturbed.

The next day, Friday, I went to the office. By that time, the riots were in full swing in Washington and elsewhere. Most of the Senate offices were closed, but Senator Russell announced that his office would maintain its normal hours as he did not intend to be affected by the lawless activities. He did allow the female employees to go home. The rest of the staff stayed for the entire day. By this time, troops were stationed in the government buildings, including the Capitol. Russell followed his usual routine. After finishing the mail, he had several drinks of Jack Daniels and water while munching on Georgia peanuts and watching the news. The evening news was, of course, filled with the story of the riots. Earlier that day, I had overheard a telephone conversation Senator Russell had with President Johnson in which he urged Johnson to have Stokely Carmichael arrested because he was allegedly inciting the riots in Washington. Apparently, Johnson told Russell that he had been advised by Attorney General Ramsey_Clark not to arrest Carmichael. I remember Senator Russell telling Johnson, "Who is president of the United States? Are you president of the United States, or is Ramsey Clark president of the United States?" Carmichael was not arrested.

After the news was over and Russell finished his cocktails, he announced that he was going home. He opened his desk drawer and pulled out a pistol. I had no idea Russell owned a gun. Bill Jordan, Proctor Jones, and I were the remaining staff members when Russell left. Being concerned about him driving alone in a car with a tag indicating a United States senator from Georgia , we devised a strategy by which I would ride in the car with Senator Russell and Bill and Proctor would follow in one of their cars. Russell parked not in the Senate garage but in the courtyard of the Senate Office Building. I accompanied him to the courtyard, but before I could get in the car, he sped off. He apparently had become suspicious about our plan. Bill and Proctor did follow Russell to his apartment in the Foggy Bottom area of Washington across the street from the Watergate Complex. The trip, which would ordinarily take about twenty minutes, took over an hour. Finally, however, he was able to get to his apartment without incident.

General William C. Westmoreland, the commander of United States forces in Vietnam, was in Washington for a series of high-level consultations about the Vietnam War. Russell had been asked by President Johnson to be at the White House at approximately 7:30 the next morning to participate in the discussions. When Russell arrived at the White House, enhanced security procedures were in effect because of the rioting. The security personnel indicated to Russell that they would be required to search him and his vehicle because of these enhanced procedures. Probably because he still had the gun either on himself or in the car, Russell indicated to the security officers that he had been asked by the president to attend this meeting, and he was happy to leave and go home. He indicated that he was well known and was not willing to be searched. After some brief discussion among the security personnel, he was waved through without being searched.

Russell participated in the meetings at the White House for about two hours. He then drove to Capitol Hill, where he encountered soldiers guarding the Capitol. He noticed one soldier who had a new rifle that had recently been authorized by the Armed Services Committee. He introduced himself as the chairman of that committee and asked to see the rifle, at which point he discovered that it contained no ammunition. Coming on the heels of President Johnson's refusal to arrest Stokely Carmichael the day before, he became incensed. When he arrived at the office, he immediately telephoned the president, who was still in the Vietnam meetings at the White House. He bitterly complained to Johnson that the soldiers guarding the Capitol had no ammunition. Johnson indicated that he had no knowledge of the matter and put the chairman of the Joint Chiefs of Staff on the phone. Russell expressed outrage to him as well. Shortly thereafter, a military vehicle screeched to a halt outside Russell's office. Two generals came into the office and asked to meet with Russell at the request of the chairman of the Joint Chiefs of Staff. They assured him that ammunition was nearby and would be issued to the soldiers if the need should arise. Only slightly placated by this assurance, Russell dismissed the generals.

The riots grew worse that day, and looting of stores became prevalent as well. I decided that I was better off to go to the Virginia suburbs and stay with a Russell staff member until the riots died down. I stayed there for the next several nights. Before long, I decided to move back to Virginia, where I lived until I returned to Georgia following Senator Russell's death.

Moving Up on the Russell Staff

In 1968, Bill Jordan decided to move to the staff of the Senate Appropriations Committee shortly before Senator Russell became chairman of that committee. At that time, I was named executive secretary in Russell's office. I was a twenty-six-year-old law student holding what was, in effect, the top staff position in the office of Richard Russell. It was a daunting challenge. While I was thoroughly familiar with the operations of the office as a result of having worked there for several years, I nonetheless had some trepidation about being named to the top staff position. I was uneasy about how I would be accepted by staff members who had been there for years. Shortly thereafter, Leeman Anderson died, and I was named administrative assistant.

There were also some things about the office that I wished to change. By that point , Russell's health was increasingly fragile and there were tremendous demands on his limited energy. He seldom saw constituents who came by the office. Many of these constituents and their families had voted for him for as long as they could recall. I did not have any problem with the fact they would not be able to see Richard Russell because that was out of the question. However, I did want them to have a pleasant experience visiting his office. Marge Warren had been in the office for years. She came from a prominent family in Georgia. Her brother, Denmark Groover, was a prominent member of the Georgia Legislature. Not surprisingly, Marge had been there so long that she was not entirely thrilled to see visiting constituents. I felt that she should be moved out of the reception room and continue to discharge her duties in another room of the office suite. She did not agree with me.

I discussed the matter with Russell on several occasions. Richard Russell was reluctant to confront staff members or to make changes. That is probably one of the reasons there was such little turnover in his office. I insisted, if I was going to continue as administrative assistant, that Marge be moved out of the reception room and that we hire a new receptionist who would be friendlier to visitors who came by the office. With great reluctance, Russell finally agreed. He discussed the matter with Marge. She was not happy, but she made the move and the problem was solved. We hired a new receptionist, Anne Prichard, who was the daughter of Georgia Commissioner of Agriculture Phil Campbell (no relation to me). Her husband, Phil Prichard, had been assigned to a federal agency in nearby Maryland. Anne was a natural for the position and did a great job. I do not believe Marge ever forgave me—or Richard Russell either for that matter—but I felt sufficiently strong about the situation to endure the consequences.

Other than certain senior members whom I have already identified, Richard Russell hardly ever saw any members of his staff. That bothered me as well. It particularly came to my attention one day after I became administrative assistant and was walking down the hall of the Senate Office Building with Russell. We encountered a young lady who had been working in Russell's office for about one year and who had previously worked for Governor Ross Bass of Tennessee. By that time, Bass had been elected to the Senate and had been to lunch with his former employee. I suffered the humiliation of having Senator Bass introduce to Senator Russell a member of his staff who had worked for Russell for over a year. That convinced me that I should look for a way to have Russell walk through the office occasionally to meet staff members whom he did not see on a regular basis. He reluctantly agreed to do so. Unfortunately, on the first occasion , one of the Warren Commission "nuts" was in the reception room. This man came by periodically wanting to see Senator Russell in connection with his belief that there was a conspiracy that resulted in the assassination of President Kennedy. I never again suggested that Richard Russell go into the reception room.

The Richard Russell I Knew

Some historians or observers have presented Richard Russell simply as a conservative and a segregationist. I believe those assessments are far short of the mark. He was, from my observation, a brilliant but complicated and complex person with some contradictions. For example, while he was regarded as a staunch conservative at the end of his career, he had been an avid supporter of the New Deal early in his career. While he was certainly a segregationist and opposed all of the major civil rights bills, he was viewed as the most reasonable of the southern senators and never raised the race question in any of his political campaigns. While he was a strong advocate of the Marshall Plan that helped rebuild Europe following World War II, he came to regard the foreign aid program as essentially a waste of money and an effort to bribe other countries. By the time I joined the staff, he routinely voted against all foreign aid. While he was regarded as the foremost authority in the Senate on national security and favored aggressive military action during the Cuban missile crisis, he opposed involvement in Vietnam and the commitment of American troops anywhere unless a vital security interest of the United States was at stake. While many viewed him as a friend of the Pentagon, he sometimes slashed military appropriations. And though he opposed many of the social programs of Lyndon Johnson, he was the father of the school lunch program, helped establish the forerunner of the food stamp program, and was a consistent supporter of federal aid to education.

Russell himself once described his political philosophy in the following terms. In times of crisis, such as the Great Depression, he was a liberal and believed that government action was necessary. In good times, he was a conservative and saw no need to tinker with the system. He was considered the quintessential southern gentleman, but he was also a tough politician. Senators knew that if they crossed Richard Russell, there would be a price to pay. I remember a certain incident that illustrates this fact. Senator Edward Kennedy, whom Richard Russell liked and predicted would become a better senator than either of his brothers, became chairman of a subcommittee of the Senate Labor Committee. He conducted hearings on the nation's labor supply, covering the impact of the military draft. Russell considered the draft to be under the exclusive jurisdiction of the Armed Services Committee and offered an amendment to the Labor Bill to make that clear. His amendment passed with over seventy votes. Russell was interested, however, in the twenty-five or so senators who voted with Kennedy. Several months thereafter, I was in Russell's office one day when he was studying the Congressional Record and a vote that had taken place the day before. To see which senators were voting in a particular way, he had placed next to that vote the vote on the amendment to the Labor Bill from several months earlier. A senator expressed it this way one time: "Richard Russell may not be the most beloved member of the Senate, but he is the most respected."

Perhaps the strangest contradiction of Richard Russell related to family. I have never known a more committed family man than him. But he was a lifelong bachelor. The happiest time of the year for Richard Russell was in the period before, during, and immediately after the annual Russell family reunion in Winder in the summer. I attended several of those reunions. After his parents died, he became the patriarch of the family. Often, up to one hundred members of the family attended these reunions, and Russell would preside. He looked forward to the reunions more than any other event of the year.

When Richard Russell was a young man, his father advised him not to marry. His reasoning was that family responsibilities would take time away from the performance of his public responsibilities. That might seem like strange advice coming from someone who fathered fifteen children. But it appeared that Richard Russell followed this advice because he never married. I heard rumors after I joined the staff that Russell had once been engaged. No one knew any details, and it was certainly not the kind of thing one would discuss with Richard Russell. It turns out that the rumor was true, and the story can now be fully told. On April 27, 1971, some three months after Richard Russell died, Pat Collins agreed to do an oral history interview for the Russell Library. She did so on one condition—that the part about her romance with Richard Russell be kept under seal until the time of her death. She died on May 27, 2009, in La Jolla, California, at the age of 101. All of the information here comes from her oral history interview, which is kept at the Russell Library in Athens, Georgia.

Pat Collins was born in Brooklyn, New York, but she moved to Atlanta with her family when she was young. She grew up in Atlanta, graduated from Agnes Scott College, and became the third female graduate of Emory University Law School. She finished near the top of her class in 1931. At that time, women lawyers were not accepted in the South. Notwithstanding her excellent academic record, Pat could not get a job with any of the Atlanta law firms. She did pro bono work for the Atlanta Legal Aid Society and had a limited amount of contract work. At some point, she met Smythe Gambrell, a prominent Atlanta attorney, a major shareholder of Eastern Airlines, a future president of the American Bar Association, and the father of David Gambrell, who would be appointed to complete Richard Russell's unexpired term when he died in 1971. Smythe Gambrell was impressed with Pat Collins. He did not, however, offer her a job in his law firm. After being unable to find full-time employment in Atlanta, Pat decided to apply for a job with the

Justice Department in Washington. She discussed it with Smythe Gambrell. He told her that for her to have any chance of getting a job in Washington, DC, she would have to have "political clearance." She had no idea what he was talking about. He explained that she would have to have letters of recommendation from Georgia's two United States senators—Walter F. George and Richard B. Russell. She said she did not know either of them. Mr. Gambrell indicated that he would help her get the letters because both senators were good friends of his.

Within a few weeks, a highly complimentary letter arrived from Senator George. Soon thereafter, a much less satisfactory letter arrived from Senator Russell. In fact, Mr. Gambrell thought the letter would do more harm than good. He asked Pat Collins if she or her family had alienated Russell in some way. Pat responded that they did not even know him. Mr. Gambrell was able to contact Russell's office and get a slightly better but still unhelpful letter. Mr. Gambrell thought they could make do with it in view of Senator George's letter. Pat Collins got her job in the Justice Department in 1934, where she worked for over forty years under sixteen different attorneys general. She became one of the first women to successfully argue a case before the United States Supreme Court. She also became a founding member of the Supreme Court Historical Society.

Several years after Pat Collins went to Washington, DC, she attended a dinner hosted by the Georgia State Society. The Georgia Congressional Delegation, including Richard Russell, was being honored at the dinner. According to Pat, all of the women were making a big to-do over Richard Russell because he was considered one of the most eligible bachelors in Washington. For her part, when she was introduced to Russell, Pat immediately questioned him about the unsatisfactory letter he had written in regard to her employment at the Department of Justice. He responded that he did not recall the letter. Several days later, Russell called Pat Collins and told her that he had investigated the letter. It seems that his administrative assistant, Leeman Anderson, had come to the conclusion that Russell should not be writing blind recommendations for people he had never met. He used the occasion of the Pat Collins request to implement that policy. He said that for all Russell knew, she could be a Republican. Russell did not feel strongly about the matter and simply signed the letter put in front of him. During his conversation with Pat about the letter, he asked her for a date.

They started dating and became increasingly serious about each other. He proposed marriage in 1938, and she accepted. She went to Georgia to meet his parents. It was the time of the annual Russell family reunion in June, which she attended. According to a letter Senator Russell subsequently wrote Collins, his father was impressed with her and liked her. Pat Collins recalled, however, that Judge Russell told his son that if he married her in the Catholic Church, he would be required to sign a statement that he would not interfere with his wife's religion and that any children of the marriage would be brought up in the Catholic Church. Richard Russell had assumed that the marriage would be conducted by his brother, Jeb Russell, who was a prominent Presbyterian minister. After the family reunion, Pat Collins and Richard Russell returned to Atlanta, where they looked at engagement rings and arranged to have a wedding announcement delivered to the Atlanta newspaper for future publication. Pat then returned to Washington, while Russell remained in Georgia since Congress had recessed and he had various speeches scheduled in Georgia.

When Pat got back to Washington, DC, she started worrying about the comment Judge Russell had made. She consulted a Catholic priest in Washington for a number of hours and came to the conclusion that the wedding would have to take place in the Catholic Church. Richard Russell had also been thinking about the comments made by his father and what he would do if the wedding took place in the Catholic Church. He was apparently worried that if he were defeated in the future in a political race after he had married a Catholic, Pat would be inclined to blame herself. Apparently, at least one member of the Russell family also advised him that it was not a good idea to marry a Catholic in Georgia at that time. Both of them grew concerned about the marriage. When they next spoke on the telephone, they reached a mutual decision not to go forward with the wedding. They were able to recall the wedding announcement from the Atlanta newspaper shortly before its scheduled publication. In the conversation in which they decided not to go forward with the wedding, Richard Russell told Pat Collins that he would never again propose marriage to anyone. And he never did. They were obviously deeply in love. They continued to see each other, and Richard Russell wrote her warm and interesting letters when he was away from Washington, which her estate gave to the Russell Library after her death.

Eventually, Pat Collins married Sal Andretti, a fellow employee at the Department of Justice. He became an assistant attorney general and was in charge of the Department of Justice budget. Richard Russell was chairman of the Senate Appropriations Subcommittee responsible for the DOJ budget and became good friends with Andretti. Andretti died several years before Richard Russell passed away. In the intervening years, Pat Collins Andretti and Richard Russell occasionally saw each other primarily because Pat was good friends with Russell's sister, Ina Stacy, who was also a lawyer in Washington. After Senator Russell died, Pat married again and moved to California, eventually outliving three husbands. She had no children in any of her marriages.

I have reason to believe that, at the end of his life, Richard Russell felt that his failure to marry Pat Collins was a bad mistake. I base that on a conversation I had with him at a time when I was struggling to juggle the responsibilities of law school and of being administrative assistant in his office. I told him one day that I was thinking about dropping out of law school so I could devote full attention to my duties in his office. He responded immediately and directly: "You stay in law school, get your law degree, and get married." Richard Russell was a lonely man during his final years. He had many friends in the Senate and was close to his family. His staff adored him. But he did not have a wife or children. While his father's advice not to get married undoubtedly helped him in his political career by allowing him to work longer hours and study the issues more thoroughly, the fact that he did not marry did not help him in his later life.

Richard Russell did have a regular girlfriend during most of his years in Washington after his relationship with Pat Collins ended. Proctor Jones told me that for many years, Russell saw Harriet Orr, a woman who worked in the Department of Defense and who was from North Carolina. According to Proctor, he double dated with the couple on one occasion. Russell and Orr had a standing date every Saturday night. On Saturday morning, Russell would have Proctor Jones go to a market on Capitol Hill and buy two steaks. He would then take them to Harriet Orr's apartment on Saturday night. They also occasionally saw each other on Sundays, often visiting Civil War battlefields in the Washington area. When Russell died on January 21, 1971, one of the first people called with the news was Harriet Orr, who had retired and moved back to North Carolina.

Richard Russell was one of the most interesting people I have ever met. He was very much a southern gentleman—retiring, patrician, reserved even to the point of shyness. However, once you got to know him and he got to know you, he was outgoing. He was so widely read that he could carry on an interesting conversation on almost any topic. His knowledge of the Civil War was legendary. But he also had read extensively about world history. Once, when he was touring a famous battlefield in Europe, the tour guide could tell from the questions he was asking that Russell knew more about the battle that had taken place there than the tour guide knew himself.

Outwardly, Richard Russell was humble and modest. A book is published at the beginning of each Congress, known as the Congressional Directory, in which each member of Congress and their principal staff are listed by state. The biographical information on many of the senators, even freshman senators, goes on for pages. During the entire thirty-eight years he served in the Senate, the entry for Richard Russell, one of the most accomplished senators of all time, was simply as follows: "Richard B. Russell, Jr.—Democrat of Winder, Georgia." This is not to say that he did not like attention. He relished praise, particularly from those in whom he had great confidence. His ability to keep confidential information confidential was legendary on Capitol Hill and was undoubtedly one of the reasons he enjoyed such a close relationship with six presidents of the United States. When the Central Intelligence Agency was established during the Truman Administration, Russell was virtually the only person in the Senate who was given the most sensitive intelligence information for many years because of the concern about possible leaks. There were no leaks on Richard Russell's watch.

Russell was extremely competitive in almost everything. This was particularly true with respect to sports. He was an avid football and baseball fan. The legendary University of Georgia football coach, Vince Dooley, once said that Russell knew more about the Georgia football team than anyone outside the coaching staff. He knew the names of all the players, their hometowns, and essential information about them. He was such a big fan of Georgia football that I remember Georgia football stars who had gone on to the National Football League coming by the office to visit him. I particularly remember Jimmy Orr, a wide receiver for the Baltimore Colts, and Francis Tarkenton, a quarterback for the Minnesota Vikings. One Saturday morning, Senator Russell and I were having a discussion—perhaps even an argument—about the weight of a certain wide receiver for the Dallas Cowboys professional football team. I argued that he weighed a certain amount, and Russell disagreed with me and stated a different amount. When I arrived at the office the following Monday morning, a Dallas Cowboys football program was on my desk opened to the page where the name of the wide receiver and his weight were listed. The information was circled with a note below it that read "for your information." Russell was right and I was wrong.

His sense of humor was also legendary on Capitol Hill. At times, he could be quite sarcastic in some of his floor speeches. For example, he once referred to columnist Drew Pearson as a "skunk." He also referred to columnist Joseph Alsop as "Alslop." I remember one Saturday morning when Russell's car was in the shop and I gave him a ride to his apartment after the office had closed around noon. He asked me to go across the street to the grocery store in the Watergate complex and buy him a box of Rice Krispies. It had just started snowing, and the floor at the entrance to the Watergate complex is marble. I was rushing along so I could complete my task and get back to my apartment to study my law books. My feet shot out from under me, and my right elbow came down hard on the marble surface. I felt excruciating pain. A person who observed the accident called an ambulance, and I was taken to the nearby George Washington University Hospital. My right elbow was dislocated. It had to be reset, at considerable pain, before I could be dismissed. This took several hours. When I arrived at Senator Russell's apartment with the Rice Krispies and knocked on the door, he opened it and said, "If I had known it was going to take you that long, I would have gone myself." I do not know if he saw that my arm was in a sling before he made that comment. He was actually quite sympathetic to my plight after he learned what had happened. I had to take physical therapy at the Capitol Infirmary for some months, and I have never been able to completely straighten my right arm again. One good thing that happened as a result of this accident was that I was able to meet and talk frequently with Supreme Court Justice Byron White, who regularly received treatment for a back problem caused by an old football injury. How many law students have private conversations with a Supreme Court justice?

As orators in the Senate went, Russell was not a particularly good speaker. He was known for having exhaustively researched and mastered an issue before he spoke. His oratory was certainly not on the same level as that of Fritz Hollings, John McClellan, or Herman Talmadge. With the written word, though, Russell was the best I have seen. He could cover more ground in a short letter than anyone I have ever met. If he had become an appellate lawyer or a judge, his writing ability would have been a tremendous asset. It was also a tremendous asset in the Senate.

Richard Russell had a fantastic memory. He had almost total recall of what he had read or been told. And he was an exceptionally fast reader. Each day, he read the Congressional Record that recorded the proceedings in Congress from cover to cover. Senator Herman Talmadge was so amazed by the speed with which he could read and the extent of his recall that he assumed Russell had undergone extensive training in speed-reading. To my knowledge, he had not. The ability was natural.

I have been asked from time to time what I would say if I tried to describe Richard Russell in just a few words. I believe Pat Collins, in her oral history interview, probably expressed it much better than I can. She said,

> Well, he just struck you as a Rock of Gibraltar, really. He was the sort of person that other people felt was the last word in integrity and sound judgment. He was the sort of person who inspired confidence and if he counseled you, you felt you had the best counsel there was. I think that was the impression you got of him, and that he was impersonal, completely impersonal in his...judgments and wouldn't pull his punches. Even in his gracious, courteous, gentlemanly way, he would still talk straight from the shoulder. I think that's the impression that I would have of him.

That would be a good description of the Richard Russell I knew in the 1960s and early 1970s.

The End of an Era

In 1969, doctors diagnosed a malignant tumor on one of Richard Russell's lungs. This would accelerate the long, downward spiral of his health. After a series of cobalt radiation treatments, he was able to announce to a press conference that the tumor had been successfully eradicated. However, it came at a heavy price. He already had diminished lung capacity from his chronic emphysema, and the radiation treatments resulted in further damage to his breathing capacity. Richard Russell had begun smoking when he was very young, and he smoked heavily until the 1950s, when he quit. When he died in 1971, several cigar boxes of vintage baseball cards, some of which are now valued at thousands of dollars, were found on a shelf in his bedroom in Winder. These vintage baseball cards came in packages of cigarettes in the early 1900s and may have been the inspiration of his habit. Even after one discontinues smoking, emphysema is a progressive disease. So it was with Richard Russell.

I noticed after the radiation treatments that he seemed to have greater difficulty walking and that the slightest exertion tended to exhaust him. On one trip to Winder, he had great difficulty climbing the steps to board the Air Force airplane. He, however, continued to put up a good front. Fortunately, by late 1969, several things had happened that made his life easier. When Senator Carl Hayden of Arizona left the Senate, Russell became chairman of the Appropriations Committee and president pro tempore of the Senate. Unlike the Armed Services Committee, the Appropriations Committee does its work primarily through a number of subcommittees. While Russell continued to be chairman of the Defense Appropriations Subcommittee, his friend, Senator John Stennis, started doing much of the work. One of the perks of being named president pro tempore of the Senate was a chauffeur-driven limousine, which meant Russell no longer had to drive. He resigned as chairman of the Southern Caucus.

As his emphysema got worse, he became increasingly dependent on treatments each day to flush out his lungs. Dr. Forrest Bird had invented a machine, called the Bird Machine, that forced medicine into the lungs and caused the patient to cough out the congestion. Russell started taking these treatments twice a day. They were not pleasant and were exhausting, but they allowed him to continue to function for a time. He was able to maintain a semblance of his prior competitiveness and combativeness. In early 1970, Russell] learned that a senator was going to give a speech on the Senate floor with respect to prison reform and was going to cite the Georgia prison system as one of the worst in the nation. Ever attentive to attacks on his home state, Russell planned to be there to defend Georgia. At the appointed time, he went to the Senate floor and was sitting in his usual seat when the senator started his speech on prison reform. That senator skipped the portion of the speech that referred to Georgia to avoid a confrontation with Richard Russell.

By mid-1970, Russell's health had furthered deteriorated, and he was often in the hospital. When he was at the Senate, he increasingly used his Capitol office and some days did not even come to his office in the Senate Office Building. I would take mail and other matters he had to address to the Capitol office. At about this time, on the advice of his doctors, we started keeping a supply of oxygen nearby for bad days. It was not long before he was taking oxygen almost every day. During this downturn, Pat Collins saw him for the last time. He had started losing weight and his appetite. He no longer enjoyed his evening cocktails. His sister, Ina Stacy, came to Washington to stay with him. Since the first husband of Pat Collins had died, Ina arranged an occasion for the three of them to go to a restaurant. In her oral history interview, Pat Collins remarked how shocked she was at Russell's appearance. He was a mere shadow of his former self.

A final concession to his deteriorating condition was when he started using a scooter to travel from his office to the Senate floor. He resisted it for a long time because the last thing Richard Russell wanted was to lose his ability to walk to the Senate under his own power. He started using the scooter so that he could continue to make Senate votes. He seldom met with constituents or other visitors during this period.

Richard Russell entered Walter Reed Army Medical Center for the final time in early December 1970. He was assigned his usual suite of rooms that he had occupied on many previous occasions. This visit would be different. Other than one time when he went to make an important Senate vote, he never left the hospital again. For a time, he continued to handle Senate business and review mail in the hospital. President Nixon visited him several times before the Christmas holidays at the end of 1970. As mentioned earlier, on one of these visits, Nixon offered Russell Air Force One to take him and his doctors to Winder so he could be home for Christmas. Initially, Russell planned to accept the offer, but his rapidly deteriorating condition made that impossible. I planned to go home for Christmas for a few days. When I spoke to him, he said he probably would not be alive when I returned. This was an exaggeration, as his doctors told me he was not in any danger of immediately dying. Otherwise, I would not have gone home. I only stayed in Georgia for a few days. When I returned, Russell seemed better and in higher spirits. Several of his brothers and sisters had come to Washington to visit him over the holidays.

It was not long, however, before he was in another black mood because of his deteriorating condition. By January 10, 1971, he seldom got out of his bed, even handling his last two official matters while lying down. His press secretary, Powell Moore, had brought a press release for him to review. After approving it, Russell told Powell that he was giving him a raise. Powell thanked him profusely and then prepared to leave. Russell said, "Aren't you going to write it up?" Powell said, "You mean right now?" Russell replied, "Of course I mean right now. I may not be here tomorrow." That reminded me of a prior occasion when I asked Proctor Jones to talk to Russell about a pay raise for me after I was appointed administrative assistant. Proctor reported back to me that Russell said, "He is already the highest-paid law student in the United States." When my next paycheck arrived, it reflected an increase in the exact amount I had requested. That was the way Richard Russell handled things.

The other final matter of Senate business was more substantive. Senator Robert Byrd was considering a race against Senator Edward Kennedy for the position of assistant Democratic leader. He had not finally decided whether to run, but there had been several articles in the Washington newspapers about the possibility. He had spoken to Russell, who had pledged his support. Russell later confirmed that commitment when I asked him following a telephone conversation with Byrd. As his condition continued to deteriorate, I raised the possibility of his signing a proxy letter with respect to his vote for Senator Byrd. He looked at me from his hospital bed and said, "Are you suggesting that I am not going to be at the caucus?" That had a way of discouraging further discussion of the matter. By about January 15, it was obvious even to Richard Russell that he would not be at the Democratic Caucus. Senator Byrd had talked to me several additional times and told me that he would not make the race unless he was assured of having Richard Russell's vote. He said he would simply run for reelection to his current position of secretary of the Democratic Caucus.

I decided to make one more effort to get a proxy signed. I prepared it and raised the issue with Senator Russell. By this time, January 18, he was not only confined to bed but could barely speak. When I showed him the letter, he approved it and indicated that I should sign his name. I told him the race was expected to be close, and I thought this matter was of sufficient importance that he should try to sign the letter if at all possible. The medical personnel propped him up in the bed, and I put the letter before him. He signed it, but it was a terrible signature and barely recognizable. It was not even correctly aligned with the signature line on the letter. The signature was so bad, in fact, that I planned to make another effort, but he slipped into a coma the next day, January 19, from which he never fully recovered. I discussed the matter with the doctors at Walter Reed to be sure they were prepared to execute affidavits, if necessary, that Richard Russell was competent when he signed the letter. They indicated that was their opinion and they would sign such affidavits.

I then went to see Russell's Senate colleague, Herman Talmadge, who would deliver the letter to the caucus on January 21 when it met. I told him I was concerned about the signature. He looked at the letter and said in the typical blunt Herman Talmadge fashion, "No one around here has ever questioned the bona fides of a Dick Russell vote. I do not believe they will be starting now." Talmadge took custody of the letter, and we agreed that he would call me at the hospital immediately prior to the vote at the Democratic Caucus. If I confirmed that Russell was still alive, he would deliver the letter to Senate majority leader Mike Mansfield. If Russell had died, Talmadge would return the letter to me. When he called shortly after 11:00 AM on January 21, I confirmed that Russell was still alive. Talmadge delivered the proxy letter to Senator Mansfield. The vote was not as close as had been anticipated. Robert Byrd defeated Edward Kennedy by a vote of 31 to 24. Senator Byrd was given the proxy letter. He had it framed, and it hung on the wall of the reception room in his office for many years thereafter. He would eventually be elected majority leader of the Senate.

Richard Russell died just after 2:00 PM on the afternoon of January 21. Other than the medical personnel, I was one of four people in the hospital room when he drew his last breath. His sisters, Ina Stacy and Pat Peterson, as well as Proctor Jones and myself were there. Death came easily with a final gulp for breath. Richard Russell left the Senate just as he had arrived—exercising power from the beginning to the end. It was the end of an era for Georgia and for the United States Senate. It had been fifty years since Richard Russell first entered elective office in Georgia. It had been thirty-eight years since he first entered the Senate.

He had become the first person to serve more than half his life in the Senate and had become the Senate mentor. For me, it was also the end of an era. The absence of Richard Russell would leave a substantial void in my life for many years to come.

When Senators pass away, their colleagues are afforded an opportunity to eulogize them on the Senate floor. The eulogies with respect to Richard Russell took place on January 25, 1971. They are all included in a book published by the Government Printing Office titled *Richard Brevard Russell, Late a Senator from Georgia—Memorial Tributes Delivered in Congress*. The eulogies are instructive with respect to the high regard Richard Russell's colleagues had for him. I will refer only to a couple. Senator Ernest (Fritz) Hollings of South Carolina said this: "...Today we mourn the passing of this century's most effective legislator. One would have to harken back to the days of Clay, Calhoun and Webster to find the peer of Richard Brevard Russell." It is perhaps not surprising that his southern colleagues would heap praise on Richard Russell. After all, he was their leader for many years.

The eulogies of senators from outside the South, both Democratic and Republican, are perhaps more illustrative. Senator Margaret Chase Smith, a Republican from Maine, was one of the few women to serve in the Senate during Russell's time of service. She knew him well because they served alongside each other for some fifteen years on both the Armed Services and Appropriations committees. In part, Senator Smith said,

> Mr. President, the death of Richard Brevard Russell marks an end to an era when the U.S. Senate achieved its greatest stature and prestige as an institution.... The decorum, the sense of dedication to the Senate as an institution, the stature, and the prestige of the Senate began to erode as the health of Richard Brevard Russell began to erode. As his failing health caused his absence from the Senate floor with increasing frequency and for longer periods, the effect on the Senate became evident. The deterioration of the Senate from an orderly and dignified parliamentary body into too often the state of an anarchistic legislative jungle is directly traceable to the absence of the calm , deliberative, and wise leadership of Richard Brevard Russell, both on and off the Senate floor. I pray to God that somehow the U.S. Senate will return to the quality that Richard Brevard Russell gave it in his fully active and healthful years.

Sadly, that did not occur. The Senate steadily deteriorated in the years after Russell's death. In 2012, a former Senate staffer, Ira Shapiro, wrote a book titled *The Last Great Senate: Courage and Statesmanship in Times of Crisis* (New York: Public Affairs, 2012) in which he places that Senate during the years 1977–1980, less than a decade after Russell's death.

Abraham Ribicoff was a liberal Democratic senator from Connecticut. Before being elected to the Senate in 1962, he was secretary of health education and welfare in the Kennedy Administration. This is what Senator Ribicoff said about Richard Russell:

> I have known very few truly great men in my life and Senator Russell was one of them. ...Several years ago, on a trip to Georgia, I had the privilege of visiting Senator Russell at his family home in Winder. I was struck by the simplicity of his home and the simple, gentle manner in which he lived. Richard Russell, the most powerful man in the Senate, lived totally without pretense, without any of the trappings of power. ...History will record Richard Russell of Georgia as one of the greatest senators who ever served in this body. In his 38 years in the Senate, he fulfilled his duties with skill, dignity, and grace. He, more than anyone else, reflected the essence of what the Senate is. By his presence he reminded us of what it means to be a senator.

In 1979, Ribicoff voluntarily left the Senate, fed up with the growing partisanship.

Jacob Javits was a liberal Republican senator from New York [and] one of the senators who fought the hardest and longest for civil rights legislation. This is part of what Senator Javits had to say: "Mr. President, his voice was an absolutely indispensable element, much as I may have disagreed with him on many occasions, of the total decision-making process which is the very pride of the Senate of the United States. This has now been lost, and will be very hard to replace. Indeed, we can only hope and pray that another Member or Members will be found who can measure up to his ability and will make his voice count as heavily as Richard Russell did in respect of the high decisions which we must make in our land."

The Funeral of Richard Russell

Richard Russell provided in his will and told a number of us that he wished his body to be immediately returned to Georgia upon his death.

This was because he wanted to lie in state at the state capitol in Atlanta. As a result of this, it is ironic that no official activities took place in Washington, DC. Otherwise, it is certain that his body would have laid in state in the Rotunda of the Capitol or in the Senate chamber itself as was done when Robert Byrd died in 2010. Several days after Russell's death, President Nixon paid tribute to him in his State of the Union address to a joint session of Congress. He referred to Russell as one of the greatest senators in the history of the country and asked for a moment of silence. He also ordered all American flags to fly at half staff. As I stated earlier in this book, Nixon also made Air Force One available to fly Russell's body back to Georgia. When we arrived in Atlanta and started our trip to the state capitol in downtown Atlanta, numerous Georgians lined the streets. Thousands of Georgians would pay their last respects by going through the rotunda of the state capitol throughout the night. Early the next morning, President and Mrs. Nixon arrived to pay their final respects. After meeting privately with the Russell family, Nixon addressed the media. He said if Russell had been born ten years later and served in the Senate ten years later, he would have been president of the United States. He also paid tribute to what Russell had meant to six presidents and referred to him as "a president's senator."

The weather was horrible on the day of the Russell funeral. It rained from the beginning until the end. The weather was so bad that two Air Force planes carrying the vice president of the United States and more than half the members of the United States Senate could not land either in Winder or at the more extensive facilities at Dobbins Air Force Base in Marietta. The planes were diverted to Charleston, South Carolina. This presented a significant problem because five of the people on those planes were participants in the funeral program. Majority Leader Mike Mansfield, Senator John Stennis, Senator Talmadge, Congressman Phil Landrum, and the Senate chaplain all had a part on the funeral program. The only two participants on the program who were actually in Winder were Georgia governor Jimmy Carter and Senator Russell's brother, the Reverend Henry Edward Russell.

We scrambled to figure out an alternative funeral program in case the participants diverted to South Carolina could not participate. Fortunately, arrangements were made whereby the participants in South Carolina could appear by remote television. Television screens were placed under tents at the Russell Cemetery. This permitted the funeral program to go forward as originally planned.

Only two members of the United States Senate appeared in person. Senator Lawton Childs of Florida, who had just been elected to the Senate and barely knew Richard Russell, had driven to Winder from his home state. Senator Hubert Humphrey of Minnesota had been away from Washington on a speaking engagement and had flown into Atlanta the prior evening. He traveled by taxi from Atlanta to Winder. There is an approximately 100-yard driveway in front of the Russell home that leads down to a public highway. That area was sealed off from automobile traffic on the day of the funeral. Therefore, Humphrey had to exit the cab and walk in the rain up the driveway to the Russell home. One of the most touching scenes of the entire funeral was a thoroughly drenched Hubert Humphrey saying that he had come to pay his final respects to his friend, Richard Russell.

It is perhaps appropriate that the weather was so bad on the day of Russell's funeral. It was a sad day and probably would not have been made otherwise by blue skies. Richard Russell was gone, buried next to the graves of his mother and father, but his legacy would live on. It would live on in Washington when, several years thereafter, Senator Robert Byrd offered a resolution to rename the Old Senate Office Building the Richard Brevard Russell Senate Office Building. This building is one of the most important in Washington. It is there that such momentous events as the hearings into the Teapot Dome Scandal, the Watergate scandal, and the Clarence Thomas confirmation took place as well as the announcement of John F. Kennedy's campaign for president. Russell's legacy would live on in Georgia through numerous facilities named in his honor, including the federal building and courthouse in Atlanta, several federal research laboratories in Athens and elsewhere, a scenic highway in North Georgia, an airport in Rome, Georgia, a Corps of Engineers dam and reservoir in Northeast Georgia, and a public school in Winder, Georgia. Even forty years later, public buildings in Georgia are still being named in his honor. The latest is the Richard B. Russell Special Collections Library Building at the University of Georgia in Athens, which opened in 2012. I have played a small part in preserving Russell's legacy through the Richard B. Russell Foundation, Inc. which is discussed in a later chapter of this book.

A young state senator from Plains, Georgia, Jimmy Carter, presents to a group in Senator Russell's office in May of 1966 plans for the development of the Civil War prison complex at Andersonville, Georgia. Attending the meeting is Senator Russell, second from the left, Secretary of the Interior, Stewart Udall, Congressman Bo Callaway and Senator Herman Talmadge. I am shown in the upper right part of the picture observing the meeting as Russell's legislative assistant. Standing behind Carter is Bill Jordan, Senator Russell's executive secretary. * *(Courtesy of UPI)*

Senator Russell giving after dinner remarks at a dinner in his honor at the Columbia Restaurant in Ibor City, Florida in March of 1967.The man seated between me and Senator Russell is the commanding general of McDill Air Force Base and the host of the dinner.*

Senator Russell with a group of interns including, second from the left, my high school debate partner, Ben Garland, and seated is one of my roommates my last year at UGA, Bill House.*

Senator Russell and his fiancé, Pat Collins, circa 1938.

Senator Russell on his scooter in September 1970 two months before he entered the hospital for the last time. As his respiratory problems worsened, he started to use the scooter so he could navigate the Senate and continue to make Senate votes.

RICHARD B.
J. ELLENDER, LA.
. MCCLELLAN, ARK.
N G. MAGNUSON, WASH.
ARD L. HOLLAND, FLA.
. STENNIS, MISS.
. PASTORE, R.I.
BLE, NEV.
T C. BYRD, W.VA.
V. MC GEE, WYO.
MANSFIELD, MONT.
M PROXMIRE, WIS.
YARBOROUGH, TEX.
M. MONTOYA, N. MEX.

MILTON R. YOUNG, N. DAK.
KARL E. MUNDT, S. DAK.
MARGARET CHASE SMITH, MAINE
ROMAN L. HRUSKA, NEBR.
GORDON ALLOTT, COLO.
NORRIS COTTON, N.H.
CLIFFORD P. CASE, N.J.
HIRAM L. FONG, HAWAII
J. CALEB BOGGS, DEL.
JAMES B. PEARSON, KANS.

THOMAS J. SCOTT, CHIEF CLERK
WM. W. WOODRUFF, COUNSEL

United States Senate
COMMITTEE ON APPROPRIATIONS
WASHINGTON, D.C. 20510

January 18, 1971

Honorable Mike Mansfield
Majority Leader
United States Senate
Washington, D. C.

Dear Senator Mansfield:

In the event it is not possible for me to be present when the Senate Democrats caucus for the opening of the 92nd Congress, I hereby tender my proxy in favor of Senator Robert C. Byrd of West Virginia if he is a candidate for the position of Assistant Majority Leader.

With best wishes, I am

Sincerely,
Richard B. Russell

Senator Russell's proxy letter voting for Senator Robert Byrd in his race against Senator Edward Kennedy for the position of Assistant Democratic Leader in the Senate. I prepared the letter and he signed it on his death bed. He died within a few hours after it was submitted to the Democratic Caucus on January 21, 1971. It was his last official act as a United States Senator.*

In the living room of Russell's home outside Winder, Georgia, where I spent so much time.

Standing beside Senator Russell's 1963 New York Chrysler automobile which the Russell family has preserved and restored.

The Russell family cemetary outside Winder, Georgia where Senator Russell, his parents and other members of the Russell family are buried.

7

Back to Georgia

At the funeral of Richard Russell, I spoke briefly with Governor Carter. He asked me to come by and visit with him before I returned to Washington. I went to his office in the state capitol the following Monday, and we had a nice conversation. Among other things, he told me that his appointment of someone to fill the unexpired term of Richard Russell would not be a political appointment but would be a person of outstanding character and ability. He did not indicate to me whom he intended to appoint or who might be under consideration.

In one of his most recent books, *White House Diary* (New York: Farrar, Straus and Giroux, 2010), Jimmy Carter stated that he offered the appointment to his longtime lawyer and confidant Charles Kirbo. Kirbo was a senior partner at the King and Spalding law firm and the lawyer who had represented Carter when he first ran for elective state office in a disputed state Senate race. Carter indicates in his book that Kirbo declined the appointment because he did not want to move to Washington, DC.

Judge Griffin Bell, who would later become attorney general in the administration of President Jimmy Carter, states in an interview published in the *Journal of Southern Legal History* (18/1–2, 2010) not long before his death that he was asked by Carter if he wished to be considered for appointment to the Senate. Bell indicates that he told Governor Carter he would be interested in the appointment only if he did not have to stand for reelection. Of course, he would not only have to stand for reelection but would have approximately one year to do so since Russell's unexpired term ended in 1972. Bell related his conversation with Carter as follows: "I couldn't get elected. All I would do is be giving up my judgeship and be in debt. And I know I couldn't get reelected because I have had so many of these unpopular cases" (p. 225). At the time, Bell was serving on the United States Court of Appeals for the Fifth Circuit and had been involved in a number of controversial school desegregation decisions. If Judge Bell, in fact, did not want to be considered for appointment to the Senate because of a fear that he could not be reelected, I think he probably sold himself short. Knowing Griffin Bell as I came to know him, I think he would have been a strong candidate because he had a South Georgia accent and a folksy sense of humor. I think there is an excellent chance he could have convinced the voters of Georgia that he was simply doing his job as a federal judge.

Former Georgia governor Ernest Vandiver told me a few years before he died that candidate for governor Jimmy Carter promised to appoint him to fill Richard Russell's unexpired term if he should die in office. Vandiver said that is one of the reasons he supported Carter in the 1970 governor's race against Carl Sanders. While I, of course, have no personal knowledge of this matter, Vandiver seemed quite sincere in his statements and was still bitter about the matter more than thirty years later.

Several days after I returned to Washington, I learned that Governor Carter had appointed Atlanta attorney and former King and Spalding partner David H. Gambrell to fill Russell's unexpired term. As a young lawyer at King and Spalding, Gambrell had helped Charles Kirbo in the disputed state Senate election on behalf of Jimmy Carter. I had never met David Gambrell and did not know much about him. He had supported Carter in his race for governor and was the son of the well-known Atlanta attorney Smythe Gambrell. Not only was the Gambrell family connected to Russell by the relationship between David Gambrell's father and Pat Collins described earlier, but David Gambrell met his future wife, Luck Flanders, because of Richard Russell. She was working in the Russell for President Headquarters in Chicago in 1952 when a young Harvard law student, David Gambrell, met her for the first time. By the time David Gambrell arrived in Washington, several of the key Russell aides had already accepted new jobs. For example, Proctor Jones had joined Bill Jordan on the staff of the Senate Appropriations Committee, and Powell Moore had accepted a job at the Department of Justice.

Shortly after his arrival in Washington and being sworn in as a United States senator, David Gambrell asked to see me. He asked me about my plans for the future. I told him that I was scheduled to graduate from the Georgetown Law School in June 1971 and that I planned to return to Georgia to enter law practice at that point. He asked if I would be willing to serve as his administrative assistant until I returned to Georgia. I agreed to do so. He also asked if I would be willing to devote the first three months after I returned to Georgia and before entering law practice to setting up his Georgia offices. I agreed to do that as well. A number of other staff people in the Russell office were also hired by Gambrell, including Joel Williams, Jim Pannell, Ray White, Craig Hosmer, Lois Riley, Lynn Larisey, and Chris Till. He also brought up from Georgia a number of outstanding people to round out his staff. When I left to return to Georgia at the end of May, Senator Gambrell hired Joe Sports to replace me as administrative assistant. Joe had served as executive director of the Democratic Party of Georgia when Gambrell was chairman of the party.

The first shock I received as David Gambrell's administrative assistant was the size of his office suite. Richard Russell had the largest office suite in the Senate—some seven rooms. Gambrell was assigned an office suite consisting of four rooms. Seniority was still quite important in Washington at that time. I found David Gambrell to be an intelligent, hard-working senator. If he had been able to hold on to his Senate seat, I think he would have been a good, perhaps great, United States senator. However, that was not in the cards.

David Gambrell also evidenced great courage in the short time I was there. Senator Henry Jackson, a close friend of Richard Russell, was pushing a supersonic transport aircraft program that would be financed by the federal government with the planes being manufactured in his home state of Washington. Richard Russell and Herman Talmadge had already committed to vote for the project. After studying it, Senator Gambrell came to the conclusion that he could not support it. That required great courage for a new senator serving an unexpired term and about to face reelection.

As I prepared to leave Washington, DC, I was touched by comments about me on the Senate floor by Senate majority leader Mike Mansfield of Montana. As reported by the *Atlanta Journal* on May 30, 1971, Senator Mansfield said, "Mr. Campbell did much to make the difficult positions of the senators with whom he served with such distinction much easier. He was an outstanding man. ...He had experience. He used good common sense." I was probably full of myself when I read these comments until I paused to reflect on the fact that by age twenty-nine, Richard Russell had already served several years as

Speaker of the Georgia House of Representatives and was about to be elected governor of Georgia.

I graduated on schedule from Georgetown in June 1971. By that time, I had already left for Georgia and did not attend the graduation ceremonies. I received my diploma in the mail. I also received several job offers, none of which I seriously considered. Several were with Washington law firms. Without Richard Russell, I had no desire to stay in Washington. I also had an offer from a large corporation headquartered in New York to join its in-house legal counsel. I went to New York for interviews not because I was seriously interested in the job but for a fun weekend in New York. It had been my plan all along to come back to Georgia to practice law.

In Georgia, I briefly considered law firms in Dalton, where I had lived for the first year of my life, and in Brunswick on the coast. I have always loved the ocean. While these were attractive firms, I knew deep down that I needed to be in Atlanta to make my mark as a trial lawyer. I only interviewed with one law firm in Atlanta—Heyman and Sizemore. On one of his trips to Washington several years earlier, the senior partner of the firm, Lamar Sizemore, had told me that if I was interested in practicing law in Atlanta after I graduated from law school, I should give him a call. I was quite surprised because I did not know Lamar well and he did not know me well. My assumption is that Herman Talmadge had said favorable things about me to Lamar. Lamar Sizemore and Herman Talmadge were as close as two people can be. Between the time Herman Talmadge was governor of Georgia and was elected to the United States Senate, he and Lamar practiced law together in a two-person law firm.

I called Lamar and told him that I had graduated from law school and planned to practice law in Atlanta. He set up a time for me to come by and interview other partners at Heyman and Sizemore. Two of the partners I met for the first time were Bob Hicks and Ted Maloof, who would be my law partners for the rest of my career, which spanned almost forty years. I was impressed with the people I met at Heyman and Sizemore. I only knew one of the lawyers—Neal Ray, the son of the state treasurer of Georgia, Jack Ray, who had been a classmate at the University of Georgia.

After accepting a position as an associate at Heyman and Sizemore, I had to decide where to live. I had the thought that I might at some point run for Congress. Therefore, I wanted to live in the Sixth

Congressional District, my home district, if at all possible. My parents owned a small house that they rented on Brookwood Avenue in Jackson. I decided to buy the house from them and live in Jackson. This would require almost a fifty-mile commute to Atlanta each way. I joined the Kiwanis Club in Jackson and served one year as the program chairman. I remember two of the programs I scheduled were a speech by Herman Talmadge and an appearance by the University of Georgia debate team.

By late 1973, the commute from Jackson was proving too much for me. I decided to move closer to Atlanta, but I still wanted to remain in the Sixth Congressional District if possible. At forty miles away, Peachtree City, Georgia, in Fayette County was the closest to Atlanta you could get in the Sixth District. I learned that a local doctor in Peachtree City who planned to move to Colorado had a condominium on the market. It turned out that the owner of this condominium, Dr. Henry Drake, was the brother of bankruptcy judge W. Homer Drake, Jr., before whom I would later have many bankruptcy cases. I was able to buy the condominium fully furnished, which was attractive to me. I did not have the time or the inclination to become involved in buying furniture. I was able to assume Dr. Drake's loan at a local bank in Peachtree City. My commute was still lengthy, but not as far as I had to drive from Jackson. I lived in the condominium until shortly after I got married in 1976, and I have kept it as a weekend place since we moved to Atlanta in 1977.

A picture in Senator David Gambrell's newsletter in late May of 1971 shortly before I returned to Georgia. Pictured on the far left with Senator Gambrell and me is Joe Sports, my successor as Gambrell's administrative assistant.

8

It's Not Easy to Get Out of Politics

When I arrived back in Georgia with my law school diploma, it was my intention to devote myself full-time to my law practice as quickly as possible and to extricate myself from political matters at least in the early part of my legal career. I was soon to learn that getting out of politics is not easy. In fact, it was well into the 1990s before I finally accomplished that task.

Senator David Gambrell

I, of course, fully intended to fulfill my obligations to David Gambrell by setting up his office operations in Georgia before entering law practice. By the time I arrived in Georgia, he had already established his Atlanta office in an office building on Peachtree Street in downtown Atlanta. The office was not fully staffed but was open and functioning. He also intended to open an office in South Georgia, which had not yet been done. He eventually decided to open his South Georgia office in Tifton, Georgia, about three hours by car south of Atlanta. I opened that office and worked out of it one day each week. In advertising that office as being available to assist constituents in South Georgia, I spoke at several civic clubs in Tifton and adjoining towns. Since I was living in Jackson, I would commute on Tuesdays of each week to Tifton. One Tuesday I was involved in a serious automobile accident. I was running late and driving entirely too fast on Interstate 75 in a heavy rainstorm. My car hydroplaned and did two complete circles on the interstate before skidding sideways into the median. If there had been traffic around me as was usually the case on Interstate 75, I could easily have been killed. As it was, my car and I survived without major damage. I did have to call a wrecker from Forsyth to extricate the car from the median, and then I proceeded on to Tifton, albeit at a much reduced speed. I arrived about two hours late.

The office in Tifton and the one in Atlanta were engaged primarily in providing constituent services, including handling of case mail relating to things such as veterans benefits and Social Security benefits. My days were frequently occupied with meeting constituents and answering inquiries with respect to federal programs. I also handled some mail myself. Senator Gambrell had a fairly large number of staff members in the Georgia offices by necessity because he had so little space in Washington. This was exactly the opposite of Richard Russell. In my five-plus years with Russell, I do not ever recall him opening his office in the People's Bank Building in Winder. He had ample space in Washington to accommodate all of his staff.

While federal law prevented me from being involved in campaign activities during business hours, my presence on Gambrell's staff necessarily resulted in my having contacts with his campaign, and I was free to engage in campaign activities at night or on the weekends. I attended a number of strategy meetings and traveled with Gambrell to several speeches in Georgia. I particularly remember one campaign meeting held at his wife Luck's family place near Swainsboro, Georgia. Most of Gambrell's key supporters were from the Carter campaign. I remember Irwin Stoltz, Conley Ingram, Bill Gunter, Charles Harris, and Philip Alston, among others. Gambrell had a difficult juggling act because he needed to be in Georgia as much as possible in connection with his upcoming campaign, but he also needed to be in Washington as much as possible to learn the ropes of being a United States senator. Under the circumstances, I think he did well.

I was certainly not one of Gambrell's key political advisers. I only provided input when my opinion was solicited. One campaign strategy with which I disagreed was the overt effort to attract supporters of Alabama governor George Wallace. Wallace was popular in Georgia at the time, and Jimmy Carter had pursued a similar strategy in his successful race for governor in 1970. Jimmy Carter, however, was a peanut farmer from South Georgia, and David Gambrell was a Harvard-educated lawyer from Atlanta. I never thought he had a good chance of getting the Wallace, vote and I feared that his efforts would cost him support or diminished enthusiasm in the urban areas of the state. I do not suggest that this is the reason for his eventual defeat. The main reason he was defeated was because he encountered a little-known state legislator from Perry, Georgia, named Sam Nunn.

The principal candidates in the race, in addition to Gambrell, were Sam Nunn and former Georgia governor Ernest Vandiver. Nunn was probably the least well known of the three. Vandiver had previously been governor and had earned credit for saving Georgia's public school system during the desegregation controversy when many in the state favored closing the public schools instead of integrating them. Vandiver, however, also had withdrawn from the 1966 race for governor because of a heart problem. That probably cost him some votes in the Senate race. He likely got the bulk of the votes from people who were close to Richard Russell because he was married to Russell's niece, Betty Russell Vandiver. He ran third in this particular race, with Nunn and Gambrell facing each other in a runoff. Nunn won the runoff.

Senator Sam Nunn

The day after Nunn defeated Gambrell in the runoff, I received a telephone call from my good friend, Norman Underwood. I had first met Norman at the University of Georgia, and he had served as an intern in Richard Russell's office in Washington, DC, before I went there. After graduating from law school, Norman was one of the first young lawyers selected by former Georgia governor Carl Sanders as he was building his law firm in Atlanta. Working in the Sanders law firm allowed Norman the opportunity to become involved in political races, as Sanders was still heavily involved in politics in Georgia. One of those races was on behalf of Sam Nunn in the Senate contest.

Norman explained to me that in the general election—in which Nunn would run against Atlanta Republican congressman Fletcher Thompson— Nunn wanted to state that, if elected, he would be appointed to the Armed Services Committee. Senator John Stennis had succeeded Senator Russell as chairman of that committee. Norman wanted to know if I would be willing to call Senator Stennis and put in a good word for Nunn in regard to his request for a commitment to be appointed to the Armed Services Committee if elected. While I did not know Sam Nunn, I was impressed with the effectiveness of his race against Senator Gambrell, and I also had confidence in the judgment of Norman Underwood. Therefore, I agreed to call Senator Stennis. I talked to Stennis on the telephone and got the impression that he had met Nunn and was impressed with him. While Stennis did not say so, I also imagined that Nunn's great-uncle, Carl Vinson, had put in a good word for him with Stennis. Vinson served in the United States House of Representatives for fifty years and was the longtime and powerful chairman of the House Armed Services Committee before he retired. His power in the House over military matters was as great as Richard Russell's power over military matters in the Senate. During the time they served in these positions, a *Washington Post* newspaper reporter described a conference committee between the House and the Senate on a military authorization bill as follows: "Two gentlemen from Georgia privately conferred with each other and resolved all the issues in dispute between the House and the Senate." Nunn defeated Congressman Thompson in the general election and was immediately appointed to the Armed Services Committee. He served in the Senate for twenty-four years and became the chairman of that committee. Like Russell, he became known as the most knowledgeable member of the Senate on national security matters. Every time I visited with Senator Stennis when I was in Washington or talked to him on the telephone, he always said the same thing about Sam Nunn: "Georgia has sent us another good one."

Shortly after Jimmy Carter was elected president in 1976, I received a telephone call from Senator Herman Talmadge in which he told me that the Carter administration was proposing a new system for selecting federal district court judges. The senators would appoint a review panel of outstanding lawyers in the state who would then review the background and interview candidates for federal district judgeships. The review panels would rank the candidates, and the senators would commit to make their appointments from the three most highly ranked candidates. Talmadge asked me what I thought about the idea. I told him that I was sure this was the wave of the future but that I did not see how it benefited the senators. I pointed out that under the then current system, the senators basically had unfettered discretion in whom they appointed, and that the new arrangement would put an intermediary in that process. I stated that while I assumed the review panels would be highly sensitive to the desires of the senators because the senators would appoint them, I nonetheless thought that this would be placing an intermediate step in the process that did not exist at the time. Talmadge told me that he agreed with me, but the new system was being pressed by President Carter, Attorney General Griffin Bell, and others in Washington. He also said that Senator Nunn was inclined to go along with it. Talmadge said that he did not feel sufficiently strong about the matter to begin a dispute over it.

Once the review panels were established, a number of new judgeships in the Atlanta Federal District Court were created. Senator Nunn was particularly interested in having his longtime friend, Marvin Shoob, appointed to one of the judgeships. The review panel apparently ranked Shoob either as unqualified or near the bottom of the list, which effectively precluded the senators from selecting him as one of the new judges. I had no idea why that happened, since it appeared to me as if Shoob was at least as well qualified as a number of other candidates who were approved. Talmadge told me that Nunn was furious over this result. Not long afterward, I received a call from Gordon Giffin, Senator Nunn's legislative director and chief counsel in his Washington office, in which he said that Senator Nunn wished to speak with me. When I spoke with Nunn, he asked if I would be willing to serve as a member of the review panel since its membership was being increased by the appointment of two new members. I agreed to serve.

The other new member of the review panel was Nathan Deal, a lawyer from Gainesville, Georgia. I had known Nathan since my college days because he was an excellent debater at Mercer University in Macon, Georgia. After graduating from law school, he had moved to Gainesville and joined William L. Norton's law firm there. When Nunn ran for the Senate, Nathan was the Hall County campaign chairman for the Nunn campaign. He was also elected to the Georgia Legislature and then to the United States House of Representatives, where he served for more than ten years. During that time, he switched from the Democratic to the Republican Party. In 2010, he was elected governor of Georgia and serves in that office at the time of this book's publication.

When the review panel met to consider additional judgeships, the name of Marvin Shoob was submitted again. No one spoke against him. He was selected as one of the best-qualified candidates, nominated by the senators, and confirmed by the Senate. He served as a federal district court judge for many years with distinction and continues to serve as a senior judge in the United States District Court for the Northern District of Georgia at the time of this writing. I had a number of cases before Judge Shoob during my legal career. He ruled with my side some of the time but also against me in several important cases. I always found him to be fully engaged, knowledgeable, and fair. Once cannot ask for more from a judge. I was told later that he was initially vetoed by Georgia attorney general Arthur Bolton, who served on the review panel.

I supported Sam Nunn in all of his subsequent campaigns for reelection to the Senate in 1978, 1984, and 1990 and contributed financially to those campaigns. He did not need my support, however, because he quickly became the most popular politician in Georgia in his time. After the first campaign in 1972, he never had serious opposition to his reelection. Even when he voted for legislative proposals that were not popular in Georgia, such as the ratification of the Panama Canal Treaties in the Carter administration, it did not seem to significantly affect his standing with the people of Georgia. They had the good sense to realize that he was an outstanding senator working hard on their behalf.

Sam Nunn was also helpful in preserving the legacy of Richard Russell. The Richard B. Russell Foundation, Inc., was set up prior to Russell's death to preserve his legacy and his papers. I became chair of the Russell Foundation in 1990. Nunn assisted with a number of matters that were important to the foundation. One was the Richard B. Russell Symposium, which was staged every two years in Athens at the University of Georgia. The focus of the programs was on some aspect of national security. The programs were televised, and a booklet of the proceedings at the symposium was printed and widely circulated among academia and public officials. Sam served as a participant on the program for the first three years. By that time, he was chairman of the Senate Armed Services Committee. He was also extremely helpful to us in recruiting top-flight speakers for the programs, including former secretary of defense Robert McNamara, former director of the Central Intelligence Agency (and later secretary of defense) Robert Gates, former United Nations ambassador Jeanne Kirkpatrick, and Senator Dianne Feinstein of California. Without Senator Nunn's assistance, the Russell Symposium would not have enjoyed such a high level of success.

Another matter on which Senator Nunn was especially helpful to the Russell Foundation was in securing authorization for the placing of a marble statue of Russell in the rotunda of the Russell Senate Office Building. When the Russell Foundation came up with this idea, we contacted Nunn's office to learn what would be necessary to gain the approvals for such a statue. Art placed in any of the historic buildings on Capitol Hill was tightly controlled. Sam put us in touch with the United

States Senate Commission on Art. We were able to secure the necessary approvals.

Before the unveiling and dedication of the statue in January 1996, Senator Nunn had announced that he would retire from the Senate and not seek reelection when his term expired at the end of 1996. When I heard this news, I was shocked, as I assumed Sam Nunn would serve in the Senate for many more years. I called him on the telephone to try to dissuade him from leaving the Senate. He was, after all, still a young man by Senate standards, and he already had twenty-four years of seniority. I will never forget what Sam told me in that conversation: "Charlie, the Senate is not like it was when you were there, and it will be even less so in ten or fifteen years." Nunn had seen the developing trends that would make the Senate of today a legislative body bitterly divided by partisanship. There is no longer much room in the center for serious legislators such as Sam Nunn or Richard Russell who are more interested in passing effective legislation than in scoring political points or adhering to some ideological agenda. In early 2013, Georgia's senior senator, Saxby Chambliss (Rep), announced his retirement from the Senate giving essentially the same reasons Sam Nunn gave me back in 1996—growing partisanship and lack of leadership that make it difficult for a serious senator to do his or her job.

When the Russell statue was dedicated on January 24, 1996, we asked Senator Nunn to serve as the master of ceremonies. Senator Robert C. Byrd of West Virginia, who served in the Senate with Senator Russell for almost fifteen years and with Sam Nunn for his entire twenty-four years, said this of Nunn during the dedication of the statue: "He stepped into some big shoes when he came to the Senate, and those shoes fit today." When it became my time to speak as chair of the Russell Foundation, I said this about Senator Nunn: "...I also can't let the occasion pass without saying, Senator, particularly in light of your retirement now, how much we appreciate your twenty-four years of Richard Russell-type service in the United States Senate." Sam Nunn had indeed proven to be more than a worthy successor to Richard Russell.

Senator Henry M. (Scoop) Jackson

One of the senators I got to know while working for Richard Russell was Senator Scoop Jackson of Washington State. He was an effective senator and a close friend of Richard Russell. They served on the Armed Services

Committee together, and Russell appointed Senator Jackson as chairman of the Military Construction Subcommittee. This was one of the most important subcommittees because it oversaw the authorization of military construction all over the world, including [that] at the numerous military installations in Georgia. While Senator Jackson was much more liberal than Richard Russell on domestic matters, they had similar views on the Cold War and national security.

Shortly after I returned to Georgia in late 1971, I received a telephone call from Senator Jackson's office asking me to assist his presidential campaign in Georgia. I did not know it at the time, but Senator Jackson subsequently said in an oral history interview he gave to the Russell Library in Athens that Richard Russell had earlier encouraged him to run for president in 1972. After checking with Lamar Sizemore, I agreed to be responsible for coordinating Senator Jackson's activities when he visited Georgia. I remember at least one trip he made to the state in early 1972. He spoke to a national Jewish organization that was having its annual meeting in Atlanta at a downtown hotel. In attendance were top Jewish leaders not only from Georgia but from throughout the nation. Jackson was a strong supporter of Israel, and the core of his support for president was partly in the Jewish community. While Senator Jackson was in Atlanta for the speech, I also went with him to visit with J. B Fuqua, a former chairman of the Democratic Party of Georgia and a well-known entrepreneur. We visited with Mr. Fuqua at his home in the Buckhead section of Atlanta.

The main candidates in the race for the Democratic presidential nomination in 1972 were eventually Senator George McGovern of South Dakota, Senator Hubert Humphrey of Minnesota, and Senator Jackson. Jackson was running third until Humphrey dropped out of the race not long before the convention. That meant that Jackson would be McGovern's chief competition at the convention. The Jackson campaign asked me to attend the convention in Miami Beach and to represent Jackson in dealing with delegations from the Southeast, including Georgia. I had previously attended the 1968 Republican National Convention in Miami Beach while working for Richard Russell. Therefore, I knew something about what went on at conventions and about the lay of the land in Miami Beach. I went with Senator Jackson when he spoke before all of the southern delegations, including Georgia. Governor Jimmy Carter was supporting Jackson and was invited to give a seconding speech at the convention in support of Scoop Jackson. Since I was the only person on the Jackson campaign staff from Georgia, I was assigned the responsibility of working with the Carter staff in connection with Carter's speech. The two principal people I dealt with were Hamilton Jordan, Carter's chief of staff, whom I had known at the University of Georgia, and Jody Powell, his press secretary. Hamilton and Jody would occupy the same positions in the Carter White House after his election in 1976.

When we received the first draft of the Carter nominating speech, the Jackson people were not happy. What they most wanted out of Carter was an attack on George McGovern, but there was no mention of McGovern in the speech and little mention of Jackson. The speech dealt more with Carter's background and the fact that his mother had volunteered and served in the Peace Corps at almost seventy years of age. We tried to get the speech revised but were unable to accomplish much in terms of an attack on McGovern. Instead, Senator Jackson had a national labor leader, I. W. Abel, beef up his principal nominating speech attacking McGovern. McGovern won the nomination by a substantial margin, with Jackson finishing second. Jackson was further put off by Carter's request that Jackson help him become McGovern's running mate. Jackson refused. These unsatisfactory dealings with Carter may have contributed to the frosty relationship and frequent clashes between the two men during the four years in which President Carter was in the White House. When Carter sought a second term as president in 1980, Senator Jackson aided and abetted the unsuccessful effort of Senator Edward Kennedy to deprive him of the Democratic nomination. McGovern was trounced in the general election in 1972 by President Nixon.

Senator Jackson had warned in his race against George McGovern that McGovern would be a disaster for the Democratic Party if he should be nominated. The fact that exactly that scenario happened encouraged Jackson to believe that he could make progress in running for president again in 1976. He really never quit campaigning. I received a call in late 1974 from Jackson's office and was asked to attend a mid-term Democratic convention in Kansas City and do the same kind of work among southern delegations that I had done in Miami Beach. By this time, of course, Jimmy Carter was running for president. While I was in Kansas City working for Senator Jackson, I met an optometrist from Fairburn, Georgia, who was at the convention supporting Carter. Dr. Del Ingram told me that one of his patients was a young lady whom I needed to meet, and that is the way I met Ann Laurel Grovenstein, my future wife.

Ironically, Jackson's main opponent in 1976 was Jimmy Carter. At the beginning of the primary process, many considered Jackson to be the frontrunner. He decided not to compete in Iowa or New Hampshire, however, both of which Carter won. With this momentum, Jimmy Carter became a serious candidate, which allowed him to withstand Jackson victories in Massachusetts and New York. Carter defeated Jackson badly in Florida and essentially ended his candidacy with a solid win in Pennsylvania. Jackson dropped out of the race before the 1976 convention at which Jimmy Carter was nominated. One of the last times I saw Scoop Jackson was in Athens, Georgia, at the dedication of the Richard B. Russell Memorial Library. He gave the keynote address on that occasion. He continued to be an important and powerful United States senator until he died in 1983. For more information, see the excellent biography of the life and career of Senator Jackson by Robert G. Kaufman, *Henry M. Jackson: A Life in Politics* (Seattle: University of Washington Press, 2000).

Senator Herman E. Talmadge

Richard Russell and Herman Talmadge served together for fifteen years in the United States Senate. They had a close relationship. They were also regarded in Washington, DC, as perhaps the most effective tandem of senators from any state. It was not unusual for senators from a state to fight like cats and dogs, even when they were from the same political party. New York State was a good example. Their Republican senators, Jacob Javits and Kenneth Keating, were barely on speaking terms. They argued over who would be first to announce federal grants or contracts in their state and about numerous other matters. In Georgia, Richard Russell and Herman Talmadge jointly announced such matters.

It was surprising that they had such a good relationship. They had completely different personalities. Talmadge's father had challenged Russell in the bitter 1936 campaign, and, when Talmadge first ran for the Senate in 1956, Russell was approached by members of Georgia's business community and requested to urge his colleague, Walter F. George, to back out of the race in favor of Talmadge. George was seventy-eight years old at the time and not in good health. He had also given up the chairmanship of the Senate Finance Committee to become chairman of the Foreign Relations Committee. That did not please the business community because of the importance of the Finance Committee to Georgia's business interests. Among the business leaders in Georgia who talked to Russell about the matter was the legendary chairman of the Coca-Cola Company, Robert W. Woodruff. Russell gave him the same answer that he had given Franklin Roosevelt in 1938. He would take no part in any effort to interfere with Senator George's reelection. Ultimately, without Russell's assistance, they were able to convince Senator George not to run, and Talmadge was easily elected.

When Talmadge arrived in Washington, Russell treated him exactly as Senator George had treated Russell in 1933. He warmly welcomed him and did everything he could to see that his colleague would get off to a good start in the Senate. He helped Talmadge secure an appointment to the Senate Agriculture Committee, which was his first choice. Shortly thereafter, he helped Talmadge secure an appointment to the Senate Finance Committee, his second choice. Talmadge served on those committees for [his] entire twenty-four years in the United States Senate, eventually becoming chairman of the Agriculture Committee and second ranking Democrat on the Finance Committee.

As senators, Richard Russell and Herman Talmadge complemented each other in many ways. Russell covered appropriations, national security, and foreign policy. Talmadge covered agriculture, trade and tax policy, Social Security, and Medicare. Their hours were also complementary. Talmadge was a notorious early riser, often arriving in his office by five o'clock in the morning. Russell, on the other hand, arrived at the Capitol usually by 8:30, but he was there until seven or eight o'clock at night, whereas Talmadge usually went home before five o'clock unless Senate votes were scheduled. Russell had enormous respect for Talmadge, particularly his keen mind and political instincts. As a measure of his respect for Talmadge, in 1970 when he was persuaded to establish the Richard B. Russell Foundation to preserve his legacy and his records, he did so on the condition that Herman Talmadge serve as its first chair. In the final two years of Russell's career during which his health was deteriorating, Talmadge could not have been more considerate. When Russell was not able to attend important meetings of Georgians when they came to Washington, Talmadge would cover for him by saying he was involved in important meetings related to national security.

Several years after Richard Russell died, Herman Talmadge had his own moment in the national spotlight as a member of the Senate Watergate Committee. Talmadge was selected for the committee primarily because of his keen legal mind and his interrogation abilities. These would be on full display in the nationally televised hearings. He was particularly effective in his examination of key Nixon aides who were involved in the Watergate cover-up. Records subsequently released by the Nixon Presidential Library in California revealed that Talmadge was the most feared member of the committee for Nixon and his advisers. And it was for good reason.

In late 1973, Lamar Sizemore asked me to come by his office. He told me he had just spoken to Senator Talmadge, who wanted me to be involved in his reelection campaign in 1974. He said that Talmadge would contact me. From the way Lamar relayed this information to me, I understood that he considered this to be a command performance and I should do whatever Talmadge asked me to do. Shortly thereafter, I heard from Senator Talmadge. He asked if I were willing to serve as the chair of his campaign for reelection. I agreed to do so. We discussed the fact that he had not had serious opposition in any of his elections in 1956, 1962, and 1968. He said he hoped he would not have serious opposition in 1974, but he had heard rumors that Georgia governor Jimmy Carter was considering a race against him. We agreed that would be a serious race, although Talmadge said that he was confident he could defeat Carter. Talmadge appointed a campaign committee, and we started raising funds and doing the other things that would be necessary if a serious race took place.

Several months later, Talmadge called me and said that Jimmy Carter had requested a meeting. Talmadge assumed this was to announce his intentions concerning 1974. On the afternoon of the day on which the meeting took place, Talmadge called me and said he had some good news and some bad news. The good news was that Carter was not going to run against him. The bad news was that [Carter] was going to run for president. The latter derisive comment was not unique to Herman Talmadge. The initial reaction of most people in Georgia upon learning that Jimmy Carter planned to run for president was shock. Some thought it was a joke. Carter, of course, had the last laugh as he ran a brilliant campaign. He won the Iowa Caucuses and the New Hampshire Primary and easily captured the Democratic nomination. He pursued to perfection a campaign strategy that had been mapped out by his chief aide, Hamilton Jordan. After securing the Democratic nomination, running as an outsider in the post-Watergate era, he defeated President Ford in the general election. Ford had pardoned Richard Nixon for his crimes in the Watergate cover-up. With Jimmy Carter out of the way, Senator Talmadge did not have serious opposition in the 1974 reelection campaign. We did run a few advertisements and he gave some campaign speeches, but it did not amount to much. It was not a serious diversion from my law practice.

The year 1980 was a different story. The intervening years were not kind to Herman Talmadge. In 1975, his oldest son, Bobby, drowned in a boating accident at Lake Lanier. This increased Talmadge's already existing tendency to abuse alcohol. It was not long before I heard rumors that there was tension in Talmadge's marriage. One afternoon in 1977, I received a telephone call from United States district court judge Newell Edenfield. Judge Edenfield had been a name partner in the Heyman and Sizemore law firm—then known as Edenfield, Heyman, and Sizemore—before he was appointed to the bench. He told me that he had just spoken to Senator Talmadge, who told him that he planned to divorce his wife, Betty. He said Talmadge told him he wanted to hire "the meanest divorce lawyer in Georgia." He was considering a lawyer by the name of Alex McLendon. Judge Edenfield expressed the opinion that Talmadge had far more to lose in a bitter divorce proceeding than Betty. He said he had reason to believe that Talmadge was going to seek my advice as to a divorce lawyer and that I could do him a favor by encouraging him to make the divorce as amicable as possible. I completely agreed with Judge Edenfield.

It was not long before Senator Talmadge called me and we had a similar conversation. I told him I did not personally know Alex McLendon, but I expressed concern as to whether it was in his interest to have an acrimonious divorce proceeding. I pointed out that he would be up for reelection again in a few years. He was clearly not in a frame of mind to receive this kind of advice. He hired Alex McLendon, and the divorce proceeding was exceedingly bitter. I was told on good authority that Betty learned her husband was suing her for divorce when she heard it on the evening news. In 1998 when my law firm combined with another firm in Atlanta, I became law partners with Stell Huie, who represented Betty in the divorce case. He told me the matter could have been settled without great difficulty if Senator Talmadge and his lawyer had not been so unreasonable.

During the divorce proceeding, Betty Talmadge testified at her deposition that her husband maintained large sums of cash in an overcoat in their home. The implication was that he was taking cash payments from someone. At about the same time, the *Washington Post* ran a story on rumors that Talmadge had misused office and campaign funds. The allegations in the divorce case and in the Washington press resulted in the Senate Ethics Committee commencing an inquiry. It was discovered that a secret bank account was maintained at the Riggs National Bank in Washington. A review of the bank records indicated that the account was opened by Daniel Minchew, Talmadge's administrative assistant. Minchew, who by this time had been appointed as a member of the International Trade Commission, stated to the Senate Ethics Committee that the account had been opened with Talmadge's knowledge and at his direction. Further review of the bank records revealed that Minchew had spent over $10,000 of funds in the account for his personal uses and had filed false expenditure reports with the Senate. Minchew was ultimately indicted, convicted, and sent to prison. Talmadge stated that he was the worst hire he had ever made. I had known Minchew since my University of Georgia days, when he taught political science in a classroom that adjoined the one where I taught while in graduate school. I did not remind Talmadge that when he was considering Minchew, I recommended that he hire George Watts, my old roommate in Washington, DC, as his administrative assistant.

The Senate Ethics Committee brought formal charges against Senator Talmadge for misusing office and campaign funds and for other irregularities. Talmadge blamed them on Minchew. I had a small role in the hearings when Talmadge's then current administrative assistant, Rogers Wade, was subpoenaed as a witness. I agreed to represent Rogers. He was not accused of any wrongdoing but was called to testify with respect to his knowledge of how the office was operated and how funds were handled. I got the sense from attending the hearing when Rogers testified that the committee, particularly its staff, thought Talmadge had engaged in wrongdoing and was probably going to take action against him. That is exactly what happened. The alternatives available to the committee were expulsion, censure, or reprimand in the order of severity. They chose something between censure and reprimand. It was one of the weaker punishments but was a bitter pill for Talmadge.

These negative developments further exacerbated Talmadge's drinking problem. Fortunately, primarily at the instance of Senator Nunn, an intervention was started. Senator Nunn contacted several of Talmadge's friends and colleagues in the Senate, including Senator Russell Long of Louisiana, who by then had dealt with his own alcohol problems, and Senator John Stennis of Mississippi. Also, members of Talmadge's family and staff assisted in the intervention. Talmadge checked himself into a treatment center in California. He was there for approximately one month. He then joined Alcoholics Anonymous and diligently attended its meetings. The publicity surrounding his personal difficulties was intense. The Atlanta newspapers had never been big Talmadge supporters. This went back to the time of his father, who had enjoyed campaigning against "those lying Atlanta newspapers." They carried publicity on a daily basis with respect to Talmadge's personal difficulties and the reprimand he received from his Senate colleagues.

It was against this backdrop that I had to consider whether to serve as chair of the Talmadge campaign in 1980. My situation had changed considerably by that time as well. Ann Grovenstein and I had married in 1976, and our first attempt at having a child had resulted in a miscarriage. We intended to try again. I also had left the Heyman and Sizemore law firm with Bob Hicks and Ted Maloof to establish Hicks Maloof and Campbell. By 1980, we had about eight lawyers, a small firm that would feel the effects of one of its main partners being out of the office for an extended period. Unlike 1974, the 1980 campaign would be much more demanding and time consuming. To further add to the difficulty of my decision were rumors that a grand jury had been convened to look at the Talmadge case and that an indictment was a real possibility. I had to consider whether to sacrifice the interests of my law practice and family for a political campaign with the risk that I would lose my candidate to an indictment before the election.

I decided to have a heart-to-heart conversation with Herman Talmadge. I flew to Washington and met with him in his office in the Russell Senate Office Building. He convincingly assured me that all of the negative information was already in the public domain, and he had answers with respect to some of the charges against him. Some of the answers seemed more compelling to me than others. Ultimately, I decided to sign on for the 1980 campaign because one thing I had learned from my parents and from Richard Russell was loyalty. Many of Herman Talmadge's friends for whom he had done so much were abandoning what they assumed was a sinking ship. I did not want to be counted in that number. I had no idea whether Herman Talmadge would be reelected, but I did not want to be on the sidelines in the most serious political battle of his career.

The first thing we had to do in the campaign was learn the full extent of the damage that had been done to Talmadge in Georgia from his personal problems and the publicity surrounding them. This can only be done reliably with a statewide poll. We employed the able pollster, Pat Caddell, who had done the polling for Jimmy Carter's presidential campaign. He conducted a statewide poll and we waited for the results. There was good news and bad news. The bad news was that Talmadge's personal problems had in fact greatly damaged him in the eyes of the people of Georgia. A majority of Georgians viewed Talmadge as arrogant, out of touch, and of questionable honesty. The good news was that an even larger majority of Georgians felt that he had been an effective senator and that his seniority and experience were valuable assets for the state. We had to figure out a way to persuade the voters of Georgia to reelect Herman Talmadge based on the latter factors as opposed to turning him out of office based on his personal difficulties.

Based on these polling results, and after conferring with the campaign staff, Pat Caddell, and our media firm, Cook Advertising of South Carolina, we settled on a strategy of running early on what became known as the "apology ads." These would be statewide television advertisements designed to make Herman Talmadge appear more human and hopefully elicit sympathy. He would not actually apologize in the ads but would state that he is not perfect and that he had made mistakes that he regretted. These ads would require Talmadge to look into the camera and make these admissions. Herman Talmadge was a proud man, and this did not come easily for him. He initially resisted the idea, but we kept at it until we convinced him that he would not be able to get a fair hearing on his merits unless he dealt with these personal problems. Eventually, he agreed to do the ads. The taping was difficult because it was clear that Herman Talmadge's heart was not in it. Because of the skill of our media advisers and because Talmadge kept trying, we eventually had television advertisements that we were told were likely to do the job.

Fortunately, we were easily able to raise the necessary funds for the polls and the television advertising. Herman Talmadge was important to the business community in Georgia and the nation because of his membership on key Senate committees. By staging early fundraisers in Georgia, Washington, and New York, we were quickly able to raise the hundreds of thousands of dollars that were necessary to pay for the polls and the television advertising. The television spots ran statewide over about ten days. We then had Pat Caddell run another poll to assess the results. The second poll showed that the advertisements had largely accomplished their purpose. The voters of Georgia had not forgotten about the personal difficulties of Herman Talmadge, but they viewed him as a more sympathetic figure and were more willing to consider his candidacy on the merits.

We knew Talmadge would have serious opposition for the first time. We just did not know who it would be. Ultimately, three serious candidates qualified to oppose him in the Democratic Primary. The first was the lieutenant governor of Georgia, Zell Miller. He had run statewide on a number of occasions and was well liked. He would be a formidable opponent. He would also be the one who would attack Talmadge most vociferously for his personal shortcomings. The second candidate who qualified, which came as a shock to me, was my good friend Norman Underwood. Norman had left the law firm of Carl Sanders to become executive secretary to Georgia governor George Busbee. After a couple of years, Busbee appointed Norman to the Georgia Court of Appeals. Norman did not attack Talmadge on his personal problems as frequently as did Zell Miller, although he did run some television advertising showing a shadowy figure stuffing money in the pocket of an overcoat. The final candidate to qualify was Congressman Dawson Mathis, who represented southwest Georgia in the United States House of Representatives. Dawson was a former television personality in Albany, Georgia, and served on the House Agriculture Committee. His entry into the race was surprising because he was supposedly a friend of Herman Talmadge who had worked closely with him on agriculture matters. That does not mean much in politics when there is blood in the water. Dawson did not attack Talmadge as much on the personal issues as did the other candidates. He ran mostly on his own experience in Congress. Dawson had a way with words. Shortly after he entered the race, a reporter asked him how on earth he hoped to defeat Talmadge since Talmadge's name was a household word in Georgia and Dawson was virtually unknown outside his District. Dawson responded, "It will be easier for me to become known than it will be for Herman Talmadge to become unknown."

The primary campaign went well. We continued to raise money at an impressive rate, with the total fundraising for the campaign, as I recall, being in excess of $2 million, the most ever raised at that time for a Senate race in Georgia. That money was required to conduct the campaign. The campaign committee, known as Georgians for Talmadge, opened an office on Peachtree Street in midtown Atlanta. It had a small paid staff as well as numerous volunteers. We continued to run television advertisements throughout the campaign. Senator Sam Nunn was supportive, doing everything we asked him to do, including taping television spots emphasizing how important Herman Talmadge was to Georgia in the United States Senate. Most of the advertisements after the initial wave related to Talmadge's experience and seniority in the Senate. We occasionally reran the apology ads as the need dictated, particularly when Zell Miller intensified his attack on Talmadge based on his personal shortcomings.

We also spent quite a bit of money on the black vote. It might seem strange that a confirmed segregationist like Herman Talmadge would think he had any chance of getting a significant black vote. It is true that he was an active participant in the southern filibusters against both the 1964 and 1965 civil rights legislation. After those bills passed, however, he was one of the first of the southern senators to hire a black on his staff, Curtis Atkinson. He also regularly spoke at black groups, including the luncheon club in Atlanta, known as the Hungry Club. Our expenditures in the black community were for two purposes. The first was to secure a place on ballots that were distributed by leaders in the black community. These ballots would list the preferred candidates for various offices. You had to pay money to get on these tickets. The second area of expenditure was to turn out votes on the day of the election. I remember we spent quite a bit of money with Billy McKinney, a black member of the state legislature from Atlanta and the father of the future congresswoman Cynthia McKinney. I was never able to determine for sure the return we were receiving from the expenditure of these funds. When you buy television time, you know exactly what ads run and you receive a detailed report. It was difficult to get such reports from the activities we financed in the black community.

We also sought support and endorsements from leaders in the black community. I remember one Saturday morning we were having a campaign strategy meeting and discussing ways we could seek the endorsement or support of Dr. Martin Luther King, Sr. Known as "Daddy King," he had quite a bit of influence in the black community. Senator Talmadge suggested that we contact superior court judge Osgood Williams. Judge Williams looked like Ichabod Crane. He was originally from Taliaferro County, Georgia, about one hundred miles east of Atlanta. He was elected to the state legislature but was far too progressive for his constituents. For example, Judge Williams introduced legislation to disrobe and unmask the Ku Klux Klan in Georgia. He was defeated for reelection and moved to Atlanta. After practicing law for a while, he was appointed to a vacant seat first on the Civil Court of Fulton County and then to the Superior Court of Fulton County. He ran successfully countywide several times for reelection and had broad support in the black community. Following Talmadge's suggestion, I contacted Judge Williams, who agreed to help us with Daddy King. Eventually, we were able to secure the support not only of Daddy King but also of other members of the King family.

I traveled quite a bit with Herman Talmadge during the campaign. He had a lot of energy for a man who was almost sixty-five years old. The only breaks he took from campaigning were to attend meetings of Alcoholics Anonymous and to return to Washington for important votes in the Senate. He stayed on the wagon for the entire campaign and did an excellent job. During his campaigning in rural areas of the state, I noticed people would come up to him and put money in his pocket without saying anything to him at all. That is one of the explanations Talmadge had given me in our heart-to-heart talk with respect to the money in his overcoat. I did not consider the explanation very credible at the time because I had not noticed this practice when I accompanied Richard Russell on campaign trips in 1966. Much to my amazement, it happened frequently when Talmadge was campaigning. These were primarily older supporters. Talmadge explained to me that it went back to the time of his father's campaigns when there were no campaign finance disclosure laws.

We, of course, could take no chance on having any problems with respect to the handling of campaign funds. We brought into the campaign the former Sam Nunn legislative aide, Gordon Giffin, who by the time of the campaign had returned to Georgia to practice law. Gordon had become an expert on campaign disclosure requirements of both the federal and state governments. He established a program of strict disclosure with which we rigorously complied during the campaign. The names of contributors did not have to be disclosed unless the contribution exceeded $100, although all funds contributed had to be listed in the totals contained in the financial disclosure reports. Thus, we were able to comply with the law in regard to the money placed in Talmadge's pockets at campaign rallies because those individual contributions almost never exceeded $100.

The goal of the campaign was to win without a runoff. That was not realistic with three formidable opponents running against Talmadge. As the date of the election approached, our polls showed Talmadge would finish first but without 50 percent, Zell Miller second, and then Norman Underwood and Dawson Mathis. Our opponents' polls must have shown similar results because Norman and Dawson started attacking Miller instead of Talmadge. It was good to have someone else under attack for a change. It was during this period that Norman started to refer to Miller as "Zig Zag Zell" because Miller had allegedly switched his position on so many issues. When the votes were counted on election day, Talmadge received 42 percent of the vote. Zell Miller received 25 percent of the vote. Norman Underwood received 20 percent and Dawson Mathis received 13 percent. While we had not avoided a runoff, it was an impressive result considering the situation we faced at the beginning of the race. We sought endorsements from Norman Underwood and Dawson Mathis. Norman declined to endorse either candidate in the runoff. Dawson endorsed Talmadge. We felt we had an excellent chance of defeating Miller in the runoff if we could just hold the Talmadge and Mathis votes, since they totaled 55 percent. The problem with runoffs is that you never know whether your voters will turn out for the runoff election. This was a problem for us because there was a high level of confidence and complacency among the Talmadge supporters that he was going to win.

Since Talmadge was an excellent debater and knew the issues related to the federal government better than Zell Miller, we decided to accept the invitation for five debates during the runoff. At Talmadge's suggestion, we insisted that the format of the debates be such that the candidates could directly confront each other and question each other. The Miller campaign agreed to this format. The five debates would be held at television studios in Atlanta, Columbus, Macon, Augusta, and Savannah. I accompanied Talmadge to each of the five debates and was in the TV studio on each occasion. Prior to the first debate, we decided to have a preparation session at my condominium in Peachtree City. There were about five people involved in the Talmadge campaign in attendance, as well as Dawson Mathis, who had endorsed Talmadge. One humorous occurrence that took place during the prep session involved Talmadge's administrative assistant, Will Ball, who had succeeded Rogers Wade. We were sitting in a semicircle in the living room of my condo when the chair in which Will Ball was sitting collapsed. Will was somewhat overweight. Dawson Mathis turned to him and said, "Son, you have to do something about that weight." Actually, the collapse of the chair had less to do with Will Ball than the condition of the chair.

The debate prep session was somewhat of a disaster in hindsight. There were too many people giving Talmadge too much advice as to what he should do or not do in the debate. As a result, Talmadge did poorly in the first debate, which was held in Columbus. I thought Zell Miller clearly won that debate. On the way back to Atlanta afterward, I told Talmadge I thought we should dispense with any further debate preparation sessions and he should just be himself. He had so much greater knowledge of federal issues than Zell Miller based on his twenty-four years of experience in the Senate and was such a great debater that I was confident he would do well if he were not hamstrung by too much advice. Talmadge agreed. He decisively won the four remaining debates. The chief strategy of the runoff campaign against Miller was to paint him as a tax and spend liberal. To drive this point home, we developed a chart that listed the cost of the various programs Zell Miller had supported. We thought this would be shocking to the people of Georgia, who were generally conservative. We placed the chart in the TV studio starting with the second debate and covered it with a sheet of paper so that its contents would not be revealed until Talmadge used it. Talmadge forgot to use it during the second debate. I noticed that Zell Miller seemed fixated on what was on the chart, and that seemed to me to be a distraction to him. Therefore, we decided to do the same thing in the next few debates and not unveil the chart until the final debate in Savannah. The strategy worked well.

When the runoff votes were counted, Talmadge had achieved a smashing victory. He garnered 58.5 percent of the vote. Zell Miller later said that Talmadge had taken him to the woodshed and given him a sound whipping. He said he learned important lessons from that campaign. He would go on to be elected governor of Georgia twice and to the United States Senate before he voluntarily retired from politics. Many of the hardcore Talmadge supporters never forgave Miller for running against Talmadge, as many of the Russell supporters never forgave Carl Sanders for considering a race against Russell. That was not true of me. I supported Zell Miller in his future races and thought he was one of the best governors in Georgia's history. It was also not true of Ovid Davis of the Coca-Cola Company, who was a strong Talmadge supporter but also a friend of Zell Miller. Ovid encouraged Talmadge supporters not to hold the race against Miller in the future. Even Norman Underwood, who had labeled Miller "Zig Zag Zell," became a strong supporter of Miller and was named as chair of the review panel to screen applicants for state court judgeships and district attorneys during Miller's two terms as governor.

Having won the primary in good fashion, it was generally assumed that Talmadge would be reelected to the Senate. Georgia had not elected a Republican senator since the Reconstruction period following the Civil War. His Republican opponent, Mack Mattingly, had never held elective office. He had unsuccessfully run for Congress and had been chairman of the Republican Party in Georgia. He was originally from Indiana and had worked for the IBM Corporation. Talmadge derisively referred to him as "that typewriter salesman from Indiana." Since Mattingly was given virtually no chance of defeating Talmadge in the general election and since the primary had been so bitter and long, we decided to ignore Mattingly and have Talmadge return to Washington and be a United States senator. This was not a strategy adopted lightly but was discussed extensively with Talmadge, the campaign staff and advisers, and key outside supporters. I remember a meeting we held with House Speaker Tom Murphy, Commissioner of Agriculture Tommy Irvin, and others where the strategy was discussed in detail. There was unanimous agreement that it was the proper strategy because Mattingly was virtually unknown in Georgia. As a result of this strategy, Talmadge declined an invitation to debate Mattingly because it would have given Mattingly free publicity.

While the runoff strategy was perhaps defensible, the way in which we implemented it was not. We quit polling as frequently as we had done in the primary, and we practically closed down the fundraising operation. We had already pressured the Talmadge supporters for contributions, and many of them had maxed out. Looking back on it in hindsight, I realize now that I had a significant conflict of interest with regard to the runoff strategy. I desperately wanted to get back to my law practice, which I had neglected. This strategy gave me the opportunity to do so. The result of the strategy was that when there was movement in the direction of Mattingly, we were slow to pick up on it. When we finally ran a poll about a month before the date of the general election, Mattingly had closed the gap to about ten points. That was still a formidable lead for Talmadge but much less than it had been earlier. Since we had not continued to raise significant funds, we did not have on hand enough money for a robust media buy at the end of the general election.

Because the Republicans had been polling all along, they were able to use these polls with the Republican Senatorial Campaign Committee in Washington to successfully solicit additional funds for the Mattingly campaign. The opportunity to defeat a senior Democrat who had been in the Senate for twenty-four years was attractive. Indeed, these funds from Washington made a major difference in the final television advertising by the Mattingly campaign. And the money was spent wisely. Mattingly's message was that it was time for a change in Washington. He spent almost no money on Talmadge's personal shortcomings, as those matters had already been thoroughly aired in the primary. Ronald Reagan was running for president, and the message was that the country needed new blood in Washington, DC. That was Mattingly's message as well.

With the race within ten points, we had to decide whether to change our strategy. It still looked like Talmadge would win, but it was no longer certain. There was not enough time left to raise significant money, but we did have the option of borrowing money to finance a more robust advertising campaign. I discussed the matter with Talmadge. Ever the fiscal conservative, he was opposed to borrowing any money. We simply spent the money we already had raised, which resulted in a much less intense television advertising campaign than Mattingly was able to finance. Still, we felt good about the likely outcome of the election.

On election night, I had the flu and did not go to the campaign headquarters. I did, however, talk to Herman Talmadge on the telephone several times during the evening. The initial returns looked promising, and Talmadge mounted a substantial lead. In fact, two television stations in Atlanta and the Atlanta newspapers projected Talmadge as the winner. He was not so sure. I remember a telephone conversation with him at about ten o'clock that evening. He had been tracking the returns in about twenty precincts around the state, which he did in all of his races. While he was winning in the precincts that he had historically carried, the margin of victory was not nearly as great as he had expected. The returns from the Metropolitan Atlanta suburbs where the Republican vote was the strongest had not yet been reported. Talmadge thought the race could turn out to be too close for comfort. While some urged him to claim victory that night, he declined to do so. I went to bed about midnight. When I woke up the next morning, Mattingly had a slight lead. Still suffering from the flu, I stayed at home. I talked to Talmadge on the telephone several times in the morning after the runoff election. He had returned to his home in Lovejoy. With practically all of the vote reported, Mattingly was ahead by about 1 percent. Some of Talmadge's key supporters urged him to seek a recount, which he was entitled to do given the closeness of the election. I remember receiving a telephone call that morning from Oscar Persons, an attorney at the Alston and Bird Law Firm and the general counsel of the Georgia Republican Party. He wanted to know if Talmadge was going to concede. I told him I did not know as Talmadge was still weighing his options. Mattingly claimed victory. Later that morning, Talmadge announced that he would not seek a recount but would accept the vote as reported. Thus ended the political career of Herman Talmadge and the Talmadge Dynasty in Georgia.

Looking back on the election, it was a perfect storm. The personal problems and the intense and continuing press coverage of them substantially weakened Talmadge, and Mattingly was the ultimate beneficiary. Our general election strategy was not well implemented. Many new voters had moved into Georgia, and a great many of them were Republicans. Fayette County, for example, where my condo is located, was an old Talmadge stronghold with key supporters such as the Redwines and Buck Murphy. Mattingly decisively carried the county. This pattern was repeated in the suburban counties throughout the state, where many newcomers had settled. The only thing they knew about Herman Talmadge was what they had read in the newspapers about his personal difficulties. While Jimmy Carter carried the state in the presidential race, he lost nationally in a landslide to Ronald Reagan. The Republican victory nationwide was so complete that the Republicans took control of the United States Senate, sweeping out not only Talmadge but also senior Democratic senators who were almost a who's who: Warren Magnusan in Washington State, Birch Bayh in Indiana, Frank Church in Idaho, George McGovern in South Dakota, and John Culver in Iowa. Two years later, in 1982, Howard Cannon, a World War II hero and a twenty-four-year Democratic senator from Nevada, went down in a race frighteningly similar to the Talmadge race in 1980. He had been accused of personal indiscretions and ethical lapses that received widespread publicity. He weathered a strong challenge in the Democratic Primary based largely on his personal problems only to be defeated by an unknown Republican opponent whom he ignored and refused to debate. I had known Senator Cannon and members of his staff when I worked in Washington because his office was located around the corner from Senator Russell's office and because he served with Russell on both the Armed Services and Space committees. Cannon's former press secretary, Michael Vernetti, has recently written a book on Senator Cannon's career and last race titled *Senator Howard Cannon of Nevada* (Reno: University of Nevada Press, 2008).

While Georgia would miss his ability, experience, and seniority in the United States Senate, the defeat may have been a blessing in disguise for Herman Talmadge. If he had been reelected, he would no longer be chairman of the Senate Agriculture Committee because the Republicans took control of the Senate. The pressures of being a United States senator under less than ideal circumstances may have led him to renew his old drinking habits. Instead, his retirement years were among the happiest of his life. The biggest reason for this was that a couple of years after he was involuntarily retired from the Senate, he met and married Lynda Cowart, a home economist with the Cooperative Extension Service from the University of Georgia. She was wonderful for Talmadge for the rest of his life.

I did not visit with him frequently in the years after his defeat because I was so busy with my law practice and other matters. He did invite me on several occasions to go fishing with him. But the invitations called for me to arrive at five or six o'clock in the morning. I am not a morning person and not much of a fisherman. The times I did visit with him were usually on Saturday or Sunday afternoons. His mind was as keen as ever. He would typically tell me about some book he had recently read and ask if I had read it. If I had, a detailed discussion of the book would ensue. If I had not, he would go over to his library shelf and hand me a copy. When I next saw him, there would be a detailed discussion about the book. And then another book, and the process was repeated again. It appeared to me that Herman Talmadge was happier and more contented than at any time since I first met him in early 1966. Friends of his who had known him far longer than me confirmed that as their opinion as well.

Several years before he died, Talmadge was in the Emory University Hospital for a heart problem. For reasons I never fully understood, when he left the hospital, he could no longer eat solid food. That was his condition for the rest of his life. This was a difficult time and would have been far more difficult had he been without the love and care of Lynda Talmadge. His funeral was a sad occasion, but he had accomplished a lot in his life. One of the last times I have seen Lynda Talmadge was in 2008 at the funeral of my old friend, roommate, and fellow Russell staffer, Proctor Jones. Proctor had died of lung cancer. He and Lynda were from the same small hometown in Southeast Georgia, Twin City. I spoke to Lynda at the funeral for Proctor Jones, and it reminded me of how much she had meant to Herman Talmadge in his final years.

Georgia Chamber of Commerce

In about 1974, Jasper Dorsey was elected president of the Georgia Chamber of Commerce. The chamber is the foremost business organization in Georgia. Its purpose is to protect and promote the interests of the business community in the state at both the federal and state level. Its Governmental Council is responsible for reviewing legislation on the state and federal level and making recommendations to the chamber's board of directors with respect to positions it should take for or against legislation. The chamber had a paid staff that assisted in this process led by Glenn Anthony. While he was president of the chamber, Jasper appointed me as chair of the Governmental Council. In addition to meetings to discuss and recommend legislative positions, the council also staged two important events each year. The first was the Eggs and Issues Breakfast held in Atlanta at which the top three state political office holders—the governor, the lieutenant governor who is president of the state Senate, and the Speaker of the House of Representatives—would speak with respect to issues in the upcoming legislative session.

The other major activity for which the Governmental Council was responsible was the Pre-legislative Forum. This was a traveling road show staged in the fourth quarter of the year to discuss legislative issues in the upcoming session of the General Assembly and Congress. Typically, top state and federal politicians were the featured speakers. For example, in 1977, which is one of the years I served as chair of the Governmental Council, the speakers were Georgia governor George Busbee and Senator Sam Nunn. I was responsible for introducing the speakers at each stop. I described it as a traveling road show because an entourage consisting of lobbyists and others who had some role in government would travel with the group around the state. At each stop, the two principal speakers would make an address to a crowd that varied from fifty to several hundred, depending on the size of the city or town. State legislators from the area also attended. In 1977, we visited nineteen towns and cities in Georgia over a ten-day period. While it took time away from my law practice, I enjoyed my activities as chair of this council.

After serving for several years as chair of the Governmental Council, I relinquished that position and was appointed to the board of directors of the chamber. I served in that position for several years until the chamber merged with the Georgia Business and Industry Association to form the Business Council of Georgia.

Other Political Endeavors

Part of being involved in politics is feeling obligated to support your friends when they run for public office. I experienced that in regard to several friends. I first supported Buddy Darden when he successfully ran for student body president at the University of Georgia. He was a former Russell intern whom I met while at UGA. After he graduated, he was elected district attorney in Cobb County and later to the state legislature. When Congressman Larry McDonald was killed in a plane crash as a result of suspected hostile fire, Buddy ran for the seat and was elected to Congress. He served in Congress for well over ten years. I supported him in all of those races. One interesting thing about Buddy and me is that we apparently look a lot alike. People who know both of us frequently confuse us. In 1998 when my law firm merged with the firm at which Buddy was practicing, we became law partners. Not long after that, a partner of the firm came up to me at a reception thinking I was Buddy and proceeded to carry on a conversation about matters he and Buddy were working on at the law firm.

Several years after he ran for the Senate in 1980, my friend Norman Underwood entered the race for governor of Georgia. I supported Norman's candidacy and served on his campaign committee. Unfortunately, he was not successful. Norman would have made a great governor. We have been friends since our UGA days, and that friendship was not affected by the 1980 Senate race. In fact, after that time, our families became much closer. Norman's late wife, Linda, was one of my wife's best friends, and Norman and Linda were godparents to our son. My wife, Ann, was the first harp teacher for Norman and Linda's daughter, Jill. Every year, we try to get together for New Year's Eve dinner with the Dardens, Underwoods, and Fred Stowers and his wife, whom I also met at the University of Georgia. Linda died several years ago after a heroic battle with cancer, and our gatherings continued but are not the same after her passing. Norman has recently married another a fine lady, Harrilee Cheshire, whom we greatly enjoy.

I came to know Mike Bowers in connection with my law practice at the Georgia Public Service Commission. He worked in the attorney general's office and represented the commission in rate cases. Later, he became attorney general of Georgia and ran as a candidate for governor as a Republican. I supported Mike until he was forced to withdraw from the race because of an affair he had while married. At the time of this writing, he is a successful lawyer in Atlanta.

I also supported Max Cleland. Max was an outstanding young Georgian who became a triple amputee as a result of his service in Vietnam. That did not deter him from significant achievements. He was elected to the state legislature and later as secretary of state of Georgia. He was head of the Veterans Administration during the Carter presidency. He then became a United States senator from Georgia. It was during that period that Max sponsored the legislation to rename the national school lunch program the Richard B. Russell National School Lunch Program. I supported Max in all of his races, and he remains a friend today.

It took me over twenty years after I returned to Georgia in 1971 to extricate myself from politics. By the mid-1990s, I had pretty much accomplished that task. Although I continued to contribute financially to various campaigns, both through my law firm's political action committee and individually, it was a good time to get out of politics because it had become so nasty, partisan, and ideologically driven that it turned me off completely. In several presidential elections, I did not vote at all. In the 2008 presidential campaign, I voted for Barack Obama. I thought highly of Senator John McCain and might have voted for him had he not named Sarah Palin as his vice presidential running mate. I was already concerned about his age and health, and to have someone so lacking in experience one heartbeat from the presidency was simply too much for me. While I was disappointed in certain aspects of Obama's presidential leadership in his first term, including giving up on the public option in his health care program without anything in exchange from the Republicans (which made the entire plan subject to constitutional challenge) and failing to support the Simpson-Bowles deficit reduction plan, I concluded that he was a better choice for president for the next four years than Governor Romney and voted for his reelection in 2012. I have always tried to vote for the candidate I believe to be best qualified regardless of party affiliation. I voted for the Republican candidate in the first presidential race in which I voted in 1960 and for Bo Calloway for governor in 1966. I do not regret any of my involvement in politics, but it became less and less attractive to me as the years went by. After I married in 1976 and became further immersed in law practice, I lost any interest in running for Congress. Serving in public office today with the extreme partisan and ideological divides cannot possibly be fun or rewarding.

Senator Herman Talmadge speaking to the Jackson, Georgia Kiwanis Club after being introduced by me during the 1974 campaign.
(Courtesy of Jackson Progress/Argus)

With Murphy Talmadge in 2012, Senator Herman Talmadge's grandson and Governor Eugene Talmadge's great grandson.

With Ann and Senator Max Cleland.

Senator Henry Jackson giving the keynote address in 1974 at the dedication of the Russell Library in Athens. Seated in the foreground are Georgia Governor Jimmy Carter and Senator Russell's sister, Ina Stacy.*

The flyer for the 1977 Georgia Chamber of Commerce Pre-legislative Forum. Participants include Georgia Governor George Busbee, Senator Sam Nunn, Chamber President Ovid Davis and me as Governmental Chairman.

9

Settling into the Practice of Law

When I arrived at Heyman and Sizemore in September 1971 to begin the practice of law, it was a midsized firm by Atlanta standards. It had approximately fifteen lawyers, whereas the largest law firm in Atlanta at the time, the predecessor for what is now King and Spalding, had slightly over fifty lawyers. My initial salary was about $25,000, and my initial billing rate was $20 an hour. By the time I retired at the beginning of 2009, my billing rate was $570 an hour. This reflects the tremendous changes that took place in the practice of law between the time I started and retired. I will discuss some of these changes and the reasons for them in a later chapter of this book.

During summer 1971, while I was working for Senator Gambrell, I took the Georgia bar exam. This was required to become a practicing lawyer in Georgia. I had assumed that because I graduated with decent grades from a nationally recognized law school, I would not need to study for the bar exam. That turned out to be a bad mistake. My longtime law partner, Ted Maloof, had three cardinal rules for the practice of law: 1. Never assume anything. 2. Do not get involved romantically with your secretary. 3. Do not go into business with a client. I had violated the first of these rules by assuming I did not need to study for the Georgia bar examination. I flunked the exam. In addition to being embarrassing and humiliating on a personal level, as the results were published in the newspaper, it also had real-world consequences. Well over 90 percent of the graduates of accredited law schools in Georgia passed the bar exam on their first try. One could not appear in court or give legal advice to clients until after passing the bar exam. I was relegated to doing such things as research in the library or administrative tasks that did not require a lawyer. In addition, my salary was substantially reduced, and it was made clear to me that I would need to pass the bar exam on my next try. Fortunately, I could take the bar exam within a few months after I received the bad results. This time I left nothing to chance. I studied intently and took a bar review course. I was able to pass the bar exam on my second try.

When I joined the firm as its newest associate, the offices of Heyman and Sizemore were located on the third floor of the Fulton Federal Building on Pryor Street in downtown Atlanta. My office was initially in a part of the suite that was referred to as the "dungeon." This was because it had no windows and was one of the least desirable parts of the office. The firm had a meeting every Friday morning at 8:00 AM at which all lawyers, partners and associates, were expected to be in attendance. Associates would discuss the activities in which they were engaged for the week, and everyone would discuss new cases brought into the firm. After that part of the meeting, the associates were excused and the partners met.

On one of the first days I was in the office, Bob Hicks was appointed trustee in a major bankruptcy case. That was a frequent occurrence at that time. As the newest lawyer in the firm and someone who had not even passed the bar exam, I was introduced to bankruptcy law by assisting Bob in this case. I had not the slightest interest in nor knowledge of bankruptcy law. Prior to that time, I had not taken any bankruptcy or creditor rights courses in law school because I never envisioned practicing bankruptcy law. Under Bob's tutelage, however, I came to enjoy that area of practice, and it remained a major part of my practice throughout my career. The other area of practice that I became involved in early in my career was administrative law at the Georgia Public Service Commission (PSC). The PSC was a five-member body that regulated public utilities that sold electricity, gas, or telephone services to the public. Until the trucking industry was deregulated during the Carter administration, it also regulated the trucking industry. The firm and Bob Hicks had a substantial practice in the transportation field and represented both the United Parcel Service and the Purolator Courier Corporation before the PSC. Bob had gained a great deal of experience in administrative law at the federal level when he was the right-hand man to Captain Eddie Rickenbacker when he ran Eastern Airlines. During that time, Bob lived in New York for a number of years. Bob also served a term as president of the Interstate Commerce Commission Practitioners Association.

When I entered the law practice, it was my intent and desire to be a trial lawyer and try jury cases. There were no juries in either the bankruptcy court or in cases before the PSC. Therefore, that part of my practice would have to wait until later. In these early years, I also represented various clients in matters in Washington, DC. I had a good many contacts on Capitol Hill, and Heyman and Sizemore had political law as a major part of its practice. I was often in Washington during those early years, but that part of my practice slowly dissipated.

Immediately across the street from the firm's offices was the historic Kimball House[, the] remnant of a historic dwelling that many years previously had included a hotel or boarding house where political figures stayed when the legislature was in session. Senator Russell's father had stayed there when he served in the Georgia legislature. By the time I started my law practice, the building was a restaurant and bar. Several of the lawyers frequently went to the Kimball House in the evenings after work for cocktails. It was a good way to get to know the lawyers in the firm with whom I did not work on a daily basis.

After having lived in or around Washington, DC, for more than five years, I did not consider Atlanta to be a particularly dangerous city. I often parked in an old garage about a block from the office and worked late at night. One night as I was leaving the office on the way to my car, I stepped on a dead body in the garage. I soon transferred my parking space to a well-lighted surface lot nearby.

My main recreation was playing golf. I joined the Flat Creek Golf Club in Peachtree City, which was located immediately adjacent to my condominium. I played golf there on the weekends, and I also occasionally played golf with my friends from the University of Georgia, Norman Underwood and Fred Stowers. Fred and I usually played on Sunday mornings with an 8:00 AM tee time at his course on Lake Lanier north of Atlanta. Since I was single at the time and often out late on Saturday evenings, I was not in the best of shape to compete with Fred on Sunday mornings. Fred was also a much better golfer than me, but his greatest skill was in negotiating the bet on the first tee before the competition commenced. I seldom prevailed.

In these early years, I dated a number of girls in Atlanta, including Nancy Braselton, Earl Leonard's secretary at the Coca-Cola Company, and Judy Woodruff, a television reporter for the local CBS affiliate in Atlanta. Judy went on to become chief White House correspondent during the Carter administration for one of the three major television networks. She subsequently joined the Mcneil Lehrer News Hour on public television, where she is still a contributor at this time.

While I got off to a rocky start in the practice of law because of my failure to pass the bar exam the first time, I rapidly adjusted and became increasingly comfortable with it. In 1974, I was named a partner at Heyman and Sizemore.

10

Family Life

A Bachelor No More

By mid-1974, I was thirty-two years of age and still single. While I had dated various girls after returning to Georgia, I had not met anyone with whom I felt comfortable making a lifetime commitment. Some of my friends feared I was going to follow Senator Russell's example and be a lifelong bachelor. That changed when I met Ann Laurel Grovenstein. As related in an earlier chapter, I met Ann by accident through her optometrist, Dr. Del Ingram. That was as a result of our chance encounter at the midterm Democratic Convention in Kansas City in late 1974. Shortly after we returned to Georgia, Dr. Ingram and his wife, Bev Ingram, who was a member of the Georgia state Senate, arranged for a blind date for Ann and me. We had dinner at a nice restaurant on the Chattahoochee River in northwest Atlanta. I was immediately attracted to Ann because she was very good-looking. I also quickly learned that she had a work ethic that would have made my grandparents and even Richard Russell proud. She was a high school economics teacher and had a night and weekend job at Rich's Department Store. As if that were not enough to keep her busy, she was an accomplished harpist who had played with the Winston Salem Symphony Orchestra when she and her family lived in North Carolina. She still played harp at special events such as choral works at churches and weddings.

After the blind date, we started dating each other regularly, and I learned more about her family. Both her father and mother came from prominent families in Georgia, although neither of them was particularly affluent. Ann's father was a noted food chemist who, among other things, invented what was to become Nucco Margarine. His father had previously served in the Georgia legislature from Effingham County in Southeast Georgia near Savannah. His family had come to that area a century earlier as part of the Salzburgers who settled there. Ann's mother, the former Ruth Allen, was from Atlanta. Her family had been in the grocery business in Atlanta. An 1881 phone directory for the city of Atlanta had as one of some 150 listings "E. C Allen, Grocer." Ann had one brother, Allen Grovenstein, who worked for a time for the Coca-Cola Company in Atlanta before moving to Florida to work for the Southern Bell Telephone and Telegraph Company.

When Ann was born, her parents lived in Minneapolis. That is where she spent her first few years before moving to Illinois and then to North Carolina. She attended high school in North Carolina and, after graduation, attended Salem College in Winston-Salem, graduating with a degree in history. (Her original major was music before she switched to history.) Soon thereafter, she became a teacher at a girls' private school in Florida. After teaching for several years at that school, she moved to Atlanta, where she accepted a position as teacher and department chair at Headland High School in College Park. She was teaching there when we met.

Ann's father died before I met her. Before his death, he had retired and he and his wife had moved back to Effingham County. Ann's mother, Ruth, continued to live there after her husband's death. Living next door to her was her sister, Pauline Allen, who had worked for many years for the Atlanta school system before retiring. Ann's mother was herself an accomplished harpist, which is how Ann first developed an interest in playing the harp. Her mother was also an accomplished painter. One of her paintings of a river scene still hangs as the principal painting in our living room in Atlanta. Finally, Ann's mother was the best cook I have ever known. She could cook all kinds of different foods, from southern dishes to the most sophisticated offerings. I particularly enjoyed the shrimp dishes she prepared when we visited her.

By the end of 1975, Ann and I had a serious relationship. We decided to take a trip to Europe during the holidays. Since we were not married, this raised the eyebrows of both Ann's mother and my mother. We took the trip anyway. We visited London, Paris, Berlin, and Switzerland. It was a wonderful trip and allowed us to get to know each other better than our hectic schedules in Atlanta permitted. The only unpleasant experience on the trip occurred when we were in Berlin. It was very cold and I was ill. We took a tour of both West Berlin and East Berlin. That was before the Berlin Wall was torn down. When the tour bus left West Berlin to cross the border, the West German tour officials were required to disembark and be replaced by East Berlin tour officials.

The contrasts between West Berlin and East Berlin were startling. West Berlin was a modern city, whereas East Berlin had the appearance of an antiquated city not much different than it must have been at the time of World War II. The last stop on our tour of East Berlin was the Russian War Memorial. By then, my cold was getting the best of me and I decided to stay on the bus. The East German tour officials took this as some kind of slight to the Russian war dead. After they huddled, they told me I would be required to exit the tour bus. I did so reluctantly, and I am sure that did not help my cold as it had started to rain.

Shortly after we returned from our European trip, Ann and I decided to get married. We set the date for April 12, 1976. We were to be married at the Savannah home of a friend of Ann's mother, Don Chambers. Ann's mother had met Don in connection with his gold leafing on one of her harps. He had a shop in his home where he did this kind of work. His home was one of the old row houses on Jones Street in Savannah. April 12 was on a Monday, perhaps an odd day to get married, but we selected that day because I was scheduled to be at the Masters Golf Tournament the entire prior week in Augusta, Georgia. One of my clients, Columbia Nitrogen Corporation, entertained its lawyers, accountants, and other professionals at the golf tournament each year. We would play golf in the mornings at the Augusta Country Club adjacent to the Masters famous A'Men Corner, attend the tournament in the afternoons, and party at night. By the time I arrived in Savannah for our rehearsal dinner late on Sunday, I was sunburned and exhausted. This was at a time when I had a good deal more influence in our relationship than would be the case later, after Ann had observed my obvious lack of judgment on a number of occasions.

What passed as our rehearsal dinner was an evening meal at the Pirates House Restaurant in Savannah. In attendance, in addition to Ann and me, were my parents, Ann's mother, aunt, and brother, plus Chuck and Evelyn Metcalf. The wedding was set for 6:00 PM the following afternoon. Approximately fifty people attended, including family and close friends. My best man was my old roommate in Washington, George Watts, and Ann's matron of honor was her friend from her Florida teaching years, Evelyn Metcalf. Since it was holy week, we had to import a minister from Atlanta to conduct the ceremony. I have never been a fan of big weddings, so our wedding day suited me fine. Ann deserved better, but she seemed pleased as well.

On the day following the wedding, we left for our honeymoon, which was another example of my less than stellar judgment. As a result of Ann's employment at Rich's , we planned our honeymoon trip through its travel department, utilizing Ann's employee discount in the process. When we met with the gentleman at the travel office, I noticed a brochure of a resort in the Dominican Republic that had a picture of a seaside golf course. I convinced Ann that the Dominican Republic would be a good place for our honeymoon. Little did she know what was in store for us. We flew from Savannah to Miami and then on to Santo Domingo. It was then about an hour and a half by jeep over extremely poor roads to the resort, Casa de Campo. As we were approaching the resort, I noticed an unusual smell permeating the air. It was coming from a sugar refinery located immediately adjacent to the resort. When the wind blew the right way, or the wrong way depending on your viewpoint, the sweet smell of refined sugar was quite prominent. It did not bother me much at first, but I must admit it became annoying during the week of our honeymoon. The resort was quite large and had a number of restaurants that visitors would access by boarding small buses. The buses also contained the workers who worked in the sugar refinery. If our honeymoon trip had occurred later in our lives, this arrangement would have been annoying, but as newlyweds, we did not mind.

We planned to fly back to Atlanta on Saturday because I had to be in court on Monday. When we arrived at the airport in Santo Domingo Saturday morning, we were told our airplane was "sick." When I asked the airline officials when they thought the airplane would be well, they were quite evasive. I became worried that it might still be sick the next day. In one of the few good decisions I made about our honeymoon, I decided to explore alternative flights to get out of the Dominican Republic. I determined that there was a flight on Saturday afternoon to New York. We flew to New York and then on to Atlanta Saturday night. The flight to New York was on a huge aircraft that was virtually empty. We had the equivalent of first-class seats.

Shortly after we arrived back in Atlanta, we had a most distressing and shocking development. Someone broke into Ann's apartment and burned it. We had decided to keep the apartment for a short time before moving into my condo in Peachtree City. The fire essentially burned all of Ann's clothes and other belongings. She was devastated. I tried to make a joke of it by telling her it was probably one of her old boyfriends and that at least she would be able to buy all new clothes. She did not see the humor. The police never determined the identity of the responsible party. With the apartment gone, we lived in my condo for several months. Ann continued to teach, and she decided to finish a Master's degree at Georgia State University in Atlanta. Since many of her classes would be at night, we decided to buy a condominium at Landmark Condominiums located at 215 Piedmont Avenue, which is across the street from the site of the hospital where I was born in 1942. The Landmark is an approximately twenty-five-story condominium building. Our condo was on the twentieth floor. A number of legislators stayed at the Landmark when the legislature was in session, and it was also the home of at least one federal judge. We lived at the Landmark until 1979, when we bought a house in the Buckhead section of Atlanta, where we still reside today. High-rise condominium living was fine with me, but it did not suit Ann. The purchase of the house turned out to be a good decision because we bought it at a good price, and it is located within easy commuting distance of downtown Atlanta, where my office remained for my entire career.

Ann and I traveled frequently in the years after we married. I remember a trip to California where we stayed at the famous Pebble Beach Lodge and I played golf on the Pebble Beach Golf Course. We also took a trip to New England, where we stayed at bed and breakfasts throughout the area. One of the highlights of the trip was a visit to Camden, Maine, where Ann had taken harp lessons from the famous harpist, Carlos Salzedo, when she was a teenager. We also stayed in Boston for several days on that trip. Later, we started an annual trip in the winter to Puerto Rico, where we stayed at a resort about an hour from San Juan. The resort, Palmas Del Mar, was located right on the ocean and had a good golf course that I enjoyed playing. The three or four holes that were the furthest from their clubhouse had armed guards to protect the golfers.

Miracle of a Son

Within a few years after we were married, Ann and I decided to start a family. Unfortunately, our first attempt ended in a miscarriage. By early 1982, Ann was pregnant again. It was a very difficult pregnancy. She was on bed rest much of the time, and the doctors were concerned as to whether the pregnancy could be sustained for nine months. In late August, the doctors decided that the baby would have to be taken by Caesarean section at Piedmont Hospital. We knew the baby was a boy from tests that had been conducted, and we decided to name him Garrett McPherson Campbell. He was born on August 30, 1982, approximately three months premature. This was a level of prematurity at which most surviving babies were severely handicapped. Many did not survive at all. Many who did survive were blind because the eyes and nervous system are the last to fully develop in a baby and because of the high levels of oxygen taken through a respirator. Since we did not receive any counseling on what we could expect, we had no idea what was in store for us and Garrett. It is perhaps just as well that we did not receive such counseling because we would not have aborted the pregnancy in any event, and it would simply have been a cause of greater concern during what was already a stressful time.

Garrett's head doctor at Piedmont, Dr. Leonard Sacks, recommended to me immediately after Garrett's birth that he be transferred to the Scottish Rite Children's Hospital in North Atlanta, since it had a much more extensive neonatal unit than Piedmont. Since Ann was still unconscious as a result of the birth, I made the decision to accept the recommendation and have Garrett moved that afternoon to Scottish Rite. It would be Garrett's home for the next three months, including two months in intensive care on a respirator. When he was born, he weighed just over two pounds. He was kept in an incubator device, and we were not allowed to touch him for a substantial period. He was cared for by an extremely competent and caring team of neonatal nurses with whom we became close friends. They are real heroes. I cannot imagine working with those babies every day only to have one die, which happened several times while Garrett was in the hospital. We were fortunate indeed.

Within a couple of weeks after Garrett was born, he developed a heart problem that required a surgical procedure known as a patent ductus arteriosis (PDA) ligation. It was difficult for me to understand how a surgeon could operate on a heart within a baby so small. It was decided that the operation should be conducted at the Northside Hospital across the street from Scottish Rite. During Garrett's early days, Father Dan Mathews, the rector at St. Luke's Episcopal Church where Ann was a member, was a source of constant strength. He is the finest man of the cloth I have ever known. After he completed his mission at St. Luke's, he became the rector at Trinity Episcopal Church in New York at the foot of Wall Street. It is reputed to be the best-endowed church in the United States, with extensive real estate holdings in Manhattan. Father Mathews baptized Garrett and prayed with the three of us on more than one occasion when it appeared that he would not survive. As a result of the heart operation at Northside, Garrett's weight dipped below two pounds. He was in an intensive and critical condition. One occurrence that would have been humorous if it had not been such a stressful time took place when we visited Garrett after his surgery. A nurse greeting us and taking us to the intensive care unit said, "Oh, you must be Garrett's grandparents." We felt more like great-grandparents.

I have always been reluctant to question the judgment of doctors. That is one of my many weaknesses. Ann, on the other hand, has always believed that the first line of defense for a patient is for the patient or his or her caregivers to be intensively involved in medical decisions. In the period after his heart surgery, Garrett seemed to experience a series of ups and downs. Ann questioned whether part of the problem was some of the drugs he was given. She questioned the doctors with respect to one drug in particular that she thought might be contributing to his problems. At her insistence, the doctors quit administering that drug on a trial basis, and Garrett seemed to begin to improve almost immediately. He was not out of danger by any means, but he seemed to stabilize. One of the many problems he had was a wild swing in his heart rate from a very low heart rate[, called bradycardia, to a very high heart rate, called tachycardia. It is unusual for premature babies to have both, but Garrett did. He was kept on a monitor that would activate if the heart rate dipped below or rose above a certain level. The alarms were not infrequent. When we were finally able to take Garrett home after some three months, he remained on a heart monitor for many more months.

After about two months, we were finally able to hold Garrett for brief periods, as he was then off the respirator. He had started to gain some weight and was looking more like a real baby. By early December, he was ready to go home. It was one of the best Christmas presents we had ever received. Ann seldom left him in the months after he was released from the hospital, and when we did go out, we would hire one of his neonatal nurses to babysit. We would not have been comfortable with any other sitter because of Garrett's condition and the heart monitor.

By the time we celebrated Garrett's first birthday on August 30, 1983, he had made a lot of progress. He still had serious difficulties, including being legally blind, having mild cerebral palsy, and being hyperactive. However, given the condition of some of the other babies who were born about the time he arrived and who survived, he was a miracle of a son. One couple with whom we became close friends had a son born about the same time as Garrett. He is completely blind and so severely handicapped that they had to place him in a children's home in Alabama, presumably for the rest of his life. For several years after Garrett was born, we attended reunions of premature babies who had been born at Piedmont. Each time, we were reminded of how incredibly fortunate we were with Garrett. He was a joy and was making a significant positive influence on our family.

One problem that Garrett struggled with was eating solid food. We were quite concerned about this problem. A friend of Ann's in North Carolina recommended that we visit the Bowman Gray Medical School in Winston-Salem to consult with a doctor there. This doctor suggested that we visit the National Institutes of Health in suburban Washington, which was conducting a study on eating and swallowing problems. We visited NIH, where Garrett was examined. They thought his problem might be caused by the manner in which his feeding tube had been positioned when he was a newborn. They speculated that he would probably grow out of it, which turned out to be the case. Today, Garrett has almost completely overcome this difficulty. It was not easy, and there were several stops and starts. At one point when he was in high school, his class studied how to administer first aid when someone chokes on food. After hearing this lesson, Garrett was unable or unwilling to eat any solid food for a week. Fortunately, he was soon back to normal.

When Garrett was seven years old, he and Ann were at an eye doctor appointment at Emory University in connection with the continued monitoring of his vision problems. A tornado alert sounded while they were in the doctor's office, and everyone, including the doctors, was ushered into a shelter until the danger passed. While they were in the shelter, the doctor noticed that Garrett was hyperactive and asked Ann if he had been evaluated. Several doctors in Atlanta had seen him but given us no definitive results. The doctor told Ann of a program run by a classmate of his in medical school that did complete evaluations of special-needs children. He recommended that we consider admitting Garrett to that hospital program. After visiting Johns Hopkins in Baltimore, we decided to have Garrett evaluated in the program. This required leaving him for a period of four to five weeks, which was a traumatic experience for all three of us. He had not been away from Ann for any period. During the first week, the parents could not see the children at all, and visits thereafter depended on how well the child was adjusting to the program. After a difficult beginning, Garrett adjusted well, and the program helped him in a number of respects, including providing assistance with respect to his eating problem. In addition, we received an extensive evaluation on what the future likely held for Garrett and us. The bottom line was that he should be able to finish high school. Attending college was an open question. While it was not easy to leave Garrett on the first day, the experience was worthwhile for our whole family.

When Garrett was about four or five, we placed him in an informal school that was conducted for about five students at a woman's home. This was Garrett's equivalent of kindergarten, and he went to that school for one year, interacting with other children. When the time came for Garrett to go to elementary school, we chose the Howard School on Ponce de Leon Avenue in Atlanta, a private school for special-needs children where Garrett attended until he reached the age for high school. At this point, Ann and I decided to try North Atlanta High School, a public magnet school for the performing arts located within about a mile of our house. Among Garrett's greatest interests were music, theater, and film. While we were somewhat uneasy about placing him in a large public high school, we felt that it was a good opportunity for him to explore his interests.

Since Garrett had a favorable experience his first year, we decided to leave him at North Atlanta for the duration of high school. He was active in the North Atlanta Chorus, which performed in New York in addition to other venues. He also participated in the theater at North Atlanta and enjoyed it greatly. Well-known figures often visited the school. One was the cellist Yo-Yo Ma, whom Garrett met and talked with about his career. While Garrett did well in literature and related subjects, his most challenging classes were in mathematics. We were fortunate that his loving mother was a former schoolteacher and knew most of the tricks employed by students to get out of studying. She may have even learned a few new ones from Garrett. To help with his math problems, we hired a tutor. Ann decided that he should attempt to earn a regular high school diploma, which would require about two additional years in high school. He successfully completed that program as well.

After we purchased our home in Atlanta, we retained the condo in Peachtree City as a weekend place. Since Ann had become a full-time mother and caregiver for Garrett, he and I started going to Peachtree City together on the weekends so I could see more of him and Ann could get a break. Our next-door neighbor in Peachtree City, Eddie Miller, owned the local distributorship for Club Car golf carts. He always had a fancy golf cart at his condo and took Garrett on rides. Peachtree City is a planned community similar to Reston, Virginia. It has an extensive network of cart paths that go throughout the city and the surrounding area. In 1988, I decided to purchase a golf cart primarily for Garrett and me to use in Peachtree City and for me to use when playing golf. Some of our best times were spent riding the golf cart during our weekend visits.

While Garrett was legally blind, he could see well enough to get around and could see the blackboard at school from the front row. His eyesight, however, was a major obstacle to participating in sports. Baseball was out of the question. Even golf was a challenge. I talked him into taking golf lessons on our visits to Peachtree City, but he never had much of an interest in it. One sport we enjoyed was basketball. We had a basketball goal erected in our backyard in Atlanta, and Garrett and I competed to see who could successfully hit the most shots. While I would shoot from roughly twice as far away as Garrett, he actually became quite proficient and held his own against me.

When Garrett was growing up, he developed a number of interests that became a focal point of our lives. One was music. To this day, he loves classical music and listens to it every day. He also became interested in film. His favorite actor was Jack Nicholson and his favorite director was Stanley Kubrick. We often went to movies. A friend of Ann's in North Carolina recommended the National Public Radio syndicated program, *A Prairie Home Companion with Garrison Keillor*, since it featured not only classical music and other kinds of music but also skits, impersonations, and sound effects. Garrett grew quite interested in the program, which aired on Saturday nights on the radio, and I developed an even greater interest in it. While Garrett eventually moved on to other things, I am still an avid listener of the program each week. During the time Garrett was most interested in it, we had an opportunity to go to St. Paul, Minnesota, the home base of the program. Tickets are difficult to come by, and there is a long waiting list. One of my law partners, Barbara Gallo, was able to secure front-row tickets for us to attend the program through her husband, Tom, a partner in the Atlanta office of a Minneapolis-based law firm that was a substantial supporter of public radio. From our excellent vantage point, Garrett could hear and see the program well. We thoroughly enjoyed it. Thereafter, any time the program came to Atlanta, we usually attended. We even attended one of the programs in Birmingham, Alabama, after Garrett moved there.

We also occasionally went to New York so that Garrett could attend Broadway theater productions and performances at Lincoln Center. A scary but revealing incident took place on one of our visits to Lincoln Center. When the program ended, Garrett wanted to meet one of the performers. In the process, we became separated from him. After searching frantically for him in the lobby, we contacted the security detail at Lincoln Center. Garrett was nowhere to be found. Ann was in favor of calling the New York City police, but for some reason I had the idea that he had gone back to our hotel about twenty blocks away on Broadway. I finally convinced Ann that we should at least check the hotel before calling the police. When we arrived, we found Garrett in our room watching TV. Once Ann recovered from her anxiety and anger, she and I were both impressed that when he could not find us, he had the presence of mind to try to make his own way back to the hotel. He told us that he had gone to the front of Lincoln Center to try to find us and then, failing that, to catch a taxicab. Because of his eyesight problems, he carried his impaired vision cane, and one of the operators of the horse and buggy tourist facilities asked if they could help him. He told them the name of the hotel, and the operator gave him a buggy ride back to the hotel. Though Garrett did not have enough money to pay the normal charges, the driver accepted what he had as full payment.

When Garrett graduated from high school, we had to decide what he would do next. He took the Scholastic Aptitude Test, a prerequisite for college. We visited several colleges, including Lagrange College and Reinhardt College, where my mother had finished her high school years. His SAT scores were excellent in verbal, over 675, but poor in math, less than 300. As opposed to enrolling him in college, we decided it was better to enroll him in a program in Birmingham, Alabama, that taught independent living. He had become so dependent on his parents, particularly Ann, that we felt he would struggle in college and have a bad experience. The program in Birmingham, run by the Horizon School, was established as a part of the University of Alabama at Birmingham. The school later separated from UAB and became independent. Its students were primarily special-needs children, some of whom had tried college, who needed help learning to live independently and perhaps to earn a living. Garrett was somewhat reluctant about this drastic move, but he agreed to it. His first year was difficult for a variety of reasons, including his eyesight problems, roommate problems, and girl problems. Most students encounter and learn how to handle similar issues in high school, but he never had those experiences. After the first year, he adjusted well and completed the three-year program. He liked Birmingham and lives in the Five Points area adjacent to the UAB campus and medical school. This area was less challenging than Atlanta and easier for him to navigate with his vision problems. He liked Birmingham so much that he decided to stay there after he graduated. He enjoys the same types of activities he did in Atlanta, including going to the symphony and seeing movies. His friends are the students at Horizon as well as other people he has met. He volunteers twice a week at a local church in the seniors program, which he enjoys.

Since Garrett is now off on his own and living independently of us, Ann and I retained a service in Birmingham, Triumph Services, that looks in on him at least once a week and more often if necessary. Since he cannot drive an automobile, they take him grocery shopping once a week and also provide counseling or other services as needed. Garrett has adjusted well to this routine and lives a happy life there. While he could have come back to Atlanta, we saw no reason to disrupt a settled and satisfactory existence. We visit him periodically in Birmingham, and he comes back to Atlanta from time to time, including all holidays. He has accomplished far more than we thought was possible for him, even recently completing the script for a short film.

One of the unfortunate side effects of being an extremely premature child is continuing eyesight problems. As a result of the extent of his prematurity and the large amount of oxygen he received during the first weeks of his life, Garrett has almost no vision in his left eye and far less than perfect vision in his right eye. His eyesight is monitored on a continued basis for changes. The eye doctors warned us about possible issues with his retina. Premature children are more prone to detached retinas in their eyes than full-term children. Cataracts are also more frequent. The doctors advised us about the danger signs of such problems. On Easter Sunday in 1997, Garrett reported to Ann that he was seeing shading in his right eye. At the time, I was at our condo in Peachtree City preparing for an upcoming trial. It was my habit when I had an important trial to go to Peachtree City with my case files and seclude myself to avoid distractions. Ann called me and said that she was taking Garrett to Emory to have his eye examined. I rushed to Emory as well.

Garrett's problem was diagnosed as a detached retina, which required immediate surgery to avoid complete loss of eyesight. The chief retina surgeon at Emory was with his family in church for Easter services. He was summoned back to the hospital to conduct the surgery. It was our first meeting with Dr. Dan Martin, who is one of the finest doctors and one of the kindest people I have ever known. He explained after the surgery that Garrett's alert reaction with respect to the signs in his eye and our quick transportation of him to the hospital had permitted surgery that probably solved the problem. It would still require close monitoring, but Garrett seemed to have dodged another bullet.

In 2009, while Garrett was at home visiting during the Thanksgiving holidays, he told us that he was experiencing similar symptoms in his left eye. Dr. Martin, in the meantime, had left Emory to become the head of the prestigious Cole Eye Institute at the Cleveland Clinic in Cleveland, Ohio. We took Garrett to another doctor in Atlanta, who stated that he could not tell if Garrett had retina problems in his left eye because he had a substantial cataract that obscured the view of the retina. He recommended that the cataract be removed. When we were back in his office a week or so later to prepare for the procedure, he looked at Garrett's right eye that had undergone retina surgery in 1997 and said that it looked great. Garrett then told him that he was actually beginning to see some changes in the right eye. Upon closer examination, the doctor said he saw the beginning signs of a tear in the retina, which he quickly repaired with a laser in the office.

Neither Garrett, Ann, nor I particularly liked this new eye doctor. His initial failure to diagnose the problem in Garrett's right eye concerned us, and the hasty nature of the procedure he performed did not give us much comfort either. Desperate to preserve the vision in Garrett's right eye, we made an appointment with Dr. Martin and flew to Cleveland, Ohio, to see him. Dr. Martin diagnosed the beginning of a hole in the retina of the right eye and performed surgery a day later. After such surgery, it is necessary for the patient to sit or sleep upright, which of course made it difficult for Garrett to rest. After seeing Dr. Martin once more, we were ready to return to Georgia, where he arranged for a follow-up review of Garrett's eye by a doctor he recommended at Emory.

After retina surgery, a patient cannot fly on an airplane for some time because of the pressure in the eyes from flying. Therefore, we rented a car and started our trip back to Atlanta shortly after noon on Friday. We stopped Friday night south of Lexington, Kentucky, and checked into a hotel. Garrett was doing fine and we went out to eat dinner. When he awakened the next morning, he complained about a headache and a high heart rate. We ate breakfast and started the rest of our trip home, though our progress was delayed by an overnight snowstorm. When we reached Knoxville, Tennessee, about one o'clock in the afternoon, we stopped for lunch. Ann, who has a medical condition I will discuss below, carries a machine that can monitor pulse and heart rate. She took Garrett's at our lunch stop and discovered that his heart rate was above 160 beats per minute (bpm), which is abnormally high, particularly when the person is at rest. We nonetheless forged on southward and arrived in Atlanta at about seven o'clock that evening.

Ann thought that a prednisone-based eye drop Garrett was taking as a result of the surgery might cause the elevated heart rate. She called Dr. Martin in Cleveland and our local doctor, who discounted the eye drop theory and advised us to take Garrett to the emergency room. We arrived at the Piedmont Hospital ER at approximately nine o'clock Saturday evening. Garrett entered under his own power and was calm and even joking. Within an hour, he would be on the verge of death. His heart rate rose above 260 bpm. The hospital did not have available the preferred drug to suppress the heart rate and had to use a substitute drug. In addition, Garrett received substantial volumes of fluid. Soon his breathing was compromised and his lungs began to fill with fluid, which caused respiratory failure. He was placed on a respirator, and the doctors made it clear that his condition was extremely critical. This was, of course, quite a shock since he had entered the hospital on his own just two hours earlier.

Throughout Saturday night, his condition continued to deteriorate. Since the respirator did not appear to be doing the job, the medical personnel replaced it with a later model. It literally looked as if someone were jumping up and down on Garrett's chest. The new respirator slightly improved his condition. By midday Sunday, he had stabilized and was no longer in danger of imminent death, although he was still considered critical. Ann and I went home for a couple of hours since our house is within several miles of Piedmont Hospital. We were, of course, praying constantly, and Ann contacted our friends to ask them to pray for Garrett.

When we returned to the hospital Sunday afternoon, his condition was stabilized but not improving. That was the case for the next several days. The biggest issue was pinpointing the reason for the rapid heart rate. Since his tachycardia and bradycardia as a newborn, Garrett had showed no evidence of heart problems. Infectious disease doctors and heart specialists consulted on his case. For a while, the infectious disease doctors thought he might have the H1N1 virus or the swine flu, which was a new development at the time. The Centers for Disease Control and Prevention (CDC) was in the process of authorizing an experimental drug for swine flu patients who were in imminent danger of death. The Piedmont Hospital officials asked for permission to give Garrett that drug. By the time it was approved , Garrett was better. We decided not to accept the drug since it was not fully tested and no one knew the possible side effects. When final test results were received, it did not appear that Garrett had an infection. The heart doctors also did not believe that he had a noticeable heart problem. They speculated that the rapid heart rate was caused by Garrett being under the pressure of the eye surgery, losing hours of sleep, and taking the automobile trip back to Atlanta immediately thereafter. They made it clear, however, that this was merely speculation.

Garrett gradually improved. Because he had fought the respirator, they decided to basically paralyze him for a time. They had some difficulty getting him out of the state of paralysis and weaning him from the respirator. After about a week, they had accomplished both of these tasks, and he was transferred from intensive care to a regular hospital room. One concern was the effect this extended stay in the hospital bed might have on his eye surgery. Piedmont retained a retina specialist to examine Garrett. The specialist reported that the retina surgery seemed to be holding. However, we learned that Garrett had developed blood clots in both legs because of the long period he was in the bed. They gave him blood thinners for the clots. By the second week in December, Garrett was released from the hospital and went home. Ann and I agreed that his homecoming was the best Christmas present we had received since Garrett initially came home from the hospital as a baby. We decided not to exchange Christmas presents that year. Garrett stayed at home recuperating with us until after the first of the year, when he returned to Birmingham.

When we were in Cleveland for the retina surgery, Dr. Martin had confirmed that Garrett had cataracts on both eyes. While Dr. Martin did not perform cataract surgery, we decided to have the procedure done in Cleveland so he would be on standby if anything happened to the retina. The cataract removal went smoothly in 2009, and we returned to Atlanta without further incident. Garrett has not had any significant new problems with his vision since the cataract removal, and his distance eyesight is now actually better than it was before the second retina surgery.

Loss of Family Members

During the Senate campaign in 1980, Ann's mother, Ruth, was diagnosed with pancreatic cancer. The prognosis was not good. After surgery and treatment, she moved in with us for her final months. We rented a hospital bed and placed it in our den. Since she had not lived in Atlanta in many years, she did not have a doctor in Atlanta. We persuaded the longtime doctor for the Campbell family, Tully Blalock, to take her on as a patient. This was quite a concession on his part as he was nearing the end of his career as a doctor and was not taking new patients. This old-school doctor came to our house on a number of occasions to give Ruth pain shots and other treatments. His care made a big difference in her last months.

Not long after Ann's mother died, her aunt and her mother's sister, Pauline Allen, had a recurrence of her breast cancer. She died in less than a year. These two deaths were sad for all of us but particularly devastating for Ann, who had already lost her father. More bad health news came in 1999 when her brother, Allen, also died. As a young man, he had contracted Hodgkin's disease, for which he received extensive radiation treatment. Apparently, this caused lasting damage to his heart, and he suffered four heart attacks immediately prior to his death. By this time, Allen had moved to Florida, remarried, and had a daughter, Christie. Allen was buried alongside his father, who had died many years earlier, and his mother. They were buried in the cemetery in Guyton, Georgia.

I also experienced difficult health news in my own family during these years. Like Richard Russell, my father had been a heavy smoker earlier in his life. In fact, he had smoked the worst kind of cigarettes—unfiltered Camels. He quit smoking on advice of his doctors in the 1960s, but, like Senator Russell, he did not avoid the scourge of emphysema. My father's disease followed a pattern similar to Richard Russell['s]. As the years went by, his breathing became labored and he had difficulty clearing his lungs. He had essentially the same treatment Russell received, and it undoubtedly postponed death for a substantial period. By 1990, he was in a seriously weakened condition. After my mother joined him in retirement in the 1980s, they moved to my mother's home place outside Bremen, Georgia, and built a home across the road from my mother's sister, Aunt Nig. During my father's last illness, my mother took care of him and was his only caregiver. He died in peace at home.

My older brother, Borden, died in 2002. It was perhaps the saddest of all these deaths, as his was a life of unfulfilled promise. He was without question the ablest of the three Campbell boys. He was the valedictorian of his high school class and finished number four in his class at the University of Georgia. He did so well in chemistry and related courses that he was talked into applying to medical school. He applied to and was accepted at the Medical College of Georgia in Augusta, Georgia. While he was in medical school, however, his mental problems surfaced. In his second year, he started having phobias that the government was conspiring against him. Soon he became so distracted that his medical school grades suffered, and it was not long before he withdrew from school. He taught public school for a year in Butts County and for another year in Clayton County south of Atlanta. This was during the height of the Vietnam War, which he also thought was part of the government conspiracy. He fled to Canada to evade the draft, where he lived until the war ended. He then moved back to Georgia and lived with my parents for a few years. They tried to get treatment for him, including at one point having him admitted to a mental institution. He refused to take any of the medication, however, because he thought it was a part of the government conspiracy. The medical personnel at the mental institution said they could not hold him against his will because they had judged him not to be a threat to himself or others.

It was not long before friction with my father resulted in Borden moving to Atlanta, where he lived in a series of substandard apartments for many years. He eventually became an alcoholic after he befriended the homeless people of Atlanta. My parents could not give him spending money because he would either use it to buy liquor or the street people would get him drunk and steal his money. I got him released from jail on a number of occasions for public drunkenness. He did maintain his intellectual curiosity and went to the library in Atlanta to check out and read numerous books. My mother or I visited him at least once a month, but it was never a pleasant experience. We finally found a place for him to live that was a great improvement—the Ponce de Leon Hotel on Ponce de Leon Avenue not far from the old Sears Roebuck store location where we shopped on our trips to Atlanta many years earlier. Transients coming into the hotel in the evening after hours were prohibited, and this policy was strictly enforced. This was the best living arrangement Borden had during the time he lived in Atlanta. An African-American lady who worked at the hotel took an interest in him and kept my mother and me informed if he did not return to his room at night or if he had other needs. We arranged for him to be able to eat at a nearby cafeteria, which served southern foods that he liked and which we could pay directly without giving the money to him.

In September 2002, I received a telephone call from the lady at the hotel one afternoon while sitting in my law office. She told me that Borden had collapsed on the street and was taken to the hospital. She was not positive which hospital but assumed it was Grady Memorial Hospital, which was the large public hospital that treated most of the indigents or the uninsured. I rushed to Grady but could not find him. After about an hour, I concluded he must have been taken to a different hospital. In the meantime, Ann was calling the other hospitals in Atlanta and was told by the emergency room at the Crawford Long Hospital that an unidentified white male, about sixty years of age, had been brought to the emergency room earlier that afternoon. He fit the general description of Borden. I went to Crawford Long and found Borden unconscious in the emergency room.

I was later told that he had a viral brain infection that was probably fatal. While he was eventually transferred to a room in the hospital, he never regained consciousness. He died several days thereafter. He was buried in the cemetery in Bremen next to my father. When we were growing up, he seemed to have everything going for him. He was an excellent athlete and very smart. While the medicine to treat paranoid schizophrenia was not as good then as it is now, I am confident that he could have been helped if we had persuaded or forced him to take the medication. Instead, a promising life was lost.

A Cruel Disease

In 2003, Ann complained of pain in her hands that began to interfere with her sleep. She went to her doctor, but there was no conclusive diagnosis. Having learned from our medical experiences with Garrett, she knew that a patient is his or her own best advocate. She researched her symptoms on the Internet and learned about scleroderma, an autoimmune disease that occurs when the body's immune system treats the blood vessels and other healthy tissues as an attack on the body and starts to fight them. This results in the deposit of a substance called collagen, which is a part of the healing process. The difficulty with scleroderma is that there is no infection, but the body's immune system, for reasons unknown, continues to act as if attacked and deposits more collagen. As would be the case if you cut yourself, the deposit of collagen causes a hardening of the areas of the cut to enhance the healing process. With scleroderma, however, there is no healing process and no way to stop the attack of the immune system. The causes of scleroderma are unknown, as it is fairly rare and little research has been done.

Convinced by her own research that scleroderma was a real possibility, Ann made an appointment with a rheumatologist, Dr. Hays Wilson. He confirmed the diagnosis. We visited two places where people have done research on scleroderma and are knowledgeable about cutting-edge treatments: one in Baltimore, Maryland, at Johns Hopkins University and one at the University of Houston adjacent to the M. D. Anderson Cancer Center. We decided that Ann would be treated at Johns Hopkins. The head of the practice there and one of the leading scleroderma researchers in the country is Dr. Fredrick Wigley. We promptly made an appointment for Ann to see him. A visit to his reception room is not a comforting experience. We saw many people in the reception room in wheelchairs, on oxygen, and/or with amputations of fingers, feet, or limbs. This was a particularly devastating diagnosis for Ann because it meant she would never be able to play the harp again. The three large harps in our music room have been largely unused since her diagnosis.

The details Dr. Wigley told us about the disease were alarming and comforting at the same time. He told us that the disease generally runs its course in about six years and is often confined to the hands without spreading internally or to other parts of the body. He did say, however, that in some people the disease spreads to internal organs such as the heart and lungs and can be fatal. He said some research was being done, including his own, but there was no known cure for scleroderma. Most of the treatments were designed to slow the disease. Because the pain in the hands is so intense and continuous, it is necessary for patients with scleroderma to take painkillers on a regular basis. Cold temperatures, which compromise blood flow to the fingers, particularly heighten pain. The principal painkiller prescribed for Ann was Fentanyl, which can be administered two ways: through patches placed on the body or through a lollipop-type sucker placed in the mouth. The advantage of the latter method is that the painkiller gets into the bloodstream quicker. The disadvantage is that the flow is not as steady and regulated as with the patches. Also, one effect of scleroderma is to harden the skin on the hands and potentially other parts of the body, which interferes with the body's ability to absorb painkillers through the patches. Ann experienced substantial hardening not only in her hands but also on her feet and back. Thus Ann used the lollipops to help control her symptoms.

Ann has done far better with the disease that I would have if I had been in her shoes. However, it has been a trying experience. There is no known cure, and her pain has continued for years, becoming quite intense at times. She has also lost some use of her hands. For example, not only can she not play the harp, but she has difficulty opening a bottle or performing other tasks that require dexterity. When the disease began cutting off circulation to one of her fingers, enhancing the risk of infection, she had that finger amputated. Fortunately, there has not been widespread and serious involvement of her internal organs. While no treatment does away with the effects of the disease, researchers in Germany used an existing treatment (IVIG) whereby a patient is periodically given parts of blood from up to about fifty different donors in an effort to confuse the body's immune system and turn off the deposit of collagen. The treatments are very expensive—more than $6,000 for each one. When the disease became very pronounced and painful, Ann had five of these treatments each month at Piedmont Hospital for a substantial period. She thought they helped in terms of mitigating the effects of the disease. We were fortunate to have good medical insurance through my law firm to pay almost all of the cost of these treatments and her other expenses.

Dr. Wilson in Atlanta and Dr. Wigley in Baltimore continue to treat Ann. Her scleroderma and resulting pain have diminished. Today she is largely off the drugs. She does not use any of the lollipops and only uses the patches infrequently in small doses.

While Ann has suffered greatly with the disease, she has been lucky. The sister of one of my law partner's wife died of scleroderma while Ann was undergoing her treatment. It had spread internally to various organs. Ann appears to have had some minimal internal organ involvement, but this has not compromised any of her essential organs. For that, we are exceedingly grateful. We both hope she is coming to the end of her battle with scleroderma. If so, she is entitled to a tremendous amount of the credit for conquering this disease and its related problems. She has become an avid supporter of the Scleroderma Foundation in Boston and of the local chapter in Atlanta.

Mother Turns 100

My mother was one of the most amazing people I have ever met. She was born in 1910 on a farm in Northwest Georgia and grew up during the Depression. Her father had received little formal education, and he was determined that his children would at least have an opportunity to graduate from high school. When my mother was about eight years old, he decided that she should attend the schools in Bremen, Georgia, as opposed to what he viewed as the less adequate small rural school several miles from their house. Each morning , he would hitch up the family's horse and buggy, and she would drive it some six miles to Bremen to the house of some kinfolks and then walk to the school from there. After school in the afternoon, she would ride the horse and buggy home. During her junior year in high school, a more affluent uncle offered to pay her expenses if she attended her senior year at the Academy, which was part of Reinhardt College in Waleska, Georgia. She graduated from high school there. As a graduation present, another uncle gave her a typewriter and an instruction booklet. He wanted her to have job skills so that she would not have to be a housewife if she preferred to work. This was at a time when few women worked outside the home.

After graduating from high school and learning to use the typewriter, Mother accepted several secretarial jobs for the Southern Railroad in Birmingham, Alabama, and in New Orleans, Louisiana. When the Depression hit, she returned home and soon landed a job in Rome, Georgia. She met my father, who was working in the county agent's office there at the time. He had a business degree from Georgia Tech and had been hired to help administer the new farm assistance programs that were part of Franklin Roosevelt's New Deal. My mother and father married in 1937. My father became interested in becoming a county agent and decided to go back to college to get an agriculture degree at the University of Georgia. They moved to Athens, Georgia, where my mother took a job to help support my father while he worked on his agriculture degree.

After graduating from the University of Georgia, my father took jobs with the Cooperative Extension Service and the Tennessee Valley Authority in North Georgia. During this time, my mother continued to work outside the home when she was not giving birth to their three sons. I can never remember a time when my mother was not working full-time until she was in her seventies. When I was growing up, she worked six days a week and into the evening on Wednesday and Saturday. She probably would not have retired in her seventies, but the owner of the department store where she worked died, and his estate decided to sell the store. She reluctantly retired. After my parents moved to Bremen and my father died, my mother announced one day that she was moving to a retirement home that she had already selected. We had not encouraged her to do so; she made the decision entirely on her own.

I thought she would finally be able to rest and relax after years of working and being the sole caregiver of my father during his last illness. Not long after she moved to the retirement home, however, I learned that she had taken a job as a monitor. Her responsibility was to be sure all the residents at the retirement home showed up for their meals. If they did not, she had to investigate their whereabouts and be sure nothing was wrong. She began referring to certain people as her "patients." I discovered that she was keeping up with and administering the medicine for retirement home residents who could not remember what medicine to take and when to take it. Almost all of them were younger than my mother. I asked her if she was concerned about being charged with illegally practicing medicine. She responded, "Not at all."

My mother drove her car until well into her nineties. The area around the retirement home was extremely congested, and I barely missed being hit by a car several times when I visited her. When she was approximately ninety-two, Mother had an accident while returning to the retirement home from the drugstore. She claimed that the lady driving the other car was speeding, and that was the cause of the accident. Since my mother had apparently cut in front of the other car, I had my doubts that her position would stand up in court. The police officer gave her a traffic citation and assigned a court date. Being a dutiful lawyer son , I offered to represent her in court. She told me that she did not think it was necessary, as she could handle it herself. I was hoping through good legal representation to get her off with a small fine. On the afternoon of the hearing, I called her at the retirement home to inquire about the results of the hearing. She said there were no results. I asked if she had been fined and she said she had not. I later learned that she told the judge she had decided to give up driving. She told me that was the most difficult decision she ever made, as it mortgaged her independence. It was not long after that conversation that she introduced me to her "boyfriend." I thought it was quite late in life to have a boyfriend, but when I learned that her boyfriend had a car and still drove, it made all the sense in the world.

On June 14, 2010, my mother celebrated her 100th birthday. When I took her for one of her periodic checkups, her doctor told me that some of his patients had reached 100, but none had reached that age with the quality of both physical and mental life that my mother enjoyed. A few days before her birthday, we decided to have a party for her at a Carrollton, Georgia, restaurant. Family and friends from the retirement home were in attendance. She thoroughly enjoyed it. A church she had become affiliated with near the retirement home, Sardis Baptist Church, had a luncheon for her several days before the party. I was asked to make some remarks about my mother on that occasion. At the end of my remarks, I indicated that I had said about all I had to say. In a loud voice from her seat of honor, my mother said, "Good, you have already said too much."

On the occasion of her 100th birthday, my mother was interviewed by a newspaper reporter. She emphasized the importance of faith in her life and said, "God has blessed me all my life." When the reporter asked her what she enjoyed doing, she indicated that she played bingo once a week, walked every day, and went to church on Sunday, sometimes twice. She also said she enjoyed reading books. At the time of the interview, she identified the most recent book she had read as *FDR's Funeral Train*.

She lived completely independently until after her 102nd birthday. Shortly thereafter, she had a fall. While she did not break any bones, she suffered serious bruises and a strained back. She moved into an assisted living section of the retirement home, where she received assistance with her medicines and bathing needs. In October 2012, my mother complained of intense back pain and was admitted to the hospital. An MRI disclosed two compress fractures in her back. She died in the hospital from an infection and kidney failure on October 23, 2012. She was a remarkable lady who led a remarkable life.

The 1912 Georgia State Senate on the steps of the State Capitol in Atlanta. The page second from the right on the first row is Ann's father, Stafford Grovenstein. The state senator fourth from the right on the second row is Ann's grandfather from Effingham County, A. N. Grovenstein.

With Ann during our courting days.

Ann's mother, Ruth Allen Grovenstein from Atlanta, with her harps.

Ann with her brother, Allen Grovenstein, at our wedding in Savannah on April 12, 1976.

With Garrett on his first birthday on August 30, 1983.

Garrett when he was about four years of age in 1986.

With Ann and Garrett in the lobby of the Plaza Hotel in New York when he was sixteen years of age in 1998.

My parents, Bonnie and Borden Campbell.

My aunt Edna Barton, uncle Babe McPherson, younger brother Kenneth and mother at her birthday party for her 100th birthday on June 12, 2010.

11

Law Firms with which I Practiced

During my career, I had the privilege of practicing law with four fine law firms in Atlanta—Heyman & Sizemore (1971–1977), Hicks Maloof & Campbell (1977–1998), Long Aldridge & Norman (1998–2002), and McKenna Long & Aldridge (2002–2009). Each of these firms had good lawyers and clients. Each was successful economically, as I never missed a payday, even when we were starting our new firm in 1977. I also was blessed to practice with fine partners in each of these firms, many of whom remain friends today. In this chapter, I will describe some of my memorable experiences practicing in these four firms.

Heyman & Sizemore

As stated in an earlier chapter of this book, when I arrived at Heyman & Sizemore in fall 1971, it had between fifteen and twenty lawyers and was considered a midsized firm by Atlanta standards. It had a varied practice, which included litigation, corporate, bankruptcy, and public regulatory. The firm was a good fit for me because, among other reasons, it was considered one of Atlanta's "political" firms. The senior partner, Lamar Sizemore, was active in political circles and known throughout the state as being a confidant of Senator Herman Talmadge. Much of the firm's practice was before various agencies of the state government, including the Georgia Public Service Commission and the office of the Georgia Insurance Commissioner. Probably because of my political background, Lamar took a special liking to me and basically gave me free reign to engage in political activities as described in chapter 8 of this book.

My law practice quickly settled into three areas of law—trying jury and nonjury cases in state and federal courts, trying cases in the bankruptcy court, and trying public utility and transportation matters before the Georgia Public Service Commission. In the first couple of years of my practice, I was frequently engaged in cases in the bankruptcy court and before the Public Service Commission. Initially, the bankruptcy cases were primarily attributable to the bankruptcy business originated by Bob Hicks. My Public Service Commission practice was a mixture of cases I generated as a result of my prior political experience and established transportation clients of the firm such as United Parcel Service and Purolator Courier Corporation.

I also did other kinds of legal work that did not fit into these three categories. For example, Ted Maloof did a lot of work for an Atlanta-based company known as Interfinancial Corporation. It was involved in the nationwide acquisition and packaging of real estate projects into partnerships that had tax advantages at that time. At the end of the year, there was always a push to close as many of these deals as possible for tax reasons. One year I went with Ted Maloof to Los Angeles for a series of closings. I am pretty sure this was late 1972, because I remember George McGovern had just run for president. While Ted and I were in Los Angeles, we had dinner with his cousin, Sam Maloof, the famous custom furniture maker. Some of Sam's rocking chairs and other works are in the Smithsonian Institution in Washington, DC. His rocking chairs sold for thousands of dollars. Sam and his wife lived on one of the highest hills above Los Angeles and had a spectacular view of the city at night. We also toured his workshop, which was located on the premises and where he created his custom-made furniture. At one meal, we had a spirited political discussion in which I was the only one who stated that I had voted for Richard Nixon instead of George McGovern, the last of three votes I cast for Nixon for president.

Another area of legal work in which I participated was the representation of the Georgia Railroad. The right-of-way of the railroad was owned by the state of Georgia but leased to a bank in Augusta, Georgia, that operated the railroad. The firm regularly represented the railroad, and I handled a number of its cases. I particularly remember being involved in the condemnation proceedings when the Metropolitan Atlanta Rapid Transit Authority (MARTA) was condemning some of the railroad right-of-way for Atlanta's new rapid transit system. When the parties could not reach an agreement, that involved trying cases as to the value of the property being condemned. The Georgia Railroad ran essentially from Atlanta to Augusta, and its right-of-way through downtown Atlanta happened to be the exact path of the planned rapid transit system. Therefore, there were a great many condemnation proceedings that involved the Georgia Railroad. There was also a political aspect to representing the Georgia Railroad because periodically the state lease would come up for renewal or amendment, and there would invariably be a spirited fight in the Georgia legislature over who would be favored with the new lease. I remember working with Lamar Sizemore on several of those matters.

In my first several years of practice, I did not get to try as many jury cases as I would have liked. That is primarily because of the time I devoted to bankruptcy and Public Service Commission cases as well as my political activities. The first jury case I can recall trying happened around 1974. I served as the understudy of Bob Hicks, who was the lead trial lawyer in that case. It involved a client in Fort Valley, Georgia, who owned a peach-processing plant in the region of the state that grew the most peaches. The client was the Markham family from South Florida, who had extensive fruit and vegetable farms in Florida as well as the peach-processing facility in Fort Valley. The finished product of the peach-processing plant, canned peaches that would be sold to retail outlets such as grocery stores, was shipped by rail. There were several sidetracks by which the railroad accessed the processing facility. The case Bob and I tried arose out of a derailment by one of the trains that crashed into the peach-processing facility and virtually destroyed the building. In turn, the inclement weather resulted in condensation in a large inventory of processed peaches, which virtually destroyed the inventory. We sued the railroad for essentially destroying the business, claiming that its negligence in causing the accident had put the facility out of business at a critical time of the year. The Markhams were in the process of introducing a new variety of canned peaches known as the Cling peach. This new variety had the advantage of being much easier to separate the fruit from the pit during processing. The year of the accident was to be the first year in which the plant would have marketed the Cling peaches. An Atlanta firm that did a lot of railroad defense work represented the railroad. The attorneys were Burt Deriux and Greg Diegel, seasoned railroad defense counsel. Senior state court judge, Bowie Gray of Tifton, Georgia, presided over the case. During the course of the trial, Bob and I felt good about the jury, but we were uneasy about how Judge Gray viewed the case. That turned out to be a well-founded concern. I particularly remember one morning when most of the jurors were late in arriving at the courthouse. Bob and I smiled when they arrived and announced that the reason for the delay was a railroad train that had blocked a downtown intersection the jurors had to cross to get to the courthouse, apparently a frequent complaint in Fort Valley.

I learned a lot from observing Bob trying this case. I examined a couple of witnesses, but Bob did most of the work. Judge Gray made a number of unfavorable rulings during the trial, which we were concerned might adversely affect the result. When the jury rendered its verdict, however, we had been given almost everything we asked for in our complaint. We were overjoyed until Judge Gray set most of it aside in ruling on several motions filed by the railroad. The central areas of contention were whether the business had any real value since it had been losing money and whether the jury had used the correct standard for damages to the inventory. As a result of the post-trial rulings, our damages were severely reduced, and we decided to appeal the case to the Georgia Supreme Court. Bob argued the case in the Supreme Court and secured a reversal and the opportunity to try the case again. As a result of the appellate ruling, the parties settled the case before a retrial, and our client received most of the damages the jury had awarded it in the trial. This experience in a jury trial case reinforced my long-held intention to be a trial lawyer before juries. That is one reason I did not devote my practice entirely to bankruptcy: there is almost never a jury trial in the bankruptcy court.

I also learned a great deal about trying cases from the lead litigation partner at Heyman & Sizemore, William H. Major. Bill was one of the most successful graduates of the Atlanta Law School, a night program in Atlanta, and was sought by other lawyers to try cases in which their firms were disqualified. Bill tried a number of high-profile divorce cases as well as some criminal cases. He was known as one of the best trial lawyers in Atlanta. His son, Billy Major, is a successful trial lawyer in Atlanta today.

Lamar Sizemore frequently invited me to join him for dinner at the Capitol City Club in downtown Atlanta, where we discussed politics in addition to law. The only thing I did not like about the dinners was how long they lasted. We would generally go to the club at about 6:30 in the evening and have a couple of drinks before dinner. After dinner, Lamar would have a number of after dinner drinks over a period of several hours. This violated the rule for drinking liquor that I had learned from Richard Russell—never drink before six o'clock in the evening, and never drink after dinner. Lamar was just getting started when the evening meal ended. His whole approach to alcohol was odd, because I was told that he absolutely prohibited liquor in his home. Being one of Lamar's favorites at the firm, of course, did not hurt me. I was made a partner in 1974.

Lamar's method of running the firm kept it in constant turmoil. He was skillful in playing one partner against another. He was so dominant in this that he was able to keep the firm together even though considerable discontent bubbled up from below. I wondered what would happen when Lamar was no longer there. I got my answer in 1975 when Lamar died in his hotel room, suffering the effects of a stroke while on a business trip to New York City. Ted Maloof was traveling with him. The bubbling discontent that Lamar so skillfully controlled came to the surface after his death. Within two years, Bob Hicks and Ted Maloof announced that they were leaving the firm to form a new one. They asked me to join them as a name partner. The new firm would be known as Hicks Maloof & Campbell. While it might appear that I faced a difficult decision of whether to launch out on my own the year after I was married, it was an offer I could not refuse. I got along well with all the partners at Heyman & Sizemore, but there was little reason for me to stay after Lamar's death, especially with Bob and Ted leaving. Even when Lamar was living, the firm frowned on the bankruptcy practice, and Bob and Ted were taking all of the bankruptcy work with them. By 1977, bankruptcy cases were an important part of my practice, and I had started originating significant bankruptcy work on my own, as well as assisting with the cases originated by Bob or Ted. I agreed to join them at the new firm, which was established in May 1977.

Hicks Maloof & Campbell

I practiced at Hicks Maloof and Campbell for twenty-one years, over half my career. It was a great place to practice law with hardly any disagreements and plenty of good legal work to keep its lawyers busy. The first two decisions Bob, Ted, and I had to make were which lawyers at the old firm, if any, to invite to go with us and where to locate the new office. We wanted to keep the new firm small and to concentrate the practice in the bankruptcy field. It would also have a corporate and non-bankruptcy litigation practice as well as some public regulatory work, but we did not start out intending to be a general-purpose law firm. We decided to invite three young associates at Heyman & Sizemore to join us as associates at the new firm. Bob Bartlett, originally from New York City, had joined Heyman & Sizemore about a year after I came to the firm. His father was a New York City policeman, and he had attended prep schools in New York, where he was a star athlete. He went to Yale on an athletic scholarship and then attended law school at George Washington University in Washington, DC. The second associate we invited was Charles E. Wilson III, who was from an Atlanta family that owned properties in downtown Atlanta. Chuck received his undergraduate degree from Vanderbilt University and his law degree from the University of Georgia. He had come to Heyman & Sizemore about two and a half years after I arrived. The third associate we invited was Robert E. Tritt. Bob, born in San Diego, California, had attended both undergraduate and law school at the University of Georgia. His father was a college professor, consultant, and businessman. These were three excellent young lawyers, and Bob, Ted, and I were gratified when they agreed to join the new firm. In a period in which lawyer mobility increased significantly and lawyers increasingly switched firms, it is noteworthy that the six of us practiced together for the rest of my career—more than thirty-five years.

In regard to the location of the offices of the new firm, we knew we wanted to stay in downtown Atlanta and eventually settled on a fairly new office tower located at 101 Marietta Street, about five blocks from the offices of Heyman & Sizemore. We were originally located on the 24th floor but soon moved to the 34th. We shared a library with a small firm that included the brother of Bob Hicks, John Hicks. Bob and Ted took their longtime secretaries, Pat Baswell and Jackie Pollack, from the old firm, but I hired a new one.

Bob Hicks, Ted Maloof and I enjoyed an excellent relationship with each other for my entire legal career. Bob and Ted had already been practicing law together for more than ten years when I joined Heyman & Sizemore. By the time each of them retired, they had been practicing law together for well over fifty years. They were quite a pair. Bob Hicks loved the practice of law more than any lawyer I have ever met. His father was a lawyer and judge in Dublin, Georgia, and Bob graduated from both undergraduate school and law school at Mercer University in Macon, Georgia. He was editor of the Law Review in law school and a fine student. Bob is also one of the best people lawyers I have ever encountered. He was skillful in playing the good guy/bad guy routine with Ted. Bob would be the friendly, amicable southern gentleman in complicated bankruptcy cases, while Ted would be his no-nonsense lawyer.

Ted Maloof is the most brilliant lawyer I have ever met. He is originally from Copper Hill, Tennessee. He attended undergraduate school at Notre Dame and law school at Emory University. Ted could do anything in the practice of law, and he did at one point or another in his career. After clerking for a superior court judge in Atlanta, he became a litigation lawyer and assisted the well-known libertarian Georgia lawyer, Morris Abrams, in trying some of his most important cases, such as the one invalidating the county unit system in Georgia. After this litigation experience, Ted continued to litigate constitutional cases and also became a corporate lawyer. Then, when the need arose, he became an expert bankruptcy lawyer. Later, when the firm expanded into technology law, Ted mastered that area of the law and became one of the most respected practitioners in Atlanta. He also did quite a bit of real estate and estate law practice. In short, there was not anything Ted could not do, and that ability was indispensable to the success of Hicks Maloof & Campbell. Bob could originate the business, and Ted could handle it as well as originate substantial legal work.

I particularly remember one case in the mid-1970s that illustrated this point. The bankruptcy case of North American Acceptance Corporation (NAAC) came into the firm while we were still at Heyman & Sizemore. NAAC was a large, diversified company based in Atlanta that had extensive real estate holdings in Mississippi, Arizona, Washington State, and Hawaii. It financed its business through what were known as "thrift notes," which were essentially above-market interest-rate unsecured demand notes sold to the public. Well-known celebrities in the sports community advertised them on television in Atlanta. NAAC was not, strictly speaking, a Ponzi scheme because it did have a real business and substantial properties. Its ability to continue to operate, however, was dependent on its ability to continue to sell notes to the public. Since the notes could be called at any time, the business shared one of the characteristics of a Ponzi scheme in that it could not continue if there was a run on the notes. That is exactly what happened in the mid-1970s, which resulted in its bankruptcy filing. Bob Hicks was named bankruptcy trustee, and Ted Maloof was his principal counsel.

NAAC had entered into millions of dollars of transactions with a company in New York named Security Mortgage Investors. These transactions either sold or pledged the thrift notes to SMI depending on one's interpretation of the legal documentation. This was an important issue in the bankruptcy case because if the notes had simply been pledged, they would still be owned by the bankrupt company, whereas if they had been sold, the notes would be owned by SMI. Since SMI believed and had legal opinions that the transactions were sales, it did not file UCC financing statements that would be required to make it a secured creditor with a perfected security interest. It was in danger of being an unsecured creditor. Millions of dollars of collections from the notes were received each year in a lockbox account. Based on Ted Maloof's legal advice, Bob, as bankruptcy trustee, took the position that North American Acceptance Corporation still owned the notes and that he was entitled to the collections. This was a shock to SMI and brought about a hostile and immediate reaction from its lawyers. The trustee was sued by SMI, and I helped handle the litigation. The seizing of the collections by the trustee significantly endangered the business of SMI and almost required that company to negotiate a settlement. During the settlement negotiations, Bob was his usual jovial, friendly self. But he made it quite clear that he had complete confidence in the legal advice he had received from his attorney. Ted, on the other hand, had little to say in the meetings other than repeating the legal advice he had given the trustee. One annoying habit Ted exhibited during these negotiations was tearing off a piece of clear tape and affixing it to the center of his forehead above his eyes. He would leave it there for a few minutes, slowly peel it off and go through the same process again. It was extremely disconcerting and annoying to the SMI attorneys and must have caused them to wonder about Ted's stability and the lengths to which he might go in resisting their right to the collections. Eventually, a settlement was agreed to that resolved the litigation.

It was also in the bankruptcy case of North American Acceptance Corporation that we first met William G. Hays, Jr. Bill had extensive experience in the finance business, including owning his own company before he sold it and established a consulting company. That had happened at about the time of the filing of the NAAC bankruptcy. He was recommended to Bob by one of the partners at Heyman & Sizemore, Dan Greer, who was from the same hometown—Covington, Georgia—as

Bill Hays. Bill was an ideal person to bring into the bankruptcy to run the company until it could be sold or liquidated. That started a relationship that continued for the rest of my legal career and, in fact, continues today. I employed Bill as an investigator, consultant, or expert witness in many of my cases. Bob, Ted, Bill, and I still have lunch together at least once a month and remain fast friends. For some thirty years, Bill and I attended virtually every home football game of the University of Georgia. Our wives remain great friends today as well.

For the first few years, the law firm continued to grow slowly but steadily in accordance with our plan. We added on average about one new lawyer each year until a transforming event occurred in 1979. Management Science America, Inc. (MSA) was a computer software company based in Atlanta for which Bob Hicks had served as bankruptcy trustee during the early 1970s. Before the bankruptcy, John Imlay from Honeywell had come to run MSA. Bob made a deal with John that if he and those who were assisting him were successful in paying off the creditors, Bob would recommend that they receive the stock of the company as it exited bankruptcy. The stock had been valued at zero during the bankruptcy. John, along with Bill Graves and Gene Kelly, were able to accomplish this task and owned most of the company after the creditors were paid. After the bankruptcy, the company prospered and grew. MSA became dissatisfied with its existing legal counsel. Bob Hicks happened to run into John Imlay at an airport in New York. John asked if our firm would be interested in becoming legal counsel to MSA, which would represent quite a challenge because we did not have any lawyers who were experts in technology law. We did, however, have Ted Maloof, who could quickly and thoroughly learn any area of the law. The firm accepted MSA as a client, and Ted began his crash study of technology law, including technology licensing, computer law, and trade secret law. This was important to MSA because it developed large application software programs that were licensed to users instead of being sold. It was critical that the company protect its rights to the software in its licensing agreements.

The representation of MSA substantially changed the firm. MSA wanted the firm to handle all of its legal business, and this required adding more attorneys faster than would otherwise have been the case. While Ted Maloof and Chuck Wilson did the initial technology work, the amount of the legal business also required the firm to hire additional technology lawyers. We had gone from a small boutique firm specializing in bankruptcy work to a more general practice firm. I handled a number of litigated matters for MSA. By the late 1980s, the firm had grown to such an extent that we needed new office space. In 1990, we moved into the Marquis Two Tower in the Peachtree Center office complex in downtown Atlanta, occupying essentially the entire twenty-fourth floor of the office building and part of an adjoining floor. The firm continued to do well throughout the 1980s and grew to almost thirty lawyers by the end of the decade. It was during this time that Bob was named to MSA's board of directors and Ted Maloof and Chuck Wilson did most of the legal work to take the company public. It was subsequently sold to Dun & Bradstreet Software.

One of the reasons Hicks Maloof & Campbell was so successful was our unique compensation system. If the firm had adopted a normal compensation system that recognized to a significant extent the origination of legal work, Bob Hicks would have received well over half of the firm's profits each year. Instead, Bob insisted on a compensation system that gave greater weight to the responsibility for handling legal work. This allowed younger lawyers who did not originate as much business to receive greater compensation. Bob and Ted also agreed that they would receive the same amount of compensation each year, and that was true for the entire twenty-one years of the firm's existence. I was treated more than fairly in the compensation arrangement. This helped create a culture of cooperation among partners instead of competition. None of the discontent that I had witnessed and experienced at Heyman & Sizemore was present at Hicks Maloof & Campbell.

I can only recall two substantive matters on which Bob, Ted, and I disagreed in the twenty-one years we practiced together at Hicks Maloof & Campbell. The first related to whether to establish a new category of partner below that of the equity partners. Equity partners in a law firm own the firm and share in the profits of the firm based on their percentage interest in it. Many law firms at the time were adopting a system of non-equity partners who were salaried attorneys but were allowed to attend partner meetings and other events. In some firms the non-equity partners had little chance of making equity partner in the future, and in some firms it was still realistically possible for the non-equity partners to make equity partner in the future. The establishment of the non-equity partner system was a way to avoid making the difficult decision to tell a young lawyer that he or she was not going to become a partner and would have to seek employment elsewhere. Bob and Ted were inclined to adopt the non-equity partner system, but I was opposed to it for several reasons. First, I feared it would become a dumping ground for attorneys who did not meet the firm's standards, and it would be increasingly difficult to separate them in the future. If they stayed, I feared it would create a lower class of partners who would be discontented and view themselves as second-class citizens. I preferred to go ahead and address the tough decisions of which attorneys to make equity partners and which ones to separate from the firm. Because of my opposition to the non-equity partner system, the firm never adopted it. Almost all of the attorneys who left the firm because they did not meet the requirements to become an equity partner were able to find acceptable alternative employment with our assistance. Some of them went with smaller law firms, some with universities or nonprofits, some with government agencies, and some with in-house legal departments at corporations. The fact that an attorney is not well suited for the private practice of law in large or medium-sized commercial firms does not mean that he or she cannot have a successful career in law. Even though almost all law firms today have some system of non-equity partners, I still have reservations about the system and its long-term effects.

The other matter on which Bob, Ted, and I disagreed was more serious and substantive. During our years at Hicks Maloof & Campbell, we were approached by a number of firms about possibly merging with them. One I particularly recall was the Schneider Harrison firm from Philadelphia. It was the longtime national counsel for United Parcel Service. In the 1990s, UPS decided to relocate its corporate headquarters from Connecticut to Atlanta. We were one of the few law firms in Atlanta that represented UPS at the time, and Bob Tritt headed up the real estate work that involved hundreds of UPS senior employees buying homes in the Atlanta area. The Schneider Harrison firm was obviously concerned about this move and the impact it might have on their representation of UPS in the future. They decided to open an Atlanta office and began courting us as a merger partner almost immediately. We had no real interest in merging with any firm and certainly not one whose affairs would be directed from Philadelphia. We respectfully turned down the offer and continued to do a good deal of UPS work. It was not long before UPS started beefing up its in-house legal department and spreading its legal work around to other firms in Atlanta, including King & Spalding and Alston & Bird.

One of the other firms that approached us from time to time about a possible merger was the Long Aldridge & Norman firm. Clay Long, John Aldridge, and another attorney who was no longer with the firm had started it a few years before we started Hicks Maloof & Campbell. It was somewhat like our firm in that it was entrepreneurial and had grown rapidly. It was probably a little more than twice our size by 1990. Each time Clay Long or John Aldridge mentioned a possible combination of the firms, we indicated that we had no interest. In 1997, I was at the Richard B. Russell Federal Building and Courthouse in downtown Atlanta pitching a creditors' committee representation in a large bankruptcy case. John Aldridge was there pitching the same business for his firm. There was not room for us in the waiting room, and we were relegated to sitting next to each other in an adjacent hallway. John said that he did not understand why we would not at least give them the courtesy of a meeting with no obligation whatsoever. I told him the firm had never been interested in combining with another firm and that we did not want to waste their time, but I would let him know if the situation should change.

This came at a time when I was giving a great deal of thought to the future of the firm. While we had been successful and had established a great place to practice law, things had changed from what they were when we started the firm in 1977. First, Bob Hicks and Ted Maloof, who were the heart of the firm from the beginning, were both reaching retirement age. In fact, Bob had already passed the normal retirement age, and Ted would soon be there. While we had good lawyers and a well-established firm, I did have concerns as to how well the firm would do with some thirty attorneys without Bob and Ted. A second factor involved how the firm had changed from a boutique firm specializing in bankruptcy practice to a general practice firm with a technology emphasis. Every time we went into the market to hire a new technology lawyer, we were told we would have to match the salaries offered by the larger firms such as King & Spalding to attract qualified technology lawyers. Our hourly billing rates were almost 50 percent below those of King & Spalding, and I did not see how we could pay the higher salaries and maintain our rates at the lower level. By this time, we were not only representing MSA but had also taken on other technology clients such as

Peachtree Software and KnowledgeWare, a computer firm started by Francis Tarkenton, the former All-American quarterback at the University of Georgia and an NFL great with the Minnesota Vikings. We had other technology clients as well. A third factor was the way in which the practice of law itself had changed. Tremendous consolidation was underway among law firms, and there was constant pressure to become bigger, particularly for general practice firms. It was still possible for small boutique firms to do well, but it was becoming increasingly difficult for small to medium-sized general practice firms. A fourth factor was the change that had taken place in the bankruptcy practice. When we established the firm in 1977, the bankruptcy judges controlled the lucrative appointments in bankruptcy cases such as bankruptcy trustee. When Congress rewrote the bankruptcy laws in the late 1970s and early 1980s, an office was created within the Department of Justice, known as the Office of the United States Trustee, that, among other things, took over the appointments of fiduciary positions in bankruptcy cases such as bankruptcy trustees, examiners, and counsel for official committees. The US Trustee's office established panels of bankruptcy lawyers who would be expected to take on all cases, both large and small. We were not interested in the smaller cases and never had any of our attorneys on the panels. That meant it would be more difficult to get appointments in the larger cases in the future. Finally, although I had been managing partner of the firm for several years, I did not enjoy law firm management as did Bob and Ted, and I could see this taking a greater amount of my time away from trying cases in the future as the firm continued to grow and as Bob and Ted were less active. All of these factors led me to the conclusion that we should listen to what Clay Long and John Aldridge had to say. I was not sure that I would be in favor of a merger, but I was at least in favor of listening.

When I returned to the office from my conversation with John Aldridge, I discussed the matter with Bob and Ted. They were both opposed, Bob strongly, to any discussions with the Long Aldridge firm. First, they did not want to give up the independence of our own firm, and second, they did not want the word to get out that Hicks Maloof & Campbell was in play. I considered both of those to be legitimate points, but I thought the second point could be dealt with in a tight confidentiality agreement and our emphasis to Clay and John that if word got out that we were having merger discussions, we would call them off so we could honestly say the firm was not considering merging with anyone. When I did not make much progress in convincing Bob and Ted that we ought to consider the matter, I suggested that we had a responsibility to the other partners in the firm to at least discuss it at a firm meeting of partners. They readily agreed to that. At the firm meeting, the majority of the partners who spoke on the matter supported Bob and Ted's position. But, as I recall, at least two of the partners, Bob Tritt and David Dantzler, spoke up that they thought we should listen to what Clay Long and John Aldridge had to say. This gave rise to further discussions among the partners and an eventual decision to schedule a meeting.

Bob, Ted, and I met with Clay Long and John Aldridge at their office, which was located in the same complex as ours. They made their case as to why they believed important synergies existed in combining the two firms. Some of those were that their firm had an established bankruptcy practice but it was heavily oriented toward representing secured creditors, and we had a well-established practice that was oriented toward representing fiduciaries in bankruptcy cases. Also, we had an established technology practice, which they did not have in their firm. Lawyers from both firms knew attorneys in the other firm and had friends there. For my part, I was good friends with Gordon Giffin, whom I had met when he worked for Senator Nunn and who had helped us in the 1980 Herman Talmadge campaign on campaign finance disclosure issues. Gordon and I and our wives had remained good friends. For a number of years, he and I played tennis once a week. In an ironic twist, when Gordon had called me a few years earlier to get my advice on whether he should leave his partnership at the Hansel Post firm and join Al Norman at the Long Aldridge firm, I had advised him to stay where he was because his firm was well established and you never knew what would happen at a fairly young firm. Just a few years later, the Hansel Post firm had fallen apart and was acquired by the Jones Day firm, and we were considering whether to combine with the Long Aldridge firm. Gordon rejected my advice but never let me forget it. To this day, he mumbles something about my judgment. I also had known Buddy Darden, a former member of Congress and Russell intern, since my days at the University of Georgia. Additionally, I knew Al Norman, who had become a name partner in the firm when he moved from the Hansel Post firm a few years earlier. I first met Al when he was the understudy for

Allen Post as counsel for the Atlanta Gas Light Company at the Georgia Public Service Commission. Finally, I had litigated some cases against Mark Kaufman, a bankruptcy lawyer who had come to the firm from the Troutman Sanders firm. In this first meeting, we made it clear that we would not consider any deal unless it included an invitation for everyone at our firm, attorneys and non-legal staff, to join the new firm. We were not willing to turn anyone away. Clay and John agreed to this upfront. They also agreed that any discussions would be absolutely confidential and would be maintained as such throughout the process.

The next step was to exchange financial information on the two firms. There were surprisingly few instances of conflicts of interest whereby one of the firms would have to give up an existing client because it directly conflicted with a client of the other firm. There were considerable differences in the level of the hourly billing rates, with their firm having higher rates. This would present some problems for some of the smaller clients represented by our firm, but the consensus was that it would not be an insurmountable problem. In short order, we were able to arrange the key terms of a deal from which a letter of intent was prepared and ultimately an agreement. It was not technically a merger but an acquisition of assets. Most of our partners immediately became equity partners, but a couple became non-equity partners in the new firm, which was not to my liking. It was agreed that I would serve a two-year term on the board of directors of Long Aldridge & Norman. Bob and Ted would become senior counsel but would continue to be active in the practice of law. I don't think Bob ever fully embraced the move, and I am sure he was at least initially disappointed in me. Ted eventually changed his opinion or at least told me he thought it had been a wise move. I hated giving up our firm, but I have no doubt, in hindsight, that it was the right thing to do.

Long Aldridge & Norman

The combination of Hicks Maloof & Campbell and Long, Aldridge & Norman became effective on June 30, 1998. Since there were many things to do to close the old firm, I would not move into my office at the new firm for another month. Some assets were sold, and some were transferred to the new firm. Receivables were collected. Fortunately, the offices of the two firms were in adjoining office buildings in the same complex, so it was convenient to go between them for meetings or other matters.

All of the attorneys and all of the members of the non-legal staff were invited to join Long Aldridge & Norman. Essentially, all of the non-legal staff and all but three of the attorneys did so. One litigation partner, Bruce Edenfield, went with a small boutique litigation firm primarily because of the medical malpractice defense work he did for the state of Georgia. That work was billed at hourly rates even lower than those of Hicks Maloof & Campbell and much lower than those prevailing at Long Aldridge & Norman. Bruce concluded, correctly I believe, that it would be difficult to assimilate his medical malpractice work for the state at the new firm. He had been handling that work since he was with the attorney general's office before coming to our firm and was understandably reluctant to forego it. Bruce, the son of the legendary United States District Court judge in Atlanta, Newell Edenfield, is a fine litigator, and, though I understood his reasons, I regretted that he was not able to join with us at the new firm.

Two of the young technology partners, James Harvey and James Meadows, elected not to go to the new firm because they said they did not want to have to build another technology practice from scratch. Instead, they accepted partnerships at Alston & Bird, which had an established technology practice. They practiced at that firm for a number of years but have now both left for other firms.

By and large, the Hicks Maloof & Campbell attorneys who went with Long Aldridge & Norman did well. Of course, this was a period of tremendous mobility in the practice of law, and it was not unusual for partners to go from one firm to another. Several did so. Michael Bradley, a public utility partner, went to Sutherland Asbil & Brennan, which had an established energy practice. Ed Hirsch, a corporate and estate partner, went with Morris Manning & Martin after a few years. Lisa Wannamaker, a corporate partner, went in-house with a client after a number of years, as did Jeff Cavender, who was an able bankruptcy and litigation partner. After a couple of years, one associate went with the in-house legal department at UPS. After about five years, three of the litigation partners, David Dantzler, John Hutchins, and Tim Mast, left for Troutman Sanders because they said they felt it offered better opportunities to practice in their area of greatest interest, securities litigation. In 2012 it was announced that David Dantzler would become managing partner in Troutman's New York City office effective January 11, 2013.

I joined the firm's board of directors shortly after the consummation of the deal and served on it for approximately two years. This gave me an insight into the operation of the firm that was essentially run by Clay Long, the firm's chairman. The firm had about 100 attorneys and practiced in almost all the principal areas of commercial law, including corporate, litigation, real estate, mergers and acquisitions, securities, bankruptcy, and utility regulation. What set it apart from other firms was one of the best government relations practices in the city. This practice was also facilitated by an office in Washington, DC, staffed by approximately thirty attorneys. The government relations practice was essentially a lobbying operation that represented clients before Congress, the federal government, the Georgia legislature, and state governments. The firm was well staffed by people who had extensive experience in government from both the Democratic and Republican parties. From the Democratic side, Buddy Darden, who served in Congress for more than ten years, was a partner, as was Keith Mason, who served as chief of staff for Georgia governor Zell Miller and in the Clinton White House. Gordon Giffin, who had worked for Senator Sam Nunn, had been appointed by President Clinton as United States ambassador to Canada. He would return to the firm in 2000. On the Republican side, Randy Evans, who would serve as general counsel of the Georgia Republican Party and the personal attorney for two speakers of the United States House of Representatives, had an extensive government relations practice as well as an insurance litigation practice. He later joined the firm from Arnall Golden & Gregory. Also, Eric Tannenblat later came to the firm following his tenure as chief of staff to Georgia governor Sonny Purdue. Finally, on the Republican side, the firm hired Alex Albert, who had been on the staff of Republican Senator Paul Coverdale and subsequently on the staff of Senator Zell Miller in Washington. There were other well-qualified attorneys and non-lawyer professionals in the government relations department, which deserved its reputation as one of the best in Atlanta.

My own practice changed somewhat after the combination of the two firms. In the bankruptcy area, what was first viewed as a strength turned out to be otherwise. The Long Aldridge firm's representation in bankruptcy was primarily of secured creditors, whereas the Hicks

Maloof representation was of bankruptcy court fiduciaries such as debtors or trustees. We soon determined that the banks and other secured creditor clients of Long Aldridge were not particularly interested in having bankruptcy attorneys in the firm handling high-profile assignments representing debtors or trustees. Another contributing factor to the diminution of that bankruptcy practice was the fact that fewer substantial bankruptcy cases were filed in Atlanta. Most of the larger cases were filed in New York, Chicago, or Delaware, and the smaller to medium-sized cases increasingly were disposed of in out-of-court settlements. I started doing less bankruptcy work and more non-bankruptcy litigation.

My litigation practice included more out-of-town cases than we had at Hicks Maloof & Campbell. The firm represented the Monsanto Corporation, based in St. Louis, as a result of one of its partners, Bill Ide, becoming general counsel of Monsanto. I handled a number of cases for Monsanto, including a three-party dispute that involved Monsanto, the Scotts Company, and Central Garden and Pet Company. Central Garden was a public company headquartered in California that had an exclusive distributorship agreement with Monsanto to distribute its lawn and garden products in the United States. Monsanto terminated that arrangement and entered into a similar agreement with the Scotts Company. This resulted in antitrust and unfair business practice litigation between the three companies with lawsuits filed in California, Missouri, and Ohio. We conducted discovery for several years, and I appeared in the courts in all three venues. The first case to go to trial was in Missouri, which settled on the first day of trial. This essentially resolved Monsanto's involvement in the litigation. I also had a number of other cases for Monsanto.

One day I particularly remember at Long Aldridge was September 11, 2001, the day of the terrorist attacks in New York, Washington, and Pennsylvania. Early that morning, I was convening a meeting with some clients from England who were in town to present a proposal to purchase most or all of the assets of Wolf Camera Company, a large camera retail establishment that was in bankruptcy in Atlanta. A hearing was scheduled in the bankruptcy court in two days, and we were meeting for the purpose of deciding on the details of the offer to be made on behalf of the clients. A corporate partner, Michael Rosensweig, whom I had invited to the meeting to assist with corporate matters that would be involved in the transaction, reported shortly after the meeting convened that an airplane had hit the World Trade Center in New York. We continued with our meeting without giving it any further thought until he reported approximately twenty minutes later that a second plane had hit another tower at the World Trade Center. Our meeting continued for about an hour until it was announced that we would be evacuating our building because of the fear that there might be a more widespread attack on high-rise office towers throughout the country. The conference room in which we met at the time was on the 53rd floor of the SunTrust Tower at 303 Peachtree Street. The firm had all of the floors from the 47th floor to the 55th. It was difficult for the English clients to understand why it was necessary to leave the building, but we adjourned our meeting to a different location in Atlanta. We finalized our proposal and presented it to the bankruptcy court two days later, but it was not accepted. Nonetheless, the English clients said that it was certainly a memorable visit to America.

Since the Long Aldridge firm had more than 100 lawyers and two offices, it scheduled a partner retreat each year. This was a new experience for us because we had not had such activities at either Heyman & Sizemore or Hicks Maloof & Campbell, since those firms were much smaller and had only one office. The firm retreat was the only opportunity for all the partners to meet each other during the year. We had a number of memorable retreats with the Long Aldridge firm. The one I enjoyed the most was in Ottawa, Canada, while Gordon Giffin was the ambassador there. He arranged for the top Canadian government officials to address meetings of the firm, and we stayed in a historic hotel. Even before this retreat, Gordon and his wife, Patti, had invited Ann and me and two other couples to stay with them for a few days. Ann and I greatly enjoyed both of our trips to Ottawa.

One of the things I learned from my service on the board of directors at Long Aldridge & Norman was that the pressure on firms to become bigger was more intense than I had realized while at Hicks Maloof & Campbell. During my two years on the board, there were a number of proposals either made by the firm or to the firm to combine with other firms. Nothing came of any of those proposals until 2002, when the firm agreed to merge with McKenna and Cuneo. That firm had three offices in California and an office in Colorado, Pennsylvania, Washington, DC, and Brussels, Belgium. It had slightly more attorneys than the Long Aldridge firm. The combination of these two firms would result in a firm of almost 300 lawyers. The specialty of the McKenna firm was its government contracts practice, which was recognized as one of the best in the country. It was believed that the synergies between that practice and Long Aldridge's government relations practice would be substantial. That was one of the determining factors in the merger.

McKenna Long & Aldridge

The merger of McKenna & Cuneo and Long Aldridge & Norman became effective in mid-2002. It was a merger of equals with the largest office being in Atlanta and the second largest in Washington, DC. Merging law firms is a tricky business. Often, the anticipated synergies do not seem to materialize and difficulties are encountered in combining the cultures of the two firms. Occasionally, however, there is a merger of equals that works out well. That was the case with this merger. It resulted in a firm that probably had the best combined government contract and government relations practice in the United States. It allowed the firm to present itself as an expert "where business and the government meet." Initially, the combined firm was managed through an arrangement whereby the chair of the McKenna firm was the combined firm chair for the first year and the chair of the Long Aldridge firm was the combined chair for the second year. After that, the firm elected a chair. Following the two-year period, Jeff Haidet, a corporate partner in the Atlanta office, was elected chair of the firm and remains in that position today. The firm has been successful economically and provided me the years of my highest compensation before my retirement in 2009.

The merger also brought about a substantial change in my personal practice. The new firm, McKenna Long & Aldridge, had seven offices in the United States and one foreign office. At the time of the merger, the only bankruptcy attorneys in the firm were in the Atlanta office. We started inheriting bankruptcy work all across the country, which necessitated a substantial amount of travel. After the merger, it seemed that I had few bankruptcy cases in Atlanta. From the time of the merger until my retirement, I handled bankruptcy cases in California, Nevada, Arizona, Texas, Colorado, Illinois, Indiana, New York, Washington, DC, and Delaware in addition to a number of bankruptcy assignments in southeastern states. In time, the firm started adding bankruptcy attorneys in its Los Angeles office and in its Washington, DC, office.

Several years before I retired, the firm opened an office in New York City and started adding bankruptcy attorneys there as well. In short, the bankruptcy practice became a national practice throughout the United States.

Each department within the firm was divided into teams of between five and ten attorneys. The bankruptcy practice was in the litigation department. For several years, I was the head of a team composed of attorneys who practiced bankruptcy law and non-bankruptcy commercial litigation. The merged firm allowed me to work on much larger bankruptcy engagements. For example, a partner in the Washington office, Josh Hocberg, was appointed examiner in the Refco bankruptcy case in New York, and I served as lead counsel for the examiner. The Refco case is discussed in more detail in chapter 12 of this book.

The merged firm also had a strong non-bankruptcy litigation practice. In addition to its government contracts practice, the firm had a large litigation department with litigation attorneys in all of the firm's offices who handled almost all kinds of litigation. The Washington office did a great deal of technology litigation. At the time of the merger, three litigation partners were fellows of the American College of Trial Lawyers, which is reserved for the top 1 percent of trial lawyers in America—Bob Brewer in the San Diego office and Bob Hicks and myself in the Atlanta office. Later, David Balser, then a litigation partner in the Atlanta office, was also admitted as a fellow of the American College of Trial Lawyers.

Practicing at McKenna Long & Aldridge was a good way to end my career as an attorney. By 2009, I had been practicing law for almost forty years with four different firms as described in this chapter. Under the policy in effect at the firm at the time of my retirement, equity partners could continue to practice as such until December 31 of the year in which they turned sixty-seven years of age. In my case, this would in essence be sixty-eight years of age since my birthday is on January 12. I decided to go ahead and retire a year early at the beginning of 2009.

Charles Campbell, Bob Hicks and Ted Maloof on the 20th anniversary of the founding of the Hicks Maloof & Campbell law firm in May of 1997. Bob, Ted and I practiced law together for my entire career—- almost 40 years.

12

Some of My Cases

One of the great things about practicing law is the wide assortment of characters you encounter and the interesting circumstances that present themselves in your cases. You never know from one case to the next the challenges you will face or the opportunities for success on behalf of your clients. This chapter showcases ten of my cases. Some are included because of the interesting characters involved, some because of the importance of the legal issues, and some because they are particularly memorable. I hope they will illustrate the wide range of situations encountered by trial lawyers.

Consolidated Motor Inns Case

When the real estate recession hit in the early 1970s, almost all projects such as hotels and motels, apartment complexes, and office complexes in the Southeast were adversely affected. Atlanta was no exception. Consolidated Motor Inns was a Georgia general partnership that owned approximately ten motels in three southeastern states. It had an interesting group of partners. Larry Morris, a former All-American football player at Georgia Tech and NFL great, was in the real estate business in Atlanta and Florida. Duncan Roush was a commercial pilot with Delta Airlines in Atlanta. Pug Butrill owned a construction company in Atlanta that specialized in building small and middle-sized churches. Bill Trunnell was a farmer in the middle Georgia town of Hawkinsville. Each man was a general partner of CMI, which meant they were personally liable on all the debts of CMI, and their personal assets would be exposed if CMI could not pay its debts in full.

The CMI partners came to see me for counsel with respect to how to deal with their creditor situation. I outlined the alternatives, and they eventually decided to file a bankruptcy proceeding under Chapter 12 of the Bankruptcy Act for CMI. None of them wanted to file bankruptcy individually. The CMI case was filed in the bankruptcy court in Atlanta around 1973 and was assigned to bankruptcy judge W. Homer Drake, Jr. The partnership had a large number of secured creditors because each motel property in Georgia, Florida, and Tennessee was financed separately.

This case presented two important legal issues. The first issue was the scope of the exemption under Chapter 12 for federally chartered savings and loan associations. It was clear that the exemption prevented a debtor from modifying or canceling the debt of the savings and loan (S&L). What was not clear was whether the debtor could forestall foreclosure by the secured creditor while it was formulating a bankruptcy plan to deal with its other debts. This was a particularly important issue to CMI because, if the broader exemption applied, it would almost immediately lose the motels financed by the federal S&Ls. We initiated proceedings in the bankruptcy court for a determination of the scope of the S&L exemption. Judge Drake conducted a series of hearings on the issue and received briefs from the parties. He eventually ruled that the exemption was narrow in that it did not prohibit the debtor from continuing the stay against foreclosure during the bankruptcy proceeding. This gave us some breathing room because it meant that we could negotiate with the S&L creditors while we formulated a bankruptcy plan for the other creditors. Eventually, we were able to work out deals with the S&L creditors to give back their collateral in exchange for a full release of CMI and the individual partners.

The other important legal issue in the CMI case involved whether the individual liability of general partners could be discharged in a bankruptcy plan if the partners themselves did not file for bankruptcy. There was not a great deal of law on this issue, but what was available made it clear to me that we had an uphill battle. Nonetheless, we filed a plan providing not only that CMI would be discharged if the plan were confirmed but also that the individual liability of the four general partners would be eliminated. To provide backup protection in case that position did not prevail either before Judge Drake or on appeal, we also included in the bankruptcy plan provisions that any creditor who voted for the plan or accepted a payment under the plan would be deemed, as a matter of contract between the parties, to have released not only CMI but also the partners. As further protection, we provided that the debtor could include restricted endorsements on any checks issued under the plan, such that the endorsement of the checks constituted an independent release of CMI and the general partners. The vast majority of the creditors accepted the plan, and Judge Drake confirmed it.

One secured creditor, BVA Credit Corporation, voted against the plan, objected to it, and refused to accept payment under the plan with a restricted endorsement on its check. BVA had financed the furniture and equipment in a number of the motels. In addition, BVA appealed Judge Drake's order confirming the plan to the United States District Court for the Northern District of Georgia. When that court affirmed Judge Drake's order, BVA appealed it to the next highest appellate court, the United States Court of Appeals for the Fifth Circuit. A three-judge panel of that court affirmed Judge Drake's order by a two-to-one vote. BVA promptly filed a motion for rehearing en banc before the Fifth Circuit, which was the right of an appellate party where there was a split vote of a panel of the court. Few such rehearings are granted, but, much to my consternation, this one was granted and a hearing was scheduled before the full Fifth Circuit Court of Appeals in New Orleans. There were approximately ten judges on the court. When an appellate court agrees to hear a matter en banc, it often means the full court is going to make some change in the decision of the panel.

The Fifth Circuit Court held that the discharge for the partners in the bankruptcy plan was impermissible because it exceeded the authority of the bankruptcy court. Since BVA had not accepted any payment under the plan, the court ruled that the remaining arguments relating to the restrictive endorsements on the checks were moot. This was actually a favor to CMI because almost all of the other creditors had voted for the plan and accepted their payments. This allowed us simply to reissue a check to BVA without the restrictive endorsement and then to negotiate a settlement with respect to the difference between the amount it was paid under the plan and the total amount of its debt. This successfully resolved the case, and we were able to accomplish the objectives of the client.

Two of the partners of CMI, Duncan Roush and Bill Trunnell, became so interested in the practice of law as a result of the case that they went to law school in their middle age. Duncan graduated from the Emory University School of Law in Atlanta and became a partner with the Kilpatrick Stockton firm in Atlanta before retiring. Bill graduated from the Mercer University Law School in Macon and opened a law practice in his hometown of Hawkinsville. This was one of the most interesting cases I litigated during my career, particularly since it came near the beginning.

Pinegate Associates, Ltd.

Another real estate project in Atlanta victimized by the recession in the early 1970s was the Pinegate Apartment Complex off Beaver Ruin Road in Northeast Atlanta. David Vaughn, the managing partner of the limited partnership, came to see me on behalf of him and his partners to see what they could do about the creditor situation. I outlined a number of alternatives, including the possibility of filing a proceeding under Chapter 12 of the Bankruptcy Act. That is ultimately the course of action the partners chose. We filed the case in the bankruptcy court in Atlanta, and it was assigned to bankruptcy judge William L. Norton, Jr., whom I had first met when I was working in Richard Russell's office.

The problem Pinegate faced was quite different than that faced by CMI. There was no liability personally on behalf of any of the partners in Pinegate because it was a limited partnership and because the loan with the secured creditor had been made on a non-recourse basis—that is, the secured creditor agreed to look solely to the value of its collateral for payment of its debt. Naturally, in the recession the value of all such projects diminished considerably, and we anticipated that the value at the time of the bankruptcy would be considerably less than the total debt. There was a provision in Chapter 12 of the Bankruptcy Act, known as the cramdown provision, that seemed to permit a bankruptcy court to determine the value of the secured creditor's collateral and authorize the complete discharge of its debt upon the payment in cash of that amount regardless of how much additional debt was left unpaid. This provision of the bankruptcy law had not been used successfully since the Great Depression and only sparingly at that time. We decided to give it a shot since it appeared to offer the best opportunity for the partnership to retain property with the future upside once the recession ended.

We filed a motion on behalf of Pinegate to establish the value of the property. The secured creditor was represented by a California firm and two local lawyers, Penn Nicholson and Bob Meals. I could tell early in the proceedings that Judge Norton did not approve of the arrogance and dismissiveness of the California lawyers. They basically took the attitude that the bankruptcy court did not have the authority to discharge their client's debt upon payment of any amount less than the entire debt. We also had a much better appraisal witness during the valuation hearings conducted by Judge Norton than did the secured creditor, which was a large, national insurance company. Judge Norton determined the value of the property to be significantly less than the debt. He also found that Pinegate could discharge the entire debt upon paying this amount in cash. Relying on the guarantees of some of its partners, Pinegate was able to refinance the debt with a new lender for enough to pay off the secured creditor. Of course, the California attorneys were outraged.

The secured creditor appealed the decision of the bankruptcy court to the district court, which affirmed the decision. It was then appealed to the Fifth Circuit, which also affirmed the decision. While I did not consider the case particularly revolutionary while we were litigating it, I found out otherwise after it was over. Not long after the Fifth Circuit affirmed Judge Norton's decision, he called me one day and asked if I would be interested in going with him to New York to appear on a seminar panel sponsored by the Practicing Law Institute and devoted entirely to the Pinegate decision. I thought it was considerate of Judge Norton to invite me, a relatively new and inexperienced lawyer, to go with him to such a prestigious seminar. After we arrived at the New York Hilton Hotel and I observed the audience's hostility, however, I realized that Judge Norton's real motivation in inviting me was probably so he would not be the only one in New York defending his decision.

At the time of the seminar, large secured creditors, such as insurance companies, had literally billions of dollars of non-recourse loans on their books. It was the preferred way of making real estate loans because of tax advantages at the time. If a bankruptcy judge in Atlanta, Georgia, could appraise the collateral in the depths of a recession and order the discharge of the entire debt upon paying the depressed value, what did this say about the carrying value of these loans on their books? The secured creditor community was up in arms. Virtually every major national secured creditor was represented at the seminar. Other seminar participants and members of the audience used words such as "ridiculous," "absurd," "irrational," and "unprecedented" to describe the Pinegate decision. They did not convince us and we did not convince them.

Several years later, when Congress rewrote the bankruptcy law, it killed Pinegate about three or four different ways in the new statute.

Ordinarily, I would have felt embarrassed to be associated with such a disgraced legal precedent, but then I recalled something that happened while I was working for Richard Russell. One day in the Senate, an amendment was defeated by a vote of 95 to 3. Richard Russell was one of the three members voting for the amendment. When he returned to the office that afternoon, I engaged him in a conversation about the amendment. He told me that based on his thirty-plus years in the Senate, it was his belief that any amendment that attracted 95 negative votes and only 3 affirmative votes had a good deal of merit. Remembering that, I dismissed the murder of Pinegate as just another example of our national legislative bodies not knowing what they were doing.

PSC Cases

Early in my career, I started representing clients before the Georgia Public Service Commission (PSC). I originated some of these cases myself based on my political connections, and some of them came to me through the established PSC practice of Heyman & Sizemore. Bob Hicks was particularly active in this area and was the chief counsel in Georgia for United Parcel Service and Purolator Courier Corporation. The PSC had jurisdiction over all public utility matters, including electric, gas, and telephone rates, as well as transportation companies operating in the state. I concentrated my PSC practice in these two areas.

One of the first PSC clients who retained me was Columbia Nitrogen Corporation of Augusta. The company, which was owned by a Dutch holding company, was a major manufacturer of fertilizer at its plant in Augusta and a large user of natural gas in the manufacturing process. Therefore, every gas rate case was of great concern. I do not clearly recall who recommended me to Columbia Nitrogen, but it may have been Ted Harvey, a lawyer friend in Augusta. In any event, the general counsel of Columbia Nitrogen, Clem White, contacted me and asked if I was willing to represent the company at the PSC. I agreed to do so and participated in a number of gas rate cases filed by the Atlanta Gas Light Company. Our participation was generally not in opposition to a gas rate increase but opposed to the design of the rates for the industrial class. We contended that the rate design unfairly penalized industrial customers and subsidized residential customers based on the costs of serving those respective classes. This was not surprising since the five members of the PSC were elected statewide every four years. While utility rate regulation is notoriously complex and arcane, the members of the PSC were essentially politicians. Strict rules of evidence were not followed, and it was entirely permissible to have ex parte communications with the commissioners while the case was pending for decision. In fact, the utilities regularly went to see the individual commissioners after the hearings were over to lobby for their position. In addition to its PSC work, I also represented Columbia Nitrogen or its affiliated companies in other matters. One matter I particularly recall was when I represented a senior executive of Colombia Nitrogen and its parent, Dutch State Mines, in his testimony before a federal grand jury in New York that was investigating alleged price fixing in the sale of fertilizer in the United States and abroad.

I also participated in a number of rate cases filed by the Savannah Electric and Power Company (SEPCO) on behalf of a group of industrial customers in Savannah, Georgia, known as the Savannah Industrial Group. These were large users of electricity, and their concern usually also centered on the design of the rates as opposed to the amount of the requested increase. At the hearings, we would typically sponsor witnesses (expert and lay) who would testify on the appropriateness of the rate design and offer alternative rate designs. The success or failure of our position was generally judged by whether the commission increased the subsidy that the residential class was already receiving at the hands of the industrial class.

Another area of my practice at the PSC was in the transportation arena. We represented, as stated above, both UPS and Purolator. They were generally involved in the same kind of business that was the delivery of documents and small packages on an expedited basis overnight. UPS, as now, was one of the largest such companies in the world, but it did not often protest applications of competing carriers who were seeking authority to operate in its service area. The attitude of UPS was the more the merrier. Almost all matters I handled for UPS related to limitations in its tariff with respect to its liability for lost or damaged shipments. The tariffs strictly limited UPS's liability in those cases unless the shipper had declared a certain value in the documentation when placing the shipment in commerce. UPS would go to great lengths to litigate these cases, even when the amount in a particular case was quite small, because of its concern for the precedential value if the PSC or a court determined any provision of its tariff to be unenforceable.

Purolator was another matter. Purolator routinely protested applications by new carriers in its service area on the ground that there was no "public convenience and necessity" that justified granting new authority. That was supposed to be the standard the PSC used in deciding whether to grant authority to new carriers, but it was often much more political. Purolator, headquartered in New Jersey, would typically send witnesses down to testify in cases we were protesting, or we would use the local man that headed up Purolator's Georgia operation, Paul Womack. While Purolator was the firm's client, as was UPS, it increasingly fell to me to handle its business at the PSC, as Bob Hicks became more involved in his bankruptcy practice.

One of the real characters that served on the PSC during my time of practice there was Robert C. (Bobby) Pafford. A former baseball umpire, farmer, and member of the state legislature from Southeast Georgia, Bobby was a huge man of some 300 pounds. While he did not have the background that would make one think he was particularly qualified to undertake the work of the PSC, he had probably the best regulatory mind of any of the commissioners before whom I practiced. His problem was that he always maintained a state of turmoil by his endless badgering of witnesses at hearings and by making irrelevant revelations that did not seem to have anything to do with the matter at hand. He had an astute mind and an analytical and mathematical capability. He could frequently figure out in his head the answer to a complex question posed to an expert witness before the expert witness could complete the analysis on his calculator.

Bobby and I became fast friends quite by accident. When he was elected to the PSC and faced with moving to Atlanta, he decided to buy a farm within commuting distance of the city. He selected a 100-acre farm in Butts County, my home county, and went to the livestock auction barn where my mother worked on Wednesday afternoons to buy cattle for his farm. Every Wednesday afternoon thereafter, unless he was busy with hearings at the PSC, he would return to the cattle auction barn to buy and sell additional cattle. Eventually, he became so interested in the sale barn that he bought it. At that point, my mother became his employee. In a court of law, that would probably have disqualified me from representing clients before him or at least would have required the disclosure of the relationship. But no such rules existed at the time at the PSC.

That is not to say that Bobby preferred my position in my cases at the PSC after my mother became his employee. Quite the opposite. He did not spare me or my clients in his badgering of witnesses or caustic comments. In fact, at times it appeared to me that he was targeting us. A few examples illustrate this point. One day I was handling a case for Purolator in which we were protesting an application by a new carrier to serve banks located in Middle Georgia, including one of the banks in my hometown of Jackson. One of the witnesses testifying on behalf of the new carrier was someone I had known from high school who worked at the local bank. Bobby interrupted his testimony by asking him the following question: "Do you know Mr. Campbell?" After the witness testified that he not only knew me but considered me a friend, Bobby asked him this follow-up question: "What do you think about someone who would desert his little hometown in favor of representing a large national corporation headquartered in New Jersey?" The witness allowed as how he hoped the PSC would grant the application, but he still considered me to be a friend.

On another occasion, a witness from Purolator's home office in New Jersey was on the stand opposing an application by a new carrier. Bobby broke into the questioning of my witness with the following inquiry: "Do you think Mr. Campbell's legal rates are too high?" When the witness said that he thought all lawyer rates were too high but mine were no worse than others the company routinely paid, Bobby followed up with this question: "Would it surprise you if I told you his mother considers his legal rates to be too high?" When I later confronted my mother about this, she stated that she had told Pafford no such thing.

Bobby's badgering of witnesses was by no means limited to mine. I remember one occasion when an expert witness from New York was testifying and Bobby broke into his testimony with the following question: "Do you agree that an expert is someone who is smart and who is able to express informed opinions based upon his or her education and experience?" The witness, apparently not having had any prior experience with Bobby and not knowing what was coming, allowed as how he thought Commissioner Pafford was correct. Pafford then asked him, "If you are so smart, why are you living in New York?" On one warm spring morning when the first thaw of winter had arrived, Bobby broke into the testimony of a witness to observe, "This time of the year reminds me when I was growing up on a farm and the first warm weather arrived in the spring. There was no better feeling than being able to go barefooted in the yard. There was no worse feeling than stepping on some chicken ____ and getting it between your toes."

By the early 1980s, we had hired a new public utility partner from the attorney general's office, Mike Bradley, who took over most of the utility practice. The transportation industry was deregulated during the Carter administration and this basically eliminated the work for Purolator. In addition, I was becoming increasingly busy with my bankruptcy and non-bankruptcy trial practice. My PSC practice gradually came to an end, particularly after Bobby Pafford died. I still have many vivid memories of that era.

Lawson Cotton Case

The Lawson Cotton Company was a cotton merchant and warehouseman located in Cochran, Georgia, about thirty miles south of Macon. It was owned by William Carlton Lawson, a prominent citizen in his community. He financed his business through loans from William Islein and Company, a CIT-related company based in New York. In the early 1980s, we received a call from Islein to retain us to file a suit against Lawson. We had previously done legal work for several of the CIT companies, including Islein. We were told that Lawson had falsified cotton receipts and other documents to receive loans on fictitious transactions and that the losses could be in the millions of dollars.

After requesting, receiving, and reviewing documents from our client, we filed a lawsuit against Lawson and his company in the United States District Court in Macon. The case was assigned to district court judge Wilbur D. Owens. Lawson hired Jerry Kaplan, a well-known attorney in Macon, to represent him and his company. We also retained the services of Bill Hays as an investigator since, by this time, his company had significant experience in investigations in fraud cases. We first served document requests on Lawson and his company and then began to take depositions. It became apparent that Lawson was treating sweepings from his warehouse floor as real cotton and submitting receipts to Islein to obtain loans on them. The sweepings were known as "motes." They were essentially trash and of little value. In addition, we discovered that Lawson had falsified certain invoices representing purported sales of cotton to third parties or receipts showing that cotton was held for Lawson's account at warehouses in several surrounding states.

We took the depositions of several cotton merchants with which Lawson did business in Georgia, Alabama, Mississippi, and Tennessee. We also took the deposition of Mr. Lawson himself. At this time, the court rules did not impose any limits on the duration of depositions, and Mr. Lawson's deposition lasted several days. After he had testified for two days, he arrived on the morning of the third day with the announcement that he was retracting all of his testimony and would invoke the Fifth Amendment protection against self-incrimination in refusing to answer any additional questions. This effectively brought his deposition to a halt.

It did not prevent us, however, from taking the depositions of those who worked for Lawson. One such person was W. Lonnie Barlow, an attorney in Cochran, who was Lawson's right-hand man and secretary of his company. He also maintained the minutes of the Lawson Cotton Company and other records. During his deposition, my crack fraud investigator, Bill Hays, pointed out to me that each of the letters written by Mr. Barlow had in the lower left-hand corner the initials "WLB/itm." Bill pointed out that we had not identified any employee of the company with the initials "itm" and suggested that I ask the witness for the identity of this person as someone else who might need to be deposed. When I asked Mr. Barlow the suggested question, he responded, "it means I typed it myself." So much for my crack fraud investigator.

We had sued Lawson and his company for fraud, breach of contract, unjust enrichment, and breach of fiduciary duty. The evidence was so overwhelming that his attorney, Jerry Kaplan, decided to confess judgment for the full amount of damages we were seeking on the breach of contract claim and then argue that there was no reason to have a trial on the remaining causes of action. We had a hearing before Judge Owens on that motion. Owens was known as a strict judge, and several Macon lawyers had warned me that it was not a good idea to cross him or to argue with him once he made up his mind. Judge Owens said at the hearing that it appeared to him, if the defendants were confessing judgment for the full amount of the damages we were seeking, that there was no necessity to try the other counts in the complaint. I tried to explain to him that there is a difference between obtaining a judgment based on a fraud count and obtaining one on a breach of contract count.

In the former instance, the liability generally cannot be discharged if the debtor files bankruptcy, whereas a breach of contract claim can be and usually is discharged in a bankruptcy. This did not seem to impress Judge Owens, as it was clear that he did not want to take up the time of the court in trying the case. Jerry Kaplan's clever strategy had worked.

It was apparent to me and my client that we were unlikely to collect much, if any, money damages against Lawson or his company. The blatant fraud committed, however, did raise the possibility of criminal charges against Lawson and/or his company. The office of the United States attorney for the Middle District of Georgia launched its own investigation and assigned a young assistant district attorney to the case, Lewis Sands, who would later become chief judge of the United States District Court for the Middle District of Georgia. At Sands's request, we sent Bill Hays down to Macon to brief him on the documents and testimony we had obtained in the civil case. This paved the way for a criminal indictment against Lawson to which he eventually pleaded guilty. Judge Owens had a good deal of discretion as to the length of prison sentence given Lawson. One of the things we had noticed in our discovery was that Lawson regularly gave approximately 10 percent of the money he was obtaining by fraud to churches in the area with which he was affiliated. At his sentencing hearing, a number of pastors from those churches testified as character witnesses in his behalf. This apparently did not impress Judge Owens, as he sentenced Lawson to the maximum prison sentence under the applicable federal sentencing guidelines.

One thing this case illustrated is that attorneys can vigorously litigate their cases and zealously represent their clients without degenerating into unprofessional conduct and personal animosity. While our clients fought like cats and dogs throughout the case, Jerry Kaplan and I maintained amicable relations and remain friends to this day.

Colony Square Case

Colony Square is a large mixed-use real estate development in Midtown Atlanta. Today, it includes condominiums, offices, and retail establishments. It was built in the 1970s and prospered for a while before falling on hard times. One of the principal investors was the Mellon banking family from Pittsburgh. The development filed for bankruptcy in the 1980s. Under the bankruptcy plan confirmed by the court in Atlanta,

Colony Square was able to keep its properties and to pay off its principal secured creditor, the Prudential Insurance Company of America (PRU), over time, as long as it met certain performance requirements. If it fell below those requirements, then, under the bankruptcy plan, PRU was entitled to a deed of the property. When it failed to meet the requirements of the plan, instead of complying with the plan and deeding the property to PRU, it filed a new bankruptcy in Pittsburgh to avoid the Atlanta court and several other suits in state and federal courts in Pennsylvania. PRU, represented by the Alston & Bird firm in Atlanta, filed motions to compel Colony Square to comply with the bankruptcy plan and deed the properties to PRU. Bankruptcy judge Hugh Robinson, who had presided over the original bankruptcy, conducted hearings on the motion and decided to grant it.

Instead of preparing an order himself or getting both sides on the phone or at a conference to announce his ruling, Judge Robinson called the attorneys at Alston & Bird, told them he was ruling in favor of PRU, outlined his reasons for reaching his conclusion, and asked them to prepare an order. This happened on several occasions. Ex parte communications between the court and counsel for only one side are frowned upon and prohibited today. At the time of the Colony Square matter, however, the law was not as clear. In fact, the prevailing practice in Georgia state courts at the time was to do exactly what Judge Robinson had done. That was less prevalent in federal courts in Georgia, but it did happen from time to time. At some point, the Colony Square attorneys discovered that Alston & Bird had "ghostwritten" Judge Robinson's orders and filed a motion to disqualify Judge Robinson, disqualify PRU's lawyers, and vacate the orders transferring the Colony Square properties to PRU. If Colony Square could cause the orders to be vacated, even if they were subsequently reinstated on appeal, it would mean millions of dollars to the investors in Colony Square, including the Mellon family, in tax savings.

The Colony Square motion was not filed promptly upon the entry of the orders. In fact, it came months later, and only after the Colony Square attorneys learned of a case in Chicago in which bankruptcy court orders had been ghostwritten by attorneys for one side without the knowledge or involvement of the other side. This was the so-called Wisconsin Steel Company case. Upon learning of that case, the Colony Square attorneys decided to file the motion to vacate the orders of the

Atlanta court since vacating the orders was one of the reliefs granted by the Chicago court. The motion filed by the Colony Square attorneys was filed in the United States District Court for the Northern District of Georgia and assigned to district court judge Richard C. Freeman.

Alston & Bird called our firm to represent it and PRU in connection with the Colony Square motion. Since the Alston & Bird attorneys were involved in the facts of the matter, they obviously could not handle the litigation and needed replacement counsel. Judge Sidney Smith, by then a partner at Alston & Bird, initially called Bob Hicks about our firm handling the matter. Then, Bob and I met with Frank Bird, Jr., the son of one of the name partners in Alston & Bird, with Neal Batson, and with Grant Stein to discuss the case. We agreed to take the case but with the proviso that if a conflict developed between the interests of Alston & Bird and PRU, we would resign as Alston & Bird's attorney and continue as PRU's attorney. Both clients agreed to this. Bob Hicks asked me to be lead counsel in the case.

In deciding how to defend the Colony Square motion, we had to choose whether to defend the ex parte communications or to take the position that, even if they were improper, Colony Square had waited too late to file its motion to receive any relief. We were reluctant to get into the position of defending the ex parte communications because we feared that would divert attention from other points that had a greater chance of success. It appeared that we had a good case that the Colony Square motion was filed as a tactical maneuver and was not filed timely upon its attorneys learning that Alston & Bird might be drafting some of Judge Robinson's orders. We decided to file document requests and take depositions to see if we could support that position. The main witnesses to be deposed were attorneys at the Atlanta firm of Powell, Goldstein, Frazer & Murphy, local counsel for Colony Square, and the Pittsburgh firm of Kirkpatrick & Lockhart, its lead counsel. On the theory that the younger the attorney and the less experienced the more likely he or she is to tell the truth, we decided to start the depositions with the youngest attorney who had worked on the case at Powell Goldstein.

That attorney was Ken Shapiro, an associate at the Atlanta firm who did a good deal of bankruptcy work in the Atlanta court. When I took his deposition, one of the questions I asked is whether he had personally experienced or heard of an attorney in the bankruptcy court in Atlanta receiving ghostwritten orders such as occurred in the Colony Square case. We hit pay dirt right off the bat. After some additional probing questions, Ken admitted that he had had a similar occurrence with Judge Robinson in a bankruptcy case before the Colony Square matter. This was dynamite evidence in that it showed that Colony Square and its attorneys knew or were on inquiry notice as to whether Alston & Bird was preparing some of the orders. This, at the very least, required an immediate investigation and/or filing of the motion instead of waiting months without doing anything.

When we took the depositions of the Kirkpatrick & Lockhart attorneys in Pittsburgh, we uncovered further evidence of knowledge on the part of the Colony Square lawyers that Alston & Bird attorneys were preparing orders for Judge Robinson. Documents and deposition testimony from the Kirkpatrick & Lockhart depositions show that in an elevator conversation going to one of the hearings in one of the cases filed in Pittsburgh, the Powell Goldstein and Kirkpatrick & Lockhart lawyers actually discussed the fact that they suspected Alston & Bird was ghostwriting some of Judge Robinson's orders.

By the time Judge Freeman scheduled a hearing on the Colony Square motion, we had firmly decided not to defend the ex parte conversations but to state and argue to the court that Colony Square was entitled to no relief because it had not timely filed its motion and was using it purely as a tactical maneuver. Since the witnesses at the hearing would include both attorneys from the Powell Goldstein and Kirkpatrick & Lockhart firms, Colony Square retained a well-known Atlanta trial lawyer, Nick Chilivis, as its lead counsel. I knew Nick to be a fine trial lawyer and had had a number of cases with his firm.

I did not know Judge Freeman well. I had a couple of small matters before him but nothing that gave me much exposure to him. His reputation was for being somewhat irascible, which people who knew him attributed to the fact that he suffered from arthritis and often took drugs to deal with the affliction. The hearing before Judge Freeman lasted approximately one week and went well from our viewpoint. On several days, he continued the hearing into the evening. One of the points that we made most strongly at the hearings was how irresponsible the actions of Colony Square had been after they knew of or suspected the ghostwritten orders. We decided to get all the pleadings together from the numerous cases they had filed in Pennsylvania and put them in evidence to bolster our contention that the pending motion and all the other machinations were nothing more than an abuse of the judicial process. We decided to use Neal Batson, a well-known bankruptcy lawyer with Alston & Bird, as our witness to put these pleadings in evidence. We stacked the pleadings on counsel table, and I laboriously went through each one of them with Neal, explaining each pleading to the court. When we were a little over halfway through the pleadings, Judge Freeman blurted out, "This is an outrage on the American taxpayer. And someone is going to pay for it." That confirmed to us that we were making progress in convincing the court that the Colony Square motion should be viewed as a cynical attempt to gain an advantage as opposed to rectifying alleged improper conduct by attorneys and the judge.

Several weeks after the hearing concluded, Judge Freeman issued his order. He severely criticized Judge Robinson and the Alston & Bird attorneys for the ex parte communications. But he also held that Colony Square had waited too long to bring its motion and was doing so for tactical reasons. He also held that his own independent review of the orders ghostwritten for Judge Robinson convinced him that the judge had correctly decided the matters after full and fair hearings and that the ex parte communications had not influenced any of his decisions. This was supported by sworn written interrogatory answers provided by Judge Robinson at the direction of Judge Freeman and sworn testimony and notes by the Alston & Bird attorneys who participated in the telephone conversations.

Colony Square was not yet ready to give up. They decided to appeal Judge Freeman's order to the United States Court of Appeals for the 11th Circuit. They also hired a new lawyer—Monroe Friedman, a nationally recognized ethics expert from the Hofstra University Law School in New York. I thought this was a mistake because they had a perfectly good lawyer in Nick Chilivis, who had tried the matter in the district court and knew the case. After filing briefs with the 11th Circuit, we appeared at oral argument. The presiding judge was the late Judge Robert Vance, who was later killed by a bomb mailed to his home in Alabama by a disgruntled party in one of his cases. As Professor Friedman was unpacking his briefcase and putting his documents on counsel table after the case was called, Judge Vance said that the court was not going to reverse any of the orders but that Professor Friedman had raised interesting issues that he wanted to talk about. That basically told me that Colony Square was going to lose. One of the hardest things for a trial or appellate attorney to do is to know when to shut up. When it came my time to make an argument, I made a few comments and said I would be glad to answer any questions the three judges on the appellate panel had for me. There were a couple of questions, but it was clear that the court had already decided the matter based on Judge Freeman's order and the briefs filed by the parties.

Colony Square was still not ready to give up. It filed a petition for a writ of certiorari in the United States Supreme Court. The Court seldom hears such petitions because it is a discretionary appeal. Nonetheless, we had to take the matter seriously. It is typical for parties to hire Washington counsel to file briefs and make arguments in the Supreme Court, and many of the attorneys who practice in that area are former clerks of justices of the Supreme Court. PRU had used for a long time the Washington, DC, firm of Howry & Simon to do such work, and they were retained to help us with the briefs and to appear at argument if argument was granted. This was my first opportunity to work with the Howry & Simon lawyers, with whom I was impressed. I would later try a number of cases with them in Atlanta. They did an excellent job in helping us on the brief, and I was confident that the Supreme Court would not grant certiorari. That was confirmed shortly thereafter when we received an order denying the writ of certiorari. This ended the Colony Square case.

Burt Reynolds Case

Alexander A. (Sandy) Simon, Jr., is a close friend of my law partner, Ted Maloof. He had lived in Atlanta and in Savannah for a time and had been active in real estate projects in both cities. When his father died in Florida, he returned home to manage the family investments and businesses with his three brothers. The movie actor, Burt Reynolds, owned a theater and ranch in nearby Jupiter, Florida, and was introduced to Sandy by mutual friends. When he decided to make a change in his business manager, he hired Sandy for that position. Sandy's duties as business manager included managing and investing the assets Reynolds owned, as well as keeping up with his houses in Florida and California. This was at a time in the latter half of the 1980s when Reynolds was still in demand as a movie actor and was earning considerable monies as royalties on movies he had previously made. He also had investments in a restaurant chain and in various stocks and bonds. One thing Sandy did was to open a brokerage account at the national investment and brokerage firm, Shearson Lehman Brothers, Inc., in Little Rock, Arkansas. The broker assigned to the account was one Michael Swofford, who did not have much to recommend himself as a broker, other than an ability to talk. He was a former schoolteacher.

Sandy not only opened accounts at Shearson for Reynolds but also opened accounts for himself and a family partnership, EASSA Properties. Almost from the beginning, Swofford mishandled the accounts by improper trading and other misdeeds. It was not long before he was stealing considerable sums of money from the Reynolds account. When the thefts were detected by an internal Shearson investigation, the Little Rock office notified two senior executives in Shearson's home office in New York, its general counsel, Peter Kajawski, and its director of compliance, Joseph Del Duca. Instead of alerting Sandy to the thefts and the trading in his own account and that of the family partnership, Kajawski and Del Duca bypassed Sandy and called the attorney for Burt Reynolds in California. Depending on whose testimony you believe, they either told or implied to the attorney for Reynolds that Sandy was implicated in the wrongdoing. Burt Reynolds promptly fired Sandy as business manager. Sandy contacted Ted Maloof for legal advice. Ted asked me to investigate the matter as best we could without the filing of a suit. Primarily based on talking to Sandy and reviewing documents, I concluded that Sandy had various causes of action against Shearson, Swofford, Kajawski, and/or Del Duca. Ted asked me to take charge of the litigation. We signed a retention agreement with Sandy whereby we agreed to take the case on a contingency basis—that is, the attorneys would not be paid anything for our services unless there was a recovery. Sandy would be responsible for the expenses of the litigation. Our legal fee would be one-third of any recovery without an appeal and 40 percent of any recovery in the case of an appeal.

The first thing we had to decide was where to file the suit. We could have filed it in Florida where Sandy resided, in California where the telephone call to the attorney for Reynolds was received, in New York where the telephone call was placed, in Arkansas where the thefts occurred, or in Atlanta where Shearson had an office. Since Atlanta was where Sandy had previously lived and worked and would be more convenient to us as his attorneys, we decided to file the case in the

United States District Court in Atlanta. The case was assigned to Judge Orinda Evans. I did not know Judge Evans well, but I had served on the judicial review panel during the Carter administration when the panel interviewed her and deemed her qualified to be a district court judge. I had never had a case before her previously. She had been a litigation partner at the Alston & Bird firm before President Carter appointed her to the bench.

The complaint we filed stated causes of action against Shearson and/or the other defendants for breach of contract, fraud, breach of fiduciary duty, defamation, and tortuous interference with contract. Ordinarily, this kind of case would be referred to compulsory arbitration because the security industry rules required claims against brokers for the mishandling of accounts to be arbitrated. There is no right to a jury trial in arbitration. We were able to file the case in the United States District Court with the right to a jury, however, because there were independent claims for defamation. Shearson retained Peter Anderson to represent it and the other defendants. Anderson was a well-known securities lawyer in Atlanta with significant experience defending brokerage firms. Two young female associates, Louise Matte and Sarah Ford, assisted him. I was assisted by Peter Quist, an associate in Hicks Maloof & Campbell.

After filing the suit, we served document requests on all the defendants and prepared to commence depositions. I took depositions in Florida, California, Arkansas, New York, and Georgia. The most important depositions were those of Burt Reynolds and his attorney, Donald Petroni, and those of Shearson, Peter Kajawski, Joseph Del Duca, and Michael Swofford. Swofford was indicted and convicted for the thefts. Prior to his reporting to federal prison, I took his deposition in Little Rock. While he was a good talker and evasive in some of his answers, he contradicted himself on numerous occasions, and I caught him in a number of outright lies during his deposition. He claimed that he thought some of the transactions had been authorized by two people who worked with Sandy on the Reynolds accounts—Keith Bell, an accountant, and Labe Mell, a consultant. He never directly accused Sandy of any wrongdoing or knowledge of the thefts.

Before taking the deposition of Burt Reynolds, we decided to depose Donald Petroni, his attorney who received the telephone call from Shearson. Petroni was an experienced business lawyer in Los

Angeles with a large firm and was a good witness. Prior to taking his deposition, we subpoenaed his documents, including any notes of the telephone conversation with Shearson. While certain documents were not produced because of a claim of attorney-client privilege, his notes of the telephone conversation with Shearson were produced and were helpful. It was clear that Petroni had been led to believe, if not told directly, that Shearson believed Sandy Simon was involved in the wrongdoing. We next deposed Burt Reynolds. He was not an impressive witness. He was defensive and seemed to assume that the lawyers were trying to make a fool out of him. In my opinion, that was not necessary, as he did a pretty good job himself. On the critical question of why he fired Sandy, his testimony was equivocal. He certainly emphasized all the negative information about Sandy that he could, but he did not deny that the Shearson phone call was the precipitating factor in Sandy's termination. He said that he considered a number of things, including dissatisfaction by some of his associates with respect to Sandy's performance. I was able to impeach him somewhat with respect to this testimony by showing him letters or memos he had written Sandy commending him for his good job as business manager. Reynolds was a much smaller person in physical size than I had assumed based on seeing some of his movies. He was well short of six feet tall and probably weighed around 150 pounds.

The depositions of Kajawski and Del Duca in New York were interesting. They were completely different witnesses. Del Duca was an aggressive, vocal, and in-your-face witness. He started his deposition with an announcement to this effect: "Mr. Campbell, I am a busy man and I do not have time for this foolishness. I expect you will finish your questions by noon today." I responded with something like this: "Mr. Del Duca, I have a lot of questions to ask you, and you will be here until I get answers to them regardless of how long it takes." The deposition lasted several days. He was extremely combative and uncooperative, and I formed the opinion that he would not go over well before an Atlanta jury. He was much more personable during recesses in the deposition and revealed that he had a daughter who was attending Emory University in Atlanta. But when we went back on the record, he returned to his combative, hostile self. He acknowledged that he had no idea whether Sandy was involved in the thefts, and he denied telling or implying to the attorney for Burt Reynolds that Sandy was involved.

Kajawski was a low-key, calm, and smooth witness. As would be expected of an attorney, he was comfortable with giving testimony and with the deposition procedure. I noticed, however, that when I got to the critical questions of what he and Del Duca told the attorney for Burt Reynolds, his calmness evaporated and he evidenced a number of nervous habits. I formed the opinion that if this occurred at trial, the jury was likely to conclude that he was not telling the truth in regard to what he and Del Duca told the attorney for Burt Reynolds. Like Del Duca, Kajawski denied that they told Petroni Sandy was implicated in the thefts. It was clear that both Del Duca and Kajawski were offended that they had been sued personally. I also heard that repeatedly from their attorney, Peter Anderson. We felt completely justified in suing them individually because they made the telephone call in which the alleged defamation occurred. In addition, with them as defendants in the case, it would be nearly impossible for Shearson to defend on the ground that their statements were not authorized by the corporation and thus were not the legal responsibility of the company without throwing them under the bus. The fact that they were individually defendants in the lawsuit apparently complicated their lives in terms of reports that had to be made to regulatory authorities, including the Securities and Exchange Commission.

Prior to this case, I had found that deposing the highest executive officers of major corporations often bore fruit because they were either so busy, or thought they were, that they did not adequately prepare for the depositions. Therefore, I noticed the deposition of the chairman of Shearson on the grounds that he was the most senior official of Shearson ultimately responsible for the supervision of Shearson brokers and the establishment of procedures that would prevent misdeeds of the kind in which Swofford was engaged from taking place. Shearson vigorously opposed the deposition and argued to Judge Evans that it was simply harassment. After a hearing, Judge Evans allowed me to take the deposition but limited its length to one hour. While this substantially hamstrung the deposition, I did get some testimony that I thought was helpful in the case, as it was obvious the witness had not given Shearson attorneys enough time to prepare him adequately. A number of the depositions in this case took place on the 105th floor of the World Trade Center that would later be hit by terrorists on September 11, 2001.

After discovery was completed, Shearson filed a motion for summary judgment, arguing that the facts did not warrant sending the case to a jury but should be decided by the court. Judge Evans denied this motion and scheduled the case for trial. Prior to the trial, a pretrial conference was held with counsel for both sides. The purpose of a pretrial conference is to work out the details of the trial, including the scheduling of witnesses and other such matters. During the pretrial conference, in the presence of Peter Anderson, Judge Evans said that she did not think much of my case and urged me to settle it. Of course, it is difficult to get a reasonable settlement offer when the presiding judge says the court does not think much of the case in the presence of opposing counsel. No serious settlement discussions took place.

Peter Anderson continued to lobby me to dismiss Del Duca and Kajawski. He said that his client would agree to any reasonable protection that would prevent Shearson from arguing that the statements made to the attorney for Burt Reynolds were not authorized by the corporation. Eliminating these two defendants would simplify the case somewhat, but I was not willing to take any risk in doing so. One danger in dismissing defendants is that they might not show up at trial or only at a time advantageous to the other side. If they remained as defendants, they still would not have to be in the courtroom at all times, but they would certainly be expected to be there during most of the trial. I gave the matter a good deal of thought and came up with some conditions under which I would dismiss Del Duca and Kajawski without prejudice—that is, the claims could be brought against them at a future date. The conditions were, first, that Shearson agree that the corporation authorized the statements made in the telephone conversation and that Shearson would not defend on the grounds that they were not so authorized or that Shearson was not liable for them if the court or jury determined them to be actionable. Second, I insisted on an agreement by Shearson, and the two individual defendants being dismissed, that they would be produced at the trial on twenty-four hours written notice from me at a time of my choosing. If agreed to, this was a significant advantage because it meant I could be assured of their presence when I wanted them and when they would best fit into the presentation of my case. Shearson immediately accepted my proposal, and Del Duca and Kajawski were dismissed without prejudice prior to trial.

The trial lasted for approximately three weeks in the Richard B. Russell Federal Building and Courthouse in Downtown Atlanta. As plaintiff, we put on our case first. Sandy Simon was my first witness, and I thought he did a good job. I then called Del Duca and Kajawski for cross-examination. They were disastrous witnesses for Shearson. Del Duca was not only combative and hostile but was not adequately prepared. There were a number of instances where he tried to give testimony inconsistent with his deposition testimony, and I was able to show the jury that he was changing his story. Kajawski was not much better. His nervous habits during critical questioning were in sharp contrast to his earlier calmness during the preliminary questions. I prolonged the preliminary questioning somewhat to be sure his calm demeanor was firmly fixed in the jury's mind before I got to the critical questions. I felt that the decision to dismiss these two defendants and be able to control their appearance at trial had worked in our favor.

I was, of course, concerned about the testimony of Burt Reynolds. Since he was outside the subpoena power of the court, his attendance could not be compelled. Instead, in its case, Shearson read portions of his deposition and I read other portions. I was concerned about the effect his criticism of Sandy might have on the jury. When we interviewed the jury after the trial was over, I discovered that most jurors simply interpreted his hostile attitude toward Sandy as evidence of the damage that had been done to Sandy from the telephone call. Trial lawyers often are not the best judges of the effect of trial testimony on jurors.

Another episode during the case that surprisingly worked to our advantage was the appearance of Swofford. Shearson brought him in as a witness during their case from prison, which I never understood. The only conceivable way he could help Shearson was in some of his statements that his dealings with Keith Bell and Labe Mell led him to believe that Sandy agreed to some of the actions and that he told that to Shearson in good faith. There were so many contradictions in his testimony, however, and he had told so many lies in his deposition that it was easy to impeach him. After I had gone through the first couple of lies he told, Judge Evans told me she thought that was enough on that subject and I should move on to something else. I was shocked at this direction since I was cross-examining the defendant who handled the accounts and stole the money, and the general rule is that, on cross-examination, you are entitled to a full and complete examination. I went on to other questions but then came back to a first cousin of one of Swofford's lies in his deposition. At this question, Judge Evans asked counsel to come to the bench and lectured me that she thought I understood her directions and she expected me to follow them. When we retreated from the bench, Peter and his co-counsel had wide smiles on their faces and gave thumbs-up in full view of the jury. I thought this was unprofessional conduct, and Peter should have known better. In interviews with the jury after the case was over, they were highly critical of this conduct and of Judge Evans for cutting off my cross-examination of Swofford. Before dismissing Swofford, I paused for at least a minute to study my notes so the jury would understand that I had a lot of additional questions that I was not allowed to ask. In later interviews with jurors , several said they thought the judge was against us and had treated us unfairly.

One of our best witnesses in the case was Sandy's wife, Donna. She is originally from Massachusetts and a delightful lady. Her testimony was important in outlining for the jury the damage Sandy's firing by Burt Reynolds did to him and to their family. She testified that after the firing, he was no longer as trusting of people and that he was humiliated by rumors that were circulated as to why he was fired. They divorced not long after the case.

One of the things I had learned in trying previous cases is that in the closing argument, it is effective to use analogies that lay jurors can understand in simplifying complex legal issues. One important legal issue in the case was the amount of punitive damages that should be awarded against Shearson if the jury found in favor of the plaintiff. Punitive damages are not designed to compensate the prevailing party but to punish the wrongdoer and deter others who may be situated in similar circumstances from engaging in such conduct. In setting the amount of punitive damages, jurors are authorized to consider the worldly circumstances of the defendant. In this case, that meant Shearson's size and wealth. We placed in evidence information with respect to Shearson's assets, profits, and cash, which were enormous. In my closing argument, in addressing the question of how much in punitive damages was appropriate, I used an analogy to our son, Garrett, who was about six years old at the time. I told the jury that he loved the *Sesame Street* television program. If he misbehaved and I did nothing more than tell him not to do it again or even spank him, he would soon forget it. But I also told the jury that if I deprived him of seeing *Sesame Street* for a week, he did not forget the punishment. Therefore, I argued to the jury that the amount of punitive damages it set should be the amount it believed would make Shearson remember this case if future similar situations should occur. "The next time something like this happens and the Shearson senior executives in New York receive a telephone call from one of its offices around the country," I said, "whether the call comes from Little Rock, Arkansas, Atlanta, Georgia, or Los Angeles, California, will they recall what happened in that case down in Atlanta? Will they say we came out of that pretty well or we don't want to get hit like that again? It is not for me to tell you how much in punitive damages is necessary to deter this corporation from wrongdoing. That is a decision for you to make based on the evidence you have heard in this case."

The jury returned a verdict of over $10 million, including almost $8 million in punitive damages. We were, of course, overjoyed, and Sandy was happy and relieved. As I previously stated, we learned a lot from the jurors when we interviewed them after the verdict was rendered. They thought the testimony of Del Duca and Kajawski had been damaging to Shearson, and they did not believe the testimony of Reynolds or Swofford had hurt Sandy's case. One juror, an African-American nurse, told me, "Mr. Campbell, I thought to myself at the end of your closing argument that it was time for prayer meeting." There is no better feeling for a trial lawyer than to have prevailed in a major trial and to have jurors say positive things about the way in which the trial was conducted. This was certainly one of the proudest days of my legal career.

One of the most depressing days of my legal career occurred several months thereafter. I was vacationing with my family at the Cloister Resort at Sea Island, Georgia, when I received a telephone call from the office stating that we had received an order from Judge Evans setting aside every dime of the verdict. She had directed that a verdict be entered for Shearson principally because the telephone call, in the court's opinion, was not the reason for Sandy's firing. I was shocked at this blatant substitution of the court's opinion on legitimate contested issues of fact in a jury case. The jury could have decided that Sandy was not fired because of the telephone call, but it could equally well decide that the telephone call was a proximate cause of his termination. If jurors are not entitled to decide those kinds of questions, why have juries at all?

We, of course, appealed the order entered by Judge Evans to the United States Court of Appeals for the 11th Circuit. I was confident that we would get some relief from her order, although I recognized the legitimate issues with respect to the amount of damages. We filed our brief, and Shearson filed its brief. The matter was argued before a three-judge panel chaired by the senior judge on the panel, the late Judge Thomas Clark. I thought the oral argument went well. In an order entered approximately six months later, the 11th Circuit severely criticized Judge Evans for substituting her opinion for the opinion of the jurors on the reason for the firing of Sandy Simon. Her order was reversed. The appellate court gave us a choice—we could retry the case or accept approximately $2.5 million in damages. Sandy was inclined to retry the case. I advised against that, saying it was perfectly obvious that Judge Evans was going to figure out some way to make it difficult for us to recover. Sandy suggested that we move to disqualify her on the grounds of prejudice. I explained that this is difficult and almost impossible based on a court's rulings unless you can show actual prejudice or some improper interest in the case. I said a disqualification motion was almost certain to be denied and would simply inflame the court further. I also said that since Shearson had been given one look at our strategy in the trial of the case, much of what worked well in the first trial would probably not work as well in a retrial. While I said I was certainly not satisfied with $2.5 million in damages, candor required me to say that it was as much as we would probably get out of a retrial or more. Ted Maloof agreed with me and so advised Sandy. We accepted the reduced damages.

Bob Kern Case

The approximately ten-acre tract of land located at the intersection of Peachtree and Piedmont roads in North Atlanta, known as Peachmont, is today the home of a substantial hotel, condominium, and retail development. In the 1980s, the Prudential Insurance Company of America (PRU) assembled and purchased the property for future development. PRU was assisted in the acquisition of the property by an Atlanta real estate broker and developer, Bob Kern, and his company, Kern and Company. After the property was acquired but before it was developed, Kern claimed that PRU had agreed that he would be an equity investor in the project. PRU disputed that, claiming that he was only a broker in the transaction. Kern filed suit against PRU in the United States District Court for the Northern District of Georgia. The case was assigned to district court judge Jack Camp. PRU retained the Washington law firm of Howry & Simon to represent it in the case. Based on our earlier work together on the Colony Square case, Howry & Simon retained our firm as local counsel.

There was essentially no documentation to support Kern's claim that he was to be an equity investor in the project. His case was based almost entirely on alleged comments a senior PRU executive made at a reception in Atlanta. Kern claimed that the PRU executive described him as PRU's "partner." It seemed preposterous to me that a large corporation would make someone a partner in a multimillion-dollar development without any partnership documents. My role in the case was to examine the "political witnesses" who attended the reception. They were former governor Carl Sanders, whose firm regularly represented Kern, former Atlanta mayor Andrew Young, chairman of the Fulton County Commission Michael Lomax, and president of the Atlanta City Council Marvin Arrington. These witnesses were expected to provide important testimony about what was said at the reception and the circumstances under which it was said. Ordinarily, an oral promise of this nature would not be enforceable, but Kern claimed that the comments made at the reception were part performance, which might make the promise enforceable even without an agreement in writing.

I took the depositions of Mayor Young, Chairman Lomax, and city council president Arrington. All three of them generally supported Kern's claim except for Mayor Young. Michael Lomax supported Kern's case by stating that he recalled the comments at the reception of the PRU executive to the effect that Kern was PRU's partner. Marvin Arrington went even further and gave the most outspoken testimony in favor of Kern by stating that there was no doubt in his mind from what was said at the reception that Kern was PRU's partner. Andrew Young, who before being elected mayor of Atlanta had served in the United States House of Representatives, as ambassador to the United Nations, and as a close advisor and ally of Dr. Martin Luther King, Jr., testified that he could not recall exactly what the PRU executive had said but that, in any event, he would not necessarily have interpreted such comments in that setting to mean that they were partners in a legal sense. Young's testimony was not helpful to Kern, and Mayor Young was not called as a witness at the trial. We could have called him as a witness in PRU's case, but we elected not to do so since his testimony, while favorable to PRU, was not critical and we did not want to further impose on his time. I took his deposition at his offices in the Merchandise Mart in Atlanta where he was playing a major role in the winning and staging of the 1996 Olympic Games in Atlanta.

At the end of discovery, we felt good about our case and thought we might even get summary judgment. Judge Camp denied the motion, however, and scheduled the case for trial. Prior to the trial, PRU decided to participate in an exercise to test the central themes of its case and to get juror reaction to its lawyers. This practice is often used in large cases where the exposure justifies the expense. A company that specializes in this kind of work uses the same procedures to select mock jurors that will be used by the court in the trial of the case. The mock jurors are brought into a facility where lawyers for each side make abbreviated statements of each side's case and then the jurors deliberate. The attorneys and client representatives observe the deliberations through one-way windows and can actually send in questions to see what the jurors thought about certain arguments or attorneys. One of the purposes of this exercise was to see whether the lead counsel for PRU from Howry & Simon, Bill Wallace, would go over well before a southern jury. He had tried numerous cases for PRU around the country and had been successful. In fact, he was somewhat of a hero at PRU. I discovered this when I was walking down the hall with him at PRU's corporate headquarters in Newark, New Jersey, and witnessed numerous PRU executives coming out of their offices to shake his hand and greet him. They appreciated all the successful defenses of PRU in the cases he had tried. There was no question about Bill's capabilities as a trial lawyer, but he was the quintessential northerner with a noticeable accent. He had not previously tried a major case in the South, and PRU wanted to be sure that he would be well received by a southern jury. I did not have much doubt about that, because from experience I knew that Atlanta juries had changed a great deal as a result of the influx of people from throughout the country. At the mock jury exercise, I argued the case from Kern's side and Bill argued the case from PRU's side. Bill was well received by the mock jurors, and this alleviated any concern about using him as lead counsel in the case. The mock jury exercise also gave us comfort that our central theme in the case—that no one would ever make someone a partner in a deal of this size without a written partnership agreement—would be well received by the jury.

This was the first trial in which I used or witnessed the use of new, cutting-edge technology for the impeachment of witnesses on the computer. Usually, when a witness was impeached for giving testimony contradictory to what he or she said in an earlier deposition, the attorney simply showed the witness the prior testimony on a written transcript. This new technology allowed a deposition, which had been videotaped, to be separated into snippets of key testimony that were burned onto a disk and could be immediately replayed on a screen in the courtroom if the witness contradicted the prior testimony. This new technology is effective with a witness who is making up testimony and having difficulty keeping track of what he or she has previously said in a deposition. This was particularly true of Mr. Kern in his testimony at trial, and he was effectively impeached based on his prior deposition testimony by Bill Wallace using this new technology.

At the trial, Kern was represented by Neal Pope, an experienced trial attorney from Columbus, Georgia. Neal, who would later be named as a fellow of the American College of Trial Lawyers, was not in good health at the time of the trial. In fact, I wondered for several days whether he would be able to continue. I also noticed that his wife was in the courtroom several times during the trial. Immediately after the trial was over, he had major heart surgery at the Emory University Hospital.

I cross-examined Governor Sanders, Michael Lomax, and Marvin Arrington at the trial. At the beginning of my cross-examination of Governor Sanders, he referred to me as "Charlie." This is a technique often used by attorneys when they are being cross-examined to suggest that the opposing lawyer and the witness are friends and on good terms. To offset that impression, I said at the beginning of my questioning of Sanders that I would refer to him as Governor Sanders. His testimony was consistent with what I had expected, and my cross-examination of him was designed to show that Bob Kern was a major client of his law firm and paid large sums in legal fees. It was my hope that this would lead the jury to discount the testimony of Governor Sanders as not being an entirely disinterested party. The testimonies of Lomax and Arrington were consistent with their depositions, but I did not think the testimony of any of these witnesses was credible, and this was confirmed when the case was over and we interviewed the jurors.

During the trial, Judge Camp tried to get us to settle the case by calling all counsel into his chambers. We thought we were in good shape with the jurors and saw no reason to make a significant settlement offer, particularly since PRU strongly felt that the suit was nothing more than an attempted shakedown. When the jury returned with its verdict, it was a complete victory for PRU. Kern did not recover any damages. Our interview with the jurors after the verdict was rendered revealed that they did not consider the testimony of any of the political witnesses to be credible and they did not believe that a corporation like Prudential would make someone a partner in a major real estate development without a written partnership agreement.

A sad postscript of this case involves Judge Camp. I had known him since he was a lawyer in Newnan, Georgia, and represented local banks in some of my bankruptcy cases. He went on to have a distinguished career as a federal judge in Atlanta and to serve as chief judge of the district court. After having been on the court for almost thirty years, he was caught in an FBI sting operation involving prostitutes and drugs. He apparently was not only involved with the prostitutes but was apparently assisting with the drugs. He resigned in disgrace and pled guilty. He was sentenced to time in federal prison. I have never been so shocked in my life, as Jack Camp would have been one of the last people I would have thought could be involved in any such activities.

Aiden Emmett Barnes III

Emmett Barnes is one of the most interesting clients I ever represented. Born in Macon, Georgia, his father was prominent in the insurance business through a substantial insurance agency office he owned in Macon. Emmett received a business degree from Harvard Business School and fought in the historic Battle of the Bulge in World War II. He was a highly decorated war veteran. He then returned to Macon and joined his father in the family insurance business. After his father's death, he continued the business and, in addition, established his own insurance company. He made millions when he sold that company in the early 1980s. In addition to his home in Macon, he had large residences at Sea Island, Georgia, and at the Breakers Resort in West Palm Beach, Florida. He owned a number of farms, shopping centers, apartment complexes, and an extensive art collection. He traveled by his own private plane. After he sold his insurance company, however, he over-invested in real estate, particularly in downtown Macon. It was said that if you walked down the street in Macon and pointed randomly at a property, there was a good chance Emmett Barnes owned it.

In the early 1990s, Frank Jones, a senior litigation partner at King & Spalding who was originally from Macon, was representing Emmett in a dispute with the Zürich Insurance Company concerning premiums collected by Emmett's insurance agency that were supposed to be treated as trust funds. During the course of this litigation, it became apparent to Frank that Emmett had problems beyond the Zürich litigation. He suggested that Emmett should consult an attorney experienced in dealing with creditor problems. Frank called Bob Hicks one day when Bob was out of the office and, in his absence, asked for me. He described the situation and asked if we were in a position to talk to Emmett Barnes. I called a lawyer friend of mine in Macon to see what he could tell me about Barnes. He strongly discouraged me from representing him and stated that he was hardheaded, uncooperative, and would be difficult to represent. When Bob came back to the office that afternoon, I discussed the matter with him, and we agreed that if Frank Jones was representing Barnes, then he was someone to whom we should at least afford an audience. I called Frank back, told him we would be glad to talk with Barnes, and outlined the kind of documentation we would need prior to the conversation. I received that documentation shortly thereafter.

The situation Emmett Barnes faced was highly complex on a number of fronts. He owned extensive property of all kinds, and there was no unified way in which it was held. Some was in his individual name, some was held in partnerships with others, and some was held in corporations. In addition, more than thirty secured creditors had financed various properties. His principal residence in Macon, on which there was a multimillion-dollar bank loan, was on a thirty-day demand note. He was in bad need of help, and Bob and I decided to take him on as a client. Bob asked me to take responsibility for the case.

After reviewing the documentation, I traveled to Macon and met with Emmett Barnes at his residence. Also at the meeting were Frank Jones and Barnes's brother, Dr. Waddell Barnes, a prominent physician in Macon. When I first met Emmett Barnes, he was sitting at a table in his kitchen and feeding one of his dogs part of a leftover Wendy's hamburger. He was in his seventies and was completely estranged from his two children, Nancy, who married Pierre Howard, the lieutenant governor of Georgia and a former classmate of mine at the University of Georgia, and Emmett IV, who had married the daughter of a prominent King & Spalding litigation partner, Byron Attridge. Barnes had divorced his first wife and the mother of his children, who was from a prominent family in Virginia, and married his secretary, Edwina. His family affairs were in no better shape than his business affairs.

Emmett lived in a fashionable section of Macon in a simple, ranch-style house on about fifteen acres of land. He had a set of fountains on the property the likes of which I had never seen. At night when they were illuminated, it was a sight to behold. Just operating the fountains cost several thousand dollars a month in utility expenses. He also had his own private chapel on the property. In earlier times when he was doing well financially, every time he went on a foreign trip he would buy so much art that he had to build a new wing onto his house. He had a Russian wing, a Japanese wing, and others.

At the meeting, I outlined the alternatives available to Emmett Barnes. The first was to move to Florida and protect his assets under that state's favorable law. In Florida, at the time, you could basically shield from creditors an unlimited amount of assets as long as they were in a principal residence and surrounding property or in investments such as annuities. Many prominent people moved to Florida to take advantage of its law in this regard, including the former commissioner of baseball, Bowie Kuhn. Emmett quickly said that he was not willing to leave Macon. I told him the second alternative was to file a proceeding in the bankruptcy court, which would be complicated because of the way in which he held his properties. He said he would under no circumstances file a bankruptcy and seemed to be offended that I would even suggest it. We were not off to a good start. He then asked for the third alternative. I told him we could try to do an out-of-court workout with his creditors, but that such efforts seldom succeeded and it would be particularly difficult in his situation because of the large number of different secured creditors and properties. He stated that he wanted to take that approach. I told him we would try but that experience had taught me it was critical to do the things necessary to file a bankruptcy in the event that the workout negotiations fail. I explained that it only took one creditor to move against its collateral to create a stampede. If that happened and he was not immediately in a position to file bankruptcy, he was at risk of losing all of his properties. I told him that the ultimate decision of whether to file would rest with him, but we would not represent him in workout efforts if he did not agree that the bankruptcy papers were to be prepared and ready to file. He reluctantly agreed that we could complete the documentation, which would put us in a position to file a bankruptcy if an emergency required it, and he approved. At the same time, he was adamant in insisting that he was not going to file bankruptcy but would pay his creditors in full.

Mike Levengood, a detail-oriented person with extensive knowledge of the Bankruptcy Code, was a young partner at Hicks Maloof & Campbell with whom I had previously worked on bankruptcy matters. I asked him to assume responsibility for assisting me with the case and for immediately commencing work on the documentation that would be necessary to file a bankruptcy. Jeff Cavender, a young associate who had just joined the firm from law school, was lined up to help Mike on the bankruptcy documentation and research. In the meantime, I would review detailed information on the different secured creditors, their collateral, and the performance of the properties in order to be in a position to advise Emmett as to the kinds of offers that made sense in this situation. While a number of his properties were performing well, others were losing money and seemed to be candidates to give back to the secured creditors in exchange for a release. I went back to Macon to meet with Emmett at his office, which was on the second floor of a building above a first-floor retail space. Emmett had an impressive office with a large mural that depicted his daughter and son-in-law. We discussed his situation and arrived at the general contours of proposals to be made to the different secured creditors. Each time we discussed a particular creditor, Emmett said something to the effect that the president of that bank was a good friend of his and there would be no problem with that creditor. Finally, I said, "Emmett, you are in a situation where you are about to discover the truth of the old saying that if your best friends are bankers, you are largely without friends." After the case was over, Emmett said I was right, although he did not know it at the time. I told him that at some point we would want to get all the creditors together to be sure they were all hearing the same thing and did not feel one was being played against the other. I explained, however, that there was a danger in getting all of them in one place, as it gave them an opportunity to talk and plot against him. I also repeated what I told him earlier that it would take only one creditor to torpedo the whole effort by moving against its collateral.

We scheduled a meeting of all the secured creditors in the conference room facility of a motel in Macon. We had good attendance, and I felt that the meeting went well. To my surprise, I was actually hopeful following the meeting that we might be successful in accomplishing an out-of-court workout agreement with the creditors. The largest secured creditor was Empire Mortgage Corporation, which held liens against a number of the apartment complexes and shopping centers. Not long after this meeting, with no advance warning, Empire moved to claim the rental proceeds from the apartment complexes in which it had secured positions. This is exactly what I had feared and what I had warned Emmett might happen. When he called me and told me what had happened, I told him he had no alternative but to file bankruptcy immediately because the other secured creditors would soon move to claim the proceeds from their collateral and any possibility of reorganization would collapse. He reluctantly authorized us to file the bankruptcy papers that had already been prepared. We were able to file the bankruptcy before any of the other secured creditors took action, and we successfully litigated with Empire over whether the actions it had taken before the filing were sufficient to divest the bankruptcy estate of its interest in those rental payments.

The bankruptcy case was assigned to Judge Robert F. Herschner, who had previously been a law partner with Jerry Kaplan during the time we litigated the Lawson Cotton case. I did not know Herschner well, but he had an excellent reputation of being fair to debtors and giving them a reasonable opportunity to reorganize. That is all we could hope for or expect. The initial period of a bankruptcy is hectic because a tremendous amount of documentation and information has to be filed with the bankruptcy court. Mike Levengood and Jeff Cavender assumed responsibility for this substantial task and did an excellent job. I was busy advising Emmett as to what I thought we should do about the various properties. We immediately agreed to sell the two farms because Emmett would not have time for them anyway. He and I visited the condominium at Palm Beach. It was a beautiful property on the ocean, but I urged him to auction it. He readily agreed to do so. We also identified a number of the downtown Macon properties that we would offer to return to secured creditors in exchange for a full release.

A good many of the properties would need to be sold and a real estate broker retained to do that. Emmett came up with the idea of retaining several different brokers on a non-exclusive basis so there would be competition to get the best price. I had never used that approach and was skeptical, but that is what we did, and it worked out well. Contrary to the advice I had received from the Macon lawyer about representing Emmett Barnes, he was an ideal client. He was optimistic throughout and fully engaged. Each time he testified in the bankruptcy court, he was prepared and articulate. He took legal advice readily and seemed genuinely to appreciate the efforts made by the attorneys on his behalf. The bankruptcy proceeding went well for the first few months. We were just beginning to formulate our bankruptcy plan when Empire struck again.

Empire filed a motion to convert the bankruptcy proceeding to one under Chapter 7. Unlike Chapter 11, under which we had filed, Chapter 7 is a liquidation in which the court appoints a trustee, usually a local attorney, who essentially displaces the debtor. This would be a disaster in Emmett's case. It would mean he would lose control and incur much additional expense that would be paid from his properties. For the first time, I think he was genuinely frightened that he might lose everything. I tried to explain to him that while this was a serious move on the part of his largest secured creditor, it was also an opportunity for us. I told him that, in my experience, when a bankruptcy court denies the motion to convert a Chapter 11 case to Chapter 7, it usually means the court is going to give the debtor every opportunity to reorganize. Therefore, we geared up to fight the motion filed by Empire and were able to defeat it. Empire was represented by a partner in the Atlanta firm of Troutman Sanders, Mary Grace Deihl, who is now a bankruptcy judge in Atlanta. Mary Grace was a fine lawyer and is now a fine judge. Filing the motion to convert was a mistake, however. Her client may have insisted upon it. When the bankruptcy court denied it, I was confident that Judge Herschner would give us a fair opportunity to confirm a plan.

Not long thereafter, we filed our bankruptcy plan. It called for Emmett to sell certain properties, give some back to secured creditors for a full release, and retain a number of apartment complexes, shopping centers, and downtown Macon properties. It called for us to auction the

Palm Beach condo, sell the art collection at auction, and give the Macon house back to the secured creditor. The hardest sell for Emmett was to dispose of the art collection, which was dear to him. I explained that there was no way the unsecured creditors would allow him to keep the art collection and any other properties as well. And I pointed out to him that the Macon residence without the art collection would be a huge house he did not need and could not afford to maintain. We employed Alfred A. Robinson Auction Company from Knoxville, Tennessee, to auction the art collection. It was quite an event that was held on site at Emmett's Macon home and lasted several days. Emmett owned many fine pieces of art (paintings, sculptures, antiques, and one of the largest collections of Beam porcelain in the country), and there were buyers from all over the United States and international buyers participating by telephone in several foreign countries. The art collection sold for several million dollars. This, and proceeds from the sale of certain other properties, was used to pay the expenses of the bankruptcy and make a significant down payment to the unsecured creditors at the time of confirmation of the plan.

We employed Bill Hays as our expert witness for plan confirmation on the question of the feasibility of the plan. Among many other requirements, to obtain confirmation of a bankruptcy plan, a debtor must show that he or she is not likely to need further reorganization proceedings because he or she can perform under the plan. Since we had already negotiated agreements with almost all the secured creditors, the feasibility related to the unsecured creditors. Under the plan, we proposed to make a significant down payment of approximately $2 million to the unsecured creditors (they were owed about $8 million) at the time of confirmation from the auction proceeds and then to pay the net income from the properties that were retained over a period of six years without interest. At the end of the six years, if the unsecured creditors had not been paid in full, they would be given deeds to the properties remaining in satisfaction of their debts. This was a favorable deal for the debtor. But it was not obtained because of great attorney work. It was possible because of the circumstances of the case. Tom Byrne of the Atlanta firm of Sutherland Asbil and Brennan represented the unsecured creditors committee. Tom was an experienced bankruptcy lawyer and was no fool. The main reason he agreed to the long-term payout with no interest had to do with the age of the properties being retained and the fact that they had been almost completely depreciated for tax purposes during the lengthy period Barnes had owned them. If they had been liquidated and sold, there was equity in some of the properties, but it would have been consumed by the payment of taxes. By agreeing to a long-term payout and the receipt of the properties remaining at the end of the payout, coupled with a requirement that Barnes be prevented from leaving the properties to anyone in his will other than his wife so as to minimize estate taxes, this was the best assurance that the unsecured creditors would be paid in the final analysis. The plan was confirmed on that basis. In a strange twist on this issue, Emmett did not make any net profit payments to the unsecured creditors during the six-year period because he plowed all the monies back into the properties and maintained them like they had never been maintained before. After about four years, with judgment day coming, he came up with the ingenious idea of having his friend, John Ramsay, whom I had known at the University of Georgia, buy the creditor claims at anywhere from 10 to 25 cents on the dollar. It took a little over $ 1 million to do so. John then sold these claims back to Emmett for exactly what he paid for them. Emmett raised this money by refinancing his Sea Island home. Thus he was free of any remaining obligations under the plan.

Emmett was, of course, overjoyed with the successful conclusion of his bankruptcy, although he told me our legal fees of about $1.5 million were the largest he had ever paid. The most important thing I had accomplished for him was helping him keep the Sea Island house. I told him I thought that was the property most likely to appreciate in the future and was also a property that I thought he would enjoy as the years went by. Under the agreement with the unsecured creditors, he had to rent the Sea Island house sufficiently each year to generate revenues to pay the upkeep of the property and taxes. The proceeds from his other properties could be used to pay the mortgage on the Sea Island house, which was several million dollars. The house was rented through the Sea Island Company, and the rental price was approximately $30,000 a month. By renting it about four or five months out of the year, he could pay the upkeep of the property and use the house for the remainder of the year himself. It turned out to be the best advice I gave him during the bankruptcy.

A sad occurrence that took place toward the end of the bankruptcy was litigation between him and his children. His father had left a trust for him and a separate trust for his brother, Dr. Barnes. He had placed about $750,000 in each trust and had provided that his sons would be the principal beneficiaries and their children would be the secondary beneficiaries. During the bankruptcy, Emmett took quite a bit of money out of the trust to live on since he was not earning much from his properties. The children, from whom he had become estranged much earlier, objected to the withdrawals and filed suit against the trustee to prevent them. During the bankruptcy, I tried to negotiate a settlement with Pierre Howard, and I thought we had agreed on a deal under which Emmett would limit his withdrawals. His children never agreed to the proposal, however. I assume that Pierre was not able to sell it either to his wife or her brother. We defended the suit filed by the children in the superior court of Bibb County. The judge ruled against our position, and we appealed it to the Georgia Supreme Court. The Supreme Court reversed the lower court and held that Emmett was entitled, as the primary beneficiary of the trust, to withdraw such monies as were necessary for him to continue to live as he was living at the time of the bankruptcy. This essentially allowed him to withdraw all the funds from the trust, which he eventually did.

After the conclusion of the litigation with the children and the bankruptcy, we had a victory party at our house in Atlanta. It was a wonderful occasion, and it was good to see a client who was genuinely grateful for the work of his attorneys. Emmett and I remained good friends until the day he died. He also took a liking to our son, Garrett, and he invited us on several occasions to stay a week at the Sea Island house, which Garrett enjoyed. It was a huge house right on the beach, and I remember one year we were there at Halloween, which was a special time for Garrett to investigate the nooks and crannies of the house and search out goblins. The last time I saw Emmett was about a year before he died when he invited Ann, Garrett, and me to join him at dinner in the dining room of the newly reopened and rebuilt Cloister Resort. We enjoyed the evening immensely. He suffered a massive stroke at his Sea Island home about a year later and died in a Brunswick hospital that night. He was not only one of the most interesting clients I have ever represented but also a good friend.

United Companies Financial Corporation

United Companies Financial Corporation (UCFC), a public company based in Baton Rouge, Louisiana, was in the business of originating, servicing, and selling subprime home mortgages. These were loans made at above-market interest rates to borrowers who had a questionable credit history. The secret to the business was in making loans to qualified purchasers and effectively servicing the loans. Many of the loans were packaged into what were known as "securitizations" and sold by Wall Street to the investing public. UCFC generally retained the servicing rights for the mortgages included in the securitizations. Over time, UCFC became lax in the criteria used in making loans, used inflated or fraudulent appraisals, and did a poor job of servicing its loans. This eventually forced it into bankruptcy in 2000.

One day in 2000, my law partner, Gary Marsh, asked me to come to the firm's large conference room, where he introduced me to Rich Johnson, a UCFC shareholder who had helped organize an unofficial shareholder committee prior to the bankruptcy. One of the first such committees to be organized on the Internet, it received a good deal of press publicity. Subsequently, the unofficial committee convinced the office of the United States Trustee and the bankruptcy court in Wilmington, Delaware, where the case was pending, to appoint an official equity committee in the bankruptcy. This was fairly rare because shareholders in a bankruptcy share in the assets only if they are sufficient to pay creditors in full. Rich was conducting an interview of several law firms as possible counsel to the official equity committee. Gary asked me to participate in the interview to help outline the firm's bankruptcy and litigation experience. Our firm was selected as counsel for the committee.

I have always teased Gary about trying to slough off his most difficult cases on me. I was only half joking. In a moment of weakness, I allowed Gary to convince me to become responsible for the UCFC equity committee representation. It would be one of the most difficult of my career. The first difficulty was that the assets of the company did not appear to be sufficient to pay the unsecured creditors and leave anything for the shareholders. The second difficulty was that the debtor in possession and the official creditors committee felt so strongly about that position that they both vigorously opposed the appointment of an equity committee and then refused to cooperate with the committee and its counsel after it was appointed. Finally, there were a number of hotheads on the equity committee who had little knowledge of or interest in bankruptcy law. Several of them had purchased their UCFC stock after the problems surfaced and the stock plummeted in price so that they bought at a low price and thus stood to make a windfall if the shareholders got anything in the bankruptcy.

From the beginning, counsel for the debtor, the Weil Gotshal firm from New York, and counsel for the creditors committee, the Wachtel Lipton firm from New York, treated the equity committee and its counsel as if they did not exist. These were two of the most powerful law firms in New York. The debtor and the creditors committee failed to cooperate with the equity committee and its counsel on pending litigation in the case and in regard to requests for documents submitted by counsel for the equity committee. The lack of cooperation became so serious that on one occasion the bankruptcy judge, Mary Walrath, sanctioned counsel for the debtor by announcing that the court would not approve legal fees sought by counsel for the debtor in connection with a motion brought by the equity committee to compel compliance with document requests submitted to the debtor. Notwithstanding this admonition, the lack of cooperation continued. If anything, the creditors committee and its counsel were even less cooperative.

In this hostile environment, it was difficult for the equity committee to do its job. I decided to bring the matter to the attention of the bankruptcy court again and ask for relief. Judge Walrath was a relatively young and new judge, having been appointed only a few years earlier after working as an attorney with a small firm in Philadelphia. The other attorneys and I discovered, however, that she was tough as nails and not easily intimidated. When the hearing with respect to the lack of cooperation from the debtor and the creditors committee was held, Judge Walrath was not pleased, particularly since she had already admonished both parties at the earlier hearing when she sanctioned counsel for the debtor. She announced at the second hearing that because of the lack of cooperation, she was terminating the exclusive right of the debtor to file a reorganization plan and opening up the process to the equity committee. This was a significant ruling because the debtor in a bankruptcy case typically has a certain amount of time in which it has the exclusive right to file a plan, and other parties are relegated either to opposing the plan or trying to negotiate changes in it. When the court ruled that the equity committee could propose its own plan, the dynamics in the case shifted significantly.

Since one of the matters that would determine the level of assets in the case and the likelihood that they were sufficient to reach the shareholders was the value of the loan portfolio serviced by the debtor, we quickly determined that the best way to generate additional value from the assets would be to improve the servicing of the loans. That would not be difficult since the debtor had a substandard servicing system with the result that numerous defaulted loans often sat idly by with no attention for months. This not only resulted in no income being received on the loans that were in default but also in the underlying homes that served as collateral sitting unoccupied and unmaintained with a diminished value. We recommended to the equity committee that the best plan would be to bring in a new and qualified servicer that could do a better job of collecting the outstanding loans and servicing delinquent loans. I requested Brian Olasav, a non-lawyer professional in our law firm who had Wall Street experience with these kinds of assets, to help me locate a respected and effective servicer of subprime loans. We eventually identified such a company in Florida and visited its offices there. We were impressed. It had the latest technology to keep track of defaulted loans and had an excellent record of servicing subprime mortgages. We commenced negotiations with this firm to serve as the new servicer in the equity committee plan. We were able to reach a nonbinding letter of intent on the principal terms. This letter of intent was subject to definitive documentation, and the finished contract would serve as the main feature of the equity committee plan.

Not long after the letter of intent was signed, I received a telephone call from the servicer. The company was not willing to go forward and negotiate a contract after all but was withdrawing. I was, of course, surprised and immediately suspected that the firm had been pressured to withdraw by either the counsel or a member of the creditors committee. Information that had been provided to the equity committee during our due diligence of the servicer indicated that members of the creditors committee had business connections to the servicer. Since the elimination of the centerpiece of the equity committee plan would cripple our efforts to offer a competing plan, we decided to file motions with the bankruptcy court for permission to take what are referred to in bankruptcy cases as Rule 2004 examinations. These are depositions that can be taken before the filing of a lawsuit to see if there are sufficient grounds for filing. We asked the bankruptcy court for permission to take a 2004 examination of the servicer and the chair of the creditors committee. Counsel for the creditors committee vigorously opposed the motion. A senior partner of the Wachtel Lipton firm, Chaim Fortgang, came to the hearing to argue on behalf of the committee. He was hostile, dismissive, and even, in my opinion, insulting to the bankruptcy court. He essentially lectured the court that he was busy and did not have time to come down to Delaware to oppose a motion from an equity committee that should never have been appointed. He said that granting the motion to take the 2004 examinations would be a waste of time and money and demanded that the court deny the motion. After hearing him out, Judge Walrath leaned forward and looked him straight in the eye and said something like this: "Mr. Fortgang, if the allegations Mr. Campbell has made are true, someone is going to be in big trouble in this case." She granted the motion.

This gave me a perfect opportunity to get even with Gary Marsh for getting me in this mess in the first place. Since I would have to give my deposition as part of the discovery on the motion filed by the equity committee, the committee would have to have a different lawyer prosecute and defend the motion. I told Gary that he would have to take responsibility for the motion and handle the depositions and the hearing. He ably did so. While the servicer denied that it had been pressured to withdraw its participation in the equity committee plan and the chair of the creditors committee professed that he did not know anything about it, we were able to discover enough documents and other information to suggest that pressure had indeed been applied to the servicer. We decided to seek authority to take additional 2004 examinations and filed such a motion with the bankruptcy court. After a hearing, Judge Walrath said she was concerned about the allegations and the information presented but did not want the matter to sidetrack the court, or the parties, from the confirmation of a plan. She said that she would give the equity committee additional time to find a replacement servicer and would refer the evidence that had been generated thus far to the office of the United States attorney in Delaware for possible criminal or other charges. It would, of course, be difficult for the equity committee to locate another qualified servicer who was willing to become involved in such an acrimonious situation.

Not long after this hearing, I received a telephone call from the attorney for the debtor. He asked whether the equity committee would be willing to consider a compromise and settlement. That is what we had wanted all along, but neither the debtor nor the committee had been willing to talk to us until this point. I assumed they had gotten the message that we did not intend to go quietly and that the judge could not be intimidated. I told him that I thought the equity committee would be willing to consider any fair and reasonable settlement. We commenced negotiations that were heated at times but eventually resulted in us reaching a settlement that I thought was fair to the equity committee. It would have involved the equity committee withdrawing its plan and agreeing to support an amended plan by the debtor. The amended plan would provide for a cash payment to the shareholders at confirmation of the plan and the potential for further payments in the future depending on how much the liquidation of the assets yielded. We had been so accepted into the fold that we were able to persuade those in charge of liquidating the assets of UCFC under the debtor's plan to employ Bill Hays as litigation trustee to pursue litigation on behalf of the bankruptcy estate and as disbursing agent to make distributions to creditors and shareholders. As a result of litigation filed by Bill, he recovered almost $100 million for the bankruptcy estate. In one of the major trials held in Baton Rouge, Louisiana, I testified as the first witness on behalf of the bankruptcy estate. I thought this was as good as we could possibly hope for, and I was proud that we had been able to achieve this result for the shareholders. I assumed my troubles were over in this case, but I was soon to learn otherwise.

The hotheads on the equity committee accused me and my law firm of abandoning the shareholders in exchange for a token settlement that was obviously inadequate. After a number of acrimonious committee meetings by telephone, cooler heads on the committee prevailed and the committee agreed to accept the settlement. We were then able to work out the final documentation with counsel for the debtor and the creditors committee. After we reached the settlement, one amusing but pathetic occurrence took place. Throughout the case, anytime I called the office of the attorney for the debtor and spoke to his secretary, she was as rude and uncooperative as her boss. After we reached the settlement, each time I called his office the same secretary could not have been nicer and always said it was good to hear from me. Such transparent "courtesy" did not impress me, but, unfortunately, by the turn of the century it had become rather frequent in the practice of law.

The debtor's amended plan was confirmed, and the equity holders received a substantial payment at confirmation. In addition, the liquidation of the assets provided additional payments in the ensuing years. Even after I retired in 2009, I received a telephone call from the firm liquidating the UCFC assets in which I was advised that the level of recovery was such that even further payments could be made to the shareholders. Since I had retired, I gave this individual the name and number of Gary Marsh at the McKenna law firm. At the end of this case, I could not help contrasting the feeling I had at the end with the feeling I had at the conclusion of the Emmett Barnes representation. I felt that our firm had done an excellent job in both cases and had benefited our clients. In the case of Emmett Barnes, he was grateful. I cannot say the same of the UCFC committee.

Refco, Inc.

Refco, Inc., was a New York-based financial services company, primarily known as a broker of commodities and futures contracts. By October 2005, the company's books indicated that it had over $4 billion in approximately 200,000 customer accounts and was the largest broker on the Chicago Mercantile Exchange. The firm's balance sheet showed about $75 billion in assets. Refco became a public company on August 11, 2005, when it sold 26.5 million shares of its stock in an initial public offering at $22 per share. The stock shot up over 25 percent higher than that, with the company's resulting valuation being about $3.5 billion. On October 10, 2005, less than two months after it had gone public, the company announced that its chief executive officer and chairman, Philip R. Bennett, had hidden approximately $430 million in bad debt from the company's auditors and investors. This had been discovered by a low-level employee in the company's accounting department and reported to the board of directors. Refco shortly filed bankruptcy as the price of its stock plummeted.

Refco had earlier been a private company since 1969 but was regulated to a certain extent by government agencies because of its brokerage business. One part of its business was to stand behind the trades of customers in regard to their liabilities to counterparties. In the 1990s, when the Russian debt crisis occurred, Refco suffered massive losses when it had to make good on trades entered into by its customers after they defaulted. Instead of writing these bad debts off as losses, Refco kept them on its books on the premise that they would be collected in the future. When it became apparent that they would not be collected, Refco still did not write them off but continued them as assets in the form of affiliated debts. It further complicated the situation by adding fake bonds and other expenses to the account. While Refco was not a public company at the time, it engaged in significant financing transactions with large banks that conducted due diligence with respect to the accuracy of Refco's financial statements. To disguise this affiliated debt that is not viewed as favorably as debts owed by third-party independent debtors, Refco started entering into loan transactions with ostensibly independent third-party creditors at the end of each quarter and year-end reporting period so as to disguise the nature of the indebtedness. These "round-trip loans" occurred in the following manner. Shortly before the end of the quarter or year, Refco would take out a loan with an independent third party and pay off the affiliated debt on its balance sheet. Shortly after the end of the reporting period, it would then reverse the transaction and place the affiliated debt back on its books. To insulate the third-party creditor from loss, a Refco affiliate guaranteed that Refco would timely pay the third-party creditor and deposited amounts sufficient to collateralize its guarantee obligation. Thus, the third-party creditor earned interest on its loan to Refco with no real exposure. This process was repeated for years and apparently went undetected by auditors or outside creditors. By October 2005, the amount of this affiliated debt was over $400 million.

It is shocking that this fraud could have occurred for as long as it did without detection. In fact, even before Refco did its Initial Public Offering (IPO), it entered into a Leveraged Buyout (LBO) with a sophisticated venture fund based in Boston, Massachusetts. This company purchased control of Refco for approximately $500 million but failed to detect the fraud during its due diligence process. Even more shocking was the failure to detect the fraud during the SEC-led due diligence during the IPO. When Refco filed bankruptcy, it was clear that a serious investigation would be required to determine who perpetrated the fraud, who knew about it, and whose complicity or negligence permitted it to continue. The office of the United States Trustee moved for the appointment of an examiner in Refco's bankruptcy to conduct an independent investigation. Under the bankruptcy law, the appointment of an examiner was required for a company of the size of Refco and with the apparent fraud having occurred. The office of the United States Trustee decided to interview a number of potential examiners and counsel for the examiner. It was interested in getting someone qualified but not in New York, if possible, because several of the possible subjects of the investigation were large professional firms in New York such as attorneys and accountants.

Joshua Hochberg is a partner in the DC office of McKenna Long & Aldridge who had joined the firm a year or so earlier after a career as a government attorney with the Department of Justice in Washington. He had risen to the level of head of the Criminal Division of the Justice Department and had participated in criminal investigations of many large companies, including Enron. The United States Trustee's office contacted Josh and indicated that it was interested in interviewing him as a possible examiner in the Refco case. Our law firm would be required to provide the attorneys to staff the investigation and handle matters related to the bankruptcy case that affected the investigation. While Josh was experienced and thoroughly knowledgeable about investigations, he had little knowledge about bankruptcy law or the workings of the bankruptcy court. He, therefore, would require an experienced bankruptcy lawyer in the firm to serve as his lead counsel. I was asked to fulfill that role as lead counsel to the examiner. My duties would include assisting the examiner in coordinating the investigation, handling all appearances in the bankruptcy court, attending meetings with other parties in interest—including the debtor, the creditors committee, and various government agencies—advising the examiner with respect to his final conclusions, and assisting in the writing of the examiner's final report. This would be a formidable assignment if Josh were selected for this important engagement.

In November 2005, I was on a holiday break with my family at our beach place on St. Simons Island, Georgia. I was called and told that Josh's interview with the United States Trustee's office would take place on the day after Thanksgiving and that I should plan to be in New York. I drove from our condominium at St. Simons to the Jacksonville, Florida, airport on Thanksgiving afternoon to fly to New York. The temperature when I left the Georgia coast was approximately 80 degrees and was in the teens when I arrived in New York. I met Josh and another partner from our Washington office at the Ritz-Carlton Hotel in lower Manhattan. We divided the responsibility for the presentation the following morning, with me being responsible for describing the litigation and bankruptcy expertise of the firm. Josh would cover his own experience conducting investigations in the Justice Department.

The office of the United States Trustee in New York is located in lower Manhattan near the bankruptcy court. From the office of the United States Trustee, the top officials in the New York office as well as Cliff White, the head of the national office in Washington, were in attendance. Josh outlined his experience in conducting investigations, and I summarized the firm's experience in litigation and bankruptcy matters. I thought the interview went well, and we were told at the conclusion that it might be several weeks before a decision was made.

Several weeks later, Josh was advised that he had been selected as the examiner for Refco. The next step was to develop a plan for the investigation and a budget. While the bankruptcy statute required an examiner to be appointed in a case like Refco if the United States Trustee filed such a motion, the bankruptcy court was left with some discretion as to the scope of the investigation and the budget. The creditors committee in the Refco case, represented by the New York firm of Milbank, Tweed, Hadley & McCloy, LLP (Milbank Tweed) took the position that the committee was already conducting an investigation and that the examiner should merely monitor the investigation as opposed to conducting his own. The debtor, Refco, was represented by the firm of Skadden, Arps, Meagher & Flom, LLP (Skadden Arps), which also generally supported the committee position. This position was unacceptable not only to Josh but also to the United States Trustee. The bankruptcy statute obviously intended that the examiner conduct an independent investigation and not simply be an adjunct to the creditors committee. During negotiations with the counsel for the debtors and creditors committee, it became clear that we were at a stalemate. Other attorneys in the case had warned us that the bankruptcy judge assigned to the case, Robert Drain, almost always seemed to support counsel for the creditors committee when there was a dispute. However, since we were not able to reach an agreement on the scope of the examination or a budget, we had no alternative but to take the matter to the bankruptcy court.

In our first hearing before Judge Drain, he did indeed seem to side with the creditors committee and was critical of the examiner for not reaching an agreement with the committee. He sent us back for further negotiations. In these negotiations, the examiner offered to limit his investigation to the professional firms involved as opposed to conducting a full-scale investigation of all aspects of the matter, including the role of Refco's officers and directors. This did not satisfy counsel for the creditors committee, and the stalemate continued. We had no choice but to go back to the bankruptcy court for a second time. At this hearing, I sensed that Judge Drain thought the creditors committee was being unreasonable after the examiner had offered to compromise. After a rather heated hearing, Judge Drain said that he was not going to impose a specific scope of the examination or budget on the examiner. He did note, however, that the fees of the examiner, and his counsel, would ultimately be subject to the approval of the bankruptcy court, and he would depend on Josh to conduct himself in a responsible manner and be sure his activities were making an important contribution to the bankruptcy estate.

After the second hearing, Josh decided to limit his investigation to the compromise he had proposed to the committee and to limit his expenditures to no more than approximately $10 million. While this sounds like a lot of money, it was miniscule compared to the fees being charged by other professionals in the case, which would eventually greatly exceed $100 million. After we agreed to limit the investigation essentially to the professionals in the case and limit the budget, our relations with counsel for the creditors committee and the debtor improved immensely. To minimize expenses further, the examiner agreed to use the professionals that had been retained by the debtor and the committee to advise them in the bankruptcy as opposed to retaining a completely new set of accountants and other advisors. We did retain the right to hire other professionals if the debtor and committee professionals did not have the time to be responsive to the examiner's needs or for new areas of inquiry. As a practical matter, utilizing professionals that were already working in the bankruptcy case and familiar with the case was helpful to the examiner because we only had approximately eight months within which to conduct the investigation and submit the final report to the court.

The principal professionals that would be the target of the examiner's investigation were accounting and law firms. These included some of the nation's largest auditing and accounting firms, such as Ernst & Young, Price Waterhouse Coopers, and several smaller accounting firms as well as the law firms of Mayer, Brown & Platt, LLP (Mayer Brown), the longtime outside counsel for Refco, and Weil, Gotshal & Manges, LLP (Weil Gotshal), the law firm that represented the acquirer in the LBO transaction and thereafter represented Refco, along with Mayer Brown, in the IPO transaction. To investigate the exposure or lack of exposure of these firms meaningfully, it would also be necessary for the examiner to understand thoroughly how the fraud originated and how it was concealed. This required a full understanding of the round-trip loans and related transactions.

To staff the investigation, Josh decided to have five investigative teams at the law firm. One would investigate the accountants and two would investigate the attorneys. Another team would be responsible for understanding the round-trip loan transactions, and another helping to write the examiner's final report. Attorneys in the firm's Atlanta and Washington offices generally staffed these teams. The accountant team, however, was chaired by Chris Humphries, a former CPA who was a partner in the firm's San Diego office. A conference telephone call would be scheduled each week for the teams to report to the examiner and discuss any problems incurred in the examination. These calls proved to be indispensable in ensuring that everyone was on the same page and that adequate progress was being made given the limited time available for the investigation.

The stages of the investigation were generally as follows. The first stage was document review, which was a tremendous undertaking. There were literally hundreds of thousands of documents for review. We were fortunate in that the examiner was given access to the database of documents of the Skadden Arps firm and more limited access to the database of the Milbank Tweed firm. These two firms had already amassed many of the documents needed for the examination, saving the examiner a tremendous amount of time. Additional documents had to be obtained by subpoenaing them from the targets of the investigation to the extent they had not already been produced to the debtor or the committee. Most of the parties were cooperative in providing documents, although we did have to go to the bankruptcy court for orders to enforce subpoenas on a number of occasions. I handled all of those hearings.

The second stage of the investigation was to begin to research the numerous legal issues involved in determining whether viable causes of action existed against any of the professionals. This research was conducted primarily by associates in the Atlanta and Washington offices and supervised by a senior associate. I will discuss later some of the legal issues involved. After completion of the review of documents and the necessary research, the next stage of the investigation was to conduct depositions or interviews with witnesses. Among other reasons, Josh was appointed because of the confidence that he would be able to coordinate his investigation with the various government agencies that were conducting their own inquiries and not interfere with those investigations. We were particularly sensitive with respect to the criminal investigation conducted by the office of the United States Attorney for the Southern District of New York. That office was primarily investigating criminal liability of the principal officers of Refco. We were not investigating officers as such, but we were cognizant of not inquiring into areas that might compromise the criminal investigation. Josh met with the attorneys in the United States Attorney's office who were responsible for the Refco criminal inquiry on a number of occasions, and I attended those meetings with him. The meetings were helpful to the examiner because they gave him a good idea of where the criminal investigation was going. Josh and I also had a number of meetings with the Securities and Exchange Commission with respect to its ongoing investigation. The level of cooperation was good, and the examiner was given access to numerous documents that had been provided to the SEC. Several officers of Refco, including Philip Bennett, would eventually be indicted and convicted.

The final phase of the investigation by the examiner was reaching conclusions and writing the examiner's report. That was an intense period because it came at the end of the allotted time and we were under tremendous time pressure. We also had to coordinate the examiner's final report with the government agencies and preview it not only with those agencies but also with counsel for the debtor and the creditors committee. The examiner concluded that viable claims existed against the Mayer Brown firm and against the Ernst & Young firm. He also concluded that there probably were claims for negligence against the Weil Gotshal firm, although that was a close question and the firm would have formidable defenses. All of those parties, of course, disagreed with the examiner's conclusions.

The most important of the areas of inquiry related to possible claims against the Mayer Brown law firm. Its partner, Joseph Collins, had been Refco's attorney for many years and handled almost all of Refco's transactions, including the round-trip loan transactions. Numerous documents indicated that all of the round-trip loan transactions were prepared either by Collins or by younger attorneys at Mayer Brown under his supervision. In addition, Collins reviewed the monthly billing statements that went to Refco that described the legal work being done and resulted in millions of dollars of legal fees being charged to the firm's client. The attorney selected to head the team investigating Mayer Brown was tenacious, detail-oriented Robert A. Bartlett. Thousands of documents did not intimidate him, and he had an uncanny ability to review and absorb them. Josh and I attended some of the testimony of witnesses, including that of Joseph Collins and other Mayer Brown witnesses. They were represented by the Williams and Connolly firm from Washington, which was one of the best-known firms in these kinds of cases in the country. I was surprised at the testimony of the Mayor Brown lawyers that all of them professed to have little recollection with respect to the key transactions. Bob had assembled numerous documents that showed these attorneys had prepared or reviewed the round-trip loan documentation and engaged in extensive correspondence and internal memos with respect thereto. No credible explanation was ever given as to what the attorneys thought the legitimate business purposes of these round-trip loans were at the time they took place. When a witness testified, we gave him or her the choice of whether to have the testimony taken down verbatim by a court reporter. That was our preference because otherwise the examiner would have to rely on the recollections and notes of him and his counsel. Mayer Brown declined to have a court reporter.

The Weil Gotshal lawyers (with court reporters present) testified that the Mayer Brown attorneys misled them and concealed information in connection with the LBO and the IPO. This testimony appeared to be credible. Certainly, at the time of the LBO, the Weil Gotshal attorneys would have no reason to ignore the fraud had they known about it because their client was about to invest $500 million in Refco. After the LBO closed and their client became the controlling shareholder of Refco, the firm was in a different situation with respect to its legal work. It was then representing Refco, both in regard to the IPO and other matters. While the examiner discovered no evidence to suggest that anyone with the Weil Gotshal firm knew or even suspected that the fraud was occurring, there was a question, as stated in the examiner's final report, as to whether Weil Gotshal had been negligent in not discovering the fraud in its work after the LBO. One of the problems was that the team that had represented the acquirer in the LBO was a different team than the one who did the IPO work, and there was not the greatest coordination in sharing information between those attorneys. It was further complicated by the fact that they were in different offices.

Even with respect to the viable claims the examiner concluded existed against certain professionals, the examiner stated in his report that there were substantial possible defenses to any such claims. One of those defenses discussed in the report was based on the legal principle of in pari delicto, which in turn is based on the principle of imputation. In layman's terms, a party is ordinarily prevented from suing others for damages caused by fraud participated in by that party. In this case, it was clear that certain executives of Refco not only started the fraud but also perpetuated and concealed it. The legal question, therefore, was whether Refco or its representative in the bankruptcy case were barred from suing the lawyers and/or accountants for negligence or other claims because of the complicity of the Refco officers. The doctrine of in pari delicto was recognized in the Second Circuit Court of Appeals, which established controlling law for the Refco bankruptcy case, but the parameters of the defense and certain exceptions to it were not entirely clear. Even if imputation applied, there were two possible exceptions. One was called the adverse interest exception. That is where the corporate officers complicit in the fraud were acting entirely on matters to benefit themselves and not the corporation. Bennett and the other officers in Refco received substantial sums of money at the time of the LBO and other benefits. On the other hand, it was also arguable that Refco had received certain benefits and this exception might not apply. The second exception was the so-called "sole actor" rule. That is, if there was no one else in a corporation that would have been able to address the fraud had it been discovered because the corporation was so dominated and controlled by the one committing the fraud, then those acts would not be imputed to the corporation. In Refco's case, this defense was not clear because Bennett arguably controlled Refco up until the LBO, but after that point independent directors were added to the board during the period of the IPO. Thus, based on the foregoing, the examiner warned in his report that any professional sued on the claims discussed in the report could assert the in pari delicto defense and might prevail. That is exactly what happened. Numerous suits were filed against professionals and others on behalf of the Refco bankruptcy estate, and, except for several that were settled, they were dismissed under the doctrine of in pari delicto.

The Refco case was the subject of tremendous press scrutiny. Constant articles were written, and people tried to speculate on whom the examiner would find liable and whom he would exonerate. Josh decided that all press inquiries would be directed to me. Up until the time of the issuance of the examiner's report, I had an easy answer: we are not in a position to discuss the examiner's investigation until it has been completed. Nonetheless, the press did speculate based on certain subpoenas we filed with the bankruptcy court and the hearings held on those subpoenas.

The examiner's final report and the appendices exceeded 1,000 pages. It was an exhaustive treatment of the subjects of the examination, and I believe they set forth an understandable and accurate portrayal of how this fraud was perpetrated. Before its public release, we previewed the report with the office of the United States Trustee, the SEC, the United States Attorney for the Southern District of New York, counsel for the debtors, and counsel for the creditors committee. In addition, at the request of the United States Attorney's office, we redacted for a time the version released to the public to eliminate certain items that the United States Attorney's office thought might implicate the criminal proceeding. Eventually, those redacted portions were released as well. We filed the report within the time permitted for the examination, and the total fees and expenses requested by the examiner were less than the $10 million threshold in the compromise budget proposal.

Other than the reaction of the parties against whom the examiner concluded possible claims existed, the response to the examiner's report was quite favorable. The United States Attorney's office thought it was helpful, and the debtors and creditors committee thought it was helpful in connection with possible claims that would be brought on behalf of the Refco bankruptcy estate. At the final fee hearing on the application for fees and expenses by the examiner and his counsel, there were no objections filed by any party in interest. Judge Drain observed at the hearing that the fact that there was no objection was evidence that the parties in interest in the case felt that the examiner's investigation had delivered value to the estate and had been appropriately conducted. He commended the examiner and his counsel and approved the fees in full.

With the submission of the examiner's report, our involvement in the Refco case was over. The criminal proceedings resulted in the conviction of at least three officers of Refco. In addition, the Mayer Brown partner, Joseph Collins, was indicted, convicted, and sentenced to seven years in federal prison. Josh testified as a witness for the prosecution. This compares to a sixteen-year sentence for Refco's former CEO, Philip Bennett, who pleaded guilty to conspiracy to commit securities fraud. The conviction of Joseph Collins was reversed on appeal because of juror issues. He was indicted, tried, and convicted again in a second trial. It is rare that an attorney is the subject of a criminal indictment because of work he performs as the attorney for a client. However, Refco was an unusual case.

Emmett Barnes, his wife Edwina, and the team that worked on his bankruptcy case at the victory party at our home in Atlanta in 1995. On the far left is my law partner, Mike Levengood, and next to him is associate Jeff Cavender.

Dining with my friend and former client, Emmett Barnes, at Bennie's Red Barn Restaurant on St. Simons Island, Georgia in 2003.

My client in the Burt Reynolds case, Sandy Simon.

13

Civic and Professional Organizations

Richard B. Russell Foundation, Inc.

The Russell Foundation, the primary purpose of which is to preserve the legacy of Richard Russell and his official papers, was the brainchild of Judge William L. Norton, Jr., before whom I tried some of my most important bankruptcy cases. The Norton and Russell families had been friends for many years, and both hailed from Northeast Georgia. Judge Norton's family, which made its mark in business, real estate, insurance, and legal and political circles, was from Hall County not far from Richard Russell's home in Winder, Georgia. Judge Norton's wife, Adelaide, had worked at the Russell for President headquarters in Chicago in 1952.

By the late 1960s, Richard Russell was grappling with what to do with his official papers after his death. His growing emphysema problem and a bout with lung cancer had convinced him the time had come to make a decision. Several years earlier, the president of the University of Georgia, Dr. O. C Aderhold, approached the senator about leaving his papers to the UGA Library. Russell was inclined to do so, but he worried about the papers becoming buried in a large university library. His main concern was that his papers be readily available to students and researchers.

Based on a study he did of libraries established by former senators and presidents, Judge Norton came up with a solution. He recommended the establishment of an independent foundation that would receive Russell's papers from his estate and enter into an agreement with the university for the housing, preservation, cataloging, and display of the papers. In late 1968 or early 1969 on one of his visits to Winder, Judge Norton came to see Senator Russell and brief him on the idea of an independent foundation. Russell was attracted to the idea and told Judge Norton he would think about it and get back in touch with him. When he returned to Washington the next week, he asked me what

I thought about the proposal. I told him it seemed like an ideal solution to his problem. He thought about it for about another week and agreed to the establishment of the foundation on two conditions—that no money be raised while he was still in the Senate and that his colleague from Georgia in the Senate, Herman Talmadge, agree to be the first chair of the foundation. Senator Talmadge readily agreed.

In 1970, the official papers for the foundation were filed. Senator Russell selected the initial board of trustees with input from, among others, Judge Norton, Senator Talmadge, and me. Russell wanted a diverse board that would include young people. He selected two young attorneys, James Blanchard of Columbus and Wyck Knox of Augusta; two women—Mrs. Ivan Allen, wife of the mayor of Atlanta who had been Russell's friend since college, and Mary Gregory Jewett, who was president of the Georgia Trust for Historic Preservation; and one African American—Jesse Hill, who was president of the Atlanta Life Insurance Company. The remainder of the trustees was a who's who of leaders in Georgia's business, legal, political, and academic communities. In addition to Jesse Hill, the leaders from the business community included J. Paul Austin, president of the Coca-Cola Company; Morris Bryan, president of Jefferson Mills; Lawton M. Calhoun, president of Savannah Sugar Refining Company; James M. Cox, Jr., a member of the family that owned the Cox newspapers; Jasper N. Dorsey, head of Southern Bell in Georgia; Richard H. Rich, owner and chairman of the Rich's Department Store in Atlanta; and Bert Struby, who ran the *Macon Telegraph* newspaper. Leaders from the legal community included Robert Troutman and Charles L. Gowen, partners at the King and Spalding law firm; William L. Norton, Jr., an attorney from Gainesville and bankruptcy judge; and Lamar W. Sizemore of the Heyman and Sizemore law firm in Atlanta. Leaders from the academic community included Warren Boes of the UGA Library; Fred C. Davison, president of the University of Georgia; and George L. Simpson, Jr., chancellor of the Georgia Board of Regents. Public officeholders were also represented by Senator Herman E. Talmadge, Congressman Howard H. Callaway, and Congressman Phil Landrum. Shortly after the initial board of trustees was established, one of Richard Russell's favorite nephews and a co-executor of his estate, Hugh Peterson, Jr., was added to the board.

As had been agreed with Senator Russell, Herman Talmadge served the first four years as the chair of the foundation and almost single-handedly raised the approximately $1.5 million that made it possible for the Russell Foundation to launch its efforts. Congressman Landrum succeeded Talmadge and served as chair for four years. In 1978, Jasper Dorsey was elected chair of the foundation and served until 1990, when he passed away. At that point, I was named as chair of the foundation and served for seventeen years until 2007. I was succeeded by William H. (Dink) NeSmith III, who served five years. In 2012, Norman L. Underwood, a former Russell intern and Georgia Court of Appeals Judge, became the sixth Chair of the Foundation.

I formally joined the foundation in 1980, when, at the behest of Jasper Dorsey, I was named as a trustee. Not long after that, a vacancy occurred in the office of secretary, and, again through Jasper's efforts, I was named to that position. That paved the way for me being named as chair of the foundation in 1990 when Jasper passed away. I never intended to keep the position for seventeen years, but of all of the extracurricular activities outside the law in which I was engaged, the work of the Russell Foundation was the most enjoyable and rewarding. Dink NeSmith was a fitting successor to me as chair for several reasons. First, he was well known at the University of Georgia, where he had served as president of the UGA Alumni Society and as a member of the Athletic Board. After he was named chair of the Russell Foundation, he was also appointed by the governor of Georgia to the Georgia Board of Regents. Finally, Dink was the first chair of the Russell Foundation who was not closely associated with Richard Russell or worked for him. That is important because it will not be long before the work of the Russell Foundation will be entirely in the hands of those who never knew Richard Russell. Dink did an outstanding job as chair.

Almost all the activities of the Russell Foundation are based at the University of Georgia. The foundation has contributed almost $8 million to the university during its existence and funds a number of activities that I will discuss below. This wonderful partnership has paved the way for accomplishments in his name that Richard Russell never could have imagined. I believe he would be pleased with the way in which Judge Norton's idea for an independent foundation has been brought to fruition. The foundation has continued Richard Russell's original intent in having a diverse board of trustees, which today includes four women, an African American, and a number of young Georgians. Of the original trustees, two still served on the board—at the beginning of 2012 Jesse

Hill, who was an emeritus trustee, [Mr. Hill passed away on December 17, 2012] and Judge Norton, who in 2012 became an Emeritus Trustee when he was replaced on the board by his son, William L. Norton III who is a prominent bankruptcy attorney in Nashville, Tennessee. The following are some of the activities of the Russell Foundation in the past and / or the present.

Richard B. Russell Library for Political Research and Studies

The library established to house Russell's papers, memorabilia, and personal effects from fifty years in public office was created through the joint efforts of the Russell estate, the Russell Foundation, the University of Georgia, the Georgia Board of Regents, and the Georgia Legislature. It was dedicated on June 22, 1974. Among those appearing on the dedication program were senators John Stennis, Herman Talmadge, and Henry Jackson as well as Georgia governor Jimmy Carter. It was originally referred to as the Richard B. Russell Memorial Library in recognition of the fact that its purpose was to house the papers of Richard Russell. It was not long, however, before the mission of the library greatly changed. Two Georgia congressmen, Maston O'Neal and John J. Flynt, Jr., were the first to leave their papers to the library when they left the House of Representatives in Washington. The process intensified following the 1980 defeat of Herman Talmadge in his bid for reelection to the United States Senate, when he decided to give his papers from twenty-four years in the United States Senate and his years as governor of Georgia to the Russell Library. Soon afterward, Dean Rusk, former secretary of state in the Kennedy and Johnson administrations, contributed his papers to the Russell Library. Very quickly, numerous present and former officeholders were deciding to deposit their papers at the Russell Library as well. Today, it has more than 300 collections that include those of United States senators, members of the United States House of Representatives, governors of Georgia, state legislators, judges, and many others. It has become the foremost center for political research in the state, far surpassing anything Richard Russell could have imagined. In recognition of this increased role, the library was renamed the Richard B. Russell Library for Political Research and Studies.

The library's collections include the papers of primary participants in four of the great congressional investigations in the country's history in four different decades: Richard Russell's papers as chair of the Joint Committee to investigate President Truman's dismissal of Army General Douglas McArthur in the 1950s; his papers as an important member of the Warren Commission to investigate the assassination of President Kennedy in the 1960s; the papers of Herman Talmadge as an important and senior member of the Senate Watergate Committee during the Nixon Administration in the 1970s; and the papers of Congressman Ed Jenkins, a member of the Iran-Contra Investigating Committee in the Reagan Administration in the 1980s. I could give numerous other examples of how these additional collections have enhanced the totality of the Russell Library. The Russell Library has been so popular that the most recent governor of Georgia, Sonny Perdue, insisted that all of his papers, both official and unofficial, be deposited in the Russell Library. Since Georgia law specifies that the official papers of all governors are to be deposited in the state archives, this required a special licensing arrangement between the Russell Library and the Georgia State Archives. Because Governor Perdue wanted all of his papers in one location, the state archives licensed the Russell Library as a depository for his official papers.

The Russell Library has become a center for political research of a number of well-known books. Probably the best known of these books are the four written by Robert Caro on the career of Lyndon Johnson. A fifth book is now in progress. Much of the research for the Caro books was done at the Russell Library. In fact, his principal researcher, his wife, Ina, was so appreciative of the assets and efforts of the Russell Library that she nominated Sheryl Vogt, the library's director , for the national archivist of the year award, which Sheryl subsequently received. Richard Russell's niece, Sally Russell, has used the library extensively to research three books she has written about the Russell family, including a compilation of letters written to her children by Senator Russell's mother, a biography of Senator Russell's father, and more recently a biography of Senator Russell himself. Much of the research for this book took place at the Russell Library.

When I became chair of the Russell Foundation in 1990, the library's mission had already changed, and many additional collections were already on hand. I was supportive of this expanded role. My only concern was the adequacy of the facilities as the number of collections grew and the demand for more space grew with them. Many of the collections were stored off site and waiting to be catalogued. I felt strongly that a new facility was necessary to provide state-of-the-art storage space under climate-controlled conditions and also additional exhibit and research space. Fortunately, a relatively new librarian at the University of Georgia, Dr. William G. Potter, came up with the idea of a special collections library building that would house the Russell Library and two other special collection libraries at the university that were then housed in the main UGA library facility. He later presented this proposal to Dr. Michael Adams, who had also recently come to the university as its new president. Dr. Adams was enthusiastic about the need and feasibility for a new special collections library building.

The proposed building was projected to cost approximately $36 million, with two-thirds provided by the state of Georgia and one-third provided through private money that would have to be raised from donors. The Russell Foundation Board of Trustees had always considered the library to be the foundation's most important activity. By this time in the late 1990s, the foundation had between $6 and $7 million in its investment portfolio. The original funds contributed primarily as a result of Senator Talmadge's efforts had been wisely invested and had grown over time, notwithstanding the fact that several million had also been spent on activities. I thought the new proposed special collections building was so important that I discussed with several individual Russell Foundation trustees the possibility of the foundation kicking off the private fundraising efforts by pledging $3 million to the facility. This would be a major commitment for the Russell Foundation—almost half of its portfolio. I wanted to be sure that the foundation could continue to carry on its work and other activities after the contribution. Therefore, I requested that the portfolio manager, an affiliate of SunTrust Bank, conduct an analysis of whether adequate funds to continue the foundation's other activities would still be on hand after the $3 million contribution. The report submitted indicated that even under a most pessimistic assumption as to the future growth of the portfolio, sufficient funds would remain. I presented the matter to the executive committee of the foundation, which enthusiastically endorsed it, followed by the endorsement of the full board at its annual meeting.

One of the things we requested in exchange for this contribution is that the new special collections library building would be named in honor of Richard Russell. The University and the Georgia Board of

Regents approved this naming. The initial $3 million pledged from the Russell Foundation helped prompt other early contributions, including a $3 million pledge from the Walter J. Brown Trust. Mr. Brown was the father of Atlanta lawyer Tom Watson Brown, who administered the family trust following his father's death. Other significant contributions were also received early, and it was clear that UGA would be able to raise the $12 million in private funds. The process for the authorization of such a building is complex and time consuming. It first has to be approved by the university and placed on its priority list of new construction projects. It also has to be approved by the board of regents and placed on its list of approved projects, which includes new construction for all of the thirty-odd institutions of higher learning that are state supported in Georgia. It took more than ten years for this building to work its way to the top of the UGA and board of regents lists and be eligible for funding by the state legislature. Then the legislature had to fund it. By the time it was approved by the board of regents and the legislature, the overall cost of the building had increased to $45 million, which meant that another $3 million in private funds were needed. That money has been raised as well, and the new Richard B. Russell Special Collections Library Building was dedicated in early 2012. It is a wonderful facility with adequate storage spaces for the three special collections libraries for at least forty years. It also will permit more extensive programming and display of the collections. One of the last actions taken by the Russell Foundation during my tenure as chair was to authorize a $1 million programming endowment for the Russell Library when it moved to the new building. One of the most interesting things in the new building of the Russell Library is a full-scale reproduction of Richard Russell's personal office in Suite 205 of what is now the Russell Senate Office Building in Washington. It is so much like the original office in which I spent time over forty years ago that sometimes when I am there, I almost think I have returned to my days in Washington. My wife, Ann, and I contributed $150,000 toward the recreation of the office.

The three special collections located in the Richard B. Russell Building are of great importance to the University of Georgia and the state and complement each other in significant ways. I have already written about the collections present in the Russell Library. The Hargrett Rare Book and Manuscript Library is an outstanding special collection of its own that includes some of the most important historical and cultural documents in Georgia's history. Among them is one of the few remaining original copies of the Constitution of the Confederate States of America, an extensive collection of maps of colonial Georgia, one of the best collections anywhere of Civil War correspondence, and many of the original papers of Margaret Mitchell in connection with her historic novel *Gone with the Wind*. The third special collection is the Walter J. Brown Media and Peabody Award Archives, which is probably the best known of the three outside UGA. The Peabody Awards are given each year in New York to recognize excellence in broadcast journalism (now including the Internet). The awards were started some seventy years ago by the legendary dean of the Georgia Journalism School, John Drury. The awards are still administered by the UGA Journalism School and a blue-ribbon panel of journalism leaders and are presented each year at a luncheon at the Waldorf Astoria Hotel in New York. I have attended three of these events, including the one in 2011. The master of ceremonies for the awards is always a well-known journalism personality. In 2011, it was Larry King of CNN, and the year before it was Diane Sawyer of ABC News. In 2011, thirty-eight awards were given that recognized outstanding journalism—from local TV programming in towns and communities across the country to major national coverage such as the CNN coverage of Hurricane Katrina. I do not know of anything that brings more positive attention to the University of Georgia nationally than the Peabody Awards.

Much of the success of the Russell Library is due to Sheryl Vogt, the library's longtime director. Sheryl joined the library on August 1, 1974, shortly after it opened and became the acting director in 1979 and director in 1981. She has spearheaded the effort to expand the collections and has also helped make the library a center for civil rights studies by joining with others at UGA to record the contributions of unsung heroes in the civil rights movement through the Foot Solider Project. In addition, she has been instrumental in continuing an extensive oral history interview program that records oral histories of those who have been active in Georgia politics through the years. This program actually started in interviews with Richard Russell's Senate colleagues and with three former presidents—Gerald Ford, Richard Nixon, and Jimmy Carter—after Russell died. More recently, the library has directed this program in a joint effort with Young Harris College to record numerous interviews of those who have been active in Georgia politics in one role or another. Bob Short, a legendary Georgia political figure for decades, has generously donated his time and expenses in conducting most of these interviews in Georgia and Washington, DC. I gave one of the oral history interviews based on my experiences working for Richard Russell, other political activities, and my career as a lawyer. Sheryl Vogt has also been active nationally. Under her leadership, the Russell Library was one of the founding members of the Association of Centers for the Study of Congress, and she has served as president of that organization.

A Chair and a Professor

In 1970, the organization documents for the Russell Foundation provided for the establishment of a chair in American history in Russell's name. It has been held by four distinguished historians. The first holder of the Russell Chair was Dr. Gilbert Fite, who wrote the definitive biography of Russell's life. From Arkansas, Dr. Fite was an expert on southern agriculture and politics. His biography of Russell was so well received that it was given the D. B. Hardeman prize for the best book on the United States Congress in the year in which it was released (1991). Following Dr. Fite's retirement, Dr. William McFeely was named to the Russell Chair. Dr. McFeely was a Pulitzer Prize-winning historian who was an expert on the life and career of Frederick Douglass, the former slave, abolitionist, and black leader. When Dr. McFeely was named the Abraham Baldwin Professor at the University of Georgia, Dr. Edward Larson was named the holder of the Russell Chair. Dr. Larson held a joint appointment in UGA's law school and history department and is an expert on evolution. He had also received a Pulitzer Prize for his book on the Scopes monkey trial in Dayton, Tennessee, which featured the former presidential candidate, Williams Jennings Bryan, and the famed Chicago trial lawyer, Clarence Darrow. Larson was popular with the Russell trustees and attended most of the annual meetings during his tenure. After he left to go to Pepperdine University in California, Dr. Claudio Saunt was named to replace him. Dr. Saunt is an expert on the American Indian and has written a number of highly acclaimed books and publications. He currently holds the Russell Chair.

By 1997, the Russell Foundation had contributed more than $1,300,000 to the Russell Chair, which was more than the $1 million required to establish a chair. At that point, the University of Georgia agreed to maintain the Russell Chair in perpetuity without any further financial contribution from the foundation. The foundation agreed to contribute $250,000 to establish a Richard B. Russell Distinguished Professor of Public Policy in a college of the university to be agreed upon between the foundation and UGA. Following five annual payments of $50,000, the professorship was established in 2005 in the School of Agricultural and Applied Economics. Dr. John C. Bergstrom was named as the first Richard B. Russell Distinguished Professor of Public Policy. He has expertise in conservation and management of natural resources as they relate to agriculture and public policy. In light of Richard Russell's extensive involvement with natural resource conservation, Dr. Bergstrom is a fitting first holder of this position.

Richard B. Russell Statue

In the years after 1971 when I returned to Georgia, I was frequently in Washington on business and would almost always go by the Russell Senate Office Building to visit with Herman Talmadge, Sam Nunn, John Stennis, and/or Scoop Jackson. During those visits, I noticed that there were a number of busts in the Russell Senate Office Building. These included busts of Senator Carl Hayden of Arizona and Scoop Jackson of Washington State. Though a magnificent carving on a wall of the Russell Senate Office Building between the second and third floors pays tribute to Richard Russell and his career, there was no bust of Richard Russell. I thought this was somewhat strange. After I became chair of the Russell Foundation in 1990, I decided to try to do something about the omission. We soon decided that a life-sized statue placed in the rotunda of the Russell Senate Office Building would be better than a bust. I assumed that the placing of art objects in any of the historic buildings on Capitol Hill would be strictly regulated. Therefore, I contacted Senator Nunn's office to find out the procedure for obtaining permission. His staff advised me that it would have to be approved by the Senate Commission on Art as well as the Capitol Architect, and they assured us they would be glad to assist with trying to get these approvals.

I next discussed the matter with the executive committee of the Russell Foundation and found them enthusiastic about moving forward with the statue. We were advised through Senator Nunn's office that the foundation would have to raise the funds and that the artist as well as the final product would be subject to Senate approval. We were also told that placing a heavy life-sized marble statue on a four-foot marble pedestal in the center of the rotunda would require reinforcement of the floor[,] which would increase the expense and the time involved in the project. They advised locating the statue in a conspicuous place toward the rear of the rotunda, where the floor was already reinforced, and we agreed.

Next, we had to select an artist. We contacted a number of recommended sculptors, including one suggested by a friend of my wife, Patricia Pence Sokoloff, who lives in Winston-Salem, North Carolina. The name of that artist was Frederick Hart, who was originally from Atlanta. He already had a number of public works to his credit, including the creation figures at the entrance to the National Cathedral in Washington, the soldier figures at the Vietnam War Memorial in Washington, and a statue of former President Jimmy Carter on the Capitol grounds in Atlanta. Following the review of materials from a number of sculptors and interviews with them, a committee of Russell Foundation trustees, which I had appointed to help me with this project, selected Frederick Hart. Hart was enthusiastic about the project. Interestingly, his father had been the media advisor for Senator Estes Kefauver in his race in 1952 for the Democratic presidential nomination. Russell had deprived him of most of the southern delegates at the convention by defeating him in the Florida primary. Rick Hart lived with his family on a farm in Hume, Virginia, approximately fifty miles from Washington, and that is where he maintained his studio. We visited with him and commissioned him to do the statue. As Rick prepared the clay model , our committee made a number of visits to the studio to review his progress. We were generally satisfied with the end product, except for the facial expression. Several members of the committee, myself included, felt that the expression was not Richard Russell. After a few modifications, we were satisfied. Rick Hart had never met Richard Russell and created the statue based entirely on photographs and film footage.

The next step was to select a stone carver. Rick recommended Joseph Palumbo, the Master Stone Carver at the National Cathedral, with whom Rick had worked there. We interviewed him and approved him. The stone carver takes the model prepared by the sculptor and, using intricate and detailed measurements of the model, carves the final statue from a block of white Italian marble. Because of the exactness of the measurements and the angles, a qualified stone carver produces an exact replica of the model in marble, and that is precisely what happened here.

We then had to raise the funds to pay for the statue and the dedication ceremony. We estimated the cost would be between $250,000 and $300,000. Then Georgia governor Zell Miller and Senator Nunn were of immense help in raising the money. They co-hosted a fundraising luncheon at the Governor's Mansion in Atlanta. I remember sitting next to CNN founder Ted Turner at the lunch. We raised more than $200,000 in private contributions. The largest contributions were by the Coca-Cola Company and former Atlanta mayor Ivan Allen. The Russell Foundation contributed the remainder of the funds to pay the sculptor, the stone carver, and the expenses of the dedication ceremony and an elaborate reception that followed.

The dedication and unveiling of the statue took place on January 24, 1996, in the rotunda of the Russell Senate Office Building. This was a presidential year, and two of the expected participants in the program were casualties to the presidential race. We received preliminary indications that President Bill Clinton would speak on Richard Russell's relationship with presidents, but he backed out at the last minute. Vice President Al Gore took his place. The Republican majority leader of the Senate, Bob Dole, was supposed to speak on Richard Russell's relationship with Republican senators during his career, but Senator Dole was running for president in 1996 and could not attend because of campaign commitments. He was replaced by Senator Ted Stevens of Alaska, who would go on to become the longest-serving Republican senator in the history of the country. The late senator Paul Coverdale, Republican from Georgia, was instrumental in helping us to obtain Stevens as a last-minute replacement for Dole. The other principal speakers included Senator Robert Byrd of West Virginia and Georgia governor Zell Miller. Senator Sam Nunn served as master of ceremonies.

As might be expected, the speakers were lavish in their praise of Richard Russell. Vice President Gore, whose father, Albert Gore, Sr., served for more than eighteen years with Russell in the Senate, said this:

> ...my father's service in the Congress overlapped with his for thirty-two years. These two men had a great deal in common. Eighteen of those years my father served in the Senate with Senator Russell. I remember often hearing my father say that whatever their occasional

> disagreements—and they did have some. On occasion, they stood toe to toe, but when it came to certain core ideals—love of country, devotion to duty, respect for principles—they always saw eye to eye. But whatever the occasional disagreements, on one matter, my father was resolute whenever he spoke about Senator Russell. Dick Russell had a heart of gold and was one of the most honorable individuals ever to serve in the United States Senate throughout its more than two hundred-year history.

While they were all excellent, the highlight of the speeches for me was that of Senator Robert Byrd. Known as one of the finest orators in the Senate, he served for some fifteen years with Russell. He said of Russell,

> He was as truly a Senate man as was Henry Clay or Daniel Webster or John C. Calhoun or Thomas Benton or any of the other giants who had preceded him.... Richard Russell followed his own star. He did not pander. His confidant was his conscience. He was always the good and faithful servant of the people. He was good for the Senate, and he loved it dearly. I can say without any hesitation that he was a remarkable senator, a remarkable American, a remarkable man who enjoyed the respect and the affection of all who served with him. In the death of Senator Russell, I felt a great personal loss. From my first days in the Senate, I looked upon him as my mentor, and he was the man I most admired in Washington, a man of great intellect, the finest of public servants, and his patriotism and love of country will never be excelled.

By the time of the dedication ceremony, Senator Nunn had already announced that he would retire from the Senate when his term expired in 1996. There were almost as many accolades for Nunn as there were for Russell. Senator Byrd put it simply: "...and I thank Sam Nunn. He stepped into some big shoes when he came to the Senate, and those shoes fit today." When it came my time to speak as chair of the Russell Foundation, I said this about Sam Nunn: "...I also can't let the occasion pass without saying, Senator, particularly in light of your retirement now, how much we appreciate your twenty-four years of Richard Russell type service in the United States Senate." Following my remarks, the statue was unveiled by Rick Hart and two of Senator Russell's sisters, Pat Peterson and Carolyn Nelson. Following the dedication and unveiling ceremony, Senator Byrd hosted a lavish reception in the historic Caucus Room of the Russell Senate Office Building, the same room where the announcements of the presidential campaigns of John F.

Kennedy and Robert F. Kennedy, the Watergate hearings, and the Clarence Thomas confirmation hearings all took place.

The Russell Statue will stand as a lasting memorial to Richard Russell in the rotunda of the building that bears his name in the nation's Capitol.

Richard B. Russell Leadership UGA Program

The Richard B. Russell Leadership UGA Program was established in 1985 and is the oldest and most distinguished leadership program at UGA. Approximately twenty-five student leaders are selected to undergo a yearlong intensive leadership training program that involves meetings on campus and elsewhere in the state. There is a theme to the program each year. In 2010, it was "Leading in times of crisis." The Russell Foundation underwrites the expenses of the program, which permits its participants to meet with political and business leaders in the state and to learn firsthand the attributes of leadership. This is particularly fitting since strong leadership characterized Richard Russell's fifty-year career in public office.

Richard B. Russell Symposium

In the mid-1980s, the Russell Foundation established a biannual program on national security that became known as the Richard B. Russell Symposium. The program was directed by political science professor and director of the University of Georgia Center for International Trade and Security, Dr. Gary Bertsch. Dr. Bertsch headed a committee to select a topic for each program, recruited the speakers, and arranged for publicity, both in a written publication of the program and in television coverage. He was also responsible for handling all the logistics for staging the program at the Georgia Center for Continuing Education in Athens. Gary did a fantastic job in organizing and conducting this program. It was also immensely helped in the early years by Senator Sam Nunn, who was chairman of the Senate Armed Services Committee. He participated in the first few programs as a member of the faculty, and, equally important, he assisted in the recruitment of outstanding speakers. Among the participants in the program have been former secretary of defense Robert McNamara, former CIA director (and more recently secretary of defense) Robert Gates, former United Nations ambassador Jeanne Kirkpatrick, and Senator Dianne Feinstein. These programs were well attended by students and others in Athens, and a number of the Russell trustees feel that the symposium is one of the best things the foundation has done. Members of the Russell family have also been supportive of the program and attended a number of the symposia. A copy of the transcript of the programs was widely circulated to leading government officials and academia. The program has not been staged since Dr. Bertsch's retirement, but discussions are ongoing with respect to starting it again.

Richard B. Russell Teaching Awards

In 1992, shortly after I became chair of the Russell Foundation, leaders at the University of Georgia suggested that the foundation consider funding three annual teaching awards for younger members of the UGA faculty. These awards would recognize outstanding performance in the classroom and thereby encourage increased devotion to teaching by faculty members early in their careers. We thought this was an excellent idea and agreed to establish the Richard B. Russell Teaching Awards. Three such awards have been made each year thereafter. In the fifteen years before my retirement as chair of the Russell Foundation in 2007, I served on the selection committee each year and presented the checks at the spring faculty recognition banquet every year except one. These awards have become the second most prestigious teaching awards bestowed at UGA. When I visit the campus now, it is not unusual for a member of the faculty to come up to me and tell me how important the Russell Teaching Award was to his or her career. Many of these award winners have gone on to become some of the most prominent and respected members of the UGA faculty. Currently, each recipient is given a $5,000 check and a plaque that is presented by the president of the University of Georgia at the spring banquet. Richard Russell often talked about how important a number of good teachers he had in his early years were to his development. I think he would be pleased with the Richard B. Russell Teaching Awards. The program is set up where the awards are made throughout the different parts of the campus and not concentrated in any one school or college. A number of African Americans have won the award, and it is not unusual for female members of the faculty to dominate the award winners in a given year. It is one of the Russell Foundation programs of which I am the proudest.

Scholarships

Through the years, the Russell Foundation has awarded various scholarships and fellowships. The ones being awarded today are as follows. Two scholarships are awarded each year at Gordon College, one in the name of Richard Russell and one in the name of his brother, Robert L. Russell. Both brothers attended and graduated from Gordon. These scholarships are restricted to Georgia residents, and the recipients are selected each year by the school.

The foundation also currently awards four debate scholarships to debaters at the University of Georgia. Each of these scholarships is in the amount of $2,500 and is awarded to encourage excellence in college debate at UGA and to assist in the recruitment of outstanding high school debaters. The Georgia debate program is one of the best in the country and almost always finishes in the top ten teams in the United States. Several years ago, a two-person debate team from Georgia was selected as the most outstanding in the nation. To give you an idea of the excellence of the Georgia debate program today, we never made the national tournament in the three years I debated at Georgia. Today, the program always qualifies at least one team for the national tournament and frequently more than one. Richard Russell was not known as the best speaker in the Senate, but he was known as a fearless debater because of his preparation and mastery of the subject being debated. This is one of the skills learned in college debate.

In 2006, the Russell Foundation established the Senator Sam Nunn Security Leadership Fellow, which awards a fellowship each year to an outstanding UGA student who is studying some aspect of international affairs. This fellowship program was established in recognition of Senator Sam Nunn's outstanding service for twenty-four years as a United States senator and in appreciation for his assistance in various endeavors of the Russell Foundation. At about the same time, the Russell Foundation endowed a student achievement award that is presented each year to a student leader who is a member of the Blue Key Chapter at UGA.

The Richard B. Russell Georgia High School Debate Championship

For some twenty years, the Russell Foundation has sponsored the Richard B. Russell Georgia High School Debate Championship, bringing together each year the most talented high school debaters in Georgia from every classification of school—both public and private. The Russell Foundation underwrites the expenses of the tournament, which is administered by the director of debate at West Georgia University and held in Atlanta. The top speakers of the tournament are awarded trophies in the form of a replica of the Richard B. Russell Statue that was placed in the rotunda of the Russell Senate Office Building in Washington, DC. Many of the high school debaters who participate in this tournament go on to become successful college debaters.

Distribution of Books

In furtherance of its mission to preserve the legacy of Richard Russell, the Russell Foundation has paid for the distribution of a number of books about Richard Russell and his family free of charge to public and private libraries in Georgia. These include the libraries at both public and private high schools and public and private colleges. The first book distributed was the biography of Richard Russell by Dr. Gilbert Fite. The Russell Foundation purchased a sufficient quantity of the books to distribute to each public and private library in Georgia. Georgia governor Zell Miller assisted in this project with some of the funds in the governor's contingency budget. In addition to the Fite biography, the foundation has made a similar distribution of a book by two University of Georgia professors who did a compilation of Richard Russell's speeches from 1929 until his death. Two other books distributed by the Russell Foundation are Sally Russell's biographies of Richard Russell's father and of Senator Russell. Finally, the foundation distributed a book by a former UPI newsman and Senate staffer, John Goldsmith, on the relationship between Richard Russell and Lyndon Johnson.

Dean Rusk and Lectures on the United States Constitution

From a modest upbringing in Cherokee County, Georgia, Dean Rusk went on to become a Rhodes Scholar, a college professor, a top official in the State Department, and for eight years the president of the Rockefeller Foundation in New York before being selected in 1960 by president-elect Kennedy as his secretary of state. He served for eight years in that position through the Kennedy and Johnson administrations. I have never known a more unassuming or less pretentious person than Dean Rusk. I got to know him casually when I worked in Washington and much better when he was appointed as a trustee of the Russell Foundation. He once said of Richard Russell, "For about twenty years, he was the second most powerful person in Washington, second only to presidents."

Unfortunately for Rusk, he became the public face and chief defender of Lyndon Johnson's Vietnam War policies. While Richard Russell certainly did not agree with those policies, he admired the job Dean Rusk did as secretary of state. I can still remember attending some of the hearings before the Senate Foreign Relations Committee when Dean Rusk, sitting alone, would undergo rigorous questioning by senators for hours on end. Senators who were members of the Foreign Relations Committee would question him for about an hour or two before leaving and being replaced by different senators. The questioning was combative and hostile, but Dean Rusk sat through it all with only a notepad and a handy pack of cigarettes. Sometimes the hearings continued for eight or ten or even twelve hours a day. One of the reasons he became so severely disliked by the war opponents and protesters was that he did such a good job of articulating Lyndon Johnson's defense of the war.

When the Johnson administration concluded at the end of 1968, one would have expected someone of Dean Rusk's background and talents to be selected to head one of America's most prestigious universities or nonprofits, or at least to be named to an endowed chair at one of America's leading universities. Because he did his job as secretary of state during the Vietnam War, however, he was boycotted and ostracized. One of the few job offers he received was to become a member of the faculty at the University of Georgia School of Law. I can remember his wife, Virginia, calling me one day and telling me that she and her husband were going to move into a certain apartment complex in the Five Points area of Athens. They knew I had recently been in school there and thought I could give them some intelligence on the wisdom of the move. I was horrified at the thought of the former secretary of state and his wife living in the apartments for even a brief period before buying or building a house. I had attended raucous parties there that were characterized by heavy consumption of alcohol. Since I did not have any better suggestion to make, however, I did not discourage Mrs. Rusk.

In my opinion, the best thing that has happened to the University of Georgia School of Law during my lifetime was the arrival of Dean Rusk. Even so, certain reactionary forces in Georgia opposed his appointment not because of the Vietnam War but because his daughter had married an African American. Fortunately, the Georgia Board of Regents ignored these protests and approved the appointment. Most of the senior cabinet members of the Kennedy and Johnson administrations wrote books and collected huge royalties or exorbitant speaking fees on the lecture circuit. Dean Rusk did none of this. He devoted himself to his responsibilities as a law professor at UGA. He quickly became one of the most popular members of the faculty, partly because he spent so much time with his students. The rise of the UGA Law School to the fine center for the study of law it is today can be directly traced to the period when Dean Rusk taught there. The university administrators were so appreciative of his services that a few years before his retirement, they named a new law school building the Dean Rusk Center. It was fittingly located immediately adjacent to the Russell Library, where buildings named in honor of these two great Georgians who worked so closely together in Washington would be forever linked.

While I had known Rusk casually in Washington, DC, I got to know him much better when he and I joined the Russell Foundation Board of Trustees. He was an active trustee and attended almost all meetings during his terms of office. He made many suggestions of worthwhile activities for the foundation to consider. One I particularly recall was that the foundation recruit outstanding scholars of the United States Constitution to come to Athens to deliver lectures on the Constitution on the bicentennial of its adoption. These lectures were highly successful and brought to Athens some of the most widely recognized constitutional scholars in America. In addition to giving these lectures, they met with students and members of the faculty. This is just one example of constructive suggestions Dean Rusk made during his years as a trustee of the Russell Foundation.

Southeastern Bankruptcy Law Institute

The Southeastern Bankruptcy Law Institute (SBLI) was established in the early 1970s to put on an annual seminar on bankruptcy law and to enhance the study of bankruptcy law. Bankruptcy judge W. Homer Drake, Jr., conceived of the idea for the institute, and several Atlanta bankruptcy lawyers organized it. At the institute's annual seminar, the most prominent bankruptcy lawyers and judges are recruited to appear on the two-and-a-half-day program held each spring in Atlanta. The seminar has been successful and grew steadily until it was the largest private seminar in the country devoted exclusively to bankruptcy law. In some years, there were almost as many as 1,000 people from most states in the country in attendance. The seminar tries to strike a balance between programs on reorganization in bankruptcy for corporations and other businesses and cases involving consumers and individuals.

Bankruptcy lawyers in Atlanta and surrounding southeastern states were recruited for the institute's board of trustees, who are responsible for planning and staging the seminar each year. It is a working board. As the prestige of the seminar grew, the prestige of serving on the SBLI board also grew. Only about twenty-five members of the board are allowed to serve at any one time, but there was initially no mandatory term or exit date. This resulted in a great many of the trustees serving for long periods, which was good and bad. It meant a high level of expertise and knowledge on the board. But it also meant a minimum of infusion of new talent. Finally, by around 2000, the board decided to require directors to accept emeritus status at a certain age so new directors could be appointed. This turned out to be beneficial because it introduced new concepts and new talent to the board. I was added to the SBLI board in the late 1980s and served as president in 1993–1994. I took emeritus status approximately five years ago and still serve in that capacity today.

In addition to putting on the annual bankruptcy seminar, the SBLI also awarded scholarships from time to time and endowed a chair in bankruptcy law, first at Emory University in Atlanta before moving it to Mercer University in Macon. The chair today is named in honor of Judge Drake, who is still active in SBLI. All of the bankruptcy judges in Atlanta are advisors to the SBLI.

One of the enjoyable things about serving on the SBLI board was the opportunity to travel as a group. Until recently, the SBLI board met during the annual National Conference of Bankruptcy Judges meeting, which was held in various locations around the country. We would frequently take a retreat for several days after the meeting to plan future activities. One year after I became a director, we also traveled internationally to Amsterdam and Brussels for about a week, during which we received briefings on bankruptcy law in those countries and in Europe.

Norton Bankruptcy Law Institutes and Publications

A few years before he retired, bankruptcy judge William L. Norton, Jr., established a national bankruptcy publication called *Norton on Bankruptcy Law.* He recruited as authors and editors for his publication judges and well-known bankruptcy attorneys from around the country whom he had met while serving on the bench. I would have thought it would be difficult to establish a viable national bankruptcy journal because one publication, *Colliers on Bankruptcy,* had dominated the field for many years. Judge Norton, however, was successful in establishing a highly effective and widely read publication. In time, it came to rival *Colliers* and is today frequently cited by the United States Supreme Court in bankruptcy cases.

Judge Norton also established a series of bankruptcy seminars to supplement and complement his bankruptcy publications. The faculties of these seminars were generally the writers and editors who appeared in his publications. I became involved when Judge Norton asked my law partner, Mike Levengood, and me to be co-editors of the portion of the Norton bankruptcy publication that contains forms that bankruptcy attorneys can use for various purposes in their cases. I also appeared at a number of the Norton bankruptcy seminars in California and Nevada. There was no appearance fee paid for these programs, but it gave a bankruptcy attorney national publicity, and all the expenses were paid. I enjoyed participating in the seminars for about ten years. Judge Norton suffered a serious stroke several years ago, and today, the Norton publications and seminars are run by Judge Norton's son, William L. Norton III, a prominent bankruptcy lawyer in Nashville, Tennessee.

American College of Trial Lawyers

The American College of Trial Lawyers (ACTL) was established in 1950 as the premier organization in the United States of the trial bar. It was subsequently expanded to include Canada. Its membership is by invitation only and is reserved for trial lawyers who have been practicing for at least fifteen years and are recognized as exemplifying the highest ideals of civility, ethics, professionalism, and effective trial practice. At any one time, no more than 1 percent of lawyers in any state can be fellows in the ACTL. When one is nominated to be admitted as a fellow, an intensive investigation is conducted, including interviews with attorneys who have practiced against the nominee in cases as well as judges who have presided over the nominee's most important trials. The nominee then must pass muster with the state chapter before being reviewed at the national level. The slightest ethical lapse or questionable conduct is often a final disqualification. I was inducted as a fellow in 1992 in Boston.

One of the most enjoyable aspects of the ACTL is its collegiality and trips. Ann and I made a great many of those trips after I was inducted. There is an annual meeting in the fall and another in the spring. In addition, Georgia, Florida, and South Carolina fellows meet usually at Sea Island, Georgia, each year. Before his death, a highlight of the Sea Island meeting was a cocktail reception at the home of Judge Griffin Bell. All of the national meetings offer outstanding educational programs that feature appearances by the top judges, including Supreme Court justices and lawyers from the United States and Canada.

The meeting I recall the best and enjoyed the most was held in London, England, and Rome, Italy, in 1998. We had a three-day meeting in London and a three-day meeting in Rome. We combined this trip with a family vacation and traveled through northern Italy and on to Vienna after the ACTL activities were finished. It was one of the most enjoyable trips I have ever taken.

There is also an annual dinner meeting at the Piedmont Driving Club in Atlanta for the Georgia fellows, which I frequently attended before my retirement. It was typical for trial lawyers from all over the state to appear at this meeting, and the national president of the organization would also attend and speak. Georgia has an active chapter of the college, and a number of Georgia fellows have been president of it, including Griffin Bell, Frank Jones, and Jack Dalton. Chilton Davis Varner, a partner of the King and Spalding law firm in Atlanta, is the current president of the college.

American College of Bankruptcy

The American College of Bankruptcy (ACB) is somewhat patterned after the American College of Trial Lawyers but is limited to insolvency professionals. These are not necessarily all bankruptcy lawyers or judges but also include accountants, consultants, appraisers, and others. Like the ACTL, membership is by invitation only and is limited to those who exhibit the highest level of professionalism and ethics and practice at the highest level of insolvency. Unlike the ACTL, the American College of Bankruptcy also requires a record of distinguished writing or speaking on insolvency matters. Judge Norton was one of the people who helped establish the ACB. I was inducted as a fellow in 1997, and I am confident that Judge Norton had something to do with it.

One of the most impressive activities of the ACB is its induction ceremony. It is typically held in the Great Hall of the United States Supreme Court in Washington and followed by an elaborate reception in the Supreme Court at which, at least in the past, it was not unusual to see a justice of the Court. I particularly remember having an extended discussion with Justice Antonin Scalia one year. In addition to the induction ceremony, the ACB annual meeting also includes an elaborate educational program. It focuses on the latest developments in bankruptcy law, and the members of the faculty are usually fellows of the college who are involved in some of the most recent and important bankruptcy cases.

The American College of Bankruptcy Foundation was established to preserve the history of the insolvency practice and its most important documents. It has a program at the University of Pennsylvania[and is] actively supported by contributions from the ACB fellows.

The Georgia chapter of the ACB meets in the summer to discuss possible new fellows. Georgia fellows have been active in the organization, and Neal Batson of the Alston and Bird law firm in Atlanta served as president of the ACB several years ago. After my induction in 1997 and at least through Neal's tenure as president, I tried to attend the annual meeting in Washington each year. It also gave me another opportunity to visit the Russell Senate Office Building.

University of Georgia Library Board of Visitors

As a result of the work I did for the Russell Foundation and my involvement with the Russell Library, I became interested in the University of Georgia libraries. The UGA libraries organized a board of visitors more than ten years ago, and I agreed to serve on the board. The purpose of the BOV is to help raise funds for the libraries and to contribute in any other way possible to their well-being. There are about thirty members of the board of visitors. I served as chairman in 2008–2009. The board usually meets two or three times a year, and it has been particularly active in the last few years because of efforts related to the new Richard B. Russell Special Collections Library Building. I continue to serve on the board at this time.

The Arch Foundation for the University of Georgia and the University of Georgia Foundation

For many years, the University of Georgia Foundation (UGA Foundation) has been the official fundraising arm of the University of Georgia. Its responsibilities were to help the university raise funds from private donors and to support the president of UGA. By 2000, the UGA Foundation had almost $500 million in its endowment, which was invested to fund various activities at the university, including professorships, scholarships, and other special projects. In 2004, a dispute arose between certain trustees of the UGA Foundation and the president of the University of Georgia, Dr. Michael Adams. I was not involved and have no personal knowledge of the controversy other than what I read in the newspaper. I gathered that the dispute was generated by the decision of Dr. Adams not to renew the contract of Vince Dooley as the athletic director. Dooley had been the longtime and successful head football coach at Georgia before becoming athletic director. After he reached retirement age, Dr. Adams extended his contract for an additional two years but declined to extend it further. I had always been a great admirer of Coach Dooley, whom I first met while working for Richard Russell, not only for his contributions to the athletic program but also for his many contributions to the University of Georgia library. However, I also understood Dr. Adams was President of the University of Georgia, and he was entitled to make the personnel decisions he thought best for the university.

It appeared from the press coverage that because of this controversy, certain UGA Foundation trustees started making other charges against Dr. Adams that had nothing to do with the Dooley situation. For example, according to the newspapers, they made allegations with respect to property in Costa Rica that had been purchased by the university for student field trips and research. I am not sure why the decision was made to air all this dirty linen in public to the detriment of UGA, but it created a controversy that adversely affected both the university and the UGA Foundation. The Georgia Board of Regents, to which Dr. Adams reported, became displeased with the conduct of the UGA Foundation or at least some of its trustees. When an effort to negotiate a settlement of the controversy apparently did not suit the board of regents, it directed the university to sever the UGA Foundation as a sanctioned organization of the university and to set up a new foundation.

At this point, I received a telephone call from the university indicating that Dr. Adams would like for me to serve as one of the founding trustees of the new foundation. While I had no idea who had shot whom in connection with the controversy, I had enough experience with Dr. Adams in my capacity as chair of the Russell Foundation to know that he was a man of integrity and had the best interest of the University of Georgia at heart. I accepted the invitation to join the board of the new foundation, which was called the Arch Foundation for the University of Georgia. It would become the new sanctioned organization to assist the university with fundraising and advise the president. The three people who principally organized the new foundation were John Spalding, a member of a prominent family in Atlanta, who was the general counsel of Cox Communications; Norman Fletcher, the former chief justice of the Georgia Supreme Court; and Sheffield Hale, a former partner of the Kilpatrick Stockton law firm in Atlanta, then the chief counsel of the American Cancer Society and now president and CEO of the Atlanta History Center.

The fact that the UGA Foundation was decertified as the official fundraising organ of the university did not mean that it could not continue to accept contributions or administer its existing portfolio. This in effect meant there would be two foundations, one officially recognized and the other not so recognized. This required the administrative staff of the university to deal with two different foundations, as the UGA Foundation was obligated to continue to administer its portfolio in accordance with the purposes of the donors to fund scholarships, professorships, or other activities at UGA.

In addition to being a trustee of the new foundation, I was asked to serve as chair of the investment committee and served in that position for the first four years. The purpose of the investment committee is to establish an investment and spending policy for the new foundation with respect to the funds it raises on behalf of the university. This proved to be a somewhat demanding task, particularly when the recession started in 2007. The investment committee met multiple times each year to review the performance of the portfolio and to make decisions on future investments. The long-term endowment portfolio grew to approximately $100 million by 2011.

I believe everyone assumed that the two foundations would eventually merge back into one. It simply did not make sense in the long term to have two foundations doing the same thing with the attendant additional administrative burdens on the university staff and the possible confusion among donors. However, a merger could not take place until tempers cooled and until cooler heads prevailed. By late 2010, we were in that period, and negotiations commenced between the two foundations. The Arch Foundation was principally represented by Jack Head, then-current chair of the Arch Foundation, and John Spalding, the first chair. An agreement was reached in early 2011 and presented to the Arch Foundation board at that time. I was enthusiastic about the merger because I did not think it was in the university's best interest to have two separate foundations long term, although the total contributions to UGA through both foundations in the prior years had been the highest in the history of the university. Over $100 million a year had been contributed in each of those years. Still, I supported the merger. I also thought it made sense that the surviving foundation would be the University of Georgia Foundation because it had existed much longer than the Arch Foundation and had a much larger investment portfolio. Dr. Adams and the board of regents supported the merger, and it was consummated in mid-2011. I continue to serve as a trustee of the combined foundation and expect to do so until my term expires in 2013.

The Richard B. Russell Statue placed in the rotunda of the Russell Senate Office Building in Washington by the Russell Foundation in 1996.

Senator Sam Nunn and Senator Robert Byrd after the dedication of the Russell Statue.

Speaking at the dedication of the Russell Statue as chair of the Russell Foundation.

The new Richard B. Russell Special Collections Library Building at the University of Georgia dedicated in February of 2012.

Dr. Gary Bertsch of UGA, Senator Sam Nunn and me at a Richard B. Russell Symposium on national security in Athens.*

Dr. Michael Adams, President of the University of Georgia, presents me as chair of the Russell Foundation a certificate of membership in the Abraham Baldwin Society upon the Foundation's contributions to UGA exceeding $5 million. The contributions now are approaching $8 million.

A golf foursome at a meeting of the American College of Trial Lawyers in Palm Springs, California circa 1995. I am the golfer on the far right.

14

Trying Cases

When I decided to practice law in spring 1960, it was my dream to become a trial lawyer. By the mid-1970s, I had realized that dream. Up until the time I entered the practice of law, I had the naïve belief that trial attorneys spent most of their time in court. The reality is that no more than 10 to 15 percent of the trial attorney's time is actually spent in the courtroom. There are a few exceptions to this fact. One is the practice in the offices of state district attorneys, which try large numbers of smaller cases where the trial lawyer stays in court much of the time. Another exception is insurance defense work, and bankruptcy is yet another. In large bankruptcy cases, the number of smaller disputes makes it feasible to send younger lawyers to court to handle them since there is not large exposure if the matter is lost. I benefited from this aspect of the bankruptcy practice early in my career. On the other hand, a young litigation attorney in a large commercial firm that works on big cases might be relegated to conducting research or carrying the briefcase of a more senior lawyer for as long as five years before getting any real courtroom experience. In commercial law firms whose practices are based on representing corporations and other businesses, the cases are much larger and require far greater preliminaries prior to the trial itself. This means that most of the trial attorneys spend the vast majority of their time outside the courtroom. I will discuss in this chapter not only the trial of cases but also some of a trial lawyer's other responsibilities in his or her practice.

My greatest desire as a trial lawyer was to try jury cases. In the early period of my practice prior to 1980, the opportunities to do so were limited because of the amount of time I spent on non-jury practice in the bankruptcy court and before the Georgia Public Service Commission. By 1980, however, I was getting more into the trial of jury cases, which I thoroughly enjoyed. I am in a distinct minority among commercial trial attorneys in that I generally preferred to try my cases before juries as opposed to judges, even when I was defending large corporations or other businesses. I found that many judges, particularly after they had been on the bench for a few years, were more impatient and set in their ways. I had more confidence in my ability to convince lay jurors to rule with my client than I did judges. There were certain exceptions to this, such as defending lawyers in malpractice cases, because juries generally speaking have a low opinion of lawyers. Another example is defending a client who received widespread negative publicity prior to the trial. The views I express in this chapter are entirely my own and are based on my experience trying jury cases for some thirty years. While some of the trial practices advocated in this chapter also apply to trial before judges, I specifically have jury trials in mind.

"It Is the Story, Stupid"

The most important duty of a trial attorney is to identify the story of a case and to present it to the jury in a compelling and understandable way. When Bill Clinton was running for president, his chief political adviser, James Carville, posted the following message on the bulletin board of the campaign headquarters: "It is the economy, stupid." In the trial of jury cases, "It is the story, stupid." Every case has a story, but too few trial attorneys spend the required time at the front end identifying the story and figuring out how to present it to a jury in a compelling and clear way. If this is not done up front, the case wanders for lack of direction, and effort is wasted. Once the story is identified, everything related to the case should revolve around the objective of refining the story and presenting it to the jury in the most effective way. I liken a jury trial to a theater production. It must hold the attention of and persuade the audience.

Jury research has shown that motive is important to jurors. Therefore, a significant part of identifying the story and planning for its effective presentation is determining the motivation of the principal actors in the case. While it is possible that discovery of new facts as the case progresses may necessitate the tweaking of the story before trial, it is seldom that a well thought out strategy has to be abandoned altogether. If that is the case, it is usually because the attorney has not done his or her job properly. In coming up with the story of the case, it is obviously important to give serious consideration to what lay jurors are likely to believe. For example, in the Bob Kern case, which I described in chapter 12 of this book, it was unlikely that lay jurors would believe a large corporation like Prudential would agree to make Bob Kern an equity partner in a multimillion-dollar real estate development without a partnership agreement or some other document memorializing the understanding. A story based on an unlikely scenario of events that is counterintuitive to jurors is not likely to be successful. An experienced trial attorney will keep that in mind in summarizing the story of the case.

Initial Investigation and Research

After a trial attorney is retained, the first thing that usually happens in a large commercial case is an investigation of the facts and research of the law. This must usually be done before the lawsuit is filed and, therefore, without access to most of the records of the adverse party. The investigation usually consists at least of interviews with the attorney's client and employees as well as review of the client's documents. At times, it can also involve interviews with third parties. A seasoned trial attorney will not blindly accept a client's view of the facts, because the client is usually emotionally involved in the case and often not objective or even truthful about what has happened. This is particularly true in large corporations if the individuals who created the facts are also the ones in charge of defending or prosecuting a suit. That is one of the reasons large corporations now frequently assign responsibility for prosecution of defense of the suit to a different set of employees than the ones who created the facts. The same thing is true of the in-house legal department of the company. The lawyers who advised the company as the facts were being created are not the same as those responsible for working with outside counsel in the prosecution or defense of the case.

Once the initial investigation is complete, the attorney generally wants to conduct research with respect to the applicable law that will govern the client's rights in the case. Younger attorneys in the firm usually do this research. It can be complicated to determine what law applies to a case whose events take place in several states and in which suits can be filed in multiple states. For example, in the Sandy Simon case, we could have filed in at least five different states. The law of the state where the case is filed is not always the governing law. This is determined by a legal doctrine known as "conflict of laws." One of the duties of the attorney conducting the research is to determine the jurisdiction whose law applies to the case and then determine the particulars of that law. It is important not to assume what the law of the state is; sometimes it is quite different than expected.

Written Discovery

Once the initial investigation is concluded and the research is completed, the case is then filed in what is considered to be the most favorable venue for the party filing the case. The next stage is written discovery, where the lawyer looks for facts relevant to the case that cannot be ascertained merely by the interview of a client or a review of related documents. For example, one of the first steps in a large case is to file document requests for the documents of the adverse party. This is one of the most fruitful places to identify facts unfavorable to the opposition. This is particularly true of large corporations because almost everything is documented. Employees are notorious for covering their tracks with written records that become the adverse attorney's best friends in the case.

Written interrogatories are also available to ascertain facts from the adverse party. The opponent must answer these questions under oath. In my experience, these have largely become a waste of time because parties and their counsel have figured out ways to evade answering the questions by either objecting to them as improper or pretending not to understand them. If the evasion of the questions is flagrant, it is possible to file a motion with the court to compel a proper answer, but courts generally frown on such motions, which take so long to resolve that they are usually a waste of time.

The same is true of requests for admissions, which are written requests that the adverse party admit certain facts in the case or certain legal propositions. Again, parties in complex cases have become so skillful at avoiding direct responses that this written discovery has also become largely a waste of time. It is possible, on occasion, to get a significant admission because it is established by a document produced by the adverse party. To the extent that a lawyer is able to get the adverse party to affirmatively admit a fact in the case, it is not necessary to prove that fact in the trial of the case. The admission can be read to the jury as an admission of the adverse party.

It is also possible to file a motion to require a party filing a complaint to provide a more definite statement of its claim. Except in the allegation of fraud and a couple of other exceptions, a plaintiff does not generally have to allege in great detail the basis of a case. The theory is that the adverse party can ascertain this during the discovery process. However, the amount of detail that has to be alleged in the case is much greater than it used to be when "notice pleading" was loosely construed to mean simply putting an adverse party on notice of a general outline of the claims. Up until the last thirty or forty years, there was far less discovery, both written and otherwise, than is the case today. Today, discovery is one of the principal reasons cases take so long to conclude and are so expensive.

Depositions

Depositions are oral examinations of witnesses under oath about the facts of a case. They are probably the most fruitful discovery devices in most large cases. This is because the attorney can press the witness with respect to evasive answers, which is not possible in the case of written discovery. In most large cases today, the most important depositions are videotaped so they can be used at trial if the witness changes his or her testimony or if the witness is not available for trial testimony. Some plaintiff litigation law firms today have their own in-house capability of videotaping depositions and routinely videotape them all.

It is critically important to complete the document review process substantially before commencing important depositions. This is because the likelihood of a witness admitting an adverse fact is greatly increased if the attorney conducting the deposition has documents that restrict the witness's ability to evade the question or give contrary testimony. Most courts today limit the length and number of depositions in a case. The court also generally enters a discovery order that sets forth the time frame within which depositions can be taken. Thus, it is important for a trial attorney to plan carefully and to adhere to the plan in the conducting of oral discovery. In complex cases, the discovery period can last for well over a year, but an effective trial attorney will investigate in advance the likelihood that the judge presiding over the case will insist on a shorter discovery period or be more reluctant to extend the discovery deadline.

Many senior trial attorneys leave the taking of depositions of most witnesses to other more junior lawyers in the firm. I generally did not follow that practice because I found it was helpful to have personally taken the deposition of the important witnesses in the case. This gave me a better feel for how good or bad the witness would be at trial. I also found that taking the depositions was an excellent way to become more knowledgeable about the facts of the case and discover ways in which the story should be tweaked or changed before trial. The disadvantage of taking almost all the depositions in a large case is, of course, that it leaves the trial attorney with less time to work on other cases. Unless the rules of the court severely limit the number of depositions, it is not unusual in a large case to take fifty or more depositions before trial.

It is also possible under the rules of most courts to take a deposition for the preservation of trial testimony as opposed to a discovery deposition. This is usually employed when the witness is ill and may not be living at the time of trial or when the witness lives outside the subpoena power of the court and cannot be compelled to attend the trial. Generally, in federal court in diversity cases, a witness can be compelled to attend the trial by subpoena only if he or she resides within 100 miles of the courthouse. In large cases that involve witnesses from all over the country, that limitation obviously prevents many witnesses from being compelled to attend the trial. At a deposition solely to preserve testimony, the questions that can be asked are much more limited because the deposition can be used only to elicit testimony that would be admissible as evidence at the trial. An inexperienced trial attorney will not infrequently be embarrassed by trying to ask wide-ranging discovery questions at a deposition noticed only to preserve testimony.

Depositions are also effective in communicating to the representative of the adverse party that it has real difficulties with its case. Generally, in large and complex cases, corporations will have business representatives attend the most important depositions and observe the testimony of its witnesses and of adverse witnesses. I found that the effective questioning of important witnesses from the other side could often prompt the adverse party to seriously consider settlement of the case before trial. Therefore, these depositions were invaluable in addition to the information learned from the witness.

Motion Practice

An attorney can file various motions prior to trial either to narrow the issues in the case, affect the trial of the case, or dispose of the case entirely. Such motions are written pleadings filed with the court, generally after discovery, before the trial. Because judges are frequently displeased with what they view as unnecessary pretrial motions that may delay the trial or unnecessarily increase the workload of the court, it is important for the trial attorney to be meaningfully involved in the process of deciding which motions to file.

The least frequently filed motion of this kind is a motion for judgment on the pleadings. This, in essence, is a request that the judge rule that the pleadings do not state a viable cause of action even if everything alleged in the pleadings is true. An example would be when a complaint fails to allege an essential element of a cause of action. The problem with these motions is that, even when granted, most courts will allow a party at least one opportunity to amend the pleadings and correct the defect. This means the moving party has not accomplished much and has spent time and energy on a fruitless exercise. The only time this has a good chance of success is when a party has already been given several opportunities to amend its pleadings but still fails to state a viable cause of action.

The most frequently filed pretrial motion is what is known as a motion for summary judgment. Supported by the discovery in the case and often affidavits as well, this motion argues to the court that there is nothing for a jury to decide in terms of disputed facts that are essential to a decision. In a complex case, a motion for summary judgment is almost always filed by both sides, even where there is little chance of success. It is almost taken as an admission that the failure to file such a motion means the party agrees that the case should go to a jury. The downside to a sweeping motion for summary judgment that has little chance of being granted is that the judge will dislike having to address it, and it may delay the trial of the case. Many attorneys use these motions more as a device of warning the other side about the weakness of its case to pressure it to settle than out of any real hope that the court is going to grant the motion. At times, motions for summary judgment can be helpful to eliminate certain claims in the case even though the entire case is not thrown out by the court. A trial attorney needs to be careful about taking positions in a motion for summary judgment that are inconsistent with positions he or she may be required to take at the trial. I believe there are far too many motions for summary judgment filed in cases today, which is yet another reason litigation has become so time-consuming and expensive.

Another often-filed pretrial motion is what is known as a motion in limine. This is a motion asking the court to rule certain evidence out of the trial on the grounds that it is not relevant, that its prejudicial nature exceeds any relevance or for other legal cause. It can also apply to witnesses. I always looked carefully at motions in limine because they can be effective in affecting the trial of the case, even if the evidence in question is not excluded. For example, I sometimes asked a judge who was withholding a ruling on the motion in limine until he or she could assess the evidence in context to at least prohibit the opposing counsel from mentioning the evidence in his or her opening statement to the jury. Most judges are willing to consider such a restriction if they think there is a good chance the motion will be granted during the trial. One mistake frequently made by trial attorneys is to file too many motions in limine covering every conceivable piece of important adverse evidence. This usually backfires because the court is not pleased with an avalanche of motions in limine that should not have been filed and often simply denies them all. Thus, if the attorney had limited himself or herself to a couple of motions in limine that had real merit, the motions might have been granted.

The Trial

The most important part of a jury case is obviously the trial, where the initial and frequently the final decision is made. For me, it is also the most enjoyable part of the case. To be a successful trial attorney, it is helpful to try to put yourself in the shoes of the jury. For most if not all of the jurors in a case, a court trial is a new experience. It can be intimidating. You are summoned to the courthouse and initially put in a room with hundreds of other prospective jurors. You are asked to fill out information questionnaires and provide background on your family, education, and work experience. Under the rules of most courts today, if you report for jury duty but are not selected during the day you report, you are excused from further duty. If you are selected, you are expected to serve for the duration of the trial, which, in some cases, can last for weeks or months.

Whether you are actually selected to serve on a jury depends on a process known as "voir dire." This jury selection process begins when you are grouped with about thirty other prospective jurors and taken from the large room, where you have been waiting, to a courtroom.

There, in the presence of the judge and the attorneys representing all parties, you are further questioned with respect to your background. In other words, a prospective juror is expected to share private information in the presence of a judge, attorneys, and others he or she has never met before. Most jurors are uneasy with the process and nervous. An attorney who can put them at ease during the jury selection process will have an advantage in the trial. Voir dire is also the trial attorney's first opportunity to bond with the jury, which is as important as selecting the jury. Even for the most experienced trial attorneys, the selection of a jury is more of an art than a science. You can never be sure you have made a wise selection until the case is over. Jury selection is the opportunity to make a first good impression. I always found it was most effective to use a low-key style and to maintain eye contact with the prospective jurors. Jury selection is also a chance to educate the jury about your client's case, although courts in recent years have increasingly put limitations on attorneys in terms of the statements they can make or the questions they can ask during voir dire. In some courts today, only the judge is permitted to ask voir dire questions.

I had two experiences early in my career that emphasized the uncomfortable situation facing jurors and gave me a better understanding of their thought process. The first was when I was exposed to the mock jury exercise whereby attorneys test the themes of their case on mock jurors that are selected in the same manner as the jury will be selected for the trial. The process is abbreviated compared to the trial and essentially consists of attorneys ostensibly representing each side of the case, making arguments, and then the mock jury retiring for deliberations. The attorneys are able to view the jury deliberations through one-way glass windows and can even suggest questions for the jury to consider. These exercises can be quite expensive and are typically used only in larger cases. They are helpful in giving an attorney insight into how jurors think and the kinds of arguments that are most likely to impress them.

The second experience was when I actually served on a jury. That is rare, as most attorneys do not want fellow attorneys serving on their juries because they are afraid the attorney-juror will dominate the jury process because of his or her greater knowledge of court proceedings. In the early 1980s, I was selected for a case in the Superior Court in Atlanta before Judge Osgood Williams, whom I had met in the 1980 Senate race.

The case was a criminal drug case in which an African-American girl and her boyfriend had been indicted for possession and/or distribution of drugs. It appeared that the boyfriend was the one who was actually dealing drugs, but the drugs were found in an apartment rented by the girl, which, under Georgia law, meant she was in possession of drugs. A large number of prospective jurors were excused for cause in the case, resulting in three potential jurors for the last position on the jury—me and two ministers. I assume that the parties thought a lawyer would be better than a minister. I was surprised to be selected for the jury.

The firsthand experience of seeing attorneys try a case taught me several things that I had not focused on previously. First, trials are much too long and jurors become bored. This lesson taught me to be conscious of shortening the trial where possible and concentrating on the essential points and not on irrelevancies. Second, it taught me how much jurors resent conferences with the judge outside their hearing to discuss legal issues. Sometimes these conferences take place when counsel is asked to come to the bench and confer with the judge in whispered voices. Sometimes they take place in recesses when the jury is taken to a holding room. In either event, jurors are resentful that there are things being discussed that they cannot hear or that they are waiting for long periods for reasons they do not understand. This taught me to be careful not to request too many conferences in the presence of the jury and to try to schedule the ones I did request either during a lunch break or at the end of the day after the jury was excused. Finally, I learned that lawyers call too many witnesses and ask too many questions. In a long trial, this is particularly annoying to jurors. I also learned that lawyers object too often to questions the opposing lawyer asks a witness. Some lawyers seem to think they need to object to any improper question whether it damages their case or not. An objection to a question communicates to jurors that the attorney believes the matter is important, and thus the jurors pay particular attention. Even if the objection is sustained, jurors are left believing the answer would have been damaging to the objecting party. If the objection is denied, the jurors pay special attention to the answer and may conclude that the objecting lawyer is trying to keep information from them or does not know what he or she is doing.

I also learned a great deal during jury deliberations in this case. My fellow jurors insisted that I serve as foreman of the jury. I resisted this and eventually agreed to do so on one condition—that I would only express my opinion on an issue after all the other jurors had expressed theirs. This is the way we deliberated. The jury was composed of approximately one-half whites and one-half African Americans, and one-half men and one-half women. I had assumed that the jury might split along racial lines, with the African Americans more inclined to excuse the defendants. I was wrong in that: the African Americans on the jury were, if anything, stronger for conviction of the defendants than were the whites. The only real division in the jury was along gender lines. The women generally felt that the girl was much less guilty than her boyfriend and several were initially in favor of acquitting her. However, Georgia law is strict on possession of drugs, and the jury charges of Judge Williams made it difficult to excuse the girl. Eventually, the jury convicted both. The most important thing I learned during jury deliberations is that the story of the case, not the minute detail, is important. Trial attorneys are frequently unable to realize this, and my experience emphasized to me strongly that I should adhere to the story of the case in future trials, avoid irrelevancies, and make the trial as short as possible.

After jury selection, the next thing that happens in a jury case is the opening statement. This is the opportunity for the attorney for each side to tell the jury what the case is about and describe the story of the case. While not all trial attorneys agree, I have always felt that the beginning of the case is the most important in a trial. The jurors are most alert at this time, as it is usually a new experience and they have not been weighed down by the constant delays and disruptions that will annoy and bore them as a long trial progresses. Opening statement is the only real opportunity an attorney has to tell his or her client's story uninterrupted and unqualified by evidence the jury will hear later in the case. The plaintiff has the advantage of giving the first opening statement, which makes the statement even more important for counsel for the defendant, because this is about the only opportunity the defendant has to communicate its side to the jury before the plaintiff rests its case, which can be weeks in a long trial. Too many defense attorneys waste this opportunity by not being sufficiently prepared and organized to give a concise and coherent statement of the defendant's story.

It is extremely important for the attorney to build trust with the jury. There is no quicker way to destroy this trust than to promise the jury in opening statement to prove something that you are thereafter not able to prove or do not even try to prove. You can rest assured that the adverse lawyer will remind the jury of your failure in closing arguments after the evidence is presented. In making opening statements, if I had any doubt as to whether I would be able to offer substantial proof for a proposition, I did not bring it up. If you raise a point in opening statement and do not offer proof of it, you lose the jury's trust. If you do not mention it in opening statement but do prove it during the trial, you can still emphasize it in closing argument. Another good way to destroy trust in the eyes of the jury is to let the jury hear negative information about your client or case first from the other side. The jury will wonder what else you are keeping from them. You are far better off to disclose and explain it. Attorneys also need to be careful about being too aggressive in opening statements and throughout the trial. Jurors generally do not like aggressive attorneys, whom they already stereotype as overbearing, aggressive, and unreasonable. Doing the slightest thing to reinforce this assumption, like badgering adverse witnesses, is disastrous for one's client.

After opening statements comes the presentation of evidence. This is done through witnesses either favorable to your case or hostile witnesses through cross-examination. As previously stated, lawyers often call too many witnesses and ask them too many questions. In planning a trial, I usually secluded myself by staying at our condo in Peachtree City with the case files until I had decided which witnesses to call, the order of the witnesses, and an outline of the questions for each witness. Preparation is absolutely critical to be effective in a major trial. The idea that an attorney, no matter how experienced, can walk into a courtroom and effectively represent his or her client in a major trial without extensive preparation is a fantasy. Nevertheless, you would be amazed at the number of trial attorneys who do not adequately prepare for trial. The worst impression to give to a jury is that you are stumbling along and deciding things as you go along. It also assures that you will receive even more pressure than would otherwise be the case. In a long trial, you are unavoidably going to be in a state of constant exhaustion, even with good preparation before the trial starts. In fact, I never appreciated the weekend more than I did when I was trying a major case. While Saturdays and Sundays were among my busiest days in preparing for the next week's proceedings[,] they were spent in my law office and not under the intense pressure of the courtroom.

The order of witnesses at trial is critically important. This matter is often given inadequate attention and thought by the trial attorney. The order of the witnesses helps determine how the story is told and whether the jury's attention is retained during the presentation of the most important witnesses. I always tried to start with a strong witness, particularly if I was representing a plaintiff, because jury research indicates that many jurors make up their minds about liability by the time the first or second witness for the plaintiff leaves the witness stand. For example, in the Burt Reynolds case, I called my client as the first witness and then called the two principal defense witnesses for cross-examination. I felt that the case was pretty much won or lost insofar as liability is concerned by the time the third witness was finished. I almost always placed my strongest witnesses in the first part of the case when I thought the attention span of the jurors would be at its peak.

Cross-examination of adverse witnesses is important, but its importance can be exaggerated. In a major case, all of the principal witnesses will have been deposed, and it should not be a surprise in terms of their testimony at trial. The most important objective of cross-examination, in my view, is to create the impression in the jury's mind that the adverse witness is not effective in resisting the other side's case. I usually did this by asking a series of questions at the beginning of the cross-examination to which I knew the adverse witness would have to give the expected answers based on the deposition. I usually started those questions with the following phrase: "You would agree with me, would you not...?" A properly deposed adverse witness has to answer that question "yes" or contradict his or her deposition testimony and be impeached. A series of such questions at the beginning creates the impression in the jury's mind that the witness does have not much of an ability to contest the opponent's case. It is generally not wise to ask adverse witnesses questions that start with the words "what" or "why" because it gives them an opportunity to make a speech on behalf of your opponent's side of the case.

After all the witnesses have testified and the evidence is closed, the next stage in the case is for closing arguments unless motions are filed asking the court to throw out the case or certain defenses to the case. Many seasoned trial attorneys believe that closing arguments are the most important part of the case. I do not agree for the reasons I have already stated. In terms of liability, I do not believe that closing arguments are often decisive in the outcome of the case. If a few jurors still remain on the fence, closing arguments may affect them. The vast majority of the jurors who have already made up their minds are not likely to be swayed by closing argument. However, closing arguments are important on the question of damages. Typically, the damages in a major case are determined based on the testimony of expert witnesses, which almost always come at the end of the party's case. The calculations of damages can be complex in a large case, and jurors are often confused as to how much in the way of damages should be awarded even after they have decided liability in favor of the plaintiff. It is usually helpful to spend a good deal of time on damages in one's closing argument so that it is fresh in the jury's mind and more likely that the jury will be able to come up with damages that are consistent with the evidence. In most courts today, jurors are allowed to take notes, and that can be helpful in jury deliberations on the question of damages.

After the closing arguments, the court will instruct the jury on the law that governs the case. Usually before the trial begins, each side files proposed jury instructions for the court to consider on the law relevant to each issue in the case. The judge then reviews those instructions, usually during the trial, and schedules a conference with counsel for the parties outside the presence of the jury to decide on the final jury instructions. It is important not to be too aggressive on jury instructions, because if the court charges the jury erroneously on a point of law, it may be used on appeal to reverse a favorable verdict. I have found that it is better to stick with vanilla jury instructions that essentially tell the jury the law that governs the case. There are now pattern jury instructions in almost all courts that are relatively safe because they have been reviewed on numerous occasions by appellate courts. Some courts now are reluctant to give anything other than the pattern instructions. In any event, most jury instructions in large civil cases are so complicated and in difficult-to-understand legal jargon that most lay jurors have forgotten them before they start deliberations.

After the jury instructions, the jurors are excused and begin their deliberations. In complex cases, the deliberations can last for long periods. The longer the deliberations continue, the more likely it is that the jury is divided on some issue. Occasionally, the jurors will ask to come back to the courtroom to receive a recharge from the court on some principle of law. In addition, the jurors may ask for certain pieces of evidence to be sent to the jury room for their review. To reach a verdict, the jury must be unanimous. In criminal cases, the government has the burden of proof beyond a reasonable doubt. In most civil cases, the plaintiff has the burden of proof under the less exacting standard of a preponderance of the evidence. The same standard applies to most defenses in a civil case asserted by the defendant. Once the jury reaches a verdict, it is communicated to the court, and the jurors are brought back into the courtroom for the announcement of the verdict. Either side can ask that the jurors be polled individually with respect to whether they agree with the verdict.

One of the most fruitful exercises, where it is permitted, is to interview jurors after the verdict is announced and the jurors are dismissed by the court. Jurors are not required to speak to the trial attorneys about jury deliberations, but they are permitted to do so under the rules of most courts. I found these informal conferences with members of the jury to be valuable. They give the trial attorney insight into what was successful and what was not successful and the reasons for that outcome. In fact, I found some of the most useful exercises of this kind to be in cases where the outcome was not satisfactory to my side. This is one of the best ways to learn about mistakes and avoid making those mistakes in the future. I always tried to interview members of the jury in all of my cases if it was permitted by the court and agreed to by the jurors.

Appellate Practice

The jury verdict is not necessarily the end of the case. The losing party can almost always appeal to a higher court. The federal and state systems in Georgia largely mirror each other in terms of the appellate courts. There is a Court of Appeals and a Supreme Court. While many of the larger law firms today have separate appellate divisions within their firms that handle almost all appellate work, many other firms do not have separate appellate practices and rely on the attorneys who tried the case to argue any appeal. That was the approach I preferred because of my belief that the attorney who tried a case would be far more familiar with the record of the case and the facts. Many appellate courts, particularly in the federal system, delight in demonstrating through their questions during the appellate arguments that the lawyer does not know the record. I argued a good number of my cases on appeal in both the federal and state systems.

While the popular perception is that oral argument is the most important part of an appeal, I do not believe that is true. I believe the briefs tend to be more important, particularly in the federal appellate courts. In fact, in a majority of the cases in the federal courts, no oral argument is held at all, and the case is entirely decided on briefs. In the Georgia Court of Appeals, a party has a right to an oral argument if it is insisted on, but the briefs are still usually the determining factor. This, of course, assumes that the appellate judges are carefully reviewing the briefs or are at least reviewing memos from their law clerks. I have found that in my experience, particularly in the federal system, the appellate judges are usually well prepared and well versed about the issues and facts of the case.

The one exception to having the attorney who tried the case also argue the appeal is in the United States Supreme Court. As stated in chapter 12 in my discussion of the Colony Square case, there is a cottage industry of appellate lawyers in Washington who specialize in arguing cases before the United States Supreme Court. Many of these are former law clerks who worked for justices of the Supreme Court. While it is possible for a trial attorney to argue a case in the United States Supreme Court, that has become less frequent in the big cases. While I was on the brief in a number of United States Supreme Court appeals, I never argued a case in the United States Supreme Court. I did argue a number of cases before the Georgia Supreme Court.

Settlement

Whether to settle a case should be constantly reviewed before and during the course of litigation. Too often the possibility of settlement is neglected in the early stages of litigation, either because the client is so emotionally exercised that they are not willing to talk to the adverse party or because they are so consumed with the likelihood of success that they are not interested in settlement. As the case drags on and the legal fees increase, reality sets in for many clients. By that point, however, huge sums of money have been spent on legal fees during the discovery process, and the officers or employees of corporate parties have devoted significant amounts of time to depositions or other activities. I have long thought that clients would be well advised to focus critically on settlement at the front end of cases. Of course, lawyers do not have a great incentive to encourage settlement early in cases because it would deprive them of the legal fees from the discovery process.

As the legal process has become more time-consuming and expensive, large corporate clients have grown more sophisticated in their approach to settlement. It is now not unusual in large cases for a corporation to retain a law firm to consider settlement that is separate from the one that is prosecuting or defending the case. Or, in some cases, it will utilize different attorneys within the firm to consider the settlement options. Sometimes it even resorts to outside help in trying to settle the case in the form of a mediator. There are sometimes business motivations to settle independent of the merits of the litigation. One time, while practicing at Hicks Maloof & Campbell, I represented Management Science America, Inc., in a dispute against NCR Corporation. The litigation was acrimonious and had been going on for quite a while with numerous depositions and hundreds of thousands of dollars in legal fees. During the litigation, AT&T bought NCR and Dun & Bradstreet bought MSA. These two companies had extensive business dealings with each other and did not want two of their companies engaged in this kind of litigation against each other. Therefore, they decided to hire a mediator from San Francisco to come to New York and broker a settlement. After several days of mediation, we did settle.

In my opinion, the best way to approach settlement early in the case is to require a sophisticated cost-benefit analysis. This measures the objective and likely outcome of the case against the expense of prosecuting or defending the case and also requires the client and counsel to focus on the merit or lack thereof of the client's position. If this is truly done in an objective way, it can often settle disputes that would otherwise linger in the court system for years. I was probably more settlement-oriented than the typical trial attorney. Because trial attorneys are notoriously aggressive and not inclined to consider settlement, it is becoming the normal practice in large cases today to have a different set of lawyers evaluate and try to arrive at a settlement. In other words, it is a good cop/bad cop routine. The settlement attorneys are the good cops and the trial attorneys are the bad cops. I always considered this to be somewhat artificial, but I assume it is probably necessary in some cases to increase the odds of settlement. Where the law firm is representing a long-term and important client, the firm is well served to figure out ways to settle litigation on favorable terms where that is in the best interest of the client. Litigating cases to a conclusion is time-consuming, expensive, and frequently results in an outcome that is not considered a victory. Settlement satisfactory to both sides is frequently the best option.

Alternative Dispute Resolution

Alternative Dispute Resolution (ADR) has become popular and widely used in recent years. ADR is based on the premise that an uninvolved third party is more likely to be able to bring the parties to settlement of litigation than if left to their own representatives. There are two principal kinds of ADR—arbitration and mediation. In arbitration, one or more arbitrators, usually attorneys, are brought in to receive presentations from both sides, and then they decide the controversy. It can be compulsory, in which case the parties agree in advance to accept the arbitrator's decision as a final resolution, or it can be non-binding. The other kind of ADR, mediation, is where a third party, again usually an attorney, sits down with the parties and hears brief presentations that are followed by an interactive process by which the mediator huddles with each side separately and conducts shuttle diplomacy. Some mediators are skillful at this process and have been able to settle cases that were the subject of acrimonious litigation. I used both arbitration and mediation in a number of my cases, and several of them did settle or were disposed of by compulsory arbitration.

Multiple advantages are touted for ADR. First, it is reputed to be less expensive and less time-consuming than court cases. That may or may not be the case. Increasingly, by the time I retired, arbitrations in large cases where significant discovery is permitted were becoming almost as lengthy and expensive as court cases. The one thing ADR does tend to avoid is a long delay in scheduling the case for trial after discovery is completed. As the budgets of various court systems have been cut in recent years, the time delay in getting civil cases (which are lower in priority than criminal cases because of speedy trial requirements) to trial have increased significantly. ADR is quicker in this regard since you have a dedicated third party to hear the case. Whether it is now less expensive depends on the amount of discovery allowed and the extent to which the parties take full advantage of all of the discovery opportunities. It was my sense by the time I retired that ADR was losing some of its touted advantage of being less expensive. Another advantage is the confidentiality permitted in ADR. The case litigated in court is in the public record in most instances. It is sometimes attractive to litigating parties to be able to have a confidential proceeding where the evidence is not made public and the result is kept confidential.

It is not unusual today for experienced trial attorneys to become active arbitrators or mediators toward the end of their careers. There is considerably less pressure than is present in trying cases. I did serve as mediator several times, but I never really took to it. I much preferred to try jury cases than to mediate in a non-jury setting. Since I have retired, I have had several opportunities to serve as an arbitrator or mediator, but I have declined in each instance.

The Demise of the Jury Trial

Many observers of our legal system believe that the importance of the jury trial is diminishing and will continue to do so in the future. In fact, some predict the demise of the jury trial. In my view, this would be a shame because it is one of the bedrocks of the American judicial system and has existed since the founding of the country.

The reasons for the decline of the jury trial are not difficult to identify. The expense and the length of time to trial are two primary reasons. The perception that jurors rule based on emotion and not evidence is probably another reason. Some also believe that juries award outrageous sums in punitive damages. I am sure this happens occasionally, but there are remedies on appeal since the United States Supreme Court established permissible multiples of punitive damages to the actual damages in a case. I believe that most juries in a properly tried case arrive at the correct result and diligently perform their duties. Probably the single biggest reason for the diminishment of the jury trial is the fact that waivers of jury trials are now in many commercial agreements. Increasingly, courts are willing to enforce these waivers of jury trial if sophisticated parties such as large corporations enter into them. Even individual waivers of jury trial are enforced in most courts. In addition, some industries have been able to persuade the regulatory authorities to permit mandatory arbitration in disputes with their customers. For example, in the securities industry, it is now virtually impossible to get a jury trial in a dispute over the alleged mishandling of a customer's brokerage account. The same is true of a bank account. It will not be long before these kinds of jury waivers will probably be included in virtually every commercial agreement.

Chapter 15

From a Profession to a Business: The Practice of Law Then and Now

Enormous changes took place in the practice of law in the almost forty years between the time I started in fall 1971 and the time I retired at the beginning of 2009. Not all of these changes were for the better. Today, some observers believe that the practice of law has become essentially just another business as opposed to a respected profession. There is considerable evidence to support that view. A few years before I retired, I attended a Bar Association meeting at which the chair of a major Atlanta firm was giving a speech on the modern practice of law. In his remarks, this leader of one of the largest law firms in Atlanta used the word "business" more than fifteen times and did not use the word "profession" once. A year after I retired, my alma mater, the Georgetown Law School, published an article on the challenges of training lawyers for the twenty-first century. This article barely mentioned professionalism but constantly referred to the challenges of the current business model of law practice. Most shocking of all, a Wall Street Journal article in 2011 reported that the New York-based law firm of Jacoby & Myers had filed suit to invalidate state laws in New Jersey, New York, and Connecticut that prohibited non-attorneys from owning equity in law firms. As my longtime law partner, Ted Maloof, once observed, "Practicing law is a way to make a good living. Whether it is a good way to make a living is another matter."

The present trends obviously pose serious questions for the future of the practice of law. Are lawyers content to work in just another business with the goal of maximizing profit, or do they desire to be part of a respected profession that puts its clients first and its profits second? There is nothing wrong, in my opinion, with lawyers making a lot of money. After all, they have to devote four years to college and three more years to law school. Many leave law school today owing large sums of money in the form of student loans that must be repaid from their future earnings. In addition, practicing law is a demanding activity and requires intelligence and energy. Attorneys are among the hardest-working people I have ever known. My problem is not how much money attorneys make but how they make the money today. For those interested in this topic, Atlanta attorney Michael H. Trotter wrote a book titled *Profit and the Practice of Law—What's happened to the legal profession?* (Athens: University of Georgia Press, 1997). Michael started practicing in Atlanta in 1960, and the book was published in 1997. Therefore, while his time of practice did not precisely overlap mine since he started his practice eleven years before I did and his book was published twelve years before I retired, many issues covered in his book are equally applicable to the period of my practice. While I do not agree with all of Michael's conclusions and recommendations, it is a book well worth reading for those interested in how the practice of law has changed in the last fifty years.

In this chapter, I discuss some of those changes, some of the problems they have created, and some possible remedial actions. I do not suggest by these comments that everything was perfect in earlier periods. I recall that the first attorney I ever saw try a case, Rueben Garland in spring 1960, was held in contempt of court by judges on more than one occasion. Earlier in the century, one of America's most famous and successful trial attorneys, the legendary Clarence Darrow, was twice indicted for allegedly bribing jurors. One trial ended in acquittal and the other one in a mistrial. A number of Mr. Darrow's friends and associates thought it entirely possible that he knew about or was involved in the attempted bribes. In his famous Scopes monkey trial in Tennessee, Darrow implied that the judge was biased because he excluded certain scientific evidence. When the judge told him that he hoped Darrow did not mean to reflect upon the court, Darrow replied, "Well, Your Honor has the right to hope." He was held in contempt of court (John A. Farrell, *Clarence Darrow: Attorney for the Damned* [New York: Doubleday, 2011] 386). While we do not frequently hear today of attorneys being held in contempt of court or attempting to bribe jurors, those are hardly the standards to which we should aspire. We also should not ignore the good things that have recently happened to the practice of law, including the hiring of many more women and minority attorneys. They were few and far between when I started. Today, fully half or more of the nation's law students are young women.

Size of Law Firms

When I joined Heyman & Sizemore in fall 1971, the largest law firm in Atlanta barely had fifty lawyers. The next largest firm barely had forty attorneys. When I retired at the beginning of 2009, my law firm, McKenna Long & Aldridge, had about three hundred professionals. Today, some law firms in Atlanta have almost one thousand attorneys with offices throughout the United States and in foreign countries. In my opinion, size in and of itself is not necessarily bad. It does require, however, that the leaders of law firms understand and appreciate special challenges. It is one thing to run a law firm of thirty attorneys. It is quite another to run a firm of one thousand attorneys. Inevitably, this requires the introduction of management techniques and practices that are more frequently seen in the business community than in the legal community. The secret to managing this complexity is to be sure that the professional responsibilities of attorneys are not ignored in the rush to become a large national or international law firm.

Size also has important implications within the law firm in terms of the relationship among partners. In today's large firms, it is not unusual that a partner may not have even met some of his or her fellow partners. They may practice in faraway offices without any opportunity to get to know each other. This makes it much more difficult for the firm to maintain a collegial culture that values the contribution of each attorney. It is an invitation to judge each attorney by the bottom line, which is frequently the yardstick used. While all of the large firms have extensive pro bono programs and ostensibly encourage participation in them, a reasonably intelligent individual cannot practice long before realizing that the true judge of progress and success rests in how many dollars are brought into the firm. This increasingly means that attorneys who originate the most business are the ones who reap the highest reward. There was a time when an attorney could do well in the practice of law by being an effective attorney handling business generated by his or her partners. That is largely now a thing of the past. This also comes at a time when the large firms are making it more difficult to become an equity partner by increasing the time during which an attorney is expected to be an associate or a non-equity partner.

The proliferation in the number of offices of law firms also presents challenges. If it were not for the technology revolution that has invaded all areas of our society, including the practice of law, it would be virtually impossible to manage firms with such a large number of offices. Even with that technology, multiple offices in different states or countries present special challenges. The partners in one office are unlikely to fully appreciate the challenges in other offices. There is frequently a differential in billing rates and the profitability of offices, which inevitably gives rise to inter-office jealousy and fights over compensation. Only the strongest leadership can keep such a firm successful with a favorable environment in which to practice. Too often it leads to discord and disunity followed by loss of key partners or dissolution. An example is the Howry & Simon firm in Washington, DC, which had many fine lawyers at one time but fell apart in recent years and was dissolved. When an attorney in a faraway office is accused of some impropriety or unprofessional conduct, attorneys in the other offices of the firm often are not as sympathetic toward the attorney as they would be if that attorney practiced in the office where they practice. This results too often in the loss of good partners and the retention of not-so-good partners.

Billing Rates and Methods

For the last forty years, the practice of law in the United States has been dominated by the hourly billing rate. That is, the amount charged the client is based on the attorney's normal billing rate multiplied by the amount of time devoted to the client's matter, usually billed monthly. It has not always been that way. When I first started practicing, retainers were much more prevalent than they are today. That is, for a certain payment each year, a law firm would be available as the attorney for a client with the amount of the compensation to be adjusted if the law firm took on a particularly complex or time-consuming engagement. I remember Heyman & Sizemore was on retainer to several railroads it represented. The retainer gradually went away because large clients insisted on the hourly rate ostensibly because it would be easier to budget for the company's legal expenses. They probably shortchanged themselves in the process. An hourly rate obviously results in higher compensation for the attorney if more time is spent on an engagement than is necessary or if more attorneys are assigned to the matter than are required. That has been a big problem in recent years and continues to be so today.

As a result of increasing dissatisfaction with the hourly rate, certain clients have searched for alternative billing methods such as a set fee for a particular matter. The results have been mixed. To protect itself against loss in the event that the engagement turns out to be more complex than envisioned when the set fee is established, law firms necessarily have to build in some cushion in setting the fee. This can result in a client overpaying. Law firms, in turn, have suggested alternative billing rates of their own. For example, some firms now quote a large client a reduced hourly rate or set fee depending on the volume of legal business the client gives to the firm. At the time I retired from the practice of law, the hourly billing rate was still the predominant method of compensation, and it probably will be for some time to come. The major exception to this is in the plaintiff practice, where personal injury cases or product liability cases may be handled on a contingency basis, which means the attorney is compensated based on a certain percentage of the recovery. Plaintiff attorneys who know what they are doing and carefully screen cases can make as much or more money in the contingent plaintiff practice than attorneys make in the large corporate defense practices.

Lawyer Compensation

There is no question that many attorneys today make far more money than their counterparts did at the time I started practicing in 1971, even adjusted for inflation. There is also a significant difference in attorney compensation between attorneys who practice in smaller firms and larger firms and those who practice in urban areas as compared to rural areas. It is not unusual today for a top attorney in a large corporate firm to make more than $1 million a year. That was pretty much unheard of in 1971. When I entered the practice, my compensation was approximately $25,000 a year. At the time I retired, pay depended on how well the firm did in a given year, but there were several years when I made almost $1 million. Whether this has resulted in attorneys being better off is debatable. It certainly has increased the pressure on attorneys to perform and work long and hard hours. This often comes at a cost to their families and their health. It is no accident that there have been substantial problems in the lives of trial attorneys from alcohol and substance abuse. Unfortunately, many attorneys also engage in a lavish lifestyle and save little during their most productive years. This means they have less to show for their efforts at the end of a career.

One of the most dramatic changes in lawyer compensation involves the opening salaries of new attorneys coming out of law school. Up until the recent recession, it was not unusual for large firms in Atlanta to pay opening salaries of well above $100,000 a year, and the starting salaries in New York were even higher. Since an attorney is generally not a profit-making center for a firm in the first few years of his or her practice, this is essentially a training period during which the new attorneys are substantially overpaid. Clients often balk at paying for this on-the-job training. The result is that salaries do not go up rapidly thereafter, and it takes much longer to become an equity partner. This has resulted in a large level of dissatisfaction by young lawyers and a high turnover rate for law firms. If a young attorney leaves the firm after three or four years during which he or she is basically in training and while the firm is subsidizing the attorney, it is a lost investment to the firm. Nonetheless, this is exactly what is happening. When I started practicing, a young attorney was guaranteed to become an equity partner if he or she stayed with the firm. There is no such assurance today. Many attorneys become non-equity partners, and many eventually become merely contract attorneys—that is, not even partners or associates of the firm but independent contractors hired to work on a particular matter. This usually relieves the firm of providing benefits such as health coverage.

A recent study in the *New York Times* reported that the average hourly wages in the New York City metropolitan area for contract attorneys were between $25 and $30 an hour. This is after the attorney has spent seven years in college and law school and usually racked up significant student loan liability. This is undoubtedly not the career that a young attorney envisions when he or she decides to become a lawyer. It is another reason why there is such a high level of discontent among younger attorneys today. Of course, our society in general has become increasingly characterized by a huge gulf between the haves and have-nots, but it is somewhat shocking that the same phenomenon exists to such a great extent in the practice of law.

Client and Attorney Loyalty

There was a time when attorneys were loyal to their clients and vice versa. Increasingly, that is not the case today. If a better client comes along, most firms today have no reluctance in suing a client, even if it is necessary to give up a small amount of business currently received from that client. Clients are also less loyal to their attorneys and more willing to hire any law firm that they think can do an acceptable job representing them at a cheaper price. When I started practicing, it would have been unheard of for a law firm to accept an engagement against an existing client, regardless of the nature of the matter. Today, there are only a few exceptions to this lack of loyalty. One is the relationship between the Coca-Cola Company and the King & Spalding law firm in Atlanta. King & Spalding is Coke's long-time counsel and still does a significant amount of work for the client. I never heard of King & Spalding taking a case against the Coca-Cola Company. I remember one year Coca-Cola paid King & Spalding a significant bonus because of the quality of job it had done representing Coca-Cola in important matters that year. Today, that is almost unheard of from any client.

As a result of this lack of client and attorney loyalty, conflict of interest has taken on an entirely different meaning. Lawyers are now able to rationalize conflicts or ignore them altogether. Nowhere is this more evident than in large bankruptcy cases. In the Enron bankruptcy, the company's principal counsel filed a disclosure of its present and former clients who had a connection to the case that took almost fifty pages in the court filing. These included numerous companies that the law firm was then representing, even some it had represented in matters involving Enron. The justification for this is that a large national firm would never be able to represent a debtor in a large bankruptcy case if the prior conception of conflict of interest were strictly enforced. The view now is that if the conflict is disclosed and the court nonetheless retains the firm, there is no problem. Occasionally, remedial measures are put in place in these cases, such as a "Chinese wall" to separate attorneys in the firm who are working on the bankruptcy from the knowledge possessed by other attorneys in the firm with respect to a related representation. In times past, this would not have passed muster because the law firm is deemed to be in possession of its attorneys' knowledge. Another favorite device now is to hire a separate firm to handle a particular matter. However, where that matter is important to the overall bankruptcy, it is extremely difficult to separate it from the rest of the case.

To be fair, conflicts do present a difficult situation for a large national or international law firm that has thousands of attorneys and numerous offices. We encountered some of these problems at McKenna Long & Aldridge, and we certainly took them far more seriously than was the case in a number of bankruptcies in which I participated in Delaware and New York. As a result of the relaxation of the conflict of interest restrictions, large law firms have now become actively engaged in the bankruptcy practice. When I started practicing in 1971, most of the large law firms in Atlanta shunned the bankruptcy practice. Small to middle-sized firms had most of the bankruptcy cases at that time. That is no longer true, as almost all big firms compete for lucrative bankruptcy assignments.

Technology

As previously stated, technology has caused a revolution in the practice of law. Today, library books and the libraries in which they are housed are virtually obsolete. Almost all research is done on a computer, and the ability to generate complex documents on the computer has transformed corporate practice. Most law firms have a set of forms for almost every kind of transaction based on the work they have done in previous engagements. With a little tinkering here and there, these forms can be used for most engagements. Certainly, there are still complicated corporate transactions that require sophisticated attorney work, but technology makes it easier. One effect of the ability to generate and revise documents more rapidly is clients' increased demand for better and faster service. With advanced technology and Internet capability, clients are not inclined to listen to excuses from attorneys as to why they cannot promptly provide requested documentation.

Along with the corporate practice, technology has also revolutionized the litigation practice. I have already discussed in regard to the Bob Kern case in chapter 12 how technology has significantly changed the way in which a case is presented to a jury. It has also changed the way documents are presented to the jury. The most important documents are now placed on large screens, and portions of them can be highlighted for emphasis during the presentation of evidence to the jury, increasing the attorneys' ability to try cases effectively. In addition, as evidenced by my discussion of the handling of documents in the Refco case, technology has made possible the expeditious review of hundreds of thousands of documents in major cases. Nonprofessionals enter these documents into a database so that paralegals or attorneys can search through them using keywords or phrases. In this way, it is possible for attorneys to meaningfully review hundreds of thousands of documents in a single case. This would have been virtually impossible twenty years ago.

Technology has had another revolutionary effect on the practice of law. When I started practicing, each partner and many associates had their own separate secretaries. Today, a secretary is shared by as many as five attorneys. This is because almost all recent law school graduates come to the practice of law with a high level of proficiency in computer use. They can and do generate their own correspondence and documents using the computer. There is little need for a secretary for these attorneys. As soon as dinosaurs such as myself either retire or die, the ratio of lawyers to secretaries will undoubtedly increase even further. At the time I retired, it was, on average, between two and three lawyers to one secretary at McKenna Long & Aldridge.

The Demise of Professionalism

In my opinion, no change in the practice of law during the last forty years has been more damaging to the profession than the shocking disappearance of ethics, professionalism, and civility. All of this is not the fault of attorneys, as American society in general has become less civil. This is evidenced in business and in politics. Nonetheless, the practice of law had always been considered special. Sadly, Rambo-style litigation tactics are no longer unusual but increasingly becoming the norm. The demise of professionalism has occurred not only in litigation but in all areas of the practice. Increasingly, there has been an acceptance of the notions of winning at all costs and that the ends justify the means. Perhaps this should not be surprising since many agree that the practice of law has become a business. Those interested in the future of the practice of law, however, should be alarmed at this trend because it will not be long before the powers that be will call for the regulation of the legal profession. We lawyers have been fortunate to be largely self-regulated since the founding of the country. I fear that will end if some of the present trends continue—particularly if outside, non-lawyer investors are allowed to invest in law firms. Even without that, with the level of lawyer advertising today, many feel that there is no reason to treat the practice of law as different from any other business.

The first time I can recall being exposed personally to an attorney's unprofessional conduct occurred on a trip to New York in July 1977. Bob Bartlett, an associate at Hicks Maloof & Campbell, and I had flown to New York to review documents produced by Security Mortgage Investors in the litigation with North American Acceptance Corporation in its bankruptcy. It was an ill-fated trip from the beginning. When we landed in New York, Bob, who is originally from the New York City area, went to Long Island to stay with some of his relatives. I traveled into Manhattan to register at the Plaza Hotel on Fifth Avenue across the street from the offices where we would review the SMI documents. As usual, I had requested a room on as high a floor as possible to avoid street noise. Much to my chagrin, I was told when I checked in that the only remaining room was on the second floor. I was displeased but accepted the room because I had no alternative. As I stormed away from the registration desk and crossed the lobby, the lights went out. New York City was in the midst of a blackout that would last two nights and one day. Because I was on the second floor, I was able to sleep in my room after raising the windows. It was extremely hot, and the guests who had been assigned rooms on the higher floors were relegated to sleeping on cots in the lobby.

When the electricity was finally restored, Bob and I went to the law firm to begin our review of documents. While the air-conditioning worked in the lobby and the hallways of the law firm, there seemed to be little if any air-conditioning in the room to which we were assigned. The room was full of boxes of documents. We plunged in and began our review. At the end of the first day, we had reviewed about a third of the documents. We had tagged the documents we wanted copied and segregated them from the rest. When we arrived to continue our review the next morning, the documents had been shuffled and the tags removed such that we could not tell what we had already reviewed and what we had left to review. We had to start over. We then started making notes of documents that were particularly important out of concern that they might not be copied, even though we marked them for copying. Sure enough, after we received the documents several weeks later, some of the most valuable documents were missing. Fortunately, we had Bates numbers and the details of those documents. We asked that they be sent, and they were eventually.

It was obvious to me that the frequency of unprofessional conduct by attorneys was increasing as the years passed. This behavior, which occurred in various forms from simple incivility to flagrant misrepresentation, took a toll on lawyer credibility. When I started practicing, an attorney would think nothing of accepting an extension of time to file a pleading without memorializing it in writing. By the time I retired, no one was willing to rely on the word of opposing counsel but always insisted that it be documented. Another area that illustrates the demise of civility and professionalism relates to the concept of an attorney as "an officer of the court." This means that an attorney has duties to the court and the judicial system that can trump his or her duties to the client. For example, it is not acceptable to submit to the court a document that the attorney knows to be a forgery or to elicit testimony from a witness that the attorney knows to be false. It is also inconsistent with the attorney's role as officer of the court to misrepresent legal authority cited or to cite non-controlling authority when the attorney knows that there is controlling authority that he or she does not cite to the court.

This violation of the concept of an officer of the court was brought emphatically to my attention one day when I sat in a courtroom in Wilmington, Delaware, waiting to make an argument in a large bankruptcy case. The matter argued immediately before mine related to a motion that had been brought by a sole practitioner from Nebraska. He argued his motion in what I thought was an ineffectual way. His argument was disjointed and poorly organized, and he cited almost no legal authority to support his side of the case. I wondered if the poor fellow even had a library. When the opposing counsel stood to present his argument, it was well organized, effectively delivered, and cited several Circuit Court of Appeals decisions that were not controlling law in the Third Circuit but that the attorney argued were persuasive authority. He said nothing about any decisions on the subject by the Third Circuit Court of Appeals, which was the controlling authority in Delaware. This attorney was a partner in a major New York City law firm. At the end of his argument, he asked the judge if the court had any questions. The judge indicated that the court had one question—was the attorney familiar with a certain decision of the Third Circuit Court of Appeals on this question? The attorney, who had been so smooth, confident, and persuasive a moment earlier, turned into an exceedingly ineffective advocate as it became obvious that he had intentionally withheld acknowledging the Third Circuit decision and thereby tried to mislead the court. Unfortunately for him and his client, the court or its law clerk had discovered the Third Circuit decision as a result of their own research. On that day, that attorney gained a reputation before the judge. And his reputation, unless changed, would work to the disadvantage of every future client he represented before that judge. If he persisted in that kind of conduct before other judges, he would soon have a generalized reputation as a lawyer who could not be trusted. As I found out when working for Richard Russell and from my law school class at Georgetown, the reputation of an attorney can be either his or her most valuable asset or a decided disadvantage.

The Future

Toward the end of my career as I became more concerned about the lack of professionalism by my fellow attorneys, I started accepting invitations to speak on professionalism at seminars sponsored by various bar associations or internally at my law firm. I have continued to accept these invitations since my retirement. In these talks, I emphasize that it is important for attorneys to follow the rules and ethical standards not only because they are supposed to but also because it is in their best interest to do so. I found that if an attorney had a reputation for integrity, most judges were prepared to give him or her the benefit of the doubt and to listen seriously to an argument that might initially appear without much support. On the other hand, if that attorney had a reputation for dishonesty or unprofessionalism, I found that those same judges were skeptical about what the attorney said even when he or she had a strong case. The loser is not only the attorney but also the attorney's client. I emphasized that no client an attorney has today is important enough to jeopardize his or her ability to represent all future clients effectively.

What can be done to arrest this trend toward lack of professionalism and ethics in the practice of law? The demise of professionalism did not happen overnight or because of just one cause, and it will not be corrected overnight or by the efforts of just one person or group. It will require the efforts of all concerned. And it will require significant time to arrest the present trends and restore the legal profession to its prior status. I offer below some of my ideas about how this can happen.

Attorneys, of course, must assume a large share of responsibility for restoring professionalism in their practice. This is a battle that will have to be fought on an attorney-by-attorney basis for success to be assured. From my experience, I do not believe most attorneys engage in Rambo-style litigation tactics and other unprofessional conduct because they enjoy it. Many times they do so because they believe they are courting clients or because they believe the client has assigned such a high value to winning that is the only way the goal can be achieved. Attorneys must be disabused of this notion and convinced that they are shortchanging themselves and their future clients by engaging in this kind of conduct. Younger attorneys would be helped tremendously in this effort by more role models.

Clients have been exceedingly slow to realize that they are the victims, not the beneficiaries, of this kind of law practice. It increases the cost of the legal services they buy, delays the resolution of their cases or other matters, and creates an environment that is not enjoyable or productive for anyone. There is no doubt in my mind that 90 percent of attorneys today would assign a far higher importance to practicing at high standards of ethics and professionalism if they thought the clients demanded or even wanted it. As long as they have a contrary impression, it will be difficult to make progress.

Judges also have to take a major responsibility for moving the practice of law back to a higher level of professionalism. Under our legal system, judges in both the federal and state systems [can use] a wide array of remedial measures to deal with unprofessional or unethical conduct in the cases before them. These remedial measures range from imposing judgment against the attorney's client to sanctioning the attorney or even terminating the attorney's right to practice in the court. A lesser penalty of depriving an attorney of his or her legal fee or imposing the fees and expenses of the matter in favor of an opposing party are less severe sanctions. In my experience, even in the most egregious cases, it is rare that judges use the sterner penalties. For example, I almost never hear of a judge rendering judgment against an attorney's client because of the conduct of the attorney. Some may say that this would be unjust to the client, but the client is often the problem. When the client is not the issue, and it is truly an instance of attorney misconduct, the client has legal recourse against the attorney. I believe judges at all levels need to become much stricter in dealing with attorney misconduct in proceedings. One of the few bright spots has been the recent emphasis on professionalism by members of the Georgia Supreme Court.

Bar associations also must be active participants in this effort. One way they can do this is by sponsoring seminars on professionalism and ethics, which they are required to do to a certain extent by the continuing legal education rules applicable in most states. However, I believe far more could be done. It is particularly important for litigation sections of bar associations to be active in this area because many of them have been largely missing in action. Trial attorneys today need to know of the serious consequences of unprofessional conduct and of the possible advantages of professional conduct. In 2011, I received the David W. Pollard Award from the Bankruptcy Section of the Atlanta Bar Association. The Pollard Award has been presented each year since 1974 to a member of the Atlanta Bar Association to recognize high standards of ethics and professionalism in a career of law practice. More awards of this kind need to be presented. There is no more satisfying feeling at the end of a lengthy legal career than to be recognized for practicing at the highest ethical and professional standards. I commend the Bankruptcy Section of the Atlanta Bar Association for presenting this award, not because I received it but because of the message it delivers to attorneys who are still practicing.

One of the most important vehicles to arrest the trend toward unethical and unprofessional conduct is the nation's law schools. It is my impression that professionalism and ethics are still taught in America's law schools by acquainting the students with the provisions of the rules and urging them to follow them because they are required to do so. Not enough attention is paid, in my opinion, to the advantages to an attorney from practicing at a high level of professionalism as compared to the disadvantages of developing a reputation for unprofessional and unethical conduct. If young attorneys do not enter the practice of law with a firm foundation in this area, it is unlikely that they will pick it up in the present environment. Something that happened while I practiced at Hicks Maloof & Campbell illustrates this fact. A Washington, DC, lawyer was using our large conference room to defend a deposition being conducted by a local Atlanta attorney. The Washington attorney, undoubtedly to throw his opposing lawyer off stride and embarrass him in front of his client, persisted in mispronouncing the last name of the

Atlanta attorney in a most unflattering way. Finally, the local attorney could take it no more, and stood up and shook his fist at the opposing attorney. He shouted that if it happened again, he would come over the table and beat his ass. This was not only being recorded by a court reporter but was also being videotaped. The exchange was overheard by a young associate in our firm just out of law school whose office was adjacent to the conference room. She told me about it later. I thought at the time that it was a terrible example to set for a young attorney just entering the practice. It suggested that an attorney could be successful and engage in such conduct. For younger attorneys to be able to withstand the temptation to follow the crowd and engage in this kind of conduct, they need to enter the practice with a far firmer ethical foundation than they have previously been provided in their legal education.

The Best Judges

I practiced before many fine judges during my career. I have often been asked who I thought were the best judges. It is difficult to limit the list to just three judges as discussed below. For this purpose, I also do not include any of the bankruptcy judges in the Bankruptcy Court for the Northern District of Georgia because so many of those judges are close friends, and I probably would not be objective toward them.

The first judge is the late Judge Newell Edenfield of the United States District Court for the Northern District of Georgia. Judge Edenfield grew up in South Georgia and attended the University of Georgia Law School. After a stint in the Merchant Marine, he practiced law in Atlanta and became one of the city's most respected and successful trial attorneys. He was a name partner in the Heyman & Sizemore law firm when it was known as Edenfield Heyman & Sizemore. In 1967, President Lyndon Johnson appointed him to the Federal District Court in Atlanta, where he served until the time of his death.

The thing I remember the most about Judge Edenfield is how he stayed on top of his docket. Being a highly experienced and successful trial attorney, he knew all the tricks that attorneys used and sometimes abused. He maintained strict control of his courtroom without hamstringing attorneys in their ability to try cases. He was known among trial attorneys as one of the best federal judges in Atlanta. I shared that view. One episode I recall that involved our firm and illustrated how Judge Edenfield handled his calendar was a particularly acrimonious piece of litigation that occurred in the bankruptcy case of Management Science America. Bob Hicks had been appointed bankruptcy trustee for MSA and was engaged in litigation with the Trust Company Bank in Atlanta, which was represented by King & Spalding. Well-known King & Spalding litigation partner, Charles Kirbo, was lead counsel for the Trust Company Bank and was assisted by Felton Jenkins, a young lawyer who was a classmate of mine at the University of Georgia. This litigation involved the ownership of an important software program, and King & Spalding had sued Bob Hicks not only as trustee but also personally because of alleged misappropriation of property of the Trust Company Bank. One day during a hearing that had become rather heated, Judge Edenfield called a recess and asked Bob Hicks and Charlie Kirbo to come to his chambers. As Bob related to me later, Judge Edenfield turned to Kirbo and said, "Charlie, you have brought some very serious charges against Bob Hicks. That is fine if you can prove them, but God help you if you cannot." He then turned to Bob Hicks and said, "Bob, I appointed you bankruptcy trustee in this case because I consider you to be an attorney of integrity and ability. If these charges are true, God help you." With that, Judge Edenfield told the lawyers to go back into the courtroom and continue the hearing. Charlie and Bob asked the judge if they could have a few moments to confer before continuing the hearing. They were quickly able to arrive at a settlement that resolved the acrimonious part of the litigation.

Today, too many judges are too uninvolved in their dockets. Attorneys are left free to file voluminous papers that delay the resolution of cases. By staying on top of his cases, Judge Edenfield was able to be sure attorneys knew that the court was aware of what they were doing and how they were doing it. When Judge Edenfield spoke, trial attorneys listened because they knew he spoke from long experience as a successful and effective trial attorney and a judge who was not interested in listening to excuses.

Newell Edenfield was also a real character. The story is told about one of his last illnesses when he had been confined to the Emory University Hospital for about a week. He had become tired of the restrictions placed on him in the hospital, which included no cigarettes and no alcohol. One day, he arose from his bed, put on his bedroom shoes and his bathrobe, went to the lobby of the hospital, and called a taxi. Soon Emory Hospital was missing a federal judge. After a frantic search, Judge Edenfield was discovered at his home in Atlanta in his favorite chair, smoking a cigarette and enjoying an evening cocktail.

I became friends with Judge Edenfield as a result of my involvement with Senator Herman Talmadge. However, he did not play any favorites in my cases before him. Once I argued an appeal in the United States Court of Appeals for the Fifth Circuit where Judge Edenfield had been appointed to sit by designation, as was often done in regard to respected district court judges. This was a case in which I was representing Bob Hicks as bankruptcy trustee of the J. D. Jewell Chicken Company. Out of the three judges on the appellate panel, Judge Edenfield asked me the most difficult questions, and I could tell he was enjoying my challenge in coming up with good answers.

The second judge is Judge Sidney O. Smith, Jr., who also served as a federal district court judge in Atlanta. Originally from Gainesville where he served a stint on the Superior Court of Hall County, Judge Smith became a highly respected federal trial judge in Atlanta and served for some six years as chief judge of the Atlanta District Court. To as great an extent as any judge before whom I appeared, he combined a calm demeanor and collegiality with firm control of his courtroom. He did not pull any punches, and he did not allow any personal views he might have about a case to sway him or the jury. He decided matters right down the middle. As a result, he became a highly trusted trial judge in Atlanta.

I remember Richard Russell paying the ultimate compliment to Sidney Smith when I was working in Washington, DC. President Nixon was trying to appoint a southern member of the United States Supreme Court and had been unsuccessful in getting the Senate to confirm Clement Haynesworth or Harold Carswell. After Carswell's defeat, I remember Russell saying one day, "If he would appoint a Sidney Smith, he could be easily confirmed." That was Senator Russell's way of saying that Judge Smith avoided extreme positions or substituting his own views instead of a rigorous application of the law. After Judge Smith retired from the federal bench, he became a partner at the Atlanta law firm of Alston & Bird. He passed away in July of 2012.

The third judge I would cite is Judge Harold Murphy, who still sits in the United States District Court for the Northern District of Georgia in

Rome, Georgia. Judge Murphy originally practiced law in a small town in Northwest Georgia, served in the state legislature, and served as a state court judge before being appointed to the district court by President Carter in the 1970s. Now in his mid-eighties, he still serves on the court as a full-time judge and not a senior judge. While I was never a particular fan of the polls run by the Atlanta Bar Association that rank judges in the state and federal courts in Atlanta or elsewhere in the Northern District of Georgia, I do believe it is noteworthy that Judge Murphy was for many years consistently rated as the top trial judge in the federal court in Atlanta. He knows how to allow the court, the jury, and the attorneys to do their jobs without unduly restricting the proper role of the other actors in the case.

Judge Murphy reminds me a great deal of the late Senator Sam Ervin of North Carolina. Both grew up in small towns and tried almost every kind of jury case known to man. This included both civil and criminal cases. In an oral history interview conducted for the University of Georgia several years ago, Judge Murphy related an experience he had in a criminal case. He was representing a defendant in a murder case and had decided to call the defendant's brother to testify. He said he had prepared the witness thoroughly before examining him at the trial and thought he knew everything relevant that the witness knew. When he asked the brother if he had any reason to believe that the defendant had killed the deceased, the brother indicated that he knew he had not done so but that he had killed another fellow. Judge Murphy said he had not thought to ask him about any other murder.

The last case I had before Judge Murphy took place a couple of years before I retired. I was representing an Atlanta attorney and his firm who were accused of conspiring with another defendant in the case to deprive the other defendant's sister and her children of their rightful inheritance. Our client decided to settle, and we appeared before Judge Murphy in connection with the settlement. On the court's own motion and without being prompted by any of the parties, Judge Murphy indicated that he would not approve the settlement without a guardian being appointed for the minor children because of the possibility of a conflict between the interests of the mother and the children. That showed me that Judge Murphy was still very much on top of things in his eighties.

These three great judges—Newell Edenfield, Sidney Smith, and Harold Murphy—had at least one thing in common. Their trial experience had taught them the proper roles for the court, the jury, and the attorneys in the trial of a case. They allowed all to perform their functions in a dignified and professional manner. They were ideal judges before whom to try cases.

The Best Lawyers

If it is difficult to select the three best judges before whom I practiced, it is even more difficult to select the three best lawyers I encountered in the practice of law. For the purpose of this exercise, I eliminate for consideration any of my law partners because I am hardly objective with respect to them. This in no way suggests that several of them would not otherwise be qualified to appear on the list.

One of the finest all-around attorneys I ever met was the late Griffin Bell. He was born in Americus, Georgia, attended college at Georgia Southwestern College in Americus, and attended law school at the Mercer University Law School in Macon. After practicing for a while in Savannah and Rome, Georgia, he was recruited to become a partner at the King & Spalding firm in Atlanta, where he practiced until President Kennedy appointed him as a judge of the United States Court of Appeals for the Fifth Circuit in the early 1960s. He served with distinction on that court for about fifteen years before returning to King & Spalding. Shortly thereafter, President Carter nominated him to be attorney general of the United States. In the post-Watergate era, Judge Bell did much to restore the morale of the career Justice Department attorneys. He posted every day on the bulletin board the names of every visitor he saw. His tenure as attorney general was widely praised even by those who initially opposed his nomination. After his service as attorney general, Judge Bell returned once more to the King & Spalding law firm in Atlanta.

Griffin Bell was a counselor in the sense of the old school. He gave advice. He advised small clients at the King & Spalding law firm and earlier in his practice in Savannah and Rome just as he advised the largest corporations in the nation and even the president of the United States. He led some of the most important legal investigations, including that of the Exxon oil spill in Alaska. He had an abundance of the one thing that is required for a great lawyer—good judgment. During the time I was working in Washington, I remember that Richard Russell had great confidence in the judgment of Griffin Bell, who was serving on the Fifth Circuit Court of Appeals at the time. He frequently consulted with Judge Bell on matters relating to judicial appointments or legislation affecting the courts.

In addition to good judgment, Griffin Bell shared something else with Richard Russell. He had a great sense of humor, and much of it was directed at himself. He had an extreme South Georgia accent that could be difficult to understand for those outside the South, and it never changed no matter how much time he spent in Washington. Once he gave a speech at an annual meeting of the American College of Trial Lawyers in which he related an experience he had while serving as attorney general. He was the head of an American delegation to an international meeting where more than one hundred nations were represented. He was called to speak on behalf of the United States, and his remarks were simultaneously translated into some ten different languages. He said that he became concerned when the British representative asked for a simultaneous translation into English. Judge Bell always had an interesting story, and one never spent dull time with him.

His judgment and independence were illustrated in his final illness. He was diagnosed with pancreatic cancer and given a short time to live. Many of his friends, including his former client, the first President Bush, urged him to go to the M. D. Anderson Cancer Center in Houston for treatment. Judge Bell declined because he said that the nature of his cancer was not such that it would be cured, and he did not want to put his family through the treatments. He also said that he did not want to miss the opportunity to see his friends in Georgia before he died. Bob Hicks visited him in his last illness. Judge Bell died in his hometown of Americus, Georgia.

One of the finest trial lawyers I have ever known was Judge Bell's law partner at King & Spalding, Frank C. Jones. Frank, originally from Macon, Georgia, attended law school at Mercer University Law School in Macon following college at Emory University, and he joined his family firm in Macon, where he practiced for a number of years before being recruited by King & Spalding to come to Atlanta as a partner. He practiced there until he retired a few years ago and moved back to Macon. Frank was the kind of trial attorney who could and did try any case. From representing the Coca-Cola Company in some of its most important litigation to representing individual clients in state courts in Georgia, Frank Jones successfully argued cases before juries in his low-key, unpretentious manner. But he was no typical trial attorney. He was elected president of the American College of Trial Lawyers and president of the United States Supreme Court Historical Society. He received numerous awards and recognitions for his professionalism in the practice of law. Frank died in Macon on August 29, 2012.

One of the finest bankruptcy attorneys I have ever known is Neal Batson of the Alston & Bird Firm. Neal was born in Nashville, Tennessee, and attended college and law school at Vanderbilt University there. After clerking for Griffin Bell on the United States Court of Appeals for the Fifth Circuit, Neal joined the firm then known as Alston Miller & Gaines, now known as Alston & Bird. Before making his mark in bankruptcy law, Neal was a well-recognized and respected trial attorney in non-bankruptcy cases. In fact, he was head of the litigation department at his firm. I litigated a great number of cases in which Neal was involved, some where he was on my side and some where he was on the opposing side. As related in chapter 12, I also represented his law firm in the Colony Square case. Neal referred to attorneys he knew well as "Colonel."

Neal had a dream bankruptcy career. He handled numerous important cases in Atlanta but eventually gravitated toward even more important cases on the national stage. He represented the family that owned A. H. Robbins Company in the large bankruptcy of that company in Virginia, and he served as the examiner in the Enron bankruptcy case. He was elected president of the American College of Bankruptcy and has received numerous awards for his excellence in the legal profession and for his high degree of professionalism. Neal now lives in retirement in Colorado.

These three great attorneys—Griffin Bell, Frank Jones, and Neal Batson—illustrated what I said earlier about the importance of professionalism in a successful legal career. They all practiced at the highest level of ethics and professionalism and are compelling proof that such practice is not inconsistent with achieving the highest levels of success as an attorney. They are role models young lawyers today can emulate in terms of the kind of lawyers they want to be in their own careers.

16

Time to Call It Quits

By the time the Refco case was winding down in late 2006, I had begun to give serious consideration to retirement. I had practiced law for more than thirty-five years. My practice had become dominated by travel, and air travel was not what it used to be. On three successive Friday evenings during the Refco case, I was booked on a Delta Airlines flight from LaGuardia Airport in New York to Atlanta at 6:00 PM only to arrive home after midnight. I still enjoyed trying cases, but I did not enjoy the other parts of law practice. Having to constantly look over my shoulder to be sure I was not victimized by unethical or unprofessional conduct did not help.

Under my firm's partnership agreement at the time, an equity partner could practice until December 31 of the year in which he or she became sixty-seven years of age. For me, that was essentially sixty-eight years of age since my birthday is on January 12. As I continued to think about retirement in 2007 and in early 2008, I finally reached a decision to retire at the end of 2008. By that time, I would be almost sixty-seven years old. While I was still in good health, I was interested in doing things outside the law practice. I had a long list of books to read and constantly regretted not being able to spend more time at our beach condo on St. Simons Island, Georgia. I discussed my retirement plans with several friends and law partners. A number of them warned me that a lifelong workaholic such as myself might not do well in retirement, and I might find that I did not have enough to keep myself occupied. I doubted that would be the case. Ordinarily, when one retires from the practice of law, he or she maintains an office and the position of senior counsel for a number of years. My practice did not lend itself to part-time work, and I planned to retire cold turkey on December 31, 2008. The firm gave me a nice retirement party at a downtown Atlanta restaurant with Ann and about thirty others in attendance. Our good friends, Ann and Bill Hays, hosted another party for about one hundred people at the Cherokee Town Club in Buckhead. We enjoyed both immensely. At the request of the firm, I did agree to allow my name to be listed as senior counsel for a year, although I made it clear that I did not plan to do any legal work. Also, I agreed to keep my office for the additional one year, although I did not anticipate visiting it frequently. For the first six months, I came into the office about once a month to check my mail and be available to discuss developments in cases I had handed off to other attorneys. After the six-month period, I visited the office seldom and gave it up at the end of 2009.

I am now four-plus years into retirement, and it has been great. The best thing about it is that I can determine my own schedule without having to abide by the dictates of clients or judges. I am a creature of habit and have developed a routine schedule that I follow most days. I rise between 6:30 and 7:30 in the morning, read the Atlanta newspaper, and then read a book, usually a biography, for an hour or two. I then exercise for about an hour, which consists of stretches, sit-ups, and pushups, walking at least thirty minutes, and a weight-lifting regimen. I am probably in better physical health than I have been in more than thirty years. My afternoons are available for a wide range of activities such as visiting my mother before she passed or attending movies with Ann.

I have remained active in a number of organizations, including the Richard B. Russell Foundation, the University of Georgia Foundation, and the University of Georgia Library Board of Visitors. I also continue as an emeritus director of the Southeastern Bankruptcy Law Institute and as a retired fellow of both the American College of Trial Lawyers and the American College of Bankruptcy. I have plenty to keep me occupied. In fact, I have not even had time to resurrect my golf game or to take a long-planned tour of presidential libraries. I have made a number of enjoyable trips with Garrett. In 2009, we flew to California to hear the works of one of his favorite composers, Philip Glass, performed by the Philharmonic Orchestra of Los Angeles at the Hollywood Bowl. Garrett planned the entire trip—the travel schedule, the hotel, and the activities. The only thing I contributed was the money to pay for the trip. I did suggest that we take a tour of the homes of Hollywood personalities, which included that of Garrett's favorite actor, Jack Nicholson, and the house where Michael Jackson had died immediately prior to our trip. I also suggested a visit to the Reagan Presidential Library, which we enjoyed. For me, the highlight of the tour of the

Reagan Library was visiting a full-scale replica of Air Force One, which brought back memories of the trip from Washington to Atlanta carrying Richard Russell's body after his death. The other trip Garrett and I took was to Athens for the Robert Osborne Film Festival. Robert Osborne is a well-known Hollywood personality who is the host of Turner Classic Movies on television. Each year, prior to the recession, he hosted an event in Athens at which seven or eight movies were shown on a large screen in the Athens Civic Center. At the showing of each of the films, either a producer, director, actor, or actress who was involved in that picture was available to discuss the film. Ann, Garrett, and I have also taken several trips to New York City to see Broadway productions and/or concerts at Lincoln Center. On one of the trips, we spent a few days on Long Island, which I had always wanted to do.

Bob Hicks, Ted Maloof, Bill Hays, and I continue our tradition of having lunch together at least once a month. And I continue to attend virtually all of the home football games of the University of Georgia.

Looking back on my life and career, I realize how extraordinarily lucky I have been in both. I have a wonderful wife and son and enjoyed an exciting and challenging career as an attorney. I also had the unique opportunity of getting to know and working for Richard Russell. As I stated in the prologue of this book, I owe a tremendous debt of gratitude to the practice of law. I was able to practice in great law firms with great partners, make a good livelihood, and retire to a comfortable standard of living. Some of my comments in the previous chapter of this book may seem unduly harsh with respect to the practice of law. I do not mean them to be such. My hope is that in the future, when a young Georgian reaches the decision I made in spring 1960 to make the practice of law a career, he or she will be able to do so in a profession that is not only a way to make a good living but also a good way to make a living. For that to happen, much work remains to be done.

Garrett and me exiting the replica of Air Force One at the Reagan Presidential Library in California on July 24, 2009.

Garrett and me with Garrison Keilor in Birmingham, Alabama in 2010.

From left to right, Bill Hays, Ted Maloof, me and Bob Hicks at one of our monthly lunches in 2011.

With my UGA friends on my 70th birthday on January 12, 2012. From left to right, Fred Stowers, Norman Underwood, Buddy Darden and me.

Acknowledgments

It would be difficult to write a book, even an autobiography, without significant assistance. I was lucky to have such help. First and foremost, my wife, Ann, a former schoolteacher and fine writer, was able to provide many details that had escaped me and also to make helpful suggestions with respect to the text. My mother, who died when she was 102 years old, had an amazing mind and was able to recall many events with respect to her life, her marriage to my father, and our early lives. In addition, on more than one occasion, she was able to correct something I thought I remembered by providing accurate details. My longtime law partners, Bob Hicks and Ted Maloof, reviewed the manuscript and had some helpful suggestions, as did my good friend, Bill Hays. Ann, my mother, Bob, Ted, and Bill also gave me much-needed encouragement, without which I may have abandoned the project along the way.

I am very fortunate, as a first time author, to have had an experienced and able publisher—the Mercer University Press. It and its entire staff showed immense patience and interest in the book. Its many contributions, including extensive editing, greatly improved the final product. I particularly thank the Director of the Mercer University Press, Marc A. Jolley, and his publishing assistant, Marsha M. Luttrell.

A good deal of the research for this book was conducted at or by the Richard B. Russell Library for Political Research and Studies. Its longtime director, Sheryl Vogt, was helpful in this regard. In addition, many of the photographs and documents included in the book came courtesy of the Russell Library and Jill Severn there. I dictated the book on my home computer using voice recognition software. Technology has not only revolutionized the practice of law but also the writing of books. You can now research almost any topic in detail on the Internet. Once I had a rough draft of the book from my work on the computer, my former law partner, Mike Levengood, at the McKenna Long & Aldridge firm, and his able assistant, Sharon Brooks, converted the draft into a finished product suitable for submission to a publisher. I am grateful to all of these friends for their valuable assistance.

There is a host of literature on the life and career of Richard B. Russell, Jr., and his family. Two fine biographies have been written with respect to his life. The first was by Dr. Gilbert Fite, the initial holder of the Russell Chair in American History at the University of Georgia. His biography, *Richard B. Russell, Jr.—Senator from Georgia* (Chapel Hill: University of North Carolina Press, 1991), was awarded the D. B. Hardeman Prize for the best book on the United States Congress for the year in which it was published. A more recent biography by Senator Russell's niece, Sally Russell, is *Richard Brevard Russell, Jr.: A Life of Consequence* (Macon GA: Mercer University Press, 2011). Sally has also written or edited two other equally fine books on Russell's family. The first was a compilation of some of the many letters Senator Russell's mother wrote her thirteen children after they left home, *Roots and Evergreen: The Selected Letters of Ina Dillard Russell* (Athens: University of Georgia Press, 1999). The other is a full biography of Senator Russell's father, *A Heart for Any Fate: The Biography of Richard Brevard Russell, Sr.* (Macon GA: Mercer University Press, 2004).

The relationship between Lyndon Johnson and Richard Russell has also garnered the attention of talented authors. Robert Caro's groundbreaking books on the life and times of Lyndon Johnson have set a new standard for biographers. He has written four books thus far with a fifth one now in preparation. In *Master of the Senate* (New York: Alfred A. Knopf, 2002), his third book on the life and career of Lyndon Johnson, Caro devotes an entire chapter to Richard Russell and numerous additional references to his interaction with Lyndon Johnson during the Johnson Senate years. A fourth book by Caro covering the years of Johnson's vice presidency and the first eight months of his presidency, *The Passage of Power* (New York: Alfred A. Knopf), was released on May 1, 2012, and contains significant information about the important interaction between President Johnson and Richard Russell concerning the Warren Commission and the historic battle over the 1964 Civil Rights Act as well as other matters. The fifth book covering the remaining years of the Johnson presidency surely will have extensive coverage of the interaction between Senator Russell and President Johnson on many matters, including the disaster that was the Vietnam War, opposed by Russell from its beginnings during the Eisenhower administration. *Colleagues: Richard B. Russell and His Apprentice, Lyndon B. Johnson* (Santa Ana CA: Seven Locks Press, 1993), an excellent and perceptive book on the relationship between Richard Russell and Lyndon Johnson, was written by the late UPI newsman and former Senate staffer, John A.

Goldsmith, who knew both men well. Also, *The Walls of Jericho: Lyndon Johnson, Hubert Humphrey, Richard Russell, and the Struggle for Civil Rights* (San Diego: Harcourt Brace & Company, 1996), an excellent book by Robert Mann, the former press secretary of Senator Russell Long of Louisiana, details the interactions between Richard Russell, Lyndon Johnson, and Hubert Humphrey in the battle over civil rights legislation in the 1960s. Finally, Jeff Woods has written an interesting book on Richard Russell's views and activities in regard to foreign policy—*Richard B. Russell: Southern Nationalism and American Foreign Policy* (Lanham MD: Rowman & Littlefield Publishers, Inc., 2007).

For the relationship between Richard Russell and Herman Talmadge and the life and career of Senator Talmadge, his autobiography, with Mark Royden Winchell, is worthwhile reading—*Talmadge: A Politician's Legacy, A Politician's Life* (Atlanta: Peachtree Publishers, Ltd., 1987). *Voice of Georgia: Speeches of Richard B. Russell, 1928–1969* (Macon GA: Mercer University Press, 1997), written by two former speech professors at the University of Georgia, Calvin McLeod Logue and Dwight L. Freshley, contains selected speeches of Richard Russell from 1928 until the end of his career. Two publications by the United States Government Printing Office are the eulogies given for Richard Russell in Congress after his death in 1971 and a transcript of the proceedings in 1996 when the Richard B. Russell Memorial Statue was dedicated in the Rotunda of the Russell Senate Office Building—*Richard Brevard Russell, Late a Senator from Georgia: Memorial Tributes Delivered in Congress* (Washington, DC: United States Government Printing Office, 1971); and *Dedication and Unveiling of the Statue of Richard Brevard Russell, Jr.: Proceedings in the Rotunda of the Russell Senate Office Building January 24, 1996* (Washington, DC: United States Government Printing Office, Senate Document Number 105-8).

As indicated in chapter 15 of this book, a most worthwhile book on the changes in the practice of law in Atlanta between 1960 and 1995 is Michael Trotter's *Profit and the Practice of Law: What's Happened to the Legal Profession* (Athens: University of Georgia Press, 1997).

Index